Creole America

Creole America

The West Indies and the Formation of Literature and Culture in the New Republic

SEAN X. GOUDIE

PENN

University of Pennsylvania Press

Philadelphia

10 9 8 7 6 5 4 3 2 1

Published by
University of Pennsylvania Press
Philadelphia, Pennsylvania 19104-4112

Library of Congress Cataloging-in-Publication Data

Goudie, Sean X.
    Creole America : the West Indies and the formation of literature and culture
in the new republic / Sean X. Goudie.
        p.   cm.
    Includes bibliographical references (p.   ) and index.
    ISBN-13: 978-0-8122-3930-0 (acid-free paper)
    ISBN-10: 0-8122-3930-X (acid-free paper)
    1. American literature—1783–1850—History and criticism.   2. American
literature—West Indian influences.   3. United States—Civilization—1783–1865.
4. United States—Civilization—West Indian influences.   5. Literature and
society—United States—History—18th century.   6. West Indies—In literature.
7. Colonies in literature.   I. Title.
PS208.G68   2006
810.9′002—dc22

                                                        2005056360

For my family and the people of Dangriga, Belize

Contents

"Our Nation Is a Caribbean Nation": The West Indies and Early U.S. America

In 1993, Caribbean leaders at the White House stood in a rim around President Bill Clinton as he delivered a speech entitled "U.S. Interests in the Caribbean: Building a Hemispheric Community of Democracies." His guests' presence visually reinforced the President's claim for the U.S. Republic's Caribbean lineage: Our concern for the region is

firmly rooted in geographic proximity[:]
the resultant flows of people, of commodities, and of culture. . . . U.S.-Caribbean relations dramatically demonstrate the absolute inseparability of foreign and domestic issues. More than ever before, our nation is a Caribbean nation. (1)

By foregrounding the nation's Caribbean lineage and by claiming "Caribbean" status for the United States, Clinton attempts to mitigate the grave concerns of the Caribbean leaders around him about the perpetual underdevelopment of their island economies as a result of the unequal "flows," as Clinton euphemistically puts it, "of people, of commodities, and of culture" between the United States and the Caribbean. An imbalance in trade and human capital, they fear, will almost certainly be exacerbated by the implementation of the North Atlantic Free Trade Agreement between the United States, Canada, and Mexico. Regardless of how one interprets the President's words—as sincere and/or motivated by political and economic expedience—Clinton speaks from a position of unqualified hegemony in the hemisphere. Nowhere present are the fraught tensions marking Federalist and Republican debates in the late eighteenth and early nineteenth centuries over the United States' volatile commercial relations with West Indian plantation economies and the European empires administering them, which I examine in this study. As the political leader of a global superpower, the President two centuries later is able to a great extent to dictate the terms of relation between the Caribbean "Community of Democracies" he extols in his speech and a sprawling U.S. commercial empire.

In sharp contrast, the United States was anything but a vast commercial empire in the late eighteenth century as it sought in essence to negotiate the country's first free trade agreements, specifically between the United States and the West Indian colonies of Europe's powerful mercantile empires. If President Clinton, speaking at the end of the twentieth century, celebrates "our nation [as] a Caribbean nation," *Creole America* demonstrates that in previous centuries, the dynamic between rhetoric and ideology has contributed alternately to parallel, obverse, opposing, and even cryptic versions of the speech's governing metaphor. As we will see, there was not anything resembling unanimity of opinion among the nation's political leaders regarding the effects on the national character of a commingling of West Indian and U.S. goods, peoples, and cultures, whatever the two regions' "geographic proximity." Even so, there was a near consensus in the immediate aftermath of the Revolution about the need to reestablish vigorous trade relations between the United States and the West Indies in order to ensure the Republic's survival and future economic prosperity.

"Thoughts on the West India Trade" (1782), notwithstanding its relative obscurity, is an important document for how it illustrates the urgency of the U.S.–West Indian trade issue to U.S. political leaders in the late eighteenth century. Produced at the request of the Continental Congress by Robert Morris's Office of Finance, "Thoughts" lays bare the ways in which competing visions for the future course of the nation and national character were formed in relation not only to U.S. expansionist designs on the continent, what scholars have come to term internal colonialism, but also the push for commercial empire in the hemisphere via the roots and routes of the West Indian trades. The document presented a template of arguments that could be deployed by U.S. ministers plenipotentiary at the peace negotiations in Europe to secure for the Republic the most advantageous commercial treaties possible in relation to the West Indian colonies. In short, the text submits that free trade between the United States and West Indies is essential in order to restore the prewar levels of commercial prosperity that the former North American colonies had enjoyed. Concomitantly, "Thoughts" insists that the most profitable West Indian plantations in the post-Revolutionary era will be those administered by the European empire that resists imposing barriers to "American" trade with its West Indian possessions.

"Thoughts" was amended and adopted for various occasions depending on the exigencies of ongoing trade negotiations between the United States and the British, French, and Spanish empires. Perhaps the most intriguing version of the document, one marked by its shift from a confidential policy paper to an explicit letter of proposal, was sent to Francisco Rendón, Spain's agent to Congress at Philadelphia, and delivered by Rendón subsequently to José de Gálvez, Spanish minister of the

Indies.[1] The letter largely repeats the various arguments contained in the source document even as it tailors them to appeal to the colonial needs and desires of its Spanish audience. Especially revealing, however, is a new argument, one that responds to concerns across Europe about the potentially catastrophic consequences of affording the Americans free trade with the West Indies: namely, that the United States would infect those colonies with its liberal commercial practices and republican values, catalyzing a successive series of democratic insurgencies:

When the colonies are unable to free themselves from dependence on the Metropolis, as is the case with the [Spanish] American Islands, there is no need to fear enriching them, for these same riches pass on to the Mother Country, which does not have to fear that they may wish to be independent. It did not happen thus with the continental colonies. If England had not granted to the United States the commerce of her Islands they would still be without doubt under her dependence. Spain can commit the same fault, if it allows the inhabitants of her Islands to go looking for provisions in New Spain instead of allowing them to draw them from the United States. In truth, by that means she will be able perhaps to enrich her islands and colonies at the same time, but who will be responsible for the consequences? (Morris, Letter to Francisco Rendón 476)

Thus the Rendón letter—very possibly penned by Morris himself given his mercantile firm's longstanding investments in trade with Cuba— goes well beyond attempting to allay Spanish fears about a U.S.-inspired creole revolution in its American colonies. If European empires worried about the inter-American domino effect of the United States on would- be independent nation-states in the West Indies looking to throw off their colonial status like their creole cousins in North America, what this text provides is a blueprint for how Spain might avoid such a contin- gency precisely by opening West Indian ports to U.S. commerce.

As such, the Rendón letter ably demonstrates the kind of diplomatic maneuvering many U.S. leaders undertook in the first decades of the nation's existence in order to establish the United States as a commer- cial power in the hemisphere. The anonymous U.S. politician engages in machinations that, however desperate given that notification had arrived previously from Europe regarding Britain's fateful decision to exclude the United States from direct *legal* trade with its West Indian colonies, are counter to the Republic's foundational values. The letter argues that the U.S. drive for independence began precisely as England granted North American colonial merchants and traders access to the British West Indian trades and plantation economies. Had the mother country not afforded its Northern and Middle Atlantic colonies a mer- cantile—as opposed to an exclusively agricultural—responsibility in building the empire, the United States would "without doubt" still be colonized by the British. In other words, the "fault" of West Indian trade access did more than create a commercial role for the North American colonists in the administration of the empire's West Indian colonies. Once created, such a role could never be withdrawn or mitigated—despite Parliament's efforts to do so by passing successive navigation restrictions in the 1760s and 1770s. In essence, the writer credits intercolonial commerce with inspiring the anticolonial—or, in the terms of this study, creolizing—values that led to armed revolution and the overthrow of British empire.

By granting the United States unrestricted trade access to the West Indies, Spain, rather than fear that the "Sons of Liberty" would spark revolution there, would on the contrary be guaranteeing those colonies' ongoing colonization. Steady supplies of U.S. fish, grains, flour, timber, and other commodities essential for a smooth-running plantation economy would enable Spanish West Indian planters to focus exclusively on the business of planting, leading to unprecedented growth and expansion of their plantations and a sizable financial windfall for the "Metropolis." Without U.S. imports, planters will of necessity, the letter warns, forge ever-stronger trading relationships with creole merchants and traders on the Spanish mainland. In the former case, U.S. commerce will warrant the independence of the Spanish colonies in the West Indies and elsewhere *from one another,* whereas the latter scenario will hasten the moment when a New *Spanish* Republic in the Americas, inspired by the U.S. Revolution and an emergent spirit of independence *from the mother country,* revolts into being.

Underpinning the not-so-subtle threat of insurrection and rebellion should the United States be denied commercial access to the West Indies is the nervous recognition that the letter's governing logic might be used against itself. Should England, France, and/or Spain proscribe direct trading relations between the United States and the West Indies, the new nation, whatever its independent status, would in functional terms remain dependent on the whims and mercies of Europe's powerful mercantilist empires. Indeed, "Thoughts," the source document for the Rendón letter, stresses in anxious tones to U.S. diplomats negotiating the terms of peace overseas the reciprocal importance of the West Indies and the United States to one another's prosperity: "Every commercial man in America knows how great the consequence of the West Indian Trade is to this Country. The situation and the products of it are peculiarly crafted to an intercourse with the former. At present it must be most proper to view that America is as necessary to the West Indies as they are to us" (282). In correspondence with other U.S. governmental officials, John Adams, minister plenipotentiary to the British, characterized the situation in a remarkably similar manner. Such rhetorical overlap suggests that Adams was, as Congress intended, drawing on the talking points of "Thoughts" as he formulated his position on a future U.S. presence in the West Indian trades: "The commerce of the West India Islands falls necessarily into the natural system of the commerce of the United States. We are necessary to them, and they to us; and *there will be a commerce between us*" (*LWJA* 8:79; emphasis added).

Adams's edict serves as a warning: should his European counterparts fail to accede to U.S. demands for free and unrestricted trade with the West Indies as outlined in "Thoughts," U.S. Americans—and West Indians reliant on American goods for their own and their slaves' survival—will defy such trade bans, raising the specter of an expansion of the U.S. Revolution into the West Indies in ways otherwise not desired, according to Adams, by either U.S. Americans or Britain's West Indian colonists. What Adams, in terms that I define below and use across this study, desires for the United States in the peace settlement is not so much direct colonial governance of, but legal and unrestricted *paracolonial* access to, Europe's West Indian colonies. Rather than engaging in unwinnable commercial wars against powerful European navies for control of their West Indian colonies, the new nation wants Europe to persist in administering the colonies but simultaneously to allow the United States a paracolonial benefit. Without licit access to Europe's West Indian colonies, Adams presciently predicts an ever receding horizon in regard to his fellow patriots' utopic vision for the United States as a nation of "happiness and prosperity" (*LWJA* 8:102). In ways like and unlike many West Indian planters in Cuba, Jamaica, and Saint-Domingue desiring free and direct commercial intercourse with the Americans in opposition to restrictions on such inter-American exchanges imposed by the European mercantile centers of empire, the United States could find itself mired in what is tantamount to a prolonged colonial condition.

Tellingly, not a single European empire would in the early 1780s grant the United States free trade access to its West Indian colonies. On the contrary, each severely limited direct commerce between the islands and the upstart North American nation for reasons that are perhaps by now apparent: to punish the creole revolutionaries and thereby set an example to other would-be revolutionary creoles in their colonies across the Americas; to guard specifically against the corruption of their West Indian colonies by the liberalizing republican values, institutions, and antimercantilist commercial practices that spawned the U.S. revolution against England; and to defend the European mercantilist system itself against incursions by a free-trading, "neutral" United States on its markets. In that regard, despite reassurances from Morris's Office of Finance and U.S. diplomats that what the United States ultimately desired in the final terms of peace was unfettered trade between the

United States and the West Indies *only*, Europe's metropolitan centers of empire suspected otherwise. They believed the United States was bent on domination of *all* the lucrative West Indian "carrying" trades: not just those to and from the West Indies and the United States, but also routes between the West Indies and Europe and Africa.

Perhaps not so ironically, it would be left to the nation's first Secretary of the Treasury, arch-Federalist Alexander Hamilton, the one-time West Indian merchant clerk who according to the dictates of European natural history discourse about the New World was a "degenerate" West Indian creole, to mastermind a bold strategy for defying the hold of Europe's empires over the destiny of not just the nation's political economy but the hemisphere itself. How might Hamilton accomplish this overwhelming challenge that he set for himself and his adopted nation without the United States ultimately compromising its foundational ideals by repeating European empires' oppressive political and military policies and reproducing colonialism's exploitative economic practices? *Creole America* argues that the tensions, contradictions, and instabilities surrounding Hamilton's controversial and aggressively pro-commerce expansionist vision for addressing that formidable task form, and are formed by, much literature and culture produced in the New Republic. If Hamilton by law could not be the nation's first President, he would arguably first articulate the future vision for U.S. commercial hegemony in a hemisphere of burgeoning democracies, the exact location from which the forty-second President of the United States, whose namesake was Hamilton's political nemesis, speaks. Yet as for William Jefferson Clinton's ecumenical notion of the United States as "a Caribbean nation," Hamilton during the New Republic period in his very person came to embody the great uneasiness many white U.S. Americans— including fellow Federalist John Adams—across the political spectrum expressed about the unpredictable, and potentially disastrous, effects on the "Anglo-American" national character of extensive political, economic, and cross-cultural relations between the slave colonies of the West Indies and the democratic states of the New Republic.

Creole America begins the work of assessing the literary culture's multiple styles and forms for enacting and engaging such a phenomenon by reading a variety of texts produced by West Indian immigrants to the United States as well as North American–born writers "gone creole" in the West Indies. Perhaps no such figure inspires the focus and ambitions of this project more than Alexander Hamilton. When one examines writings by and about Hamilton, one of the nation's foremost founding "fathers" and an important intellectual and cultural icon, a paradoxical portrait emerges. A West Indian creole, Hamilton felt he might achieve his aspirations for glory and fame in the budding American republic by allowing himself to be regenerated in the crucible of an appropriated republican virtue and ennobled creole self. Key to such pursuits was Hamilton's bold design for the United States as an "empire for commerce," a plan he advanced as the most powerful—and controversial—member of Washington's cabinet. Ironically, Hamilton's vision reveals his and the emerging U.S. empire's indebtedness to their actual and imagined West Indian origins—Hamilton worked until age eighteen as a West Indian merchant clerk on behalf of New York shipping conglomerates, an occupation that prepared him for his later role as the new nation's chief economic strategist. At once sacred and profane, the contradictory figures of Alexander Hamilton as abject West Indian creole and heroic American statesman make manifest the mutually transformative encounters between the West Indies and the United States in the turbulent commercial cross-currents of the Americas in the 1790s.

Uneasiness about Hamilton's fame registered by bitter rivals like John Adams and Thomas Jefferson pivots, Chapter 2 reveals, on uneasiness U.S. Americans themselves felt about their ongoing relation to discourses about creoles generated by the various European empires in the last half of the eighteenth century for purposes of colonial and imperial control, discourses that deemed inhabitants of the "New World" inferior and "degenerated" from European Western norms. As Corneille De Pauw notoriously put the case in *Recherches philosophiques sur les Américains* (1770), "Americans" are "a race of men who have all the faults of children . . . a degenerate species of the human race, cowardly, impotent, without physical strength, without vitality, [and] without elevation of the mind" (qtd. in Commager and Giordanetti 79–80).[2] In turn, creole discourses became internalized, resisted, and/or transformed by the colonists themselves in the New World. Anglo-Americans living in North America, for example, were acutely aware of the dominant perception in England about their intellectual inferiority, and of the view—which they themselves had helped create—that their contacts with Native Americans, the wilderness, and slavery had caused them to degenerate.[3] During the Revolutionary period, Anglo-Americans began to resist the colonial hierarchy that depended on such discourse for legitimization. On political levels they asserted their "natural rights," economically they disregarded oppressive tariffs, and culturally they embraced some of the very "creole" characteristics that had been used to define their inferiority. For instance, the term "yankee" in song and literature came to signify their resistance and independence, where in Europe it denoted their backwardness.

Yet once North American creoles gained their independence, it became obvious that in the process of un-becoming creole, Anglo-

Americans had appropriated many of the same oppressive features of creole discourse that the British had used to oppress them. In that regard, the Naturalization Law of 1790 made explicit what had been implicit all along according to the racialized language of the Declaration of Independence and the Constitution: citizenship was equivalent to whiteness. In 1798, alarmed by the presence of thousands of Saint-Dominguan and other "alien" refugees in the nation's capital, and ongoing skirmishes with Napoleon's forces in the West Indies, John Adams urged Congress to increase the period of residence required for admission to full citizenship from five to fourteen years. The passage of the Naturalization Act was accompanied by the implementation of the Alien Act and Alien Enemies Act, which were designed to intimidate "foreigners," including many of the same West Indian refugees, into leaving the country.[4] These legislative acts targeting West Indians—and their slaves—reflect the ways in which newly independent U.S. "American" creoles imagined themselves to a significant extent through and against West Indians and creole discourse about the West Indies.

As the above discussion suggests, "creole" is a term with multiple and overlapping genealogies. Like creoles themselves, discourses about "the creole" migrated throughout the Atlantic world. Etymologically derived from the Latin verb "creare," to create, "creole" was first deployed in its Spanish colonial version—perhaps deriving from the Spanish "criollo"—before migrating into French and British colonial lexicons as a term of New World identity. More precisely, colonists of European descent, as well as black and mulatto slaves and freedmen born and raised in the New World, were identified as "creoles" by the British, French, and Spanish empires. Yet the term denoted much more than the birth of a colonial subject or slave outside the "borders" of national origin (Europe or Africa). Most significantly, the term "creole" was used to account for admixtures, or syncretisms, between Old and New World "races" and cultures. Indeed, a European not born and raised in the West Indies but who had spent many consecutive years there might be thought to have "become" creole-like, or degenerate, on cultural and racial levels according to the rhetorical operations of some European creole discourses.

Of course, creole cultures, races, and identities did not always signify in the same ways in their Spanish, French, and British manifestations. Spanish and French colonists, for example, although sensitive to how the term "creole" denoted inferiority in European discursive constructions, openly identified themselves and their cultures as creole by the late eighteenth century in their writings.[5] Thus while sometimes the term denoted inferiority in Latin America and the West Indies, other times it was used in more neutral tones and at still other moments creole identities and cultures were embraced as a sign of political resistance against the European "center," or by blacks and mulattos against white creoles and Europeans.[6] In the British New World colonies, the term was deployed variously as well. If colonists in the British West Indies who lived in highly exploitative plantation economy societies accepted, however ambivalently, the appellation "creole," this was never really so in the settlement colonies of North America. Even as they understood their creole status, the British colonists in North America, both before and after independence, were highly anxious about being contaminated by the cultural and racial associations of the term "creole" as deployed in discourses of creole degeneracy about the New World. Many North American colonists—particularly in the Northern colonies—recoiled from the prospect that they had "degenerated" from the European "norm" like West Indians in the "torrid zone" or their fellow North American colonists in the South. They were sensitive to the ways in which the creolization of New World cultures, languages, peoples, races, and so on were viewed by European societies and intellectuals. Thus central to political propaganda during the Revolutionary and post-Revolutionary periods was an effort to renounce any affiliation with the pejorative classification "creole." Ultimately U.S. Anglo-Americans suppressed their associations with the term "creole" in favor of a specific creole identity designating their liberation from Europe: "American."

In this way, the process of (un)becoming U.S. American in the late eighteenth century was oftentimes dependent on (un)becoming creole, something Alexander Hamilton came to appreciate on emigrating from the West Indies to North America on the eve of the United States declaring itself "independent." The Declaration of Independence, like so many utopian documents of its kind, was an unclean break from the past. Instead, U.S. claims to a pure, uncorrupted white creole identity were illuminating for how they labored to repress the inter-American cosmopolitanisms of many of its leading citizen-subjects. As the United States sought to substitute a liberating creole identity for an oppressive colonial one, creole uplift, whether undertaken by Hamilton or Jefferson, required ever-increasing sleights of hand in order to repress, through actual and epistemological violence, the formation of inter-American, cross-cultural identities inside and outside the nation's borders. *Creole America* argues that the shadowy presence of creole American identities underlies anxious efforts to construct exceptional U.S. "American" identities and literary and cultural traditions.

In arriving at such a focus, I have been guided, in part, by Edward Kamau Brathwaite's foundational notion of creolization as "a creation of attitudes which in their evolution . . . alter the very nature of colonial dependence" (*Development* 101). Yet unlike Brathwaite, I do not take for granted that this was a fully realized process for post-Revolutionary U.S. American creoles as contrasted with their British West Indian counterparts. That is, I pose to North American and West Indian creoles alike, frequently in the context of one another, the set of questions that Brathwaite uses to gauge the development of creole society in Jamaica at the end of the eighteenth century: "Can 'creole' . . . be identified with stability, with change, or with both? If with both, did this result in some kind of creative friction, or merely in the kind of ambivalence . . . [that is] a cultural attribute of 'colonial'?" (101). I ask as well another question: what is the relation between (un)becoming (U.S.) American and (un)becoming creole in the late eighteenth and early nineteenth centuries?

Creole America surveys responses to that question across a range of genres, including state papers, empire tracts, and pamphleteering; natural histories, autobiography, and lyric poetry; and drama and prose fiction. Treatments of U.S.–West Indian relations by recognizable writers like Benjamin Franklin and Charles Brockden Brown and lesser-known figures such as immigrant playwright J. Robinson and Leonora Sansay, author of two novels set in revolutionary Haiti, are quite diverse across the early national period. In these writings, West Indian bodies and "commodities" figure prominently in competing constructions of U.S. national culture and character. The archipelago proves alternately threatening and alluring, abject and desired, entombed and fetishized across geographic, epistemic, and generic borders. As such, the West Indies function as a surrogate, a monstrous double for urgent political, cultural, and economic crises, not least among these slavery. By excavating intertextual modes of figuring the West Indies, I show how U.S. American writers have formulated competing meta–West Indian notions of themselves as well as their artistic and literary traditions. *Creole America* limns an intertextual, transcolonial, and ultimately transnational cartography of West Indian representations that demonstrates how the new nation as aspiring commercial empire and its writers define themselves through and against the New Republic's profoundly unstable investments in Europe's West Indian colonies.

As I proceed, I press against the limits of "negative" West Indian creole stereotypes and "positive" U.S. American ones to expose the motivations and desires of the writers who wield them. Indeed, as the case of Hamilton demonstrates, in many instances authors' identities are formed by overlapping and shifting U.S. and West Indian affiliations that themselves contradict hierarchical distinctions between a *creole regenerate U.S. America* and a *creole degenerate West Indies* that their texts seek to reinforce, challenge, and/or reconcile. Further, the West Indies in the context of this study are not treated as mere representational effect; on the contrary, crucial to my argument about the formative presence of the West Indies in the early national period is the recognition of an actual, felt West Indies—including West Indian creole peoples and cultures and the archipelago's natural resources—that alternately inform, de-form, and re-form notions of the "West Indies" and U.S. "America" espoused by early U.S. writers. Thus Chapters 2 and 3 examine the little-known role played by the "neutral" Dutch and Danish West Indian islands in providing for the commercial well-being of the United States before, during, and after the Revolution and in shaping the inter-American identities and texts of Alexander Hamilton and poet-journalist Philip Freneau; the third and fourth chapters on Freneau and J. Robinson, as well as parts of the fifth chapter on the writings of Charles Brockden Brown, treat the long-standing commercial and cultural ties between the United States and Jamaica, the British empire's most lucrative sugar island, in their assessments of the West Indian influence on early U.S. poetry, drama, and fiction respectively; finally, several chapters and the Afterword evaluate the overbearing revolutionary presence of Haiti as "shadow" black republic to the would-be exceptional—and exceptionally "white"—U.S. nation. In that regard, the Brown family trading business was severely harmed when one of its vessels was boarded and seized by the British navy off the coast of Saint-Domingue in the 1790s, an incident stunningly reimagined in Brown's novel *Arthur Mervyn* (1799–1800), whereas Leonora Sansay's autobiographical works of fiction recount her experiences on relocating from Philadelphia to Saint-Domingue with her French West Indian husband at the height of the Haitian Revolution. In both authors' texts—and across the study's chapters—hierarchical distinctions between U.S. and West Indian bodies, races, and cultures blend and blur in the wake of the Haitian Revolution and amid ongoing U.S. participation in the treacherous West Indian trades.

In order to gauge the ways in which the early Republic's hemispheric relations with the West Indies produce meaning within and across texts, *Creole America* provides two interpretive lenses—*paracolonialism* and the *creole complex*—that in their formulation mark the interrelation between history, politics, economics, culture, and aesthetics in the early U.S. literary imagination. The first paradigm builds on recent developments in the fields of early American studies, postcolonial theory, and Caribbean studies in arguing that the emergent Republic, beneficiary of an ongoing client relationship both pre- and post-Revolution with Europe's West Indian colonies, can best be described as operating *paracolonially*. The prefix "para"—meaning "alongside," "near or beside," "resembling," or "subsidiary to"—aptly describes the United States' relationship to

European colonialisms in the Western Hemisphere during the early decades of its existence and even today in many respects. If not a "colonialist" nation (and clearly it would eventually become one in relationship to parts of the future Caribbean and the Pacific, though this would never become a dominant state-sponsored ideological enterprise), the United States according to its strong economic and cultural relations with Europe's West Indian colonies functioned in a way that was similarly, though not precisely, colonialist. As such, the elusive nature of the United States' paracolonial relationship to sites like the West Indies has ironically tended to mystify for scholars the United States' reliance and dependency on European colonialism, thus causing some to argue either that the United States is and always has been a "colonialist"—or "neocolonial" or "imperial"—nation or, instead, that the United States has never been "colonialist" but operates as a democratic republic of states and territories whose citizens and resident aliens enjoy certain fundamental rights as established by the Constitution.

In arriving at the term "paracolonial," I suggest that the United States' actual relationship to European colonialism during the New Republic period is not an either/or but a both/and: the United States is both colonialist and not colonialist, but in such a way that *exceeds* (another of the multiple meanings of the prefix "para") the ability of that term to account for the United States' hemispheric and global conduct in many arenas, but especially in the arena of political economy.[7] Received terms like "postcolonial" and "neocolonial," or "imperial" and "neoimperial," are wholly inadequate to account for the exact (and vulnerable) location of the United States in relationship to the hemisphere's dominant political economies, specifically European colonialisms in the West Indies and elsewhere. More precisely, under the leadership of George Washington, John Adams, and Thomas Jefferson, the United States operated to a considerable extent as a paracolonial nation. Because the United States' paracolonial relationship to European colonialism predates independence, it would be inaccurate to classify its behavior as "neocolonial," for there was nothing "new" about it. Also, twentieth-century notions of the United States as an "imperialist" nation anachronistically applied to the New Republic context do not jibe with the reality of ongoing European colonial and military hegemony in the West Indies and elsewhere. Nor would it be correct to categorize the United States' hemispheric conduct as strictly "postcolonial," for clearly the nation was continuing post-Independence in a paracolonialist economic arrangement with Europe's still-dependent West Indian colonies that preceded the Revolution, even as the United States' arrival at independent status rendered it a "postcolonial," if still vulnerable, nation in relationship to England and the rest of Europe. As a result of its paracolonial political economy, then, including a visible mercantile presence on many West Indian islands, the United States emerges as a para[-]site on the scene of European colonialism in the Caribbean, a complicit client nation-state that aims to benefit economically from the scene of European colonialism without ever having to corrupt itself—or its foundational principles—with overt political sponsorship of those colonies.[8]

Creole America argues that a considerable amount of literary and cultural production in the New Republic forms itself in relation to the little-examined or -understood phenomenon of U.S. paracolonialism in the West Indies. As such, these authors and texts evince a richly varied paracolonial aesthetics. To the extent that they treat U.S. paracolonialism as inconsistent with, or counterproductive to, a given view of national or regional character and culture, or a preferred course of U.S. empire building, such authors structure their texts formally and thematically by negating U.S. paracolonialism in the West Indies—alternately obscuring, mystifying, abstracting, displacing, and altogether denying U.S. participation in the West Indian trades and the Republic's complicity in perpetuating the plantation economies there. Authors also write from the point of view of paracolonial affirmation, embracing U.S. paracolonialism as consistent with the nation's character, spirit, and founding values and principles. They understand paracolonialism in the West Indies as a necessary, if precarious, transitional mercantile economy, one to be adopted until a not-too-distant moment in the future when the United States might emerge as the dominant military and commercial power in the hemisphere. Finally, whether engaging in paracolonial negation or affirmation, almost all writers who respond to or evaluate U.S. paracolonialism in the West Indies evidence a more or less ambivalent posture toward that liminal and, as the end of the century nears, increasingly volatile political economy. They betray varying measures of anxiety about the potential contradiction between U.S. republican values and principles and paracolonial involvement in the West Indian plantation economies and trades; about the not-quite-free Republic's inability to determine its own commercial destiny in the West Indies owing to ongoing European military and colonial dominance there; and about the dangerous social and cultural intersections between a putatively regenerate U.S. American republic and the still degenerate West Indies.

The second paradigm I employ in *Creole America* centers on the dual nature of what I term—drawing on theories of creolization devised by Brathwaite (Barbados) and Édouard Glissant (Martinique), as well as influential scholarship authored by historians of U.S.-Caribbean relations in the eighteenth and nineteenth centuries—the New Republic's *creole complex*.[9] Such a creole complex operates on several mutually related levels. The first level concerns the nation's postcolonial relationship with Britain. Despite the nation's independent status, U.S. commerce remained highly vulnerable to British (and French) attack. Such a paradox manifests itself in Federalist leaders' ambivalent attitudes—alternately apologetic and resentful—toward the ways in which Britain persisted in dictating the terms of U.S. commercial relations with the West Indies and Europe. It also precipitates Republican charges that Federalists are conspiring to sacrifice republican principles and the national character by effectively returning the nation to a state of colonial dependency on Britain wherein West Indian and Southern planters are beholden to not one but two "metropolitan centers": the urban North and Middle Atlantic, controlled and governed by paracolonialist Federalist elites, and London, on whose behalf Federalist colonial mimic men like Hamilton are said to function.

The second aspect of the creole complex centers on charged debates about the strategies of resistance that paracolonial U.S. traders must employ to evade British imperial dominance in the West Indies, including dangerous trading practices that Hamilton advocated U.S. merchantmen might rely on in order to subvert the predatory practices of the powerful British and French navies while the nation attempted to amass a respectable navy. Yet given the vulnerable status of U.S. merchants plying the West Indian trades to British and French attack and spoliation, such parasitic practices tend to make the United States look like, rather than distinct from, the "debased" European empires and West Indian colonies that it relied on for its economic well-being.

The final feature of the creole complex militates against the notion that the U.S. Revolution marked an absolute break in the creole condition and character of U.S. Americans. More precisely, ongoing mercantile participation in the West Indian plantation economies, on which the U.S. political economy remains reliant for its economic and social prosperity, undermines the would-be model Republic's claims to hemispheric exceptionalism and contradicts the notion that the nation has, in the New World's embrace, redeemed the degenerated political, economic, and cultural institutions of Europe. Such a reality mitigates, too, Federalist claims in relation to plantation-owning Southern Republican adversaries to be occupying the moral high ground in their pro-commerce ideological orientation toward matters involving the national character and republican values and institutions.

What I have termed the New Republic's creole complex, then, exposes the multiple contradictions inherent in a Hamiltonian empire for commerce that espouses the civilizing benefit of disseminating U.S. "American" enlightenment values throughout the hemisphere via a rapidly expanding commercial sphere on the one hand, while exploit-

ing for purposes of expansion and material gain the plantation economies of the "creole" West Indies and the U.S. South on the other. In
such a way, Federalists themselves, many of whom, including Hamilton,
were avowed abolitionists, might be said to perpetuate hemispheric slavery, despite their impulse to charge Southern Republican adversaries
with the primary responsibility for doing so. As these definitions of the
New Republic's creole complex imply, far from realizing Hamilton's
utopic vision for the United States as an empire for commerce, the
United States remained a commercial dystopia in perpetual crisis
throughout the 1790s and early 1800s. In almost every instance, these
crises pivot in crucial ways on the U.S. government's persistent efforts to
persuade the British or French to enter into, and abide by, financial
and/or military pacts or trade agreements granting the United States
more substantial, unfettered access to the West Indian trades.

Such a crisis is intensified and deepened by a revolution undertaken
by black West Indian creoles and Africans in the French colony of Saint-
Domingue in 1789, a revolt that ultimately led to Haitian independence
in 1804. That revolution demonstrated in graphic terms the ways in
which *creolizing* republican values like liberty and freedom were not, as
had been argued, the sole purview of white creole U.S. Americans alone.
In such a way, the Haitian Revolution—and other major slave rebellions
on the islands of Jamaica, Guadeloupe, and elsewhere—would have
powerful implications at "home." White U.S. Americans across regions
cited the Haitian revolution as evidence for why abolition must be forestalled in order to preserve the New Republic's character and culture
from being "blackened" or "West Indian-ized." Conversely, free and
enslaved blacks, like Gabriel Posser in Virginia in 1800 and Denmark
Vesey in South Carolina in 1823, drew on the "West Indian" example in
their own rebellions, whereas others like Absalom Jones and Richard
Allen in Philadelphia urged abolition, emancipation, and full integration of black slaves—a multidirectional creolizing of creoles, as it
were—in their incursions into the white-dominated public sphere and
literary marketplace. All these responses occurred within the context of
substantial commercial relations between Northern and Middle Atlantic
mercantilists and the plantation economies of the Middle Atlantic and
Southern states, as well as licit and illicit networks of trade and exchange
between the putatively free and independent United States and the slave
colonies of the West Indies.

Michael Hardt and Antonio Negri in their influential study *Empire*
glimpse the significance of the New Republic to the present postmodern
moment of U.S. global hegemony. It is useful to recall their distinction
between European and U.S. modes of empire building so as to gauge

more fully than the ambitious scope of their project allows how the embryonic moment of U.S. empire in the late eighteenth century predicts its present-day incarnation. In contrast to European mercantile empires, whose "territorial boundaries of the nation delimited the center of power from which rule was exerted over external foreign territories through a system of channels and barriers that alternately facilitated and obstructed flows of production and circulation" (xii), U.S. American empire relies for its prestige and power on "a *decentered* and *deterritorializing* apparatus or rule that progressively incorporates the entire global realm within its open, expanding frontiers" (xii–xiii; emphasis in original). Such centrifugal attributes of U.S. empire find their impetus in the politico-legal principles of the U.S. Constitution and their portability across territorial boundaries, as well as the socioeconomic values that provide for sprawling free trade zones and global marketplaces. In such a way, U.S. empire forms itself in relation to, and circulates through, an ever-proliferating space or "frontier," which Hardt and Negri understand to be expansion across the continent prior to the twentieth century and thereafter throughout the globe.

Yet in reconsidering the temporal and spatial axes of their genealogy of U.S. empire formation, Hardt and Negri, as well as scholars of the early national period, would do well to consider not only how Thomas Jefferson's distinctly *agrarian* empire for liberty ideology provides for a shift between European and Euro-American forms of empire but also the ways in which Hamilton's decentered, extracontinental empire for commerce ideology does so as well, albeit in different terms. If Jefferson endeavored to inscribe the Constitution's republican values in free and open spaces of land-based agricultural economies on the continent, Hamilton, well before the twentieth century, sought to inject global markets with an acquisitive, liberalizing U.S. commercial "spirit" under the guise of spreading freedom and liberty to the hemisphere's still colonized spaces—not only on land but in the trading "spaces" of the Atlantic and the Caribbean Sea. For Hamilton, the "frontier" of U.S. empire, as today, flowed south and north as well as east and west, beyond the nation's ever expanding borders on the North American continent into the West Indies and the commercial chaos of the West Indian trades.

Notwithstanding the fascinating continuities between Hamilton's empire vision and the reality of U.S. empire today, the discontinuities between the earliest and most recent epochs of U.S. empire building are as pronounced and important. The New Republic period marks a profoundly unstable moment in the cataclysmic shift from European to Euro-American forms of empire. As my readings of "Thoughts" and the Rendón letter demonstrate, European mercantilists were sensitive to insurgent creole American energies motivating the U.S. push for commercial empire. What such documents seek to reassure is that which they are least capable of reassuring: namely, that revolutionary U.S. political and economic structures will not compromise and ultimately displace the long-standing, direct lines of power between the mercantile centers of Europe and their creole colonial peripheries. Conversely, according to its precarious paracolonial posture and resultant creole complex, the United States found it necessary to exploit the extant power dynamics of European empire in the Americas, and in the process reproduced many of their oppressive tendencies. By so doing, it actively contained the most radical potentialities of the Revolution and the Constitution for freeing all creoles (and noncreoles) regardless of race from European dominance and oppression. Such contradictions lend the emergent moment of U.S. empire, and the literary culture it produces and to which it responds, simultaneous creolizing and colonizing tendencies: the early U.S. nation as "empire" is at once static and dynamic, ambivalent and resistant, in relation to preexisting European empires.

If as a twenty-first-century global superpower the United States depends on an unprecedented ability to manage "hybrid identities, flexible hierarchies, and plural exchanges through modulating networks of command" (Hardt and Negri xii–xiii), the contradictions and tensions adhering to the United States as paracolonial nation mired in a creole complex are reflective of its inability to regulate successfully such identities, hierarchies, and exchanges. As implied by this study's title, "hybridity" is far too imprecise a construct to account for the (frequently violent) ways in which U.S. American white creoles sought to define themselves in relation to Europeans across the Atlantic, Native Americans and blacks on the continent, and West Indian creoles—white, mixed-race, and black—within and without the nation's borders. Across *Creole America*'s chapters, we will see Anglo-American creoles in the United States and the West Indies strive for the retention of root European cultural traditions, and in other instances endeavor to imitate and borrow from non-European ones emanating from Africa, Native America, and elsewhere. Likewise, nonwhite creole identities and cultures exhibit both preservationist and assimilationist tendencies. Grammars of creole identification, not only in the United States but throughout the Americas, form and re-form themselves in dominant, residual, and emergent ways, just as the literature, art, and culture that this study treats evince conventional and innovative aesthetic attributes.

If white U.S. Americans display moments of "creative friction" in their resistance to European impositions on their freedoms, they simultaneously prove to be "creole ambivalents" to the extent that they erect new borders, boundaries, and hierarchies of power in relation to Native Americans, blacks, and creoles elsewhere in the Americas, particularly the West Indies. Accordingly, *Creole America* examines how U.S. American creoles are at once creolizing and colonizing in their relations with other creoles, exceptional and unexceptional in the formation of their institutions and literary and cultural forms. As Amy Kaplan remarks concerning the "anarchic" foundations of U.S. culture and empire, "If the fantasy of American imperialism aspires to a borderless world where it finds its own reflection everywhere, then the fruition of this dream shatters the coherence of national identity, as the boundaries that distinguish it from the outside world promise to collapse" (16). Amid the paracolonial chaos of the late eighteenth century, such borderlessness and incoherence are always already collapsing in on "exceptional" U.S. dreams for a coherent national identity and a rapid rise to commercial dominance in the hemisphere. If the creative tendencies that sustain the emergent empire persistently threaten to overthrow it, early U.S. authors and artists, from distinct vantage points, routinely figure the specter of such a possibility.[10] Their creole poetics infuses *Creole America*'s chapters and Afterword, which are written by a Caribbeanist who has quite purposefully chosen to spy out spaces of creolization in early U.S. American literature and culture, and by so doing claim a new space for the study of creolization in American studies.

Part I of *Creole America*, "Paracolonialism and the New Republic's Creole Complex," consists of two chapters. Chapter 1, "Locating the Prenational Origins of Paracolonialism and the Creole Complex: Benjamin Franklin's Late Colonial Encounters with the West Indies," foregrounds the paracolonial origins of early U.S. American literature and culture by locating them in the late colonial and early national writings of Benjamin Franklin. The chapter begins by examining an intriguing rhetorical strategy in Benjamin Franklin's *Autobiography* (1818): Franklin's attempt to "figure in" the West Indies as a way of "figuring" them out of his text. By reading Olaudah Equiano's slave narrative (1789) against Franklin's *Autobiography*, I map an intertextual, transcolonial, and ultimately transnational cartography of West Indian representations that demonstrates how Franklin and other writers of the new nation (retrospectively) assert their independence and self-reliance by dis-figuring their respective investments in the West Indian slave colonies. As the chapter proceeds, it reveals how Franklin's impulse toward West Indian negation in the *Autobiography* gives way to a rhetoric of paracolonial ambivalence regarding U.S. participation in the West Indian trades. In a series of important empire tracts authored during the late colonial and early national periods, Franklin urges the continental expansion of Anglo-America westward while simultaneously trying to reconcile how such expansionism depends on a proliferating Anglo-American paracolonial presence in the West Indies. The chapter's conclusion thus examines Franklin's attempts as cultural critic under the pseudonym "Richard Saunders" and as minister plenipotentiary negotiating commercial treaties in the wake of the Revolution alongside John Adams to disentangle U.S. relations with the West Indies.

Preoccupied with examining the significance of U.S. continental expansionism—the so-called Jeffersonian empire for liberty—on literary and cultural formation, scholars of the early national period have long overlooked, or otherwise misestimated, the importance of a coterminous effort in the New Republic era under the direction of Alexander Hamilton to establish the United States as the preeminent commercial empire in the hemisphere. By revisiting the charged political debate over Hamilton's empire for commerce ideology and practice, Chapter 2, "Alexander Hamilton and a U.S. Empire for Commerce," demonstrates how the creole complex defies any univocal, triumphant, or stable understanding of the national character. Against claims for U.S. exceptionalism, the creole complex highlights the ways in which the Revolution marks not so much a break from as an ongoing process of refiguring creole conditions in the former North American British colonies, with far-reaching psychic and material consequences. In its treatment of a substantial number of texts including correspondence, natural histories, state papers, essays, speeches, poems, and biographies, the chapter argues that in charting a course for U.S. commercial empire, Hamilton challenged received assumptions about republican virtue and national character. His sweeping political and economic reforms sparked widespread discussion about Hamilton's and the nation's own "West Indian" origins that pivoted, predictably, on repressed fears about creole degeneracy.

Part II, "Writing the Creole Republic," suggests the potential benefits awaiting scholars willing to situate literary and cultural production in the New Republic in relation to Hamilton's and his opponents' persistent anxieties about their creole origins. In Chapter 3, "Paracolonial Ambivalence in the Poetics of Philip Freneau," I treat Philip Freneau's "West Indies" poems, works that respond to his experiences while living on the island of St. Croix—the same stage, ironically, where Freneau's chief political adversary, Alexander Hamilton, spent his early life—and then as he sailed the West Indian trades in the last decades of the eighteenth century. These poems, including several conceived while Freneau was stranded for two months on the island of Jamaica as a result of a commercial voyage gone awry, reveal the unique paracolonial tensions and properties attaining not only to Freneau's poetry but to art and literature across the New Republic period. As such, Freneau is an especially apt figure for foregrounding the central aesthetic and thematic concerns of the literature and culture of U.S. paracolonialism. If in transparent ways Freneau's "West Indies" poems indict the tyranny of European colonialism in the West Indies at the end of the eighteenth century, less understood by readers are the complex ways in which they register, albeit ambivalently, the licit and illicit energies and profits stemming from the New Republic's own exploitative relationship to the scene of European colonialism and imperialism in the West Indies and the Caribbean Sea. The chapter shows how Freneau's paracolonial unconscious, as it were, thwarts the poet-journalist's efforts to arrive at a unifying, triumphal account of the national character according to an agricultural ethos and continental expansionism in his "Empire" poems. Across these would-be encomiastic lyrics, the ostensibly "regenerate" and "rising" U.S. empire increasingly comes to resemble the "degenerate" scene of European colonialism that it is defined against in Freneau's "West Indies" poems.

Unlike Republican party advocate Freneau, many poets, writers and artists were staunch supporters of Hamilton and his Federalist vision of the United States as a hemispheric power, an inter-American "empire for commerce." When Republicans like James Madison called for embargoes on trade with the British in retaliation for the Royal Navy's seizure of U.S. merchant vessels plying the West Indian trades, Federalist statesman Fisher Ames urged caution, mocking the self-centeredness of Virginia tobacco planters and what he perceived to be Madison's rashness and duplicity:

But the people have been led to expect an exclusion of the British rivalry, that we may force or frighten them into an allowance of a free trade to the West Indies, &c.; and the people of Virginia (whose murmurs, if louder than a whisper, make Mr. Madison's heart quake) are said to be very strenuous for a law to restrict British trade. They owe them money, [and] perhaps would be glad to quarrel with their creditors. . . . But is it not a risky measure, exposing a feeble trade, as the American is, to the shock of experiment? Will the people forbear murmuring, if the West India trade should be cut off? (1:680–81)

Chapter 4, "The West Indies, Commerce, and a Play for U.S. Empire: Recovering J. Robinson's *The Yorker's Stratagem* (1792)," shows how immigrant playwright J. Robinson in *The Yorker's Stratagem; or, Banana's Wedding* intervenes in this escalating debate between Federalists and Republicans about the proper course for U.S. commerce in the West Indies by endorsing Hamilton's empire for commerce ideology, which by the 1790s involved a pragmatic forbearance of British spoliation of U.S. commerce in the Caribbean. As Ames makes the case, "Had we not better wait till [our] government had gained strength? And then, if we can extend our own trade, by retaliating upon foreign nations their own restrictions, I would do it; but I am afraid of taking an intemperate zeal for reformation of commerce for my guide" (1:681). Robinson's zeal is not for the reformation of commerce by embargo but for the unbridled expansion of commerce according to deft "stratagems" perpetrated by the "Sons of Columbia" masquerading as Yankee bumpkins in the Caribbean. Such stratagems include the manipulation of devices like creole dialect and imposture, and blackface and miscegenation, that project onto the West Indies evolving U.S. crises centered on race, slavery, and unscrupulous commercial conduct. Robinson's play is especially notable, the chapter demonstrates, for the ways in which it evinces the substantial though little remarked-on effect of West Indian performance culture on an emerging U.S. dramatic tradition.

In contrast to Robinson, novelist Charles Brockden Brown in *Arthur Mervyn* (1799–1800) focuses on the ways in which increasingly democratic, creolized, and fractious West Indian societies and cultures from Saint-Domingue/Haiti, Guadeloupe, and Jamaica function as perhaps the most significant threats to U.S. ambitions for commercial empire and "pure" notions of national character and culture. Chapter 5, "Charles Brockden Brown's West Indies Specie(s)," shows how Brown's narrative creole complex ingeniously exposes the multiple contradictions inherent in a Hamiltonian empire for commerce that espouses the civilizing benefit of disseminating U.S. "American" enlightenment values throughout the hemisphere via a rapidly expanding commercial sphere on the one hand, while exploiting for purposes of expansionism and material gain the slave colonies of the creole West Indies on the other. Within and without the borders of Brown's novel, West Indian and Anglo-American cultures and commodities clash and cohere in ways that resist hegemonic attempts to domesticate West Indian figures within discursive constructions of a resolutely *white* empire. By limning the contours of U.S.–West Indian relations, Brown's work dares us to come face to face with disturbing affiliations between U.S. and West Indian creole characters and cultures at the turn of the nineteenth century.

Across *Creole America*'s several chapters, the West Indies emerge as an extracontinental site binding mutually constitutive regional and national issues of the early United States. Raced, gendered, and sexualized West Indian characters and bodies exist in anterior and posterior relation to Northern, Middle Atlantic, and Southern ones. As such, the West Indies are a screen on which important regional and national conflicts are reified, refracted, and/or worked through. Also, in addition to treating more established authors and texts, critical to *Creole America*'s project of constructing an innovative inter-American literary and cultural cartography is the recognition of previously untreated or less examined figures and writings, such as Robinson and his play, originating in the United States and the West Indies. Such recognition reflects ongoing efforts by critics to expand our notion of what ultimately constitutes "American" literature and culture. Finally, in accord with recently published scholarship that endeavors to locate nineteenth-century U.S. literary production in an "inter-American" or "trans-American" context, *Creole America* redirects our attention to the ways in which early U.S. literature and culture from the late eighteenth and early nineteenth centuries forms itself not only according to an East-West transatlantic axis but also a North-South hemispheric one.[11]

Ultimately *Creole America* has three main preoccupations: to demonstrate the shaping influence of the "West Indies" in early U.S. America; to reveal how inter-American "creole" energies inflect the New Republic's literary, cultural, and artistic traditions; and to devise paradigms for understanding the intricate ways in which discrete circumatlantic forces related to U.S. involvement in the West Indian trades confound estimations of regional and national character in the Republic's first decades of existence. Significantly, such paradigms—paracolonialism and the creole complex—rather than being imposed by me from without emerged in remarkably organic ways from the authors and texts themselves. In excavating interdisciplinary, intertextual modes of figuring the West Indies and the creole origins of U.S. American literature, *Creole America* aims to unsettle scholarly perceptions about how early U.S. writers and artists conceived of themselves and others, their society and culture, and the structures and forms in which they write. It accomplishes this ambition by confronting the reader with the precise antagonisms that generated the creole complex and proved so disconcerting, albeit in remarkably productive ways, to the New Republic's writers, artists, and political and economic leaders.

Part I
Paracolonialism and the New Republic's Creole Complex

Chapter 1

Locating the Prenational Origins of Paracolonialism and the Creole Complex
Benjamin Franklin's Late Colonial Encounters with the West Indies

What does Benjamin Franklin have to do with the West Indies? This was a frequently asked question when I mentioned to colleagues that although Alexander Hamilton is the inspirational figure and generative focus of this study, it would have to begin with a chapter on Franklin. Candidly, Franklin *is* a most unlikely author with whom to start. Franklin was not born in the West Indies and there is no record of his ever having traveled to the West Indies. Even so, many writers and artists who might at first seem unprofitable candidates for treatment according to *Creole America*'s "West Indies" focus are ones, on careful reexamination of their corpus according to the interpretive lenses of paracolonialism and the creole complex, who prove to have defined themselves and their texts, and conceived of a particular notion of "national character," through and against the West Indies. Thus Franklin's canonical status makes him an especially useful figure for demonstrating the efficacy of exploring the "West Indian" margins of texts in order to apprehend a more balanced, less rigidly nationalist understanding of early U.S. literary and cultural formation. In addition, given his prominent diplomatic role as an ambassador to Europe, first on behalf of the North American colonies and later the early United States, Franklin's writings are an illuminating locus for the prenational origins of paracolonialism and the New Republic's creole complex.

To many readers, Franklin remains a distinctly "national" author, a mythic figure who defied ostensibly more learned European scientists, intellectuals, and political leaders with his home-grown genius and who, as U.S. elder statesman in the 1790s, championed the cause of abolition as president of the Pennyslvania Abolition Society. Against that nationalist reading, scholars like Michael Warner have urged recently a recognition of Franklin's transatlantic, cosmopolitan status. Warner suggests compellingly that Franklin's "provinciality"—his Londoner role as North American diplomat living abroad—reveals an "English" figure, a

Franklin of the "powdered wig" whom critics of the nationalist camp refuse to acknowledge.[1] In contrast, Benedict Anderson, in the revised edition of his influential study *Imagined Communities: Reflections on the Origin and Spread of Nationalism,* identifies Franklin as someone "indelibly associated with creole nationalism in the northern Americas" (61), a chief exemplar among the many "pilgrim creole functionaries and provincial creole printmen [who] played the decisive historic role" (65) in defining a nationalist identity in opposition to European empire. Crucially, Franklin's *creoleness,* to the extent it signifies and proves portable across national borders, does so via Anderson as critic rather than by anything authored by Franklin himself.

There are merits to the arguments of critics who understand Franklin to be a transatlantic British cosmopolitan figure, as well as those who view Franklin as an emergent creole nationalist. The "British cosmopolitan" critics usefully redirect attention to the root cultural leanings that pervade Franklin's writings and his policies and decisions as a diplomat living abroad. Even so, such critics underestimate the ingenious double-voice that belies Franklin's British gentleman posture in many of his texts, particularly those on the present and future course of the British empire. Thus Anderson is right to insist on a creole nationalist Franklin, a voice that coincides with, and at times subversively underlies, a more transparently creole loyalist voice in many of his late colonial writings. In focusing on Franklin's parochial Britishness, Warner foregrounds how Franklin should not seamlessly occupy an uncompromisingly nationalist position in the critical imaginary, even as Anderson extends our appreciation for such a Franklin by suggesting how circulating print culture—Franklin's print—produced an American nationalist vernacular in North America.

This chapter argues that Franklin, while admiring of his Anglophone status, opposes certain oppressive attributes of Britishness during the late colonial period—especially the hardening attitudes toward the North American colonies of Parliament in defense of British mercantilism, as contrasted with their privileging of the West Indian sugar islands' concerns—and in so doing adapts, or in other words *creolizes,* his Britishness according to a North American context whereby he is like and unlike the British gentleman he impersonates in his texts. Further, even as Anderson's account of "creole" fails to demonstrate any concrete understanding of the historical meanings and valences of the term in its late eighteenth-century context, he nonetheless provokes a reconsideration of Franklin as "print-journalist" in relation to the hemisphere's other creole cultures and peoples (61–62).[2] Consistent with such a shift in the spatial axis of understanding Franklin, this chapter focuses on Franklin's "West Indian" writings, especially as they relate to the North

American paracolonial role in sponsoring the plantation economies of the West Indies. It argues for a creole Franklin who is at once a figure in creative friction with the metropolitan center owing to his departure from oppressive British mercantilist attitudes toward the colonial peripheries in North America, though also a figure of creole ambivalence in regard to British North America and later U.S. America's paracolonial role in perpetuating empire's excesses in the West Indian plantation economies, which in Franklin's texts do double-duty standing in for an absent-present North American/U.S. South. In his tracts on empire and the West Indies, Franklin displays a profound sense of paracolonial ambivalence and emerges as a creole *dys*-functionary printer whose poetics of North American–West Indian relations become mired in contradiction and perpetual crisis.

The first two sections of the chapter treat Franklin's foundational autobiography and Olaudah Equiano's slave narrative alongside one another. In its formal and thematic innovations, Equiano's double-voiced narrative ingeniously demonstrates how Northern and Middle Atlantic paracolonial complicity in perpetuating the hemisphere's plantation economies—not only in the U.S. South but also and particularly in Europe's West Indian colonies—undermines bold professions that the U.S. rising empire has inherited the Enlightenment that a tyrannical Europe has squandered. In such a way, Equiano's text deconstructs the binary relation between a creole regenerate U.S. nation-state and a creole degenerate West Indies that Franklin's *Autobiography* relies on for its "exceptional" structural and thematic coherence.

The third section examines two important empire tracts, "Observations concerning the Increase of Mankind" (1755) and *The Canada Pamphlet* (1760), which Franklin authored during the crucial pre-Revolutionary period. In these works, we can distill Franklin's own version of an Equiano-esque double-voiced discourse whereby a subversive creole protonationalist voice exists in tense dynamic with a surface-level loyal colonialist one. Franklin's empire tracts reveal his paradoxical impulse to urge the continental expansion of Anglo-America westward even as he struggles to reconcile the ways in which such expansionism depends on a proliferating Anglo–North American paracolonial presence in the West Indies. Franklin's anxious acts of paracolonial negation in the *Autobiography* thus provide a framework for examining his rhetoric of paracolonialism across his empire writings. The chapter concludes by considering Franklin's unsuccessful efforts as U.S. minister plenipotentiary to negotiate with his British counterparts the most favorable trade agreement possible regarding U.S. commercial relations with the British West Indies as part of peace treaty deliberations at Versailles in 1783. Collectively, the writings that comprise Franklin's prosaic encounters with the West Indies evince the complex, conflicted ways in which much literature and culture of the late colonial period forms itself in relation to British North American paracolonialism in the West Indies, providing a "primal scene," as it were, for *Creole America*'s assessment in subsequent chapters of literary paracolonialism in the New Republic.

Paracolonial Negation of the West Indies in Franklin's *Autobiography*

Inventor, institution builder, city planner, political strategist, and, perhaps most significantly, model national biographer, Benjamin Franklin was thoroughly involved in charting the course of Philadelphia, the nation-state, and the national citizen. Nonetheless, since the publication of Herman Melville's mid-nineteenth-century parody of Franklin in *Israel Potter* (1855) and D. H. Lawrence's 1920s critical account of Franklin as a con man, writers and scholars have attempted to unravel the seemingly seamless "democratic" message of Franklin's foundational *Autobiography*. Still, they have yet to identify one of the text's foremost rhetorical strategies: Franklin's attempt to "figure in" the West Indies by way of "figuring" them *out* of his text, a strategy consistent with elisions regarding slavery and the West Indian trades in the Declaration of Independence and the Constitution. From the moment the young printer establishes himself in Philadelphia—and simultaneously avoids having to fulfill an apprenticeship to a West Indian merchant he had agreed to serve—the West Indies become a contaminated site, a place to which business failures (and Franklin's enemies) are banished, a place against which he and the rising U.S. nation are measured.

Consistent with such dis-figurations, Franklin's *Autobiography* mutes the voices of West Indian slaves and freedmen like Equiano, whose narrative recounts three fascinating "business trips" from the West Indies to "Franklin's" Philadelphia during the peak of Franklin's entrepreneurial and diplomatic brilliance.[3] By treating these little-examined moments in Equiano's narrative, I demonstrate how many New Republic–era writers such as Franklin commodify not only the colonized or formerly colonized of the West Indies but also (fascinatingly enough) the West Indian colonial establishment to which the North American economy is wedded in rhizomatic fashion.

Readers of Franklin's *Autobiography* may be surprised by the claim that the West Indies emerge as an important figural presence in the text. Indeed, Franklin mentions the West Indies less than a dozen times in the entire narrative. Yet I maintain that the space the West Indies occupy in the text is inversely proportional to their ability to generate meaning in it. Franklin's unflattering West Indian allusions—to the West Indies, to people and things "West Indian," or, more precisely, to people and things from Philadelphia "gone West Indian"—represent a discursive maneuvering always already underpinning the text's paracolonialist rhetoric. Regarding Franklin's text specifically, his West Indian allusions respond to the emerging Republic's ongoing exploitative—if not precisely colonial—relationship to the plantation economies of the West Indies. Like the democratic Republic's tautological dependence on Southern slavery, its codependency on West Indian plantation economies is at odds with the nation's founding values and civilizing mission, a contradiction that Franklin discretely registers in the *Autobiography*. In order to elucidate the paracolonialist nature of Franklin's rhetoric in the *Autobiography*, I adapt David Spurr's account of colonialist rhetoric in *The Rhetoric of Empire*. By so doing, I illustrate the ways in which Franklin's paracolonialist discourse complicates not only the text's ostensibly democratic message but also its formal properties by generating a series of West Indian representations that prove anxious and disruptive.

Franklin's allusions to the West Indies in the *Autobiography* are most notable for their consistently debasing tone: the West Indies become at once metaphor and metonym for an anti-North America, the place to which the continent's undesirables remove and are removed. According to Spurr, debasement as a rhetorical trope involves the colonizer's attempt to establish a privileged, hierarchical distance between himself and the colonized by yoking the colonized with "Dark, enclosed spaces, infestation, contamination, sexual and moral degradation" (90). These biological obsessions expand, Spurr notes, "through a scale of progression that moves both metaphorically and metonymically, into anxiety over the psychological perils of going native and finally into the dystopian view of vast social movements that threaten civilization itself" (91).

Such a paracolonial pattern of debasement characterizes Franklin's dis-figuration of perhaps his foremost foe in the *Autobiography*: the printer Samuel Keimer. A chief rival in the Philadelphia printing scene, Keimer ultimately proves incompetent and ill at ease in polite Philadelphia society. In one of the *Autobiography*'s most vicious attacks, Franklin ridicules Keimer's failure to maintain a kosher Jewish lifestyle. Although Keimer wears "his Beard at full length," he proves the fool when Franklin tempts him with "dressed meats" during Lent. Writes Franklin, "He was usually a great glutton . . . [and though] I went on pleasantly, . . . Poor Keimer suffer'd grievously, tir'd of the Project, long'd for the Flesh Pots of Egypt, and order'd a roast pig" (29), eating it in its entirety. Thus Keimer's gluttony foreordains his later removal: not to Egypt but to a rhetorically charged West Indies.

"Negation" is the colonialist discursive trope that most accurately accounts for Franklin's paracolonial figuration of the West Indies them-

selves. Spurr describes "negation" as the condition whereby the colonizer "conceives of the Other as absence, emptiness, nothingness, or
death . . . clearing a space for the expansion of the colonial imagination
and for the pursuit of desire" (92–93). Later the chapter discusses in
more detail Franklin's and his beloved Philadelphia's shared paracolonial "desires" for West Indian profits; for now, it will suffice to illustrate
how Franklin conjoins a debased Keimer with a "negated" West Indies.
This is not at all to suggest that debasing conditions are nonexistent in
the plantation economies of the West Indies. Instead, I am concerned
with the ways in which Franklin's paracolonialist rhetoric seeks to binar-
ize the relationship between the emerging U.S. nation-state, for which
Philadelphia becomes the exemplar in Franklin's *Autobiography*, and the
always already debased and negated West Indies to the extent that the
West Indies (not the U.S. South, crucially) become the site of all that is
"other" to the nation, its foundational democratic and republican values, and its exceptional citizenry. "I went on swimmingly [in the printing business]," Franklin gloats, whereas "Keimer's Credit and Business
declined daily, [and] he was at last forc'd to sell his Printing-House to
satisfy his Creditors. He went to Barbados, and there lived some years in
very poor Circumstances" (54). Ever the self-promoter, Franklin strategically produces an unrelentingly negative account of Keimer, capped
off by his unceremonious epitaph about Keimer's West Indian demise.
Nowhere does he mention Keimer's more positive achievements:
Keimer was one of the first Philadelphians to found a school for slaves
(1722); he established the first West Indian newspaper in 1731, the *Barbados Gazette*; and he published a widely circulated first collection of
West Indian creole writings and verse, *Caribbeana* (1741).[4] Such details
might have provided a fuller, more balanced account not only of Keimer
but of the many circumatlantic personalities that operate within and
beyond the margins of much late colonial and early U.S. American literature and culture. Instead, Franklin relocates Keimer, according to the
cunning artifices of his text, beyond its domains to the West Indies—a
fatal destination marked by nothingness where Keimer lives out his life
in poverty, decline, and decay.

  Several other figures also endure the "Keimer treatment," whereby
Franklin anxiously disciplines, according to a pattern of debasement
and negation, the West Indies, the West Indian trades, and the attendant
flow of peoples and commodities to the West Indies from Philadelphia.
In the process, Franklin insulates himself from possible contagion by
would-be rivals and competitors. Indeed, to read Franklin's *Autobiography*, it would seem that only the most unfit to survive in the ascending
democratic republic descend to the dark and distant West Indies, never
to be heard from again. Keimer's dandified apprentice David Harry is

one such example. In his tendency toward "pride"—he is said to "dress like a Gentleman, live expensively, take much Diversion and Pleasure abroad, run into debt, and neglect his business" (54)—Harry proleptically anticipates, according to Franklin's debasing characterization of him, his ultimate relocation to the West Indies by looking and acting like the late eighteenth-century stereotype of a West Indian "nabob" or absentee planter. Like Keimer, Harry fails in the Philadelphia printing business and "finding nothing to do[,] . . . follow'd Keimer to Barbados" (55). Franklin relates as well the fate of John Collins, a childhood friend who propels Franklin to study logic more deeply by criticizing his lack of eloquence. On their maiden voyage to Philadelphia from Boston as teenagers, Collins proves an unworthy companion to a Franklin literally and figuratively on the move. We are told Collins drinks too much and is fractious and Franklin eventually throws him overboard when he refuses to help row them to safety in a storm. He leaves Franklin on their arrival in Philadelphia, "promising to remit" to Franklin a sizable debt only to abscond to the West Indies with "a West India Captain who had a Commission to procure a Tutor for the Sons of a Gentleman at Barbados" (26–27), never to be heard from again. Finally, Franklin identifies his future wife Deborah Read's first husband, John Rogers, as a "worthless fellow . . . who got into Debt, and ran away . . . to the West Indies, and died there" (41), conveniently leaving Read eligible to partner the infinitely more desirable Franklin. Franklin's catalogue of debased rivals who remove to the West Indies thereby casts the West Indies in a negative light: the region emerges as the site to which disreputable, unsuccessful, unworthy former sons of Philadelphia retreat, thereby clearing the textual space necessary for Franklin's expansive North American personality to unfold, a life more worthy of imitation than the lives of Franklin's band of West Indian castaways.

Intriguingly, Franklin seems narrowly to have avoided sharing their fate. Early on in the narrative he relates that as a young man returning from a period abroad in England, he agreed to become the protégé of Thomas Denham, a Philadelphia merchant:

[Denham] now told me he was about to return to Philadelphia, and should carry over a great Quantity of Goods in order to open a store there: He propos'd to take me over as his Clerk, to keep his Books (in which he would instruct me), . . . He added, that as soon as I should be acquainted with mercantile Business he would promote me by sending me with a Cargo of Flour and Bread, etc., to the West Indies, and procure me Commissions from others; which would be profitable, and if I manag'd well, would establish me handsomely. The thing pleas'd me, for I was grown tired of London . . . . Therefore I immediately agreed. (41)

Soon after their return to Philadelphia, however, Denham falls fatally ill, and Franklin turns to printing as a vocation. How might the identity formation that Franklin sketches in the *Autobiography* have been altered had fate not saved him from a career as a West Indian merchant clerk? What did it mean to have one's identity formed in the crucible of the volatile and frequently violent West Indian trades? Further, what does Franklin's aborted plan to ship out to the West Indies suggest about Philadelphia's, and the inchoate nation's, shadowy involvement in the colonization of the West Indies? Did they avoid being affiliated with, or corrupted by, the West Indies trade routes that form a kind of anti-Exodus in Franklin's text, tending away from the promised land of Philadelphia according to Franklin's unidirectional cartography?

The Interesting Narrative: Negating the Rhetoric of Paracolonial Negation

Olaudah Equiano's now widely read slave narrative provides a series of richly illuminating answers to some of these questions. Published contemporaneous to Franklin's late-stage writing and revising of the *Autobiography*, *The Interesting Narrative* (1789) has received much well-deserved scholarly attention in recent years. Hardly any critical attention has been paid, however, to Equiano's Philadelphia visits. A tale within a larger circumatlantic narrative of captivity, bondage, and freedom, Equiano's Philadelphia story can be read productively alongside Franklin's foundational account of a young man's entry into Philadelphia society and his subsequent refashioning of an exemplary American identity there. As I attempt such a task, I am mindful that Equiano's Philadelphia account and Franklin's *Autobiography* emanate from two widely different locations, not only in terms of American literary history but also in relation to the two authors' respective places in the eighteenth-century circumatlantic world. Whereas Franklin enjoys a life of privilege as a Philadelphia printer, entrepreneur, and statesman, Equiano attempts to liberate himself from slavery by pursuing the life of a West Indian merchant clerk that Franklin ultimately avoided. Accordingly, Equiano's narrative proves an especially apt vehicle for deconstructing the paracolonialist properties of Franklin's foundational text.

Equiano's Philadelphia story begins as he is being sold in Montserrat to Robert King, a Philadelphia merchant working the West India trades. Before reading Equiano's account of the sale, let me briefly gesture to its larger significance. First, if Franklin's anxious narrative suggests that only failing, irredeemable Philadelphians depart for the West Indies, Robert King's presence there points to a crucially different story, one centered on Philadelphia's reliance on the West Indies for its very economic survival. Second, Equiano's ultimate emergence from the West Indies and entry into Philadelphia in search of his freedom suggests a radically different set of coordinates by which to chart the formation of foundational American stories and characters—not Philadelphia via Boston, but Philadelphia via Africa, England, and the West Indies. Moreover, Equiano's revelation about the Pennsylvania Quaker King's purchase of him points to the manifold ways in which Philadelphia's participation pre- and post-Revolution in the circumatlantic slave economy extended well beyond the North Atlantic, particularly into the West Indian plantation economies to which Franklin disparagingly alludes.

Equiano provides the following protracted account of his impressions on learning he is to be sold to King by Captain Doran, his British master's agent:

With trembling steps and a fluttering heart I came to the captain, and found him with one Mr. Robert King, a quaker, and the first merchant in the place. The captain then told me my former master had sent me there to be sold; but that he had desired him to get me the best master he could, as he told him I was a very deserving boy, which Captain Doran said he found to be true, and if he were to stay in the West Indies he would be glad to keep me himself; but he could not venture to take me to London, for he was very sure that when I came there, I would leave him. . . . My new master, Mr. King, then made a reply, and said the reason he had bought me was on account of my good character; and, as he had not the least doubt of my good behavior, I should be very well off with him. He also told me he did not live in the West Indies, but at Philadelphia, where he was going; and, as I understood something of the rules of arithmetic, when we got there he would put me to school, and fit me for a clerk. (70)

Especially striking about Equiano's testimony is how uncannily it resembles Franklin's own narrative about his emerging prospects as a West Indian merchant clerk under Thomas Denham. Like Franklin, Equiano does not become a merchant clerk, at least not initially. Instead, Equiano records how King repeatedly reneges on his promise to uplift him in order to exploit Equiano's skilled-slave status indefinitely.

Gauging King's duplicity according to Franklin's portrayal of Philadelphians "gone West Indian," we might conclude that, like Keimer, Collins, and Rogers before him, King is a Philadelphia misfit, a social pariah unworthy of admittance into citizenship status in the New Republic. On the contrary, King was a highly respected Philadelphia merchant, and his behavior and participation in the West Indian trades as depicted by Equiano was hardly unusual. Writes Equiano, "King dealt in all manner of merchandize, and kept from one to six clerks. He loaded many vessels in a year, particularly to Philadelphia, where he was born, and was connected with a great mercantile house in that city" (71). As historians such as Cathy Matson, Peggy Liss, Richard Sheridan, Philip Curtin, Philip Morgan and Jack Greene have recently shown, North American affiliations with the West Indian colonies were elaborate and varied.

West Indians owned estates in Philadelphia, and prominent Philadelphians owned and operated major trading houses throughout the West Indies. Cultural connections were strong, too. As Chapter 4 demonstrates, West Indian theatrical troupes, like the Hallams of Jamaica, were major players on the Philadelphia stage. The exchange of commerce and culture between Philadelphia and the West Indies in the late eighteenth century was far more substantial, dynamic and fluid than Franklin's text indicates. Accordingly, Equiano's account exposes the partial nature of Franklin's depiction of his and Philadelphia's West Indian affairs.

Philadelphia's role in Equiano's evolution from slave to nominally free status proves crucial. Equiano eventually reaches Philadelphia on three different voyages, two of them sponsored by King. A cursory reading of Equiano's account would seem to vindicate Franklin's binary opposition between civilized Philadelphia and the uncivilized West Indies. Equiano variously refers to Philadelphia as "the elegant town" (93), "the charming town where [he] finds everything plentiful and cheap" (93), "this agreeable spot" (94), "this fruitful land" (98), and, on his final voyage, "this favourite old town" (170). There he is able, he reports, to sell profitably wares that his captain awards him for his constant "good character"—a puncheon of rum, a hogshead of sugar—in pursuit of "money enough . . . to purchase my freedom" (92). Indeed, monies that Equiano earns from his bartering in Philadelphia go a long way toward making such a goal attainable.[5]

Closer analysis of Equiano's Philadelphia story, however, reveals a carefully structured, ingeniously catalogued set of contradictions that belie Equiano's more glowing account of what was, by the time his narrative was published, the New Republic's capital city. On the basis of the above-mentioned reports, one would expect Equiano, on receiving his manumission papers, to relocate to Philadelphia in order to live out the duration of his life in prosperity and unqualified freedom. Yet Equiano speaks about Philadelphia with a "double-voice" that Henry Louis Gates, Jr. and Valerie Smith have identified as characteristic of Equiano's textual persona.[6] In this instance, the effect of his double-voicedness is to ironize the celebratory tone of much of his Philadelphia story by exposing the contradictory condition of a Philadelphia at once free and unfree, hospitable and inhospitable, and civilized and uncivilized. If in Philadelphia Equiano avails himself of the opportunity, as he says, to sell high and buy cheaply, he does so only with the Quakers. Equiano states, "They [Quakers] always appeared to be a very honest and discreet sort of people, and never attempted to impose on me; I therefore liked them, and ever after chose to deal with them in preference to any others" (97), thereby implying that Philadelphia's non-Quakers were less honest and discreet toward him than he would have liked. Also, if in his 1785 "favourite old town" visit, which he takes several years after returning as a freedman to London, Equiano is encouraged to see some of Philadelphia's citizens "easing the burthens of my oppressed Africans," he is nonetheless dismayed that such efforts seem specific to the Quakers alone: "'Go ye, and do likewise!'" Equiano, citing Scripture, shouts at the reader (170). Finally, Equiano submits Philadelphia to a stinging critique that reveals why homelessness rather than Philadelphia would remain Equiano's "home," a liminal site from which he as a not-quite-free black man would submit the various circumatlantic sites he had encountered to scrutiny without ever being at home in any of them.

He tells the story of witnessing men he calls "infernal invaders of human rights" (88–89) kidnapping and reenslaving a freed black man from a vessel he serves off the coast of Montserrat. As he proceeds, Equiano makes it clear that blacks lack the same sort of human—let alone constitutional—protections not only in "Jamaica and other islands" in the West Indies but also in Franklin's would-be land of liberty: "I have heard of similar practices even in Philadelphia," Equiano protests, "and were it not for the benevolence of the Quakers in that city, many of the sable race, who now breathe the aire of liberty, would, I believe, be groaning under some planter's chains" (89). Such a statement counters Franklin's notion that all of Philadelphia's undesirables had shipped out to the West Indies.[7] Crucially, Equiano inserts this cautionary account conjoining the injustices of Philadelphia with outrageous violence perpetrated in the West Indies proleptically: it precedes and thereby informs the reader's impressions of Equiano's *seemingly* favorable recollections of his three Philadelphia visits.

Equiano's Philadelphia story thus suggests that the West Indies should not be thought of as unimportant to the formation of Philadelphia's and the nascent Republic's economy, culture, and character, as Franklin's paracolonial discourse of negation in the *Autobiography* might tempt us to believe. Something of an absentee landlord himself, Franklin had several business interests in the West Indies. Indeed, he sent his nephew Benjamin Mecom to, in his imperial words, win "the [printing] business of all the Islands, there being no other Printer" (*PBF* 4:357). While Mecom quickly fell into debt and his mission failed, eventually Franklin succeeded in establishing printing presses throughout the Leeward Islands (Carlson 386; Eames 308).[8] Thus we must consider the West Indies as intertwined with, and a formative presence in, the New Republic's national character, as well as the New Republic's literary history, an interesting narrative that scholars have heretofore largely negated.

Caribbean writer and critic Orlando Patterson posits the following distinction between what he terms "segmentary" and "synthetic" forms of

creolization in colonial Jamaican society: "The major difference
between synthetic and segmentary creolization is that whereas in the latter each group develops its own local culture, with synthetic creolization
the group attempts to forge a local culture that combines elements from
all the available cultural resources" (318). Thus creolization emerges
not as a singular process of seamless blending and mixing but rather as
a set of interrelated, and indeed confrontational, processes between and
among various groups contingent on the shifting dynamics of power
that define a given plantation economy. In considering the contrasting
thematic and formal structures of Franklin's and Equiano's Philadelphia
stories—their divergent treatments of racial, cultural, and social relations within and between Philadelphia and the West Indies—Franklin's
Philadelphia more closely resembles a white creole American city and
society characterized by segmentary creolization processes in contest
with the synthetic creolization processes forming Equiano's account. Put
differently, the conflicted feelings toward Philadelphia that Equiano so
eloquently expresses in his *Interesting Narrative* brilliantly succeed in
countering the *Autobiography*'s West Indian negation. At the same time,
they lay bare the deep and disturbing affiliations between the slave colonies of the West Indies and the embryonic states of the not quite "free"
paracolonial Republic.

"A Nation Well Regulated is Like a Polypus": Franklin's Ambivalent West Indian Relations in his Empire Tracts

Franklin's paracolonial figurations in the *Autobiography* signify his anxiety over the ways in which the "West Indies" as abject New World colonies—as anti-Pennsylvania—function ironically as that which is abject
about Pennsylvania and the emergent Republic. Inverting the tendency
by Franklin scholars to privilege the *Autobiography* in relation to his other
writings, the *Autobiography* operates here as a framework for treating two
important late colonial empire tracts that Franklin authored in the
1750s and 1760s. Such framing demonstrates how Franklin's paracolonial negations in the *Autobiography* are symptomatic of a far more enduring, systematic, and intertextual pattern of West Indian debasement and
negation in his writings. In *The Increase of Great Britain Considered, With
Regard to her Colonies, and the Acquisitions of Canada and Guadaloupe*
(1760), also known as *The Canada Pamphlet*, and "Observations concerning the Increase of Mankind, Peopling of Countries, &c." (1755; revised
1760), Franklin anticipates the *Autobiography*'s acts of paracolonial negation. In Franklin's empire tracts, the "West Indies" emerge as a site for
registering racial, cultural, and social misgivings about the impurities
and corruptions of late colonial Anglo-American identity. In these

works, Franklin's anxious critique of the West Indies labors to muffle ongoing socioeconomic and cultural ties between Anglo-Americans in North America and the West Indies according to the West Indian trade routes that constitute the ligatures of the Anglo-American hemispheric "body" before, during, and after the U.S. Revolution. Such mystification is necessary in order to provide for a *creole regenerate* Anglo-American empire in North America formed in opposition to—according to eighteenth-century stereotype—the *creole degenerate* West Indies.

Like Patterson's differentiation between segmentary and synthetic forms of creolization, Édouard Glissant's distinctions between New World processes of creoleness and creolization as productive of opposing "poetics of relation" can be usefully related to Franklin's paracolonial aesthetics in his empire writings. Writes Glissant, "We are not prompted solely by the defining of our identities but by their relation to everything possible as well—the mutual mutations generated by this interplay of relations. Creolizations bring into Relation but not to universalize; the principles of creoleness regress toward negritudes, ideas of Frenchness, of Latinness, all generalizing concepts—more or less innocently" (89). Thus Glissant's notion of creolization as a fluid poetics of relation (a sort of perpetual version of Patterson's synthetic creolization) versus creoleness as an impulse to fix identity for nationalist or culturally essentialist purposes (not unlike segmentary creolization) is helpful for understanding Franklin's conflicted poetics of relation in "Observations" and *The Canada Pamphlet*. More precisely, Franklin's vision of a westerly tending Anglo-American empire unravels in *The Canada Pamphlet* and elsewhere in his empire tracts exactly where his subversively creative poetics of Anglo-American relation in regard to the British metropolitan center (a poetics of creolization) depends on an ambivalent poetics of creoleness in relation to the creole West Indies and black and Native American populations. Such a tension unfolds as Franklin seeks an Anglo-American empire "makeover" according to a utopian ideal of North American creole exceptionalism—a notion perhaps to some extent confirmed by reality but ultimately belied by the totality of economic, social, and cultural cross-currents between British North America and the West Indies.

Although not published until several years later, "Observations concerning the Increase of Mankind" was written in 1751 in response to Parliament's passage of a statute restricting the manufacture of ironworks in the North America colonies. Fearful that such a growth in manufactures might upset the balance of power between the metropolitan center and the colonial periphery, Parliament passed the ironworks law to reinforce fundamental principles of empire that held that the colonies existed to produce raw materials—not finished manufactured goods—for the mercantile center of London.[9] Franklin's important essay, notwithstanding its sincere professions of loyalty, embodies in incipient form the creolizing strategies of resistance that would shape North American protests of Parliament's passage in the 1760s of the despised "Intolerable Acts" that ultimately led to revolution in 1776. In "Observations," Franklin deftly appropriates for North American colonial advantage progressive Enlightenment thought about empire and commerce so as to "manufacture" a less hierarchical and more mutually beneficial and respectful relationship between the British metropole and the North American periphery.

Even so, "Observations" evinces an acute sense of anxiety that pivots on North American colonial rivalry with the British West Indies—a creole rivalry that is itself generative of Franklin's protonationalist sentiment. Franklin's insecurity owes itself to the less important status afforded the North American colonies as compared to the West Indies according to received British mercantile policy given the latter colonies' production of more lucrative raw materials—namely, sugar. Similarly, across his empire writings Franklin chafes at the substantial power wielded by the West India Interest, a lobbying entity composed of absentee West Indian landlords, British mercantile interests invested in the West Indian colonies and trades, and their advocates in Parliament— influence that the North American colonies sorely lacked. Such intercolonial rivalry informs Franklin's efforts to reform British colonial policy by urging a more "enlightened" and ethnically and racially *lightened* future course for British empire in the New World. Franklin's reforms in "Observations" hinge on displacing onto the West Indies sole responsibility for chattel slavery and on negating once more the North American colonies' complicity in perpetuating the ostensibly degenerate West Indian plantation economies against which they are defined in binary relation. Such duplicities betray the tautology underlying Franklin's recommendations for reforming the British empire by (re)modeling its expansionism and colonization in the Americas after a more enlightened North American agrarian political economy and creole character and culture.

Even as "Observations" endeavors to dislodge the privileged relationship that the sugar colonies of the West Indies enjoy relative to Parliament and British colonial and mercantile policy, Franklin simultaneously reassures anxious British mercantilists and manufacturers that he seeks not to override but modify the terms of relation that exist between the putatively agricultural North American colonies and the mercantile and manufacturing centers of empire in England. Franklin accomplishes this delicate high-wire act by mythologizing North Americans as agronomists made regenerate in the superior land and climate of the continent. Anticipatory of Jefferson's arguments in *Notes of the State on Virginia* (1785), Franklin claims that North Americans are extreme in their devotion to nonexploitative agricultural pursuits that, if expanded across the continent, might provide the impetus for a wholesale uplift of the British empire. Yet the attraction of North American creole uplift of empire ultimately rests on Franklin's appeal to a discriminatory racial and ethnic agenda. He urges that by expanding across the western portion of North America, the empire might proliferate as a robust *white* Anglo-American colonial population and culture, as contrasted with an enervated white and predominant *black or tawny* population in the degenerate West Indies.

The key figure in Franklin's essay for representing the future prosperity—or demise—of the British empire in the last half of the eighteenth century is the "polype" or "polypus." Franklin first treats this leachlike microscopic organism in *Poor Richard Improved* (1751), a natural history account published simultaneous to his writing "Observations." "The Animal's Body," Franklin's Richard Saunders persona remarks, "consists of a single Cavity, like a Tube or Gut, and what is wonderful, and almost beyond Belief, is, that it will live and feed after it is turned inside out, and even when cut into a great many Pieces, each several Piece becomes a compleat Polype" (*PBF* 4:93). Consistent with the ways in which Franklin's mastery of Enlightenment thought across disciplines informs his long-term project of creole uplift across the eighteenth century, Franklin remobilizes the "polype" in "Observations" as a figure for illustrating to Parliament the consequences of their decision making on the future course of empire building in the New World. Writes Franklin, "In fine, A Nation well regulated is like a Polypus; take away a Limb, its Place is soon supply'd; cut it in two, and each deficient Part shall speedily grow out of the Part remaining. Thus if you have Room and Subsistence enough, as you may by dividing, make ten Polypes out of one, you may of one make ten Nations, equally populous and powerful; or rather, increase a Nation ten fold in Numbers and Strength" (*PBF* 4:233). Even as Franklin deploys the figure of the "polype" as a metaphor for a "well regulated" empire, the figure ingeniously contains within it the potentially disastrous consequences of a poorly managed one.

A polype is classified in the biological sciences as a "colonial animal," defined in *Webster's New Universal Unabridged Dictionary* as "a collective life form comprising associations of individual organisms that are incompletely separated, as corals and moss animals" or, secondarily, as "any of the individual organisms in such a life form." In that they represent individual colonies/countries, polypes might logically threaten as "colonial animals" to break off from the parent to form their own polype—precisely what would transpire in North America a mere two decades later and a process always already forewarned by Franklin's double-voiced discourse in "Observations." In his *Poor Richard* account of the polype, Franklin comments on how the polype can become "infested with a Kind of Vermin . . . [that] sometimes in a long Time will eat up the Head and Part of the Body of a Polype, after which, if it be cleared of them, it shall have the devoured Parts grow up again, and become as compleat as ever" (*PBF* 4:93). Although he doesn't actually include this detail in section 23, the penultimate section of "Observations" in which the polypus is described, it surfaces in the application of the polypus metaphor to Franklin's notorious recommendations regarding the racialization of empire in section 24. In this concluding section of the essay, Franklin explicitly alludes to the notion of "vermin" as a noxious presence that threatens to devour the "Head and Part of the Body" of empire:

Which leads me to add one Remark: That the Number of purely white People in the World is proportionally very small . . . the Saxons only excepted, who with the English, make the principal Body of White People on the Face of the Earth. I could wish their Numbers increased. And while we are, as I may call it, *Scouring* our Planet, by clearing America of Woods, and so making this Side of our Globe reflect a brighter Light to the Eyes of Inhabitants in Mars or Venus, why should we in the Sight of Superior Beings, darken its People? why increase the Sons of Africa, by Planting them in America, where we have so fair an Opportunity, by excluding all Blacks and Tawneys, of increasing the lovely White and Red? But perhaps I am partial to the Complexion of my Country, for such Kind of Partiality is natural to Mankind. (*PBF* 4:234)[10]

Not until 1763 did Franklin begin to reexamine his notions of white supremacy.[11] Also, while Franklin became an abolitionist in the last decade of his long life, he remained far more concerned with the degenerative effects of slavery on the "savage" white population administering the institution than for its victims or with integrating them into Anglo-American society in North America, a poetics of creoleness over and against a poetics of creolization. Accordingly, if Franklin's "Observations" is, in part, an antislavery tract—as it seems to be in sections 12, 13, and 24—it is also anti-integrationist in the extreme. Only Native Americans—the "Red"—are allowed to be included in Franklin's vision of an expanding Anglo-American empire on the continent, "Observations" thus anticipating once more Jefferson's romantic accommodation of Native America in *Notes*. Yet Franklin's accommodation of Native Americans is provided for only because they stand in the way of white expansion westward; they must, therefore, be assimilated to "our Language . . . Customs . . . our Complexion" (233), or else risk removal.[12] Similarly, when Franklin asks his reader, "why increase the Sons of

Africa, by Planting them in America, where we have so fair an Opportunity, by excluding all Blacks and Tawneys, of increasing the lovely White and Red?," he seems to suggest that the "Sons of Africa" are not already "planted" in "America," meaning North America.

If Franklin does intend to allude to such a reality, he abstracts it to such a level that North America's Southern colonies are not the ones singled out for excoriation in the text's central and most lengthy section, section 13. An essay within the larger essay, section 13 treats the six reasons why "the Increase of People depends on the Encouragement of Marriages," marriages that cannot take place in England among working Englishmen and women because of overcrowding, unemployment, and widespread poverty. Yet much of the section specifically focuses on reason 6, in which the West Indies are figured as the "foot" of empire, its plantation economies as the "vermin" that threaten to devour the "Head" and "Body." Item 6 begins, "The Negroes brought into the English Sugar Islands, have greatly diminish'd the Whites there; the Poor are by this Means depriv'd of Employment, while a few Families acquire vast Estates; which they spend on Foreign Luxuries, and educating their Children in the Habit of those Luxuries; the same Income is needed for the Support of one that might have maintain'd 100" (*PBF* 4:230). Franklin thus foregrounds the trope of West Indian creole degeneracy prominent across the eighteenth century. In doing so, he demonstrates its portability on both sides of the Atlantic, as well as its utility to Franklin as he endeavors to invert the privileged hierarchy of value the West Indies enjoy over North America in the minds of Parliament. Such an inversion hinges, however, on Franklin's displacement of North American complicity in perpetuating the hemisphere's plantation economies. In that regard, reason 6's initial displacement of agency—"Negroes brought into the English Sugar Islands"—abstracts and by so doing negates the major role played by New England carriers in conveying African slaves to the West Indian colonies for profit. Moreover, when agency is assigned, the "Negroes" are blamed not only for degenerating the whites in the West Indies, but for depriving poor English whites of employment. Such views are a long way from any kind of progressive racial politics according to which Franklin might have urged his readers to support the emancipation and full integration of African and West Indian creole slaves as wage laborers—or as merchant clerks, writers, and publishers. Likewise, even as he condemns creole degenerate West Indians for spending "for the Support of one that might have maintain'd 100," Franklin neglects to gesture to such profligacy in the Southern or Middle Atlantic colonies of North America, themselves possessive of vast plantation estates, nor does he allow for luxury as a problem in North America's urban centers.

Franklin's account of West Indian creole degeneracy proceeds in reason 6 by focusing on the ways in which the West Indian "body," both white and black, is corrupted by the plantation economy as "vermin": "The Whites who have Slaves, not labouring, are enfeebled, and therefore not so generally prolific; the Slaves being work'd too hard, and ill fed, their Constitutions are broken, and the Deaths among them are more than the Births; so that a continual Supply is needed from Africa" (*PBF* 4:231). Once more, a strategically passive sentence construction abjures the great financial benefit attaining to the North American slave traders who fulfill this "need." Further, although Franklin grants that black "Constitutions are broken" in the West Indies, he neglects to acknowledge that so, too, are black bodies "broken" by slavery throughout the North American colonies by whites who several decades later would leave blacks further enfeebled by themselves passing a "broken [U.S.] Constitution."

When Franklin turns to procreation, or the lack thereof, in the West Indies, he seems less concerned about whites failing to procreate than about the fact that when they do, they don't procreate *white* but *mixed race, or mulatto,* bodies owing to the greater proportion of white males to white females in the West Indian colonies. In contrast, "The Northern Colonies having few Slaves increase in Whites" (*PBF* 4:231). Perhaps, but in referring to the North American colonies as the "Northern Colonies," Franklin mystifies the great numbers of slaves living in the Middle Atlantic and Southern colonies, including ever-increasing numbers of mixed-race ones owing to white male assaults on black female slaves. He concludes reason 6 of section 13 much as he begins. By granting West Indian slaves an undesired agency, Franklin emphasizes how black slaves degenerate the manners of whites rather than focusing on the violent effects of their enslavement: "Slaves also pejorate the Families that use them; the white Children become proud, disgusted with Labour, and being educated in Idleness, are rendered unfit to get a Living by Industry" (*PBF* 4:231).

Notwithstanding his subversive and otherwise progressive critique of empire's exploitative mercantilist tendencies and practices in "Observations," Franklin's vision of a great white empire in the West relies on negating North American complicity in exploiting the British West Indian plantation economies so as to allow for a (tenuous) binary relation between North American and West Indian colonial societies and cultures. So, too, his project of creole uplift depends on a parallel displacement of Southern slavery in North America onto the West Indies. Why is such an anxious contradiction significant to us? Franklin was lorded on his passing in 1790 as perhaps the figure who, through his appropriation and adaptation of Enlightenment discourses, most defied

European scientific, philosophical, economic, and political contentions that the inhabitants of the New World were creole degenerates. Franklin thus became the quintessential figure of creole nationalism in the U.S. national imaginary, and in many ways he continues to occupy that role today. Yet Franklin's creole nationalist sentiments do not suddenly ensue in the 1770s with the onset of the Revolution, notwithstanding his persistent efforts until that time to find ways to mitigate escalating conflict over Parliament's oppressive policies toward the North American colonies. Rather, in the discourse of empire tracts like "Observations," a strain of creole resistance is always already present, a subversive voice that belies professions of loyalty to all of empire. Yet what texts like the *Autobiography* and "Observations" reveal is how Franklin's incipient creole nationalism depends on essentializing differences between the creole regenerate Northern colonies and the creole degenerate West Indian ones with which the former exist in paracolonial relation. As such, acts of paracolonial debasement and negation in "Observations," as in the *Autobiography*, provide the space necessary for Franklin's regenerative model of Anglo-American empire in North America to take hold. Considered in such a light, the cartography of empire that Franklin draws across texts depends for its meaning on an anxious commodification of extensive affiliations between West Indian and North American economies, societies, and cultures.

Franklin inserts "Observations," absent the notorious section 24, between the text of *The Canada Pamphlet* (1760) and a table of comparative statistics he provides to demonstrate the increased value of the continental colonies as contrasted with the British West Indies as available markets for English manufactures by the mid-eighteenth century. Franklin's decision to attach "Observations" to *The Canada Pamphlet* is obvious enough, the two texts overlapping substantially in content and theme. *The Canada Pamphlet* also seeks to reduce the hold of the West Indian sugar colonies over the empire's colonial policy. Franklin endeavors to accomplish this goal once more by arguing that the North American colonies, in contrast to the stagnant and steadily degenerating West Indies, ought to be the most esteemed in the empire because they produce the most sizable white population, afford the most available space for Anglo-American settlement and expansion in the New World, and promise to provide the empire with the greatest available market for British manufactures with continued expansion—and improved security on the "frontier" that only the acquisition of Canada can ensure.

Unsurprisingly, *The Interest of Great Britain Considered, with Regard to her Colonies and the Acquisitions of Canada and Guadaloupe. To which are added, Observations concerning the Increase of Mankind, Peopling of Countries, &c.* (1760), also known as *The Canada Pamphlet*, features as well the double-voiced discourse of "Observations." Franklin cleverly masquerades in *The Canada Pamphlet* as a continental British gentleman seeking to serve the best interests of the empire at large by advocating the retention of Canada rather than Guadeloupe following the pending surrender of France after the Seven Years' War (known also as the French and Indian War and the Great War for Empire in North America), a war won decisively by the British. Even as such a mask suggests Franklin's loyalty to the British Crown, it simultaneously reveals an uneasy tension between Franklin's loyalties to his "countrymen" in North America on the one hand and to the welfare of the British "nation" on the other. Such tensions recur in the surfaces and depths of Franklin's pamphlet as he defies oppressive mercantile ideologies of empire building that hold overseas possessions valuable only to the extent that they provide raw materials for the mother country. Instead, Franklin argues that colonies should be valued for their capacity to grow in population and geographic holdings, their contributions to the Anglo-American national character, and their buying power across space and time. As the editors of the Franklin papers explain, Franklin posed progressive challenges to the mercantile policies of empire that sought to subordinate in perpetuity the interests of the colonies to those of England:

An island in the Caribbean, with only a relatively small white population of planters and their overseers and large numbers of lightly clad Negro slaves, offered far fewer possibilities for the sale of British textiles, metal products, and other manufactured goods than did the middle and northern colonies of the continent, rapidly filling with independent farming families and prosperous merchants, all needing to buy warm clothing and useful household goods, and eager to acquire the articles of comfort and even luxury that only the mother country could supply. (*PBF* 9:52)

What emerges in *The Canada Pamphlet* is a creole colonial rivalry whereby the British West Indies are pitted once more against the Northern and Middle Atlantic colonies in binary relation: luxury and laxity against industry and modesty; creole degenerate West Indian planters and slaves against creole regenerate North American white farmers. Accordingly, Franklin urges that Britons should not look to Europe, or to the West Indies, but to North America for a more perfect British type. Yet, to adapt Fredric Jameson's famous terms of analysis, the "strategies of containment" that mark Franklin's paracolonial "unconscious" in *The Canada Pamphlet* are ultimately exposed by his European detractors.[13] These strategies are by now familiar to us. They include Franklin's attempts to negate North American complicity in perpetuating and exploiting the debased West Indian plantation economies so as to install unsustainable barriers between North American and West Indian creole characters and cultures, barriers that allow for Franklin's claims for Anglo-American exceptionalism in the North American colonies. Franklin's vision of a westerly tending Anglo-American empire thus unravels in *The Canada Pamphlet* and elsewhere in his empire tracts exactly where his subversive poetics of Anglo-American relation in regard to the British metropolitan center (a poetics of creolization) depends on a dogmatic poetics of relation in regard to the creole West Indies and black and Native American populations (a poetics of creoleness).

The privileged concern inspiring Franklin's recommendation that the Crown and Parliament retain Canada rather than Guadeloupe is that in securing Canada and France's Western territories, the British would be able to prevent a repeat conflict later on with the French, thus ensuring the protection of North American colonists against French and "savage" Indian incursions by removing the geographic foothold from which such attacks are launched. The British empire, according to Franklin's poetics of Anglo-American–Native American relation as not creolization but *Anglo-Americanness*, would be in a position to dictate the terms of acculturation between "savage" Native Americans and "civilized" Anglo-Americans rather than have the detested French Catholics disrupt such a process. In his more sober loyalist voice, Franklin reassures those who would retain Guadeloupe that North American colonists' "jealousy of each other is so great that however necessary an union of the colonies has long been for their common defence and security against their enemies . . . yet they have never been able to effect such an union among themselves" (*PBF* 9:90). Belying such reassurance, however, is Franklin's subversive admonition that the relationship between mother country and colony entails mutual and reciprocal responsibilities and obligations. Franklin presciently anticipates the mercantile crises of the 1760s when he reassures, in a way that is not at all reassuring, that so long as "the government is mild and just, while important civil and religious rights are secure, such subjects will be dutiful and obedient. The waves do not rise, but when the winds blow" (*PBF* 9:91). To be sure, the winds would blow like a West Indian hurricane a mere fifteen years later. Like "Observations," then, *The Canada Pamphlet* is an especially apt text for examining Franklin's double-voiced discourse in his empire tracts whereby an incipient creole nationalism belies sincere professions of loyalty and good will toward the empire.

Even as Franklin devotes considerable space in *The Canada Pamphlet* to arguing for the efficacy of acquiring Canada on its own terms, a key structuring device of the pamphlet is the antithesis between a regenerative North American versus a degenerative West Indian expansionism. If the comparison is not precisely to the British West Indies, it is to the prospect of augmenting the British West Indies by acquiring the French

West Indian sugar colony of Guadeloupe. Even so, the lengthy pamphlet does not avoid explicit comparison between the character and buying power of the North American and British West Indian colonies altogether. Franklin argues that if there are North American absentees in London, they are less conspicuous and more discretionary than "the gentlemen of the West-Indies" who spend lavishly and who inhabit "large estates" (*PBF* 9:86). In contradistinction to the West Indian absentee planters, North American absentees like Franklin himself are characterized by their "mediocrity of fortune" resulting from "a more equal division of landed property than in the West-India islands" (*PBF* 9:86). If "Great merit" (*PBF* 9:86) is afforded the West Indian "gentleman" for spending excessively in London on British manufactures, the difference between West Indians or North Americans spending their money on British manufactures "*here* and *at home* is not so great" (*PBF* 9:86). Instead, the North American "gentleman" who stays at home "and lives there in that degree of luxury and expence with regard to the use of British manufactures" inculcates, unlike the West Indian absentee, "the use of those manufactures among hundreds of families around him, and occasion a much greater demand for them, than it would do if he should remove and live in London" (*PBF* 9:86–87). Franklin thus argues for the proliferation of conspicuous consumption of luxury goods on the continent that elsewhere in the pamphlet he asserts is antithetical to the pleasing mediocrity and discretionary temperament that characterizes British North American taste and manners, consumer excesses that he bemoans in explicit terms in the 1760s and 1770s in other writings.

Franklin continues the comparison by arguing that whatever the value of the British West India trade, "it has long been at a stand. Limited as our sugar planters are by the scantiness of territory, they cannot increase much beyond their present number" (*PBF* 9:87), a reality the acquisition of Guadeloupe will do little to alter. In contrast, the trade with the North American colonies "is not only greater, but yearly increasing with the increase of people . . . [and] wealth" (*PBF* 9:87). With the great increase of such an agriculturally oriented people, North Americans will for many decades, even centuries, be in great need of manufactures. In Pennsylvania, for example, colonists have "by their industry mended their circumstances" and "are enabled to indulge themselves in finer cloaths, [and] better furniture," finished products Franklin claims "for ages" will be cheaper to buy as British imports rather than to produce as domestic manufactures (*PBF* 9:88–89). Finally, as Franklin turns in specific terms to the prospect of acquiring Guadeloupe, he suggests that the island is populated by a people of "different language, manners and religion" who will never assimilate. In contrast, French Canadians will either remove themselves or be assimilated by virtue of their being "swarmed by the crowds of English settling around and among them" (*PBF* 9:95).

Franklin's forward-looking humanistic tendencies figure prominently the mercantilist challenges in "Observations" and *The Canada Pamphlet.* Critics have long recognized such aspects of Franklin's views on commerce and empire, which amount to a sort of antimercantilist mercantilism that seeks to renovate British mercantile policy so as to gain a more respectful status for the North American colonies in the orbit of empire. Critics have identified as well the self-interest underlying Franklin's purportedly disinterested set of proposals for renovating mercantile empire.[14] Still, Franklin's critiques of British mercantilism are considerably more complicated given their double-voiced nature. Accordingly, whereas Franklin's subversion of dominant British mercantilist ideology reveals a double-voiced strain of creole resistance that belies his loyalist voice, a poetics of relation characteristic of creolization, Franklin's rhetorical orientation toward the creole West Indies and Native Americans, blacks and even other, non-Anglo-American European immigrants, manifests itself frequently as a poetics of creoleness. Rather than envisioning these disparate groups as meaningful contributors to the creolization—or *Americanization* (which is not Americanness)—of society and culture in North America, such rhetoric builds a case for Anglo-Americanness. In Franklin's paracolonial debasement and negation of the West Indies, his North American creole exceptionalist discourse threatens to reduplicate the very oppressive tendencies of empire that his *Autobiography* and empire writings ostensibly militate against. Franklin's appropriation and adaptation of Enlightenment principles does not in and of itself tend toward a more or less oppressive cultural relativism in practice than that wielded by metropolitan British mercantilists in relation to North American creoles like him.

In more explicit terms, the paracolonial unconscious haunting Franklin's contrasts between the West Indies and North America on levels of character, political economy, and social culture centers on Franklin's negations of the many *similarities* between the ostensibly regenerative North American and degenerate West Indian colonies on the one hand, and between the self-seeking, exploitative London mercantilists and their upstart rivals in the Northern and Middle Atlantic colonies on the other. Given such a paracolonial unconscious, one should expect to find Franklin's contemporary critics exploiting his paracolonial unconscious for argumentative advantage. It turns out that such critics existed, many of them British mercantilists in favor of retaining Guadeloupe instead of Canada. Collectively, their critiques raise the disturbing suggestion that Franklin's optimistic vision of a creole regenerate Anglo-American empire on the continent *in theory* is countermanded *in practice* by North American complicity in perpetuating the degenerate plantation economies that Franklin debases, not only in the West Indies but also on the continent.

One critic's misidentification of the anonymous author of Franklin's texts as a West Indian is richly suggestive on multiple levels: "Upon the whole, the performance now before me seems to be full of artifice and chicane, calculated to serve the monopolizers of Jamaica, by putting the people upon a wrong scent, in order that they may prefer the shadow of Quebec to the substance of Guadaloupe;—but destitute of every solid reason and true argument" (*PBF* 9:110). That the anonymous author of this critique mistakes Franklin for a Jamaican member of the West India Interest lobby that Franklin so despised is not only ironic but ironically perceptive.[15] When the author refers to Franklin's duplicity, he suggests that the contrasts between North America and the West Indies are too partial and absolute to be believable. Yet given the relatively weak influence of North American creoles and their agents on effecting change in British mercantile policy, the critic identifies the author of *The Canada Pamphlet* not as a North American partisan but as a Jamaican. Consistent with the ways in which the West India Interest would influence Parliament's passage of the despised Sugar Act in 1764 that required North Americans to buy their sugar from Jamaica alone and not from the French West Indies, the author suspects the "Jamaican" Franklin wants to prevent Guadeloupe from joining the empire so as not to challenge Jamaica's and the other British West Indian islands' exclusive right to the British sugar market. Thus at least on the issue of the retention of Canada, the North American "interest" that Franklin represents and the West Indian Interest that he is mistaken for representing make strange bedfellows indeed, both desiring the retention of Canada over Guadeloupe, if for quite distinct reasons.

Yet the notion of Franklin's text as a Jamaican-authored stratagem is ironic on other levels, too. From a vantage point distinct from those of British mercantilists and the agents of the West India Interest, *The Canada Pamphlet* is indeed an artful performance. Such artfulness, however, is not attributable to Franklin's hidden concern, as the critic would have it, for Jamaican sugar planters but for the North American colonists as "farmers" defined through and against the former.[16] Put somewhat differently, the ironic linkage that the critic forges between North American and West Indian creole identities is precisely that which Franklin's repeated acts of paracolonial debasement and negation anxiously refuse to allow.

Franklin's paracolonial "artifice and chicane" did not withstand the scrutiny of several other critics of *The Canada Pamphlet*. His London detractors point to the pamphlet's many occlusions, abstractions, and displacements regarding the multiple set of relations between North America and the West Indies, intimacies that once exposed, as in Equiano's *The Interesting Narrative*, serve to negate the mythic vision that Franklin's two pamphlets create of an exceptional North American creole colonial character. Such tensions mark the complex and multidirectional tendencies of Franklin's subversive double-voiced discourse, even as Franklin's critics expose the ways in which his paracolonial (im)posture refuses to allow for affinities between the exploitative and oppressive tendencies of the British mercantilists and the West Indies Interest on the one hand, and the North American colonists on the other.

An unnamed vocal critic in the *London Chronicle* (May 6–8, 1760) provides four major objections to Franklin's argument in *The Canada Pamphlet* and the attached "Observations." Of the four, only one does not pertain to Franklin's impulse to negate the paracolonial affinities between the North American colonies and the British *and French* West Indies. In such a way, there is an ironic consanguinity between Equiano's act of paracolonial exposure and the unnamed critic's here. Briefly, the opposition remarks on how *The Canada Pamphlet* conveniently neglects to distinguish between the Southern colonies and the Middle Atlantic and Northern ones. As such, essential characterizations of the North American colonies as populated by "white" bodies who live modestly and work industriously on small "plantations" are belied by Southern whites who resemble in many ways the stylized characterizations of West Indians as creole degenerates. Moreover, the promercantilist critic reminds the author of *The Canada Pamphlet* that the Southern colonies are far more valuable as producers of raw materials—tobacco, cotton, rice, and indigo—than the Middle Atlantic and Northern colonies, suggesting that the acquisition of Guadeloupe, combined with the extant British West Indian colonies and the North American South, would constitute a much more powerful and profitable block of colonies according to their production of raw materials than the expansion of the Northern and Middle Atlantic colonies as the author advocates.

The observant critic identifies two other important omissions in the pamphlet. First, he once more challenges Franklin's mobilization of a mythic North American farmer expanding westward on the continent as imposture. British mercantilists are not concerned, he notes, about farmers or producers of raw materials but rather about merchants, traders, mechanics, and manufacturers who exist in increasing numbers in Northern and Middle Atlantic port cities such as Baltimore, Philadelphia, New York, Boston, and Newport. Such emergent mercantilist and manufacturing ports create friction with the interests of the mother country in that they endeavor to rival those interests. In defiance of the fundamental principles of British mercantilism, expansion westward on the continent will only embolden such rivalries by creating a tremendous market for locally produced manufactures. The critic notes in a related point how Franklin's characterization of North American colonists as mere agricultural producers cunningly ignores the critical importance of the West Indian carrying trade to the Northern and Middle Atlantic colonies' financial well-being. In that regard, he argues that North American colonists will not suffer at all from not retaining Guadeloupe, for not only does *The Canada Pamphlet* neglect to mention the important financial benefit that the Northern and Middle Atlantic colonies obtain from their legal trade with the plantation economies of the Southern and British West Indian colonies but it assiduously avoids any mention of the flourishing *illegal* trade that Middle Atlantic and Northern traders conduct with the French West Indies. Such smuggling practices result in the acquisition of much-needed hard currency, not to mention cheap sugar and rum that provide Northern and Middle Atlantic colonists the profit margins to buy and sell the luxury British manufactures that Franklin suggests are purchased from funds gained through "modest" agricultural pursuits alone.[17]

Even as this chapter has focused thus far on Franklin's rhetoric of paracolonial negation and debasement formative of the *Autobiography*, "Observations," and *The Canada Pamphlet*, expressions of overt ambivalence regarding U.S. paracolonial participation in the West Indian plantation economies in the late colonial and early national periods in these documents and elsewhere reveal Franklin's self-reflexive awareness of the unsustainable oppositions that he strategically deploys. One such example is a 1765 critique that Franklin wrote under the pen name Richard Saunders in response to Parliament's passage the previous year of the Sugar Act. Although such laws already existed prior to the Sugar Act, for the first time Parliament promised strict naval enforcement of the Sugar Act's prohibitions against North American vessels trading with "foreign" islands. Thus, if the West India Interest had proven an unexpected partner in securing the retention of Canada a few years earlier at the conclusion of the Seven Years' War, the flimsiness of that unexpected alliance was exposed by the passage of the Sugar Act and, in turn, by Franklin's *Poor Richard* critique.

In his 1765 response, Franklin addresses Parliament's argument that the Sugar Act and other related taxes and duties on the North American colonies are necessary so as to pay down the debt the empire incurred as a result of fighting the Seven Years' War on the colonies' behalf. He also treats Parliament's second major argument justifying the imposition of the Sugar Act, responding, "I have heard too, that some of our [West Indian] Trade has been illegal, hurtful to the Nation, and therefore ought to be restricted" (*PBF* 12:4). Franklin thus gestures in explicit terms to the importance of the same illegal trading practices by North American merchants that he had sought to negate for strategic advantage in his empire tracts. Things being equal regarding the representation and influence of all the British American colonies in Parliament, Richard Saunders suggests he could sustain such arguments and throw his support behind the Sugar Act.

Yet "injury" to the "Nation" by illegal North American trading practices is not the primary motivating factor behind the passage of the Sugar Act, Franklin argues. Instead, the Sugar Act is a result of the undue influence of some colonies' interests over the interests of others according to traditional mercantilist policies:

the West-India Planters, by superior Interest at home, have procured the Restraints to be laid on that Commerce, in order to acquire to themselves the Advantage of solely supplying with their Commodities, both Britain, and her Northern Colonies, and of Course a Power of raising their Prices on both at Pleasure. If so, and as we cannot help it if it is so; what are we to do, but, like honest and prudent Men, endeavour to do without the Things we shall, perhaps, never be able to pay for; or if we cannot do without them or something like them, to supply ourselves from our own Produce at home. (*PBF* 12:4–5)

Franklin's double-voiced discourse of creole colonial resistance emerges once more in this critique of Parliament's motivations for passing the Sugar Act—a desire to "look" to the interests of the rich, sugar-producing West Indian colonies at the expense of what Franklin believes should be the most esteemed of the empire's colonies, the North American ones. If in mocking tones Saunders states, "in most Cases, my political Faith is, that what our Superiors think best for us, is really best," he foreordains in his comment a crisis in empire that hinges on the upstart North American colonies' desire for unrestricted "Commerce with the foreign islands" (*PBF* 12:4).

Franklin's anxiety and ambivalence about the long-term effects of North American paracolonial participation—whether legal or illegal—in the West Indian trades and plantation economies expresses itself in his solution to the crisis brought on by Parliament's passage of the Sugar Act. First, he admonishes his North American reader to do as "honest and prudent Men" (*PBF* 12:4) should do: refuse to buy British West Indian goods, specifically sugar and rum. Yet his follow-up to that recommendation reveals his pessimism that such an injunction will be successfully adopted given the rampant consumption of these products by his readers. In such a way, Franklin's acknowledgment belies his contention in the empire tracts that the manners and tastes of the North American colonists exist in binary relation to those of West Indian creole profligates. Instead, as a compromise, Franklin notes that "if we cannot do without them or something like them" (*PBF* 12:4), then North American desires for West Indian sugar and rum might be satiated by less deleterious, home-grown alternatives. In essence, Franklin exploits his readers' outrage over Parliament's disregard of their rights and interests as participant colonists in empire in order to rid them of their addiction to all things West Indian, though he does so paradoxically by acknowledging the widespread consumption of goods produced by the West Indian plantation economies in North America. Franklin thus indicts North Americans as virtual absentee West Indian landlords once removed. If, as James Walvin holds in *Fruits of Empire*, Franklin condemned "Britain's pernicious global power" according to a mercantilist policy that encouraged "unnecessary consumption . . . [and] the creation of trade in luxuries" (46, 197), the emergence of a successful creole nationalism would seem to hinge on North American colonists' ability to wean themselves from the tastes of an addicted empire.

In an appended note to the above critique entitled "*Concerning* SWEETS," Franklin expands on his program for weaning North American consumers from toxic West Indian rum and sugar. Antithesis once more is Franklin's preferred figure of choice for stressing to his audience the corruptive influence of West Indian sugar products on the Anglo-American character in North America. Whereas "there" in the West Indies "*forced Labour* of Slaves" is used to "extract" molasses for a West Indian "Masters Profit," "here" in North America the "*voluntary Labour* of Bees" is the means by which "Honey is extracted" for the "Advantage" of its harvesters and consumers alike (*PBF* 12:9). Likewise, Franklin insists that the syrup from the "sweet apple," the "Juice of red Beets," and the sap of the "Sugar Maple" might profitably in every sense of the word replace the use of West Indian cane sugar in the North American diet (*PBF* 12:10). Crucially, what Franklin proposes in his reform-minded essay and note on West Indian sugar is an alternative, ethically sound economy that could be possible at some future date, rather than one that already exists in binary relation to the corrupted moral economies operative in Kingston or London, something he argues in his empire tracts. Franklin's telling use of the future conditional in his most charged appeal to his reader in "*Concerning* SWEETS" renders this important distinction palpable: "Could the People of the Northern Colonies see and know, the extreme Slovenliness of the West-India Slaves in making Melasses, and the Filth and Nastiness suffered to enter it, or wantonly thrown into it, their Stomachs would turn at the Thoughts of taking it in, either with their Food or Drink" (*PBF* 12:9). The West Indian slave becomes commodified as object by Franklin's "consumer" rhetoric of West Indian debasement, serving as volatile figure for an artery-clogging molasses production process that dumps "Filth and Nastiness" not only into the coffee and tea cups of the North American consumer but also into the North American body politic.[18] Thus, by weaning one's self from West Indian cane sugar, by "extracting"—a layered trope in Franklin's note—sugars from naturally occurring fruits and vegetables in the Northern colonies, the reader will in turn be performing the patriotic act of "extracting" the Northern colonies from the debased and debasing West Indian trades with which they are at the moment of Franklin's writing inextricably bound by their uncontrollable consumptive desires.

Yet Franklin never fully grapples with the implications of such an ambivalent paracolonial relation between the societies and cultures of the North American colonies—later U.S. states—and the West Indies. Although he acknowledges North American paracolonial involvement in the West Indian plantation economies in his 1765 *Poor Richard* critique of the Sugar Act, Franklin relies once more on a complicated set of rhetorical strategies characteristic of his poetics of paracolonial negation. For example, by referring to the North American colonies as the "Northern colonies" and eschewing any distinction between the Northern, Middle Atlantic, and Southern colonies, Franklin identifies North American colonists as mere consumers of the products produced by "the *forced Labour* of Slaves" and displaces onto the West Indies and the despised West India Interest sole responsibility for directly administering plantation economies in the hemisphere. In addition, Franklin fails to acknowledge how New England slave traders profit directly from West Indian "*forced Labour*" in that they transport thousands of African slaves to labor in the "Filth and Nastiness" of West Indian plantations. On the contrary, what is conspicuous about Franklin's literary consumption of the products of West Indian slaves in the above passage is not his recognition of how the slave's deplorable working conditions adversely affect the slave per se but how the products of their slave labor tend to corrupt would-be pure white North American consumers. Although an elimination of the slave trade might well be an effect of changing the consumptive desires of North Americans regarding West Indian sugar and rum, it is not an explicitly mentioned target of Franklin's diatribe against the Sugar Act. Finally, neither does Franklin expressly indict—as he does the West Indian "Master" or the corrupt West Indian Interest—Northern and Middle Atlantic merchants and traders who are responsible for ushering the corruptive products of the West Indian plantation economies into North American port cities, and whose illegal trading practices with the French and Spanish West Indies provide, in part, the logic for Parliament's passage of the Sugar Act in the first instance. Ultimately, even as Franklin registers a keenly felt sense of paracolonial ambivalence regarding North American involvement in the West Indian plantation economies at all levels—merchant, trader, and consumer—he does so by relying on a set of paracolonial negations that produce a sharper set of contrasts between the "Northern colonies" and the British West Indies, and between an exploitative West India Interest and a parasitic North American mercantile "Interest," than is warranted, negations that ironically amplify the paracolonial ambivalence informing Franklin's 1765 *Poor Richard* Sugar Act critique.

Neutralizing the West Indian Problem: Franklin at the Peace of Versailles

Such anxiousness, ambiguity, and ambivalence characterize the tenor and tone of Franklin's diplomatic efforts during peace negotiations almost twenty years later on the eve of the Peace of Versailles. As U.S. minister plenipotentiary in France in 1783, Franklin was charged with negotiating the most favorable agreement possible regarding the resumption of trade post-Revolution between the United States and the British West Indies—an issue that emerges as perhaps the single most antagonistic, and intractable, of all those debated between the various treating parties. Moreover, its irresolution held long-term consequences for the New Republic's political economy and "national character." In France, Franklin negotiated such a trade agreement according to his usual philosophy of enlightened self-interest, which meant in practice that the United States ought not to subordinate its national interest to the interests of the British empire. Just as Franklin argued that the retention of Canada was not only in the best interest of the North American colonies but of the empire as a whole, so he pursued trade agreements with Europe's empires at the conclusion of the Revolution that ostensibly accommodated the interests of all parties to the treaty of peace but especially the self-interests of the emergent U.S. Republic.

Yet Franklin was a minister negotiating on behalf of a loosely bound confederation of states; his note of "reassurance" to opponents of the retention of Canada that the empire need not worry about the colonies ever "uniting" proved prescient. As such, the United States lacked a strong central government, was without a navy to speak of, and had incurred tremendous debts from the war. Thus Franklin and his fellow ministers plenipotentiary—including John Jay and John Adams—were destined to be disappointed in their negotiations on the West Indian trade issue. This was especially so not only because conservative mercantilist policies predominated still in Parliament but also because the English sensed U.S. American vulnerability and were thus unwilling to grant concessions when the rebellious former colonists were helpless to defend against such unjust arrangements. Even as they perhaps recognized that the balance of power between Britain and the United States had not shifted merely because the Continental Army had emerged triumphant in the Revolution, Franklin and his fellow ministers plenipotentiary could not possibly have anticipated at the outset of negotiations Parliament's ultimate decision to ban all U.S. vessels from trading directly with the British West Indies. On learning of such an unfavorable verdict, Franklin and his fellow ministers could do little else but accept Parliament's decision with the reasonable expectation that the point would be renegotiated once the British West Indies, reliant so heavily on North American foodstuffs for their survival prior to the Revolution, began literally to starve.

In a postcolonial modification of his pre-Revolutionary discourse of creole colonial resistance, Franklin proposed two treaty articles to his British counterparts that sought to neutralize the West Indian trade issue as potential source of ongoing conflict. More precisely, Franklin hoped that the West Indian trades might continue to benefit the New Republic economically without the United States becoming entangled in a commercial war with Britain (or another European empire) that might jeopardize the short- and long-term stability of the nation. He worried about the potentially corrosive effects of ongoing commercial warfare and illicit commerce on a U.S. national character that, according to Franklin's vision of U.S. empire building, ought to be shaped and formed by emphasizing the productive benefits of an agrarian political economy coupled with westward expansionism and a coterminous de-emphasis of the role of foreign commerce and mercantilism. While Franklin claims to tender the proposed articles out of concern for the interests of all parties, the utter inability of the United States to defend its mercantile presence in the West Indian trades militarily coupled with its paracolonial relationship to the West Indian plantation economies lays bare the substantial degree of self-interest and duplicity motivating their design.

The first article sought to ban privateering and to confine future wartime conflicts to armed enemy combatants. Both parts of the proposal reflect Franklin's sincere hatred of commercial war and of the collateral damage caused to innocent bystanders by armed conflict. Franklin begins by addressing the privateering issue: "If war should hereafter arise between Great Britain and the United States, which God forbid, . . . neither of the powers, parties to this treaty, shall grant or issue any commission to any private armed vessels, empowering them to take or destroy such trading ships, or interrupt such commerce" (*WBF* 10:72–73). He then seeks to protect farmers, fishermen, manufacturers, and artisans—all "who labour for the common subsistence and benefit of mankind, and peaceably follow their respective employments" (*WBF* 10:72)—from unprovoked attack by an enemy army, urging financial compensation for victims of such an attack. Yet given England's hegemonic position in relation to the United States, particularly on the sea, where the British empire possessed the greatest navy in the world, the concessions being requested for beneath the proposed article's genuinely altruistic and pacific rhetoric are decidedly one-sided. Indeed, viewed from a certain vantage point, Franklin's article reads more like an indictment of war crimes committed against the people of the United States by a marauding British army during the Revolution than a viable proposal to the peace treaty.

Moreover, Franklin is being duplicitous when he suggests that the United States would surely be the side most injured by a privateering ban: "American ships, laden only with the gross productions of the earth, cannot be so valuable as yours, filled with sugars or with manufactures" (*WBF* 10:68). Franklin's attempt to assure the English that the United States, too, is conceding something in this article despite being the nonhegemonic power to the treaty suggests why he was consistently refused an audience despite his repeated attempts to get English representatives to respond to the submitted article. Briefly, privateering in (and out of) wartime involved the seizure of ships involved in the West Indian trades traveling to and from their destinations. Franklin conveniently neglects to mention how U.S. ships returned from the West Indies laden with sugar, rum, cocoa, coffee, and specie, having traded their "productions of the earth," often illegally. Thus Franklin's refashioning of U.S. privateers into would-be peaceful conveyors of non-slave-produced agricultural products, products which take on an inflated actual value during wartime owing to the great need for these things by undersupplied military personnel, elides the full range of illicit trading practices not limited to privateering that U.S. merchants and traders involved themselves in before, during, and after the war to the great financial benefit of the national economy.

Political economists have argued that calls to neutralize or create free trade zones in the late twentieth century by the United States were disingenuous in that they inevitably worked to reinforce the sole superpower's trading advantage. Franklin's second treaty proposal, albeit offered from his location as minister negotiating on behalf of a nonhegemonic United States, has a similar aura. Franklin specifically calls on the various nations of Europe to neutralize the West Indies so as to avoid commercial wars over the various islands in future. He argues, "it would be better for the nations now possessing sugar colonies to give up their claim to them, let them govern themselves, and put them under the protection of all the powers of Europe as neutral countries, open to the commerce of all, the profits of the present monopolies being by no means equivalent to the expense of maintaining them" (*WBF* 10:72). Franklin's imaginative proposal has powerful appeal in the abstract. As he suggests, by not having to defend West Indian possessions, European empires might save more money than they spend defending them, though Franklin offers no figures to support such a contention. Yet given the dominant mercantile philosophy in Parliament, and considering that the United States itself possessed not a single West Indian island, Franklin's proposal reeks of naïveté at best, and chicanery at worst. It was one thing for progressive-minded British political economists like Edmund Burke or Adam Smith to tender such a neutrality and free trade proposal; it was quite another for Franklin to do so. Moreover, as to the altruism (or not) informing Franklin's neutrality article, it is unclear what precisely Franklin means when he suggests "let them govern themselves." Who does "them" entail—white *and* black creoles, masters *and* slaves? Franklin's proposal seems less alert to such potential complications than it might be given that his main concern with the article is not chattel slavery in the West Indies but geopolitical concerns about how to create a commercial and political climate conducive to the New Republic while avoiding naval conflict with a superior European power.

Franklin's preferred course for British North American—now U.S. American—empire building clearly figures into his motivations in proposing the two articles. In neutralizing the West Indian islands, and by getting the British to agree to a privateering ban and to restricting war to armed enemy combatants, Franklin would achieve an important hidden benefit. Not only would U.S. commerce enjoy unrestricted access to all the West India islands, which, given the proximity of the United States to those islands, its capacity to build ships, and its wealth of raw materials needed by the West Indies, would be a tremendous boon above and beyond what the United States already enjoyed in terms of licit and illicit profits stemming from the West Indian trades. The adoption of Franklin's articles would also free up the nation's resources to make the push west into Native American territory and French, British, and Spanish holdings there to fulfill Franklin's mythic vision for the United States as an agrarian empire for liberty. Thus, notwithstanding Franklin's sincere nervousness about the corrupting influence of commerce and mercantilism on the emergent U.S. national character, an uninhibited U.S. paracolonial participation in the West Indian trades and plantation economies according to Franklin's proposed treaty articles would operate to fund the nation's Manifest Destiny. Unsurprisingly, neither of Franklin's proposed articles proved acceptable to his British counterparts.[19]

As the peace treaty between the United States and Britain was being signed several months later, Franklin published a propaganda tract intended to provide, according to its title, "Information to Those Who Would Remove to America" (1784). In promoting Franklin's views about U.S. nation building, "Information" evokes many of the precise arguments Franklin mobilizes in the empire tracts of the 1750s and 1760s treated above. Such argumentative consanguinity across texts suggests the earlier works' emergent creole nationalist properties, notwithstanding their late colonial date of authorship and Franklin's then impulse to revamp the future course of the *British* empire and national character.

"Information" functions at once as a propaganda *and* antipropaganda piece. Franklin conveys a celebratory notion of U.S. America while simultaneously debunking overseas writers' claims that European opportunists—those from the professional and political classes—might relocate to the United States and capitalize financially on U.S. Americans who are wealthy but ignorant about what to do with their wealth; free but unsure about how to staff their governments; and at leisure but without artistic and literary productions of their own to occupy their time. In short, "Information" denounces the idea that white creole U.S. Americans were somehow indistinct from white creoles elsewhere in the Americas, particularly the wealthy plantation-owning class of creoles operating via their overseers the sugar islands of the West Indies. Indeed, "Information" insists that U.S. Americans are industrious yeoman farmers, artisans, and local mechanics, not—as has been rumored—carefree plantation owners who parasitically live off the labor of others.

As Franklin's narrative persona relates, "most People cultivate their own Lands, or follow some Handicraft or Merchandise" (975), suggesting that what awaits the European immigrant to the United States is a vastly scaled-back mercantile sphere that operates to serve, rather than subsume, a dominant agricultural one, a political economy characterized by localized governments and small farms dotting an ever-expanding western "frontier." Readers are told that in the United States, "happy Mediocrity . . . prevails. There are few great Proprietors of the Soil, and few Tenants" (975), a notion that repeats familiar tenets of the agrarian myth promulgated by the narrative persona, Farmer James, two years earlier in the initial letters of J. Hector St. John de Crèvecoeur's *Letters from an American Farmer* (1782). À la Crèvecoeur's husbandman narrator, "Information" holds that "America" is not a land where its citizens inquire of a stranger, " *What is he?* But *What can he* DO?" (977).

"Information" is conspicuous, however, for its silence about the killing and removal of Native Americans in order to make room for America's sprawling towns and farmlands. Nor are women provided for in Franklin's distinctly masculine account of U.S. American labor and land cultivation and the formation of a national character. Moreover, the reader wonders how Franklin accounts for the massive unpaid labor force building America: what is it that slaves "DO" in Franklin's version of America? In a much-remarked-on scene in Letter IX of Crèvecoeur's text, a brutalized South Carolina "slave in a cage" emerges specterlike from an increasingly turgid landscape and thrusts himself into Farmer James's line of sight, thereby exposing the partial, violent nature of James's sentimentalized construction of British North America as a land of peaceful, happy farmers. In contrast, the abused slave apostrophized in "Information" is made to brace, rather than rupture, Franklin's nostalgic American ideal.[20]

Specifically, Franklin commandeers a West Indian slave in a way that recalls his deployment of West Indian male slaves as figures in his late colonial and early national writings. As we have seen, in the *Autobiography* Franklin negates and debases the West Indies while muting the voices of slaves and freedmen in order to promote an exceptional idea about Philadelphia as "America" that he himself is made to embody. Such a view is challenged by Equiano's act of counternegation in *The Interesting Narrative*, a tale of creolization in opposition to the *Autobiography*'s narrative creoleness that portrays white Philadelphians and the intimate relations between Philadelphia and the West Indies in considerably more compromising terms. In addition, in "Observations," *The Canada Pamphlet*, and other empire writings of the late colonial period, Franklin once more presents an exceptional—and exceptionally white—portrait of British North America according to which he expropriates the suffering of West Indian slaves for the purposes of bolstering those texts' protonationalist designs. Further, in "*Concerning* SWEETS" a pseudonymous Franklin recalls the deplorable labor conditions on a West Indian sugar plantation not so much to urge a remedy of the slave's status as to argue for the need to change U.S. American consumers' dietary habits in order to extract the United States from its addiction to West Indian sweets.

In "Information," Franklin commodifies a West Indian slave's labor once more, but he does so by co-opting the slave's *artistic* productions; rather than muting the slave's voice as he does in the above writings, Franklin ventriloquizes it, redeploying a creolized, antislavery West Indian plantation animal tale in the service of U.S. creole nationalism. In evoking the anonymous slave's tale, Franklin's narrator remarks:

[The American people] are pleas'd with the Observation of a Negro, and frequently mention it, that *Boccarorra* (meaning the Whiteman) make de Blackman workee, make de Horse workee, make de Ox workee, make ebery ting workee; only de Hog. He de Hog, no workee; he eat, he drink, he walk about, he go to sleep when he please, *he libb like a Gentleman*. According to these Opinions of the

Americans, one of them would think himself more oblig'd to a Genealogist, who could prove for him that his Ancestors & Relations for ten Generations had been Ploughmen, Smiths, Carpenters, Turners, Weavers, Tanners, or even Shoemakers, & consequently that they were useful Members of Society; than if he could only prove that they were Gentlemen, doing nothing of Value, but living idly on the Labour of others, mere *fruges consumere nati*, and otherwise *good* for *nothing*, till by their Death, their Estates like the Carcase of the Negro's Gentleman-Hog, come to be *cut up*. (977)

On initial reading, one wonders why a U.S. American would be fond of a slave's tale that seems to indict "him" as exceptional only in so much as he has the capacity to be an uncommonly brutal slave driver. Mobilized in the wake of the North American colonists' successful revolution against slave-like, and still ongoing, oppression by an English mercantilist empire, however, a more nuanced reading suggests itself. Accordingly, Franklin's putatively decolonizing discourse in "Information" intends for the slave's antislavery "Observation" to allow for a distinction between U.S. American creoles and the "Gentleman-Hog"–filled Parliament and mercantilist representatives of the British empire. Perhaps more crucially, the West Indian slave tale enables a clean distinction between U.S. Americans and the corrupt and corrupting West Indian creole—the "Boccarorra" (a variant spelling of the term for white man in black West Indian dialect, "Bakkra")—who is at once monstrously masculine in his inclination to violence toward others and not masculine enough given his proclivity toward laziness and hedonism.

The "one of them" who claims a distinct genealogy from other corrupted creole Americans in the hemisphere is Franklin's exceptional U.S. American. He descends from artisans, mechanics, and farmers, and not from Gentleman-Hogs—degenerate West Indian plantation owners and their overseers, as well as British "gentlemen" who profit by virtue of their name and title rather than producing anything of value themselves. Franklin thus defies European charges of *U.S.* creole degeneracy by evoking a stylized West Indian dialect tale and compromising its antislavery bent. Although such a reading is significant, it is clearly subordinated to the tract's efforts to shore up its claim for exceptionalist U.S. status in the hemisphere. As David Waldstreicher argues in a trenchant reading of "Information" to which my own is indebted, "this kind of appropriation of antislavery for the purpose of justifying America trumped antislavery itself. No one did it better than Franklin . . . Franklin's seizure of victimhood, of the very idea of innocence, on behalf of the United States pushed the dilemma of America's slaves off the table" (*Runaway* 221).[21]

By way of concluding, I want to focus momentarily on the charged paracolonial poetics marking Franklin's deployment of the West Indian animal tale, a cultural crossover eerily anticipatory, in many ways, of how Southern regionalist writers of the late nineteenth-century "plantation school" adapted and appropriated slave tales to support alarmingly nostalgic views of life on the plantation "befo'" the Civil War and Reconstruction. Important to note in this regard is how the West Indian plantation economies in "Information" occlude the reality of the U.S. South. Perhaps the text's most stunning irony is how its commodification of a West Indian black slave's antislavery animal tale exposes, according to its very paracolonialist design, the illogical nature of Franklin's attempt to negate the great financial windfall the United States enjoys via its licit and, post-Revolution, increasingly illicit participation in the West Indian plantation economies. Such activities, along with the unspoken plantation economies of the U.S. South and the raging "Indian" wars, belie the text's exceptionalist arguments. If "Information" unsatisfactorily answers the question as to how to account for slave labor in Franklin's vision of the United States as emergent agrarian empire, it also muffles according to its paracolonialist rhetoric the reality of U.S. merchants and traders based in urban centers like Philadelphia working the West Indian trades to such lucrative effect, much as the text itself *trades* on a West Indian black's deftly crafted antislavery plea in order to accomplish that extraordinary rhetorical feat.

In such a way, "Information"'s West Indian slave remains poised to "*cut up*" the work's tautological narrative. Franklin's ventriloquization of a West Indian slave proleptically recalls to twenty-first-century readers the Haitian Revolution, which five years following the publication of "Information" would prove so traumatic in its effects on the psyches of white U.S. Americans who believed they alone aspired to republican virtues and had the capacity to organize themselves into a collective body for purposes of fighting against the British Gentlemen-Hogs. If in Saint-Domingue, "by their Death, [white creoles'] Estates like the Carcase of the Negro's Gentleman-Hog, come to be *cut up*" (977), the specter of such rebellion exceeds Franklin's caricature of black West Indian slave culture. The animal tale's original author thus overworks efforts to expropriate his unpaid slave labor and antislavery sentiments according to the twinned rhetorics of creole nationalism and paracolonial negation by a U.S. "Gentleman-Hog" narrator on behalf of a highly stylized, yeoman farmer-mechanic.

As a minister plenipotentiary Franklin was not alone in seeking provisos in the final peace treaty at Versailles that would grant the United States access—preferably unrestricted—to Europe's West Indian islands and the West Indian carrying trade. Yet not all such ministers adopted the same paracolonial posture as Franklin. John Adams, for example, was unabashed in his insistence that the British grant the United States full trade access to its West Indian islands. For Adams, an enthusiastic proponent of U.S. commerce, the new nation's long-standing paracolonial participation in the West Indian trades was crucial not only to the financial well-being of the Republic but to the prosperity of the British West Indies as well.

U.S. commerce in the West Indies, the future Federalist Adams believed, was not something to subordinate to utopian visions of a U.S. agricultural empire on the continent. On the contrary, U.S. commerce in the West Indian trades would be the very lifeblood of the New Republic. Thus when it became apparent during negotiations that the British might ban the United States from direct trading access to its West Indian islands, Adams voiced his threatening disapproval to counterparts in the British delegation and to fellow U.S. ministers. In the following excerpt from a June 23, 1783, letter written from Paris to U.S. Secretary for Foreign Affairs Robert Livingston, Adams expresses a deeply felt anxiety over the prospect of the United States being legally prohibited from trading with the British West Indies:

The nations of Europe, who have islands in the West Indies, have at this moment a delicate part to take. Upon their present decisions, great things will depend. The commerce of the West Indian Islands is a part of the American system of commerce. They can neither do without us, nor we without them. The Creator has placed us upon the globe in such a situation, that we have occasion for each other. We have the means of assisting each other, and politicians and artful contrivances cannot separate us. Wise statesmen, like able artists of every kind, study nature, and their works are perfect in proportion as they conform to her laws. Obstinate attempts to prevent the islands and the continent, by force or policy, from deriving from each other those blessings which nature has enabled them to afford, will only put both to thinking of means of coming together. And an injudicious regulation at this time may lay a foundation for intimate combinations between the islands and the continent, which otherwise would not be wished for or thought of by either. (*LWJA* 8:74–75)

Adams's letter makes transparent what Franklin's paracolonial posture mutes: that the "commerce of the West India Islands" is the most vital component part of the entire "American system of commerce." Perhaps the most intriguing notion in the entire letter, however, is the final one wherein Adams claims that an "injudicious regulation" by European empires "may lay a foundation for intimate combinations between the islands and the continent, which otherwise would not be wished for or thought of by either." Thus Adams admonishes that harsh restrictions on U.S. commerce in the West Indies will inevitably result in the joint subversion of such measures by U.S. Americans and West Indians alike. Alert to the outpouring of patriotic feeling expressed by many U.S.

Americans prior to and during the Revolution relating to dangerous maneuvers undertaken by U.S. merchants and traders in order to circumvent British prohibitions against trading with the "foreign" West Indies, Adams gestures to a theme treated in systematic detail in the next chapter. He implies that the newly independent Republic instills fear in extant European empires by virtue of its proliferating paracolonial presence in the West Indies and its capacity to carry U.S. democratic values and principles to Europe's colonies there. Is it possible for monarchical European empires to grant the United States full and unrestricted access to their West Indian possessions without the latter being corrupted by republicanism and the liberalizing tendencies of free and unfettered trade? Adams's boisterous tone, ironically enough, suggests otherwise.

Nonetheless, for all of Adams's bold rhetoric, it is not precisely clear what *specific* "means of coming together" Adams recommends the United States employ to dislodge Europe's hold over its West Indian islands. In that regard, there is an even more intriguing note of paracolonial ambivalence that Adams strikes in the letter's final remark. Even as he suggests that neither the United States nor the West Indies can do without the other commercially, he seems to define commerce in the narrowest sense possible—a strict exchange of goods without the social or cultural effects that inevitably attend to such exchanges. Despite his pretensions about the United States infecting the West Indian colonies with its republican values, the socially conservative Adams is obviously more concerned about a reverse contagion of the ostensibly rising and regenerate Republic by the still colonial and degenerate West Indies.

In its treatment of Alexander Hamilton and his vision for the United States as an "empire for commerce," the next chapter pays special attention to the sorts of "intimate combinations" of commodities, characters, and cultures between the creole West Indies and the creole Republic that Franklin and Adams mention so ambivalently above. If Franklin frequently engages in acts of paracolonial negation in his writings, anxious to repress the potentially deleterious social and cultural effects of commercial excess on the emergent national character, Hamilton not only sustains U.S. paracolonialism in the West Indies as an affirmation of the United States' special mission to spread liberal and republican values in the hemisphere; he also strives to build a U.S. commercial empire there. The twin impulse to at once resist too "intimate combinations" between U.S. American and West Indian creoles while striving to collapse the "commerce of the West Indian Islands" into the "American system of commerce" in defiance of the "artful contrivances" of more militarily powerful European empires: such overwhelming and seemingly contradictory challenges manifest themselves, the next chapter argues, in the New Republic's creole complex.[22]

Chapter 2

Alexander Hamilton and a U.S. Empire for Commerce

Evidenced by the recent publication of the Library of America's volume of Alexander Hamilton's writings as well as a flourish of new Hamilton histories and biographies, Hamilton is enjoying something of a cultural revival. Perhaps unsurprisingly, the two most prominent concerns reflected in these works are, on the one hand, a scholarly desire to "solve" once and for all the ambiguous circumstances surrounding Hamilton's sensational duel with Aaron Burr and, on the other, a compulsion to debate the ideological underpinnings of Hamilton's vigorous pursuit of a powerful mercantile economy and a similarly imposing national defense. Such concerns are hardly new to Hamilton criticism; on the contrary, they have tended to dominate discussions about the significance of arguably the New Republic's most enigmatic, controversial, and misunderstood founding statesman.

Especially noteworthy is Joanne Freeman's *Affairs of Honor*, which endeavors to revise our understanding of the inner workings of government during the nation's first decades. As reviews have noted, although Freeman's work focuses on many politicians both prominent and obscure, its star is Hamilton. Accordingly, a culminating affair in Freeman's study is the Hamilton-Burr duel. Although she devotes only a single chapter to the duel, Freeman nonetheless provides perhaps its most provocative reassessment. She avoids apologizing for either Burr's or Hamilton's conduct. As is well known, a reluctant Hamilton on the eve of the duel hastily penned an apology that suggested he would, if necessary, proceed with it for the public good so as to preserve his honor because Burr had "compelled [him] to fight." Yet Freeman argues in wonderfully deconstructive ways that although Hamilton's actions *appear* to uphold the New Republic's code of honor, such appearances are deceiving. Like Burr, Hamilton fought not out of any innate sense of chivalry but out of cowardice, for his "honorable sacrifice to the public good was also a surrender to the power of public opinion" (196). Freeman's readings regarding the complicated and even contradictory nature of how to read Hamilton are echoed in *Alexander Hamilton and the Persistence of Myth* by Stephen Knott. Knott skillfully surveys competing—and fluctuating—representations of Hamilton since his death in 1804. Above all else, Knott argues, alternating periods of celebration and vilification of Hamilton's portraiture in the national gallery center on U.S. Americans' fundamentally ambivalent relationship to their economic prosperity and enormous military might.[1]

Like Freeman, this chapter is concerned with questions of honor and dishonor in the New Republic; with Knott, it focuses on Hamilton's place in the national imaginary and on the ways in which Hamilton figures, and is figured by, anxieties about the ambivalent status of U.S. national character. Even so, my interest in Hamilton departs from the above assessments in important ways. During the past few decades, scholars have had much to say about Thomas Jefferson's iconographic status in the U.S. literary and cultural imagination, specifically about Jefferson's mythic vision for the United States as an "empire for liberty" and the tortured racial taxonomies upholding it as expressed in *Notes on the State of Virginia* (1785) and later writings. This chapter will not argue against the significance of a Jefferson-centered understanding of the New Republic's national character. Rather, it intends to complicate such an understanding by providing an alternative locus for situating such discussions, one centered on Jefferson's archrival, Alexander Hamilton.

More precisely, about Hamilton there has always been an aura of sacrificial mystery that transcends the tragic circumstances of his death. More than any other figure in the New Republic, Hamilton embodies the manifold ambivalences and contradictions, as well as the energies and potential, that he and the new nation evince as a result, this chapter argues, of their shared *creole complex*. In invoking such a notion, I mean to signal the complicated ways in which the New Republic capitalizes on, and disavows, both its conflicted relationship to European discourses about "the creole" in the New World and its paracolonial relationship to the plantation economies of the British and French West Indies.

The opening section of the chapter argues that when one examines writings by and about Hamilton, a paradoxical portrait emerges. A "degenerate" West Indian creole, Hamilton felt he might achieve his aspirations for glory and fame in the budding American republic by allowing himself to be regenerated, as it were, in the crucible of an appropriated republican virtue and ennobled creole self. The second section demonstrates how key to such pursuits was Hamilton's bold design for the United States as an empire for commerce, a plan he advanced as the most powerful—and controversial—member of Washington's cabinet. Ironically, Hamilton's vision reveals his and the emerging U.S. empire's indebtedness to their actual and imagined West Indian

origins—Hamilton worked until age eighteen as a West Indian merchant clerk on behalf of New York shipping conglomerates, an occupation that uniquely prepared him to function as the new nation's chief
economic strategist. At once sacred and profane, the contradictory figures of Alexander Hamilton as abject West Indian creole and heroic U.S.
American statesman make manifest the mutually transformative encounters between the West Indies and the United States in the turbulent commercial cross-currents of the Americas in the 1790s. The third section
suggests the potential benefits awaiting scholars willing to situate literary
and cultural formation in the New Republic in the context of Hamilton's and his opponents' shared anxiety about their creole origins. More
precisely, it argues that the New Republic's creole complex is at once
symptomatic and productive of efforts by writers, artists, and intellectuals to respond to, critique, and contain the potentially corrosive effects
of Europe's efforts via superior military power to undermine the political economy of the still vulnerable nation. European empires' ability to
render U.S. participation in the lucrative West Indian trades treacherous
proved profoundly destabilizing on constructed ideas about national
character, a condition registered by the former colonists' lingering sensitivity toward eighteenth-century European discourses about New
World creole degeneracy. Ultimately such developments belie claims for
U.S. American exceptionalism in regard to Europe and the hemisphere's "other" creole colonial societies and cultures as betokened by
the nation's unprecedented revolutionary victory over the British
empire and its putatively superior republican values and institutions.

Alexander Hamilton's and the New Republic's West Indian Origins

When the recently liberated Olaudah Equiano shipped out as a steward
aboard the *Jamaica* to the Lesser Antilles in 1771, he might have had
occasion to exchange a word, a glance, or a bit of cargo with a precocious fourteen-year-old merchant clerk there: Alexander Hamilton (see
Equiano 127–28). During an eight-month stay on Nevis, it would not
have been unusual to make short trips to the nearby islands of St. Kitts,
St. Eustacia, and St. Croix, where Hamilton clerked, or for Hamilton to
visit Nevis, his birthplace in 1757. Whether or not the two men crossed
paths, they were both formed by the West Indian plantation economies
that Equiano scrutinizes in his slave narrative. Both men were well
acquainted with the flow of peoples, cultures, and commodities that
issued forth from merchant vessels calling on West Indian ports in the
late eighteenth century. Thus Equiano's searing text about the horrors
of West Indian slavery is a fitting complement to works authored by and

about one of the most significant, if enigmatic, founding fathers of the United States.

As historians have repeatedly remarked, we know precious little about Hamilton's life in the West Indies before he began working as a teenage merchant clerk. Throughout his life in the United States, Hamilton assiduously suppressed details about his West Indian origins. He cultivated, as scores of immigrants have done since, a series of half-truths about his beginnings, distancing himself from his West Indian creoleness by emphasizing instead his descent from a long line of Scottish noblemen. Like the commodities he imported and exported as a West Indian merchant clerk, discourses both scientific and literary about the "true" nature of the West Indies circulated throughout the Atlantic world in the eighteenth and nineteenth centuries. The illegitimate son of a West Indian mother reputed to be "whoring" throughout the Leeward Islands, Hamilton suffered the pernicious effects of such discourses in highly visible ways as a prominent figure in the newly formed United States government.

As I explained in the Introduction, the process of (un)becoming U.S. American in the late eighteenth century was oftentimes dependent on (un)becoming creole, something Alexander Hamilton came to appreciate on emigrating from the West Indies to North America on the eve of the United States declaring itself "independent." The Declaration of Independence, like so many utopian documents of its kind, was an unclean break from the past. Instead, U.S. claims to a pure, uncorrupted white creole identity were illuminating for how they labored to repress the inter-American cosmopolitanisms of many of its leading citizen-subjects. As the United States sought to substitute a liberating creole identity for an oppressive colonial one, creole uplift, whether undertaken by Hamilton or Jefferson, required ever-increasing sleights of hand in order to repress, through actual and epistemological violence, the formation of inter-American, cross-cultural identities inside and outside the nation's borders.

By analyzing colonialist discourse about the West Indies, one can better appreciate Hamilton's protracted struggle to contain the corrosive effects of his creole lineage as a newly independent American. According to the terms of eighteenth-century British and French colonialist discourse, West Indians—and by inference North Americans participating in the slave economies of the West Indies and Southern colonies—were marked as degenerate owing to the West Indies' subtropical climate and their participation in the islands' plantation economies. Significantly, such discourses were prominent not only in Europe but also in the West Indies and North America. In Edward Long's *History of Jamaica* (1774), published two years after Hamilton left the West Indies for the soon-to-be independent United States and widely circulated throughout the British empire, a portrait of the West Indian creole type emerges. In an ethnographic chapter entitled "Of the Inhabitants," Long classifies various racial types in Jamaican society according to the normative category of "White Man." He begins, predictably, by describing creole white men and women, and then proceeds to offer accounts of races that feature "the intermixture of Whites, Blacks, and Indians" (1:260). These types include "Negroe Woman," "Mulatta," "Terceron," "Quateron," and "Quinteron," all terms of identity that refer, according to Long's tortured racial taxonomy, to the percentages of black to white blood present in a given classification. As is evident from his discussions of white male and female creoles, however, all types, regardless of race, have degenerated from the European white male norm. Long identifies "supineness and indolence" as negative characteristics of creole white men and attributes these immodest tendencies to their being "*bad oeconomists*," a fact that "too frequently hurts their fortune and family" (2:265; emphasis added). If they might be said to have "a lively imagination," white creole men are nonetheless ruled by "tinctures of vanity, and . . . haughtiness" and "sudden transports of anger" (2:265). According to Long's assignations, creole men are "fickle and desultory in their pursuits," display "a strong propensity to the other sex," and "are not always the most chaste and faithful of husbands" (2:265).

For Long, the creole inclination toward reckless economic, sexual, and social behavior manifests itself in highly visible ways, especially in the "addiction . . . to expensive living, costly entertainments, dress and equipage" (2:265). British discursive formations like Long's about the character of West Indian creoles function on several levels. The most obvious level operates to reassure privileged English readers about their cultural superiority as "gentlemen" to West Indians. Less obviously, such writings mask elite fears about the growing influence of West Indians in the economic, political, and cultural spheres of the metropolitan center, where wealthy West Indian planters and their children were settling with increasing frequency. Less obvious still are the ways in which discourse about West Indian degeneracy contains within it an urgent justification for Parliament and George III to exert ever more forceful cultural, economic, political, and military controls over the upstart American colonies. Ethnographic accounts like Long's that debase the West Indian creole were thus coterminous with legislative efforts that sought to discipline the further contamination of England by its irreverent colonies. Ironically, such edicts—the stamp acts, the taxing of tea, the exorbitant tariffs on manufactured goods originating from sites other than England, and so on—became known as the "intolerable acts" in the West Indies and in the North American colonies. Paradoxically, West Indian ethnographies mystified England's own culpability for "corrupting" virtue within and without England by administering and exploiting the highly profitable West Indian plantation economies.

Equally important in terms of evaluating the elaborate controls of empire over the colonies are the ways in which European colonialist discourse marked West Indian women. Such considerations crucially affect how Hamilton's mother came to be marked by his opponents. Such discourse will be important in subsequent chapters where I discuss how the figure of the West Indian woman influences the formation of literature and culture in the early national period of the United States. *A History of Jamaica* reveals the ways in which an overdilated European colonialist (male) gaze fixes on West Indian women's bodies, fashions, interracial relations, and sexuality for purposes of social and economic mastery, however ambivalent the result. Predictably, negative characteristics of white creole women are female versions of creole male shortcomings. West Indian women display much "vanity and pride" according to Long and are prone to "fits of rage and clamour" (2:283). Their distinct lack of virtue expresses itself in highly performative ways and is characterized by excess consumption and overindulgence. They demonstrate too great a fondness for "dress, balls, and company" (2:283), and their impulse to exceed the acceptable bounds of sentiment is imputed to the deleterious environment: "the warmth of this climate . . . co-operate[s] with natural instinct to rouze the passions," resulting in "those lapses [of judgment] which happen through the venial frailty and weakness of human nature" (2:283).

Long also provides glimpses into lurid interracial encounters that became fodder for unstable tropes in late eighteenth- and nineteenth-century British and U.S. literatures. Unsurprisingly, writers and playwrights reimagined affronts posed by West Indian creoles to British and/or U.S. sensibilities by reworking scenes depicted in standard travel accounts like *A History of Jamaica* and Bryan Edwards's *The History, Civil and Commercial, of the British West Indies* (1798).[2] In his account, Long censures creole white women for challenging already unstable boundaries of race and class by indulging in "indolent" pleasures with their black servants. He also laments, "we may see, in some of these places, a very fine young woman awkwardly dangling her arms with the air of a Negroe-servant . . . her head muffled up with two or three handkerchiefs, her dress loose, and without stays" (2:279). The transgressions committed by creole white women and their slaves, according to Long, are even more monstrous in the domestic sphere. Creole white women not only don black fashions, manners, and "airs" but also allow their "Negro or Mulatto wet nurses" to suckle their children "without reflecting that [the wet nurse's] blood may be corrupted, or considering the influence which the milk may have with respect to the disposition, as well as health, of their little ones" (2:276). According to the terms of Long's rhetoric, all black bodily secretions are synonymous with "blood," and thus creole child-rearing practices threaten to contaminate the space of the home by allowing a "white" baby to imbibe a surrogate black mother's breast milk.[3] Long extends the point when he asserts that the mere presence of black servants in and around the space of the home over a span of years has a contaminative effect on mother and child alike. I would suggest that an underlying anxiety of Long's excoriations against the interracial relations between white creoles and their black servants centers on the specter of an emergent, alternative morality and domestic sensibility across racial and class lines that functions as a menace to not only colonial but domestic norms as well. The elite readers of Long's text rely on the illusion of homogeneity for power, and thus transgressive domestic relations such as the ones Long depicts register concerns about mounting threats to the purity of the eighteenth-century *English* "home," a synecdoche for the space of the English nation.

Planters or "gentlemen" of the West Indies, their wives and children, and their black servants were the specific "subjects" of nonfiction works such as *History of Jamaica.* Yet these texts' debasing effects were operational across class and racial divisions and tended to create the impression that all West Indians—rich and poor, black, white, and mulatto—were to varying degrees a degenerate or inferior species of humanity. As suggested above, West Indian histories like those authored by Long and Edwards were not the only cultural texts in the Atlantic world marking the West Indian creole in such ways. Broadly defined, literary traditions throughout the Anglo-American Atlantic world reinforced the dominant assumptions regarding West Indian creole degeneracy, though frequently for conflicting ideological purposes. For instance, British literature and drama published prior to the nineteenth century—including William Shakespeare's *The Tempest* (1611), Thomas Southerne's *Oroonoko* (1695), Daniel Defoe's *Robinson Crusoe* (1719), George Colman's *Inkle and Yarico* (1787), Robert Bage's *Man as He Is* (1792), and Maria Edgeworth's *Belinda* (1801)—depend for their literary and ideological effects on figurations of creole degeneracy. Many such works enjoyed widespread appeal with readers and audiences in North America. A review of any major U.S. theater's play list in the 1790s, for example, reveals that American audiences were particularly drawn to "New World" dramas featuring degenerate West Indian characters, a phenomenon treated in considerable detail in Chapter 4.[4]

North American literature authored before (and after) 1800 also was imagined, in part, through and against the West Indies. Venerable writers such as John Smith, William Bradford, Cotton Mather, J. Hector St. John de Crèvecoeur, Noah Webster, and, as we have seen, Benjamin Franklin; poets and essayists like Phillis Wheatley, "Connecticut Wits" Timothy Dwight and Joel Barlow, and Republican Philip Freneau; New England "Augustans" such as Fisher Ames; turn-of-the-century novelists including Leonora Sansay (Mary Hassal) and Charles Brockden Brown: these and many other writers refashion the figure of the degenerate creole for formal and ideological purposes. In most cases, they do so in order to assert an anxiously superior and discrete North American identity, even as they betray its dependence on an actual, as well as a stylized, West Indies. In addition, a group of writers "circulating" throughout the Atlantic world sought to capitalize on their own "exotic" circumatlantic identities by seizing on the degenerate creole type in their works. One such writer, the novelist Helena Wells, emigrated from South Carolina to England during the American Revolution and published two pro-British novels that center on West Indian characters and settings, *Constantia Neville* (1800) and *The Step Mother* (1798). Her use of the West Indian type, though ultimately debasing, subtextually suggests possible alliances between North American and West Indian creoles against the British empire. Also, Charlotte Smith, a friend of Abigail Adams, emigrated from the United States to England in the late eighteenth century and published two novels, *Desmond* (1792) and *The Wanderings of Warwick* (1794), which are set in the West Indies and portray degenerate West Indian characters, albeit for abolitionist purposes.

The West Indian histories of Long and Edwards; the literature and drama of native and foreign, emigrant and immigrant British, North American, and West Indian writers and playwrights: these works conspired to create—and in several instances challenge—a stylized, circumatlantic West Indian creole type. In many of these texts the "creole" is swarthy, scheming, libertine, reckless, and above all, a sign of contagion. Thus the figure of the West Indian was manipulated not just by European colonialist discourse but also by North Americans intent on asserting an Anglo-American superiority while simultaneously justifying an important though threatened paracolonial relationship with Europe's West Indian colonies. Accordingly, it is inconceivable that anyone, especially Alexander Hamilton, would have been insensitive to the variable meanings signified by the term "creole" in the various port cities along the routes of the circumatlantic trades. Nearly dead on arrival, having narrowly escaped the burning merchant vessel that transported him from St. Croix to the rebellious North American colonies, Hamilton thus developed out of necessity a facility for negotiating the cross-cultural currents of creole degeneracy. As he did so, he charted a course for the nation's political economy according to his vision of the

United States as an empire for commerce, all the while challenging traditional republican assumptions about virtue and national identity. His sweeping reforms sparked widespread discussion about Hamilton's own and the nation's origins that pivoted, predictably, on repressed fears about creole degeneracy.

The hemispheric nervousness inspired by Hamilton's ghost in the nineteenth and twentieth centuries bespeaks the creole anxieties haunting debates in the late eighteenth century over Hamilton, his national stature, and his West Indian origins. Significantly, myths involving Hamilton's questionable paternity have proven notably persistent. During his bid for reelection in 1792, mudslinging rivals resentful of Hamilton's domineering influence over Washington's political and economic policies accused the President of having fathered his illegitimate Treasury Secretary while in Barbados.[5] Early in the twentieth century, a biographical novel about Hamilton by Gertrude Atherton resurrected the political slander against Washington and ironically suggested its veracity. In *The Conqueror* (1901), Atherton suggests it was inconceivable that such a brilliant and influential American statesman could have been conceived by a dissolute West Indian father, an anxiety registered, not coincidentally, at the dawn of a new epoch in U.S. nationalism and imperialism.[6] Thus Hamilton's legitimacy rests on the unstable axis of U.S. empire building, Washington's alleged paternity marking him across the centuries as profane and sacred "creole" son of the nation's "father." Such a fluctuation also signals the exploitable and unstable boundaries between U.S. and West Indian creole identities. As has already been suggested, the very word "creole" in the circumatlantic world of ever-expanding trade and commerce denoted not just degeneracy but contagion on multiple levels, including race. Thus we should not be surprised when Hamilton's specter haunts efforts to police the borders between nation, race, and empire. In Nevis, many West Indians still insist that Hamilton's disreputable mother, Rachel Lavien, was not white but a creole woman of color (Flexner 9). Early in the twentieth century, Allan Hamilton expressed his concern that "much misapprehension exists as to the appearance of Hamilton, some of which is due to the idea that because his birthplace was the West Indies, he presented the physical characteristics of those born under a tropical sun" (29). He added that Hamilton "is referred to by various authors as 'Creole,' or a 'swarthy young West Indian,' and most of his biographers erroneously picture him as being dark in color, and 'having black hair and piercing eyes'" (29). The preoccupation with marking Hamilton's creole "race" in the West Indies and in the United States by Hamilton scholars (Allan Hamilton anxiously asserts that Hamilton's "eyes were a deep blue—almost violet—and he *undoubt-*

edly presented the physical appearance of his *Scotch* father rather than his *French* mother" [29; emphasis added]) illustrates paradoxically how Hamilton's creole status already marks him as "raced."[7] To affix to his identity the added classification "colored" merely announces once and for all Hamilton's contaminated, unretractable West Indian creole condition.[8] These creole confusions involving Hamilton's ghost are intriguing for the ways in which they correspond to assaults on Hamilton's West Indian origins during the new national period.

Southern slaveholder and Republican party leader Thomas Jefferson and Federalist rival and New England patrician John Adams vehemently opposed Hamilton's ideas about the United States as an empire for commerce outlined below, especially as the plan manifested itself in the volatile political and economic climate of the 1790s. The disagreements between Hamilton and his two fiercest rivals ran deep and derived from their time together as members of Washington's cabinet. Jefferson and Adams shared the opinion, which history has since largely credited, that Hamilton presided over the most significant domestic and foreign policy initiatives during Washington's two terms in office (1789–96). They charged that Washington was Hamilton's puppet, and that Hamilton used his power to design and implement a political economy that badly damaged the national character. In their quarrels with Hamilton, his ideology, and its practical effects, however, each man reacted to Hamilton's creole origins differently. The differing tones in their hostilities toward Hamilton are as attributable to their dissimilar origins as they are to their famously incommensurate ideological views. Nonetheless, what is similar about their preoccupation with Hamilton's creole origins are shared concerns regarding the New Republic's negotiation of its *own* creole anxieties and condition, specifically its efforts to fashion a creole identity marked not by degeneracy but by hemispheric exceptionalism owing to its successful Revolution and the formation of unprecedented New World republican and economic institutions and communities.

Like Adams, Jefferson registered his misgivings about Hamilton's hold over Washington's mind and the national character by launching into curious sallies on Hamilton's origins. On resigning as Secretary of State in 1793 and "retiring" to Monticello, Jefferson declared, "It's monstrous that this country should be ruled by a foreign bastard!" (qtd. Rogow 4). During his period of self-imposed exile, Jefferson railed against what he perceived to be the illegitimate and degenerative effects of the *Hamilton* presidency on a nation under siege. He denounced Hamilton's imperialist ambitions as byproducts of "a man whose history, from the moment at which history can stoop to notice him, is a tissue of machinations against the liberty of the country which has not only received and given him bread, but heaped its honors on his head" (qtd.

Schachner 303). "Liberty" is a loaded term where Jefferson is concerned and central to his competing ideology of empire, spelled out in a preliminary way in his carefully contrived philosophical and scientific treatise *Notes on the State of Virginia* (1785). Jefferson's diatribes against Hamilton suggest that he felt Hamilton's exotic origins and modest beginnings delimited his ability to represent faithfully the aspirations of the American people. Tellingly, Jefferson seemed unwilling to entertain the idea that Hamilton could be scheming on behalf of untold citizens to whom Jefferson and his versions of history, liberty, and political economy would and could not speak—urban Americans who derived their livelihoods and characters from U.S. participation in inter-American commerce and the West Indian trades.

The ideological gaps between Hamilton's and Jefferson's competing models for empire were far and wide. An important reason for such disparate ideological formations descends from the two men's competing locations in the plantation economies of the West Indies and the North American South as merchant clerk (Hamilton) and planter (Jefferson) respectively. Surprisingly few scholars have connected Jefferson's agrarian vision of empire and its attendant denunciation of commerce to the ever-mounting debt that Jefferson owed to mercantile interests throughout his life. On considering the two men's competing roles in the plantation economies of the Atlantic world, the foundations of their dispute over the preferred course for U.S. empire building become more apparent. Briefly, for Hamilton there could be neither "empire" nor "liberty" without economic and political stability. Where Jefferson championed humankind's innate goodness, Hamilton believed strongly in the notion that men are motivated by self-interest and the pursuit of property; where Jefferson denounced the nation's urban centers as hives of undemocratic scheming, favoring instead an empire built on farming and expansionism, Hamilton insisted on a powerful, concentrated federal government that could channel its citizens' desires such that U.S. commerce and industry would be the envy of Europe; and where Jefferson philosophized that only through an original relationship with the wilderness would U.S. Americans transform the damaging identities assigned them as Europe's degenerate creole offspring, Hamilton riled at such defensive, isolationist strategies of resistance, advocating instead that the United States teach an assuming Europe a lesson by evincing a superior political economy while surging toward commercial preeminence in the hemisphere. Importantly, Hamilton's, not Jefferson's, vision of empire dominated the political agenda during the administrations of Washington and Adams. As Secretary of the Treasury, Hamilton was given free rein by Washington to develop policies for solving the economic crises plaguing the nation's development in its early years. He did so, to the dismay of Jefferson, by boldly confronting the British, Spanish, and French empires that were stifling the nation's economic development by controlling commerce in the West Indies.[9]

Jefferson's opposition to these policies and Washington's endorsement of them reveal some of the ways that Hamilton exposed divisions within the United States about what it meant to be an "American" and about U.S. national character. Moreover, Hamilton's fiscal mania counteracts colonialist discourse like Long's about what it meant to be a "creole" West Indian. Opponents characterized Hamilton in many unflattering ways, but to suggest that he was a "bad oeconomist" or "supine," "indolent," or "fickle and desultory in [his] pursuits" is to plumb in unconvincing ways the unsteady depths of colonialist discourse about the West Indian. So, too, do Jefferson's later thoughts about Hamilton's "private virtue" destabilize prevailing notions about creole character and the authenticity of colonialist discourse about the West Indies. Although Jefferson exploits Hamilton's illegitimate birth and immigrant status in his denunciations, he resists deploying the term "creole" to account for what he perceives to be Hamilton's public indiscretions. Jefferson's own insecurities concerning stereotypes about the South, his anxieties over having conceived several illegitimate children with Sally Hemmings (behavior that tends to confirm Long's "creole" assumptions), and the Federalist media's repeated attacks on his personal character no doubt made him alert to the metonymic associations between a West Indian "creole" identity and his own. Jefferson would have been sensitive to the interconnectedness between Southern and West Indian identities and cultures. Perhaps not surprisingly, he seeks to disentangle these terms of identity according to his expansionist thrust in a westerly direction. Such a movement would tend to mitigate, so he might have thought, their mutually contaminative effect.

Adams's quarrels with Hamilton were of a far more fratricidal nature than Jefferson's. For Adams, Hamilton was metonym and metaphor for a literal "sea change" in Federalist policies that occurred during the Washington administration. The effects of this shift in the Federalist party transformed society on all levels—political, social, and economic. Hamilton's ascent to power signaled what Steven Watts has identified as the "gradual decline of republican, paternal traditions and the convergence of Protestant moralism, capitalist acquisitiveness, and possessive individualism" (8). Thus an expanding market economy—in accordance with Hamilton's empire for commerce—reflected the emergence of a new liberalism characterized by what Watts terms "materialist striving" (9) and the consequent commodification of republicanism to accommodate such a trend. In the opinion of "High" Federalists like Adams, Hamiltonian Federalism imperiled the nation by corrupting time-honored notions undergirding the structures of nationalism like "civic virtue," "self restraint," and the unendowed masses' consent to be governed by an elite "breed" of aristocratic patriots. Ultimately these antagonisms between the insurgent Federalists and the High Federalists proved cataclysmic. The highly public feud between Hamilton and Adams propelled Jefferson to victory in the 1800 presidential election and hastened the nullification of the Federalist party as a viable political organization.

Although the details of the eroding political relationship between Hamilton and Adams are fascinating, I wish to focus on the xenophobic ways in which Adams verbalized his displeasure for Hamilton. As his correspondence, diaries, and autobiography reveal, Adams found it difficult to contain himself at the mere mention of Hamilton's name. In his writings, Adams does not identify Hamilton as a patriot or founding statesman but as a "bastard Creole" whose reputed genius for financial matters is fraudulent. According to Adams, Hamilton's knowledge of both "coin and commerce was very superficial and imperfect" (Adams and Rush, *Spur* 35). Moreover, Adams believed Hamilton's self-promoting nature, characterized by a "Creolian" impulse to "hammer out a guinea into an acre of gold" (*Spur* 173), had caused the public to disregard contributions by Washington's other cabinet members—particularly his own—to the formation of the national government and character. He feared posterity's judgment would be similarly derelict. Therefore Adams repeatedly employs stereotypical creole discourse in order to denigrate Hamilton's political achievement, and specifically to suggest the need for his audience to reconsider their too generous estimation of his commercial abilities. In effect, Adams invokes Long's classification of the West Indian as a "bad oeconomist" so as to negate Hamilton's foremost talent.

In one especially agitated passage in his autobiography, Adams deploys the full force of colonialist discourse about the West Indies in order to emphasize Hamilton's "illegitimate" usurpation of power, vowing that he will never

conceal [Hamilton's] former Character at the Expense of so much Injustice to my own, as this Scottish Creolian Bolingbroke in the days of his disappointed Ambition and unbridled Malice and revenge, was pleased falsely to attempt against it. Born on a Speck more obscure than Corsica, from an Original not only contemptible but infamous, with infinitely less courage and Capacity than Bonaparte, he would in my Opinion, if I had not controuled the fury of his Vanity, instead of relieving this Country from Confusion as Bonaparte did France, he would have involved it in all the Bloodshed and distractions of foreign and civil War at once. *(Diary and Autobiography* 159)

As the tone of his comment suggests, Adams felt Hamilton was a dangerous man to have building the U.S. empire in the 1780s and 1790s. Hamilton's overreaching and duplicity Adams attributes to his origins, and to his being born a "Prodigal" to his creole mother, classified by Adams as a "Harlot," an "Original not only contemptible but infamous." His upbringing on the West Indian island of Nevis, "a Speck more obscure than Corsica," signals Hamilton's corruption and utter alienation from traditional republican principles and values. Arrogating to himself credit for having halted Hamilton's sword-waving imperial ambitions, Adams repeatedly makes the charge in his writings that Hamilton's unnatural "Creole" blood was the source of his misconduct, "there [being] as much in the breed of men as there is in that of horses" (*Spur* 158). Calling Hamilton the degenerate "bastard brat of a Scotch ped-lar" (*Spur* 48), Adams implies that Hamilton has inherited his haughti-ness and economic imposture from his father. Although he doesn't connect the signifier "creole" with the tenor of Adams's debasements of Hamilton, John Ferling suggests that "Adams looked upon [Hamil-ton] as he would a feral animal, a reckless, intriguing, megalomaniac, who . . . had frightened even Washington into complying with his every wish" (378). Ferling's assessment indicates the parallels between Adams's discursive strategy and that of the colonialist who seeks to pre-vent the contamination of ostensibly pure traditions. Adams's neocolo-nialist gaze operates to map Hamilton's "creole" interiors in order to exteriorize Hamilton's imposture as an authentic U.S. American.

Indeed, Hamilton was viewed by his enemies as "monstrous," "exotic," and "foreign,"and his propensity toward "secrecy, mystery, and intrigue" (*Spur* 47) Adams imputed to Hamilton's "superabun-dance of secretions which he could not find whores enough to draw off" (qtd. Flexner 62). The condition of "superabundant" secretions of bodily fluids was commonly ascribed throughout the Atlantic world to persons born and raised in the West Indian "torrid zone." By using such a conceit, Adams was not only impugning Hamilton's sexual conduct but gesturing to the ways in which Hamilton's debased and creolized "body" violated republican ideas about restraint and virtue. As Mary Douglas states in *Natural Symbols,* "The human body is always treated as an image of society and . . . there can be no natural way of considering the body that does not involve at the same time a social dimension. Interests in its apertures depend on the preoccupation with social exits and entrances, escape routes and invasions. If there is no concern to preserve social boundaries, I would not expect to find concern with bodily boundaries" (qtd. Gilman vii). In the ways Douglas suggests, Adams marks Hamilton's creole body by implying that his "ideological" secretions have corrupted the nation's tradeways and stained U.S. national character and history. A "Creole" Sodomite, Hamilton invades the nation's "social exits and entrances." Jefferson echoes such scatological figurations when he remarks in *Notes* that commerce's insidious effects on the "mobs of great cities add just so much to the support of pure government, as sores do to the strength of the human body" (164).

While Adams's assaults on Hamilton's creole body reveal his notorious paranoia and mercurial temper, his acidic remarks are more than transparent reflections of Adams's antipathy for Hamilton. Adams's obsessions with Hamilton's race and origins reflect deeply ingrained anxieties about not only Hamilton's heritage but also the material realities shaping Hamilton's vision of the United States as an empire for commerce. These realities include the remapping of the U.S. "body" and political landscape by Hamilton and his commercial backers. Such a remapping shifted national governance away from a paternalistic, aristocratic leadership and toward a system of patronage between the national government and an emergent class of mercantile men made wealthy by the West Indian trades. Hamilton becomes a monstrous double as well for the massive influx during the 1790s of West Indian refugees into U.S. cities as a result of the Haitian Revolution, and also for the ongoing predations by European powers on U.S. commercial interests in the West Indian theatre during Adams's presidency. These developments were embodied in Adams's mind and in the minds of his supporters by Hamilton's defiled creole personhood. The "creole" conceit becomes so overwrought in Adams's diatribes about Hamilton that the reader's focus shifts away from the object of Adams's derision to Adams himself. Adams's invocation of an entire repertoire of images denoting creole degeneracy—dark and infested spaces, contamination, sexual and moral degradation, parental wantonness—seems to foretell the imminent destruction of the nation . . . or at least of Adams, Hamilton, and the Federalist Party.

Indeed, Adams's attacks are not singular but echoed by Hamilton's other political rivals. For example, during Adams's unsuccessful bid for reelection in 1800, Hamilton was increasingly indiscrete about his opposition to Adams and his foreign policy, and about supporting Charles Pinckney for the presidency. The nation's commanding military officer at the time, Hamilton became the target of a pro-Adams letter published anonymously in the Boston newspapers. In part, the letter read:

In your daring prediction, That if Mr. Pinckney was not elected President, a revolution would be the consequence; and that within the next four years you should lose your head, or be the leader of a triumphant army—your vanity was more gross than ever your ignorance of the character of the Eastern states. . . . And you might find yourself equally mistaken, in supposing, that the mode of your descent from a dubious father, in an English island would be no bar in this country to the pretensions to the Presidency; nor interfere with the claim of virtues which in another [Napoleon], has enabled an ambitious soldier to trample upon the little that remained of public liberty. (*PAH* 25:91)

If the anonymous letter in the Boston newspaper was intended as a preemptive strike against Hamilton's designs to hurt the President, it backfired. Wounded by the letter's admonition that his origins and ambition would "bar" him from "pretensions to the Presidency," Hamilton wrote two telling documents: he published one; the other he sent to a friend for the purpose of making it semi-public.

The first document, an open letter denouncing Adams's character and his conduct as President, was redeployed by Republicans as part of their successful campaign to elect Jefferson. The second is a privately circulated letter that Hamilton wrote to a political ally and friend that provides glimpses into his early childhood life in the West Indies. Obviously distraught over the tone of the Boston letter, Hamilton wrote, "Never was there a more ungenerous persecution of any man than of myself.—Not only the worst constructions are put upon my conduct as a public man but it seems my birth is the subject of most humiliating criticism" (*PAH* 25:88–89).[10] Defensive about the ways in which his opponents, following Adams's example, maligned his politics by attacking his origins, Hamilton's curious justification of his "birth" is significant on two accounts. First, the letter is an elaborate defense of his childhood in the West Indies. Despite the fact that the Boston letter is vague and imprecise about the scene of Hamilton's nativity, Hamilton's elaborate effort to affiliate himself with an alleged Scottish noble ancestry reveals a hypersensitivity to even vague references to his West Indian creole past and identity.

Hamilton's letter is notable, too, for its excesses and half-truths. In the letter, Hamilton demonstrates a compulsion to disassociate himself from his creole past, particularly notions about his alleged creole degeneracy. Hamilton's stated purpose for writing—to convey to the reader "the real history of [my birth], that among my friends you may if you please wipe off some part of the stain which is so industriously impressed"—suggests that removing the entire "stain" associated with being creole may not be possible. Nonetheless, Hamilton intimates that by conveying what he claims is an authentic "history" of his beginnings, his letter might function as a semi-public, counterdiscursive act against the sensational public accounts "industriously impressed" on the creole surface of his body. Although Hamilton acknowledges in his letter that his blood is not "free from blemish," he also indicates his awareness that creoleness is a discursive construction; he recognizes not only the fabricated nature of what has been written about his creoleness but crucially points to the fabricated creole identities of his enemies, including Adams. He maintains that identities in the early Republic are contrived for purposes of power and prestige and goes on to claim that his creole past is more genuine and fortunate than the origins of his enemies, arguing that he has "better pretensions than most of those who in this Country plume themselves on Ancestry."

Paradoxically, Hamilton's letter is full of its own "pretensions" and reveals his proclivity for blurring "the real history" of his origins to suit his political purposes. For example, he underscores his mother Rachel's "French Huguenot [stock]," emphasizing that her ancestors "emigrated to the West Indies in the consequence of the revocation of the Edict of Nantz." She is described by Hamilton as "handsome" and "charming," and he defends her reputation (about which Hamilton's opponents seem to have had a working knowledge), saying that it was sullied by her first husband, a Dutch "fortune-hunter . . . bedizzined with gold." Hamilton also claims that Rachel and his father were married—implying that his birth was, indeed, legitimate for a time—but that the marriage was declared "unlawful" because it turned out that Rachel's first husband arranged things so that their divorce "was not absolute but qualified." Finally, Hamilton alludes to his father's awful business practices, which included "too generous and too easy a temper." He expounds on his father's "respectable Scotch descent," including his affiliation with the "ancient Baronet *Sir Robert Pollock.*" He further redeems James Hamilton by insisting that "his character . . . and manners [were] those of a Gentleman." He ends the letter simply by reporting that his father "is now dead," though still quite "alive" in the minds of Hamilton's attackers.

The examination of extant deeds and records by scholars has uncovered details about his life that point to Hamilton's talent for improvising about his birth and origins. Hamilton's father, these documents reveal, abandoned the family and moved to the island of St. Vincent when Hamilton was not yet ten years old, leaving the family destitute (Schachner 10). As Hamilton indicated in a private letter to his brother James Jr., he never saw him again. Nor did Hamilton ever invite his brother to visit him in the United States, despite putting up dozens of Scottish "relatives" at his home. Records indicate that after his mother died of fever when he was eleven, Hamilton survived through the good graces of distant relatives and family friends (Flexner 6). Hamilton's letter is anything, then, but a "real history" of his early life in the West Indies. In its European embellishments and "creole" omissions, it illustrates the creole obsession with counteracting charges of New World degeneracy in the early national period of the United States. Ironically, the assertion of an ennobled creole identity entails wielding the very discourses that Europeans inaugurated to maintain power over the creole colonists. Thus the assaults and counterassaults between Adams and Hamilton reflect the precarious task of (un)becoming creole(s) amid the ceaseless "commerce" between U.S., West Indian, and European bodies and cultures.

As part of his denigration of Hamilton, Adams inaugurated an erroneous assumption that has remained largely unchallenged. Whenever Hamilton disagreed with Adams on a policy matter, in a characteristically chauvinistic way Adams attributed their disagreement to the fact that Hamilton was "not a native of America" and thus "never acquired the feelings and principles of the American people" (qtd. Haraszti 7). Ironically, scholars of U.S. empire building have tended to repeat such a view. For example, in *The Empire for Reason,* Henry Steele Commager remarks that Hamilton was "[not] an American—not in his thinking anyway" (265). Both Adams and Commager suggest that Hamilton's ideology of the United States as an empire for commerce was somehow not "American" owing to Hamilton's unfamiliarity with epistemological and ontological assumptions unique to "native" U.S. Americans. While conceding that Hamilton was not literally a native of the United States (though "native" is a word fraught with treacherous assumptions), this chapter argues that Alexander Hamilton embodied anxieties about what (un)becoming creole meant in the West Indies and the United States during the first decades of the nation's existence.

Hamilton often spoke in specific terms about the very subjects Adams and Commager raise. For instance, when the fate of the proposal to retire the national debt hung in the balance in 1795, Hamilton wrote to Senator Rufus King of Massachusetts urging him to petition his ambivalent colleagues on behalf of the measure. Bewildered that Congress would think of assassinating "the national honor" and undermining the public confidence in government he had worked diligently to achieve by not passing the bill, Hamilton asked:

Am I, then, more of an American than those who drew their first breath on American ground? . . . Were it not for yourself and a few others, I could adopt the reveries of De Paux [*sic*] as substantial truths, and could say with him that there is something in our climate which belittles every animal, human or brute. I conjure you, my friend, make a vigorous stand for the honor of your country! (qtd. Allan Hamilton 38)

Taken together, the remarks by Adams, Commager, and Hamilton represent a crisis in what it means to be and "feel" like an "American." As noted above, Adams in his writings charges Hamilton with "frightening . . . Washington into complying with his every wish," raising the specter that Hamilton could indeed, as he exclaimed he was doing to King, "conjure" others to behave according to his desires. Adams's comment suggests that he believes Hamilton's power and influence over others is, if not supernatural, unnatural. Yet Hamilton claims to be in sympathy with the "feelings and principles" of at least some other creole Americans—the "few others" who have not degenerated in the American environment. An examination of Hamilton's experience as a merchant clerk in the West Indies suggests that Hamilton indeed had acquired feelings and principles while living outside the geographic boundaries of the United States and without having himself been a native-born American that were as "American" in many ways as the feelings and principles that Adams claimed.

What Hamilton's comments demonstrate is the competition that statesmen in the young nation felt about shaping and forming the characters of the nation and its citizens. Though in an indirect, agitated way, Hamilton asserts that different U.S. Americans "feel" and "think" in diverse ways about these things, and he implies above in his anxious jest informed by the trope of creole degeneracy that environment may indeed have something to do with those differences. Hamilton's early life provides one such example. As a young West Indian merchant clerk, his identity, and that of his North American merchant boss, were shaped differently than the identities of many colonists living and working on the mainland, though the ships shuttling between the West Indies and North America made those differences less pronounced than they might otherwise have been. How Hamilton and Nicholas Cruger came to think and feel about concepts like "becoming" and "unbecoming," "American" and "creole," "virtue" and "interest," and "nation" and "empire" did not depend on clearly defined geographical borders or nation-spaces. The formation of Hamilton's identity is connected to his role as an international merchant clerk in the circumatlantic trades on the eve of the American Revolution, in which he would play a critical role as aide-de-camp to the commanding general, George Washington.

Hamilton's attempts to distance himself from his creole West Indian origins as a founding statesman in the independent United States obscure the ways in which his vision of the United States as an empire, and his subjectivity as a "hemispheric" American, derive from his experiences as a West Indian merchant clerk. He held this position from the age of eleven to the age of seventeen, from 1766 to 1772, the year he immigrated to North America. Hamilton was employed by Nicholas Cruger, the son of Henry Cruger, who had sons living and working in satellite mercantile houses throughout North America, the West Indies, and Europe.[11] All the Crugers were born and raised in New York and returned frequently to their native city for personal and business reasons. Merchants like the Crugers of New York City embodied the paracolonial, hemispheric embrace of commerce in the late eighteenth century. The Crugers operated warehouses, docks, and a distillery in

New York; bought and sold bills of exchange; and extended credit. They used their fleet of ships for multiple purposes, including trading, privateering, and smuggling. In short, the Cruger family merchant operation challenges scholarly assumptions about what it meant to "be" a U.S. citizen in the early Republic. International merchants like the Crugers unsettle how we imagine the boundaries of "nation" and "nationalism" and the ways in which we define concepts like "empire," "liberty," "freedom," and "virtue."

The Dutch and Danish islands, like the island of St. Croix where Hamilton lived and worked, were especially important because North American merchants erected merchant houses on these islands before and after the Revolutionary War in order to trade with the French West Indies and thus circumvent English prohibitions against the practice. By 1771, Hamilton had become Cruger's chief merchant clerk. From the day he became employed by the Crugers, Hamilton never existed *outside* the reach of North American, and later U.S., political economies. Thus Hamilton is at once a figure of the empire without and the empire within. In a telling statement to his son, Hamilton's first and most celebratory biographer, Hamilton related that despite his "aversion" to mercantilism, his employment with Cruger comprised "the most useful parts of his education" because it had provided him with "method and facility" (qtd. J. Thomas 37). We can only appreciate the import of that statement by scrutinizing the material conditions in which Hamilton was raised. So many of the skills Hamilton developed while working on behalf of North American mercantile interests in the West Indies proved invaluable to him when he became the chief "West Indian merchant clerk" for the United States—Secretary of the Treasury under Washington. Hamilton alone among the nation's founding statesmen had the requisite knowledge to imagine the vast and expanding commercial empire of the United States that pivoted on the West Indies.

Given that a number of Hamilton's letters to the Crugers around the world have survived, we have some fair indication about the ways in which his merchant clerk experiences formed Hamilton's identity.[12] Those letters not only reveal his responsibilities but also indicate the sorts of commodities imported and exported by Cruger. In addition, the letters provide perspective on the enormous wealth and capital the United States derived before and after independence from the West Indian trades. From St. Croix Hamilton shipped sugar and rum around the world. From New York City he received corn, rye meal, flour, lumber, staves, and dried fish. From Bristol came the manufactured goods necessary for the plantation economy to operate. These included mules and various farming implements; clothing for creoles and their slaves; guns and ammunition; and a range of luxury items. From all corners of the world came cash and specie—British, French, Dutch, and Spanish currencies that Hamilton endeavored to exchange at the best rates possible.

Several extant letters are urgent messages sent by Hamilton to Cruger's sons and brothers on neighboring West Indian islands warning them of pirates and enemy vessels in the area. These insights into the inner workings of piracy and spoliation would prove invaluable to Hamilton as he fashioned a military policy for protecting U.S. commerce in the treacherous Caribbean waters in the 1790s. In other correspondence he chastises Cruger's brothers for shipping tainted goods to St. Croix and causing Nicholas to suffer heavy losses. Hamilton's concerns about the integrity of Cruger's business dealings anticipate his insistence as Secretary of the Treasury on the sanctity of private property and solvency so that the government might gain the confidence of investors. Elsewhere in his letters, Hamilton chases down delinquent planters for the (always sizable) past-due balances on their accounts, a constant chore given the unfavorable balance of trade under which the West Indies labored. Hamilton drew on these experiences when he drafted his revolutionary propaganda on behalf of the North American colonies, outlining in precise detail the British empire's systematic exploitation of its dependencies. In pushing for industry and a national bank, Hamilton demonstrated his sensitivity to the ways in which West Indian wealth ended up in the banks of Europe's merchant bankers, who thereby became proprietors of plantations in default. Thus, while working for Cruger, Hamilton learned to balance books that would not be balanced, to manipulate the complexities of intercolonial trade to Cruger's greatest advantage, and to earn for the Cruger empire the maximum possible benefit while minimizing losses. He also became thoroughly conversant with the workings of the slave trade. Slaves from the Gold Coast of Africa were regularly paraded in front of Cruger's trading house, and sugar, rum, tobacco, indigo, and cotton, yields of the New World plantation economies, moved through Cruger's loading docks in large quantities.

From his vantage point as a West Indian merchant clerk, then, Hamilton came to think and feel about the inequities of empire in ways that were related to, but distinct from, those of the other founding statesmen. Hamilton witnessed the trauma that resulted from the revenue acts that tightened England's hold over the political economies of its American colonies, first as a clerk in West Indies and later as an immigrant in North America. He experienced in an intimate way how legislation like the Sugar Act of 1764 and the Stamp Act of 1765 extorted badly needed currencies from insolvent West Indian economies. As his Revolutionary propaganda tracts demonstrate, Hamilton monitored the mounting pressures in urban communities throughout the hemisphere as a result of England's increasingly severe colonial policies, a task facilitated by his contacts with merchant men from New York and around the world. In the West Indies, he would have understood the devastating cultural impact of economic hardship, absenteeism, and shortages of manufactured goods and witnessed the ill effects of slavery and violent weather, portents of the coming rebellion by the North American colonies against "mother" England. Thus by aligning Hamilton's empire-building strategies with the vast North American mercantile presence in the West Indies to which they respond and on behalf of which he labored during his formative years, one can better identify their (inter-) creole *nationalist*, as opposed to degenerate or "foreign," complexion.

With the encouragement of Nicholas Cruger, Hamilton departed the West Indies in 1772, carrying a satchel of letters introducing him to Cruger's mercantile friends in New York. Assisted by the New York commercial establishment, Hamilton enrolled in King's College (which he helped rename Columbia University after the war) and two years later became an important pamphleteer for the restless North American colonists. These early writings respond, in part, to the abuses of empire he witnessed as a West Indian merchant clerk, and they contain powerful challenges to Tory propaganda supporting the economic attitudes of the British toward their colonies. During the Revolution, Hamilton learned to think and feel like an American in new ways: first as an artillery captain, then as Washington's aide-de-camp. After the Treaty of Versailles in 1783, Hamilton led the charge to overhaul the Articles of Confederation and he later played a vital role in securing the ratification of the Constitution by writing the majority of *The Federalist* (1788), his brainchild. In these writings, published under the sobriquet "Publius," Hamilton first unveiled his notions about a U.S. empire for commerce.

The West Indian Trades and a U.S. "Empire for Commerce"

Both Hamilton's empire for commerce and Jefferson's empire for liberty respond to eighteenth-century European ideas about New World creole degeneracy. Coterminous with colonialist discourse about the West Indies, European philosophies about American inferiority authored by Comte de Georges Louis Leclerc Buffon, Abbé Guillaume Thomas François Raynal, Abbé Cornelius de Pauw, and others cited environmental factors such as climate, soil, and population to account for why North Americans had failed to fulfill the ideas of the Enlightenment. Hamilton and Jefferson recognized the malignant effects such discourses had on the ways in which U.S. Americans felt about their creole nation and natures. European discourse about the American environment, coupled with Europe's trespasses against U.S. sovereignty on land and sea, had caused many of them to internalize claims regarding the degeneracy of

North America, this despite having recently achieved their political independence. Thus Hamilton's and Jefferson's expansive designs seek to reorient the ways in which creole U.S. Americans understand themselves, their nation, and their postcolonial condition. Yet if they share an impulse to remap the coordinates of national identity and character, their cartographies for empire and their terms for engaging discourses of creole degeneracy are worlds apart.

Jefferson's confrontation with theories of American inferiority in *Notes on the State of Virginia* is comprehensive and systematic. In *Notes*, Jefferson seeks to revise the key figures and terms that European theories about the North American environment and its inhabitants exploit. To that end, he develops an elaborate counterdiscourse that demonstrates the putative superiority of the U.S. American habitat and husbandman. For Jefferson, the North American continent is not an unhealthy, stagnating place as Europe had suggested but a land of infinite plenitude and possibility. Likewise, the U.S. American has not degenerated in its embrace but instead improved on the European by demonstrating a seemingly infinite capacity to adapt and respond to a varied climate. Moreover, the nation's republican system of government, according to Jefferson, reflects the ways in which U.S. Americans are reconciled to their environment in an "internally homogeneous society" (Jehlen 59). As Myra Jehlen suggests, Jefferson believed that the United States was sloughing off its Old World skin and being made anew, "incarnate" in the continent.

In the empire for liberty, "Those who labour in the earth are the chosen people of God . . . [in] whose breasts he has made his peculiar deposit for substantial and genuine virtue" (Jefferson 164–65). Implicit in such a view, Daniel Boorstin explains, is the desire to expand to new lands, made manifest by Jefferson's recurring stylization of the North American husbandman as a figure of man's equality, a figure with a "special destiny for the kind of work to be undertaken in America" (74). Accordingly, Jefferson's eye for empire is, as a matter of course, focused on the West and turned away from Europe, the stage of corruption and immorality. In such a way, Jefferson's cartography for an empire for liberty figures a divinely inspired farmer on a westerly track cultivating freedom, justice, and equality amid a sentimentalized North American landscape. Crucially, however, Jefferson's ostensibly "enlightened" vision for republican empire, as generations of scholars have noted, rests on notions of white racial supremacy, ever more insistently so in the wake of the Haitian Revolution (1789–1804). Writes Peter Onuf, "The impossibility of racial coexistence in one place" in *Notes on the State of Virginia* is "projected across space" (180) and time in subsequent writings, Virginia functioning as a synecdoche for a nascent U.S. empire. Thus blacks would have to be expatriated and colonized—preferably to Haiti—the empire for "liberty" thereby predicting racialist notions informing U.S. nation and empire building in the nineteenth and twentieth centuries.

Like Jefferson's, Hamilton's view of empire responds in explicit ways to notions about creole American degeneracy. Indeed, in Federalist 11 he suggests that such theories motivate his will to empire:

The superiority [Europe] has long maintained has tempted her to plume herself as the mistress of the world, and to consider the rest of mankind as created for her benefit. Men admired as profound philosophers have in direct terms attributed to her inhabitants a physical superiority and have gravely asserted that all animals, and with them the human species, degenerate in America—that even the dogs cease to bark after having breathed awhile in our atmosphere. Facts have too long supported these arrogant pretensions of the European. It belongs to us to vindicate the honor of the human race, and to teach that assuming brother moderation. (*FP* 91)

Thus Hamilton is in concert with Jefferson when he acknowledges the force and sway of European discourse about New World creole degeneracy, and the tendency of U.S. Americans in their minds and actions to manifest the deleterious effects of European environmentalisms. Yet according to his disparate subject formation as a West Indian creole merchant clerk, Hamilton resists the traps set by European purveyors of environmentalist discourses, traps he believes Jefferson stumbles into by marrying the stylized U.S. American farmer with an apotheosized North American West.

In order to grasp fully the significance of such a distinction between the two founding fathers of U.S. empire building, we need to appreciate the ways in which Hamilton's repeated attempts to distance himself from his creole West Indian origins as a founding statesman in the independent United States obscure how his vision of empire, and his subjectivity as a "hemispheric" American, derive from his West Indian merchant clerk experiences. Working as a merchant clerk for North American interests on a densely populated *island*, one dependent on enslaving thousands of Africans, had likely disabused him of the impulse to appropriate natural history discourses as a way of resisting their pernicious effects. Marx's comment in *Grundrisse* about utopic discourses that promote removal to island paradises—like St. Croix—as a way of remedying the ills of modern civilization is a fitting gloss on the discursive battle between Hamilton and Jefferson over how best to reinscribe European mappings of North American creole identities:

This is the semblance, the merely aesthetic semblance, of the Robinsonades, great and small. . . . Production by an isolated individual outside society—a rare exception which may well occur when a civilized person in whom the social forces are already dynamically present is cast by accident into the wilderness—is as much of an absurdity as is the development of language without individuals living *together* and talking to each other. (83–84)

In Federalist 6, Hamilton prefigures Marx's skepticism about the romanticized island traveler or solitary individual in harmony with a Jeffersonian "continent." Commenting on the impulse to seclude oneself "from the imperfections, the weaknesses, and the evils incident to society," Hamilton asks disciples of the Jeffersonian persuasion, "Is it not time to awake from the deceitful dream of a golden age and to adopt as a practical maxim for the direction of our political conduct that we, as well as other inhabitants of the globe, are yet remote from the happy empire of perfect wisdom and perfect virtue?" (59). According to Hamilton's logic, Jefferson's defiant remarking of theories about creole degeneracy—his paean to agriculture, the U.S. "American" farmer, and the landscape—is not merely misguided. By turning inward and away from Europe and the urban United States, Jefferson's cartography of empire and citizen ironically risks reinforcing the very structures of dominance that Europe depends on for control of the U.S. political economy. Hamilton's notion of political economy—formed, in part, by chasing down debtor plantation owners like Jefferson—remained sensitive to the ways in which the British empire had drained West Indian plantation economies of their wealth and resources. Thus he eschewed the concept of a U.S. empire that emphasized agriculture for its political and economic well-being.

Designed to address the unjust trade imbalances between the United States and Europe, Hamilton's model of empire is more aggressive and confrontational than Jefferson's empire for liberty. Rather than risk reifying discourses about creole degeneracy that legitimate Europe's imperial domination of U.S. commerce, Hamilton proposes the strategic expansion of commerce and a renovated republicanism in order to disrupt the hold of Europe's commerce and scientific discourses over the United States and the hemisphere. For Hamilton, the model U.S. empire flows south and east: his notion of empire is not bent on continental expansion and conquest, but on the command of the hemisphere's tradeways: its oceans, rivers, and especially the Caribbean Sea. As Hamilton envisions the future time/space of U.S. American empire, "The veins of commerce in every part will be replenished and will acquire additional motion and vigor from a free circulation of every part" (*FP* 89). The new nation is figured as the "heart" of hemispheric influence and power, enriched by a vigorous circulatory system of commerce whose "veins" and "arteries" have been purified of Europe's clotting influence. The purifying force will be a compact, potent federal republic that Hamilton exhorts his readers to endorse: "Let Americans disdain to be the instruments of European greatness! Let the thirteen States, bound together in a strict and indissoluble Union, concur in erecting one great American system superior to the control of all transatlantic force or influence and able to dictate the terms of the connection between the old and the new world!" (91). Accordingly, Hamilton's imperial gaze is focused steadfastly on the West Indies and Europe; he implicitly dismisses the westward orientation of Jefferson's expansionist vision when he notes how the territories of the West "stretch far into our *rear*" (60; emphasis added). Instead, Hamilton seeks to reterritorialize the hemisphere's commercial pathways according to the pulsating "force" of "one great American [circulatory] system" of commercial empire.[13]

As with the figure of commerce as circulatory system to the federal "body," Hamilton deploys a series of interrelated, layered figures in his empire writings that are repeated for effect. All these terms are contained in one form or another in Federalist 11. At once an economics lesson, a treatise on empires past and present, an exhortation to control the hemisphere in the spirit of republican liberalism, and a strongly worded defense against European claims of American degeneracy, Federalist 11 is an especially prescient document in early U.S. discourse about empire. It anticipates and predicts the present appetite for economic communities, the triumphal tone of U.S. global capitalism, and the attendant sway of the United States over the cultural condition of the Western Hemisphere. Federalist 11 establishes the proposition that the United States, rather than remain hostage to European colonial and imperial desire, might one day "become the arbiter of Europe in America" (87), replacing European New World despotism with a powerful, commercially driven federal republic. By so doing, Hamilton feels the nation might dislodge the exploitative political and economic relationship between Europe and the Americas that undergirds the hierarchy of values articulated by discourses of creole degeneracy.

Hamilton roughly structures Federalist 11 around the polarities of an "ACTIVE" versus a "PASSIVE COMMERCE." With the nation hampered by an impotent federal government unable to regulate commerce under the terms of the Articles of Confederation, passive commerce signifies the ways in which European empires persist in "prescrib[ing] the conditions of [America's] political existence" (88). In contrast, "ACTIVE COMMERCE" denotes Hamilton's ideal political economy, one that capitalizes on the "unequaled spirit of enterprise, which signalizes the genius of American merchants and navigators and which is in itself an inexhaustible mine of national wealth" (88). Capitalization symbolizes not only the Hamiltonian ideal of empire but the entrepreneurial "capital" the

U.S. *hemispheric man of commerce* embodies in "spirit" and that the nation might exploit in order to right itself.[14] In Hamilton's model, the "spirit" of an active commerce supersedes the enervating effects of a passive commerce made impotent over time by European mercantile efforts to exploit and dominate the Americas. Hamilton's capitalization also represents the tremendous material "capital" the North American colonies amassed prior to the revolution from their participation in the West Indian trades. Finally, ACTIVE COMMERCE augurs the even greater prosperity the commercial community in the United States would enjoy, much of it stemming from dangerous maneuvers in the West Indies during the fifteen years following the publication of *The Federalist.*

What is so singular about Hamilton's pronouncement is his proto-modern suggestion that the pursuit of wealth through trade and industry might be integral to an empowered, regenerated national character, rather than a source of guilt and anxiety as such pursuits were for Jeffersonians and Adams Federalists (and the Puritans before them). As Hamilton notes, even without the backing of a united nation and strong federal government, U.S. traders and merchants had inculcated a profound sense of uneasiness in the empires of Europe about their potentially diminished role in the Western Hemisphere. Writes Hamilton, "There are appearances to authorize a supposition that the adventurous spirit, which distinguishes the commercial character of America, has already excited uneasy sensations in several of the maritime powers of Europe" (90). In turn, Hamilton argues, European nations have become "apprehensive of our too great interference in that [West Indian] carrying trade, which is the support of their navigation and the foundation of their naval strength. Those of them which have colonies in America look forward to what this country is capable of becoming with painful solitude" (85). Hamilton suggests there is something instinctively powerful about U.S. commerce that unsettles, agitates, and frightens European colonial forces such that they apprehend the demise of their influence in the Western Hemisphere, even at the moment of their greatest naval strength and the new nation's military puniness.

Hamilton's manifesto thus pivots on the formation of a vision, to be espoused by politicians and the various commercial interests, of the U.S. American as a hemispheric man of commerce, a sort of Colossus of Rhodes striding across the ports of the Atlantic and the Caribbean. Like Jefferson's sprawling "American farmer," Hamilton's hemispheric man functions on two levels: the vocational and the avocational. On the vocational level, hemispheric man represents the assemblage of merchants, traders, and future manufacturers that functions as the core infrastructure for an empire for commerce. These men embody the great benefit of diversifying economic life that will eventually allow the United States to address the stifling trade imbalance with Europe that an exclusive reliance on agriculture only exacerbates. Commerce, too, will infuse the culture with much needed energy. In his "Report on Manufactures" (1791), Hamilton argues for the acquisitive benefits that might accrue to the American people owing to an expanded commerce. In a commercial empire, Hamilton maintains, "each individual can find his proper element, and can call into activity the whole vigour of his nature. And the community is beneffited [*sic*] by the services of its respective members, in the manner in which each can serve it with the most effect" (*PAH* 10:255). For Hamilton, republicanism is well served by a commercial empire, as the freedom and liberty that the man of commerce enjoys in his "proper element"—Hamilton did not believe in the *equality* of all men—function to energize the entire U.S. community. Given the underdeveloped state of the manufacturing base that Hamilton envisioned, this collective body places special emphasis on the merchants and traders functioning as the agents of empire in the commercial wars in and around the West Indies.[15]

The avocational sense of hemispheric man is dependent on the meaning of Hamilton's notion of "spirit." For Hamilton, "spirit" is the zeitgeist of commerce and empire that operates to regenerate the United States—its vocational men of commerce, its political institutions, and the creole character of the nation and its people. Jefferson relies on an apotheosized landscape to elevate the condition of the creole American farmer to exemplar of pure republican virtue. In contrast, Hamilton's "spirit" symbolizes the ways in which the merchant man or trader as hemispheric man is transformed in the crucible of an ever-expanding U.S. hemispheric commercial influence into an energetic, enthusiastic "Son of Columbia." U.S. Americans did not occupy a "happy empire of perfect wisdom and virtue," Hamilton admonished the Jeffersonians; "Divide et impera" (66) and "force by fraud" (90) were standard operating procedures of European empires. Yet guided by the *spirit* of the rising U.S. empire, the hemispheric man of U.S. commerce could be trusted to adapt to any given circumstance in order to defend liberty, justice, and the nation's patriotic mission. "Spirit" was the indelible imprint made on the heart of hemispheric man according to his metonymic relationship to the "great American system superior to the control of all transatlantic force" (91).

Hamilton believed that it would take fifty or more years to amass the commercial and military strength necessary to "incline the balance of European competitions in this part of the world as our interest may dictate" (87). In the meantime, efforts to decolonize the minds and bodies of U.S. Americans in the face of ongoing European predations on the nation's sovereignty meant depending on uniquely creole strategies of resistance. More precisely, the "spirit" summoning forth the U.S. commercial empire was inextricably bound up in the patriotic spirit of nationalist resistance that precipitated revolution. One mercantile figure that embodies the revolutionary origins of the "spirit" guiding the hemispheric man in his navigation of the treacherous waters of the Atlantic and the Caribbean Sea is the smuggler. Prior to and during the Revolution, the "sons of liberty" deployed a full range of deceptive practices in order to thwart imperial efforts to regulate and limit the liberalizing tendencies of trade. The British suggested these illicit practices were attributable to American creole degeneracy. The colonists, however, transformed the smuggler into a figure of rebellion and defiance.

One particularly dangerous maneuver was the smuggling practice that involved ships "losing their identity." According to this practice, North American vessels would temporarily change their "bottoms," or national affiliation, in foreign ports like Martinique—from American to French, for example—in order that they might trade freely with the French colonies without fear of seizure by British naval vessels. Also, by trading with "neutral" islands like St. Croix, many North American merchant ships—like those operated by the Crugers—secured false "conduct passes" and were thus able to proceed to the French islands and from thence to southern Europe in violation of British law. A related activity involved North American vessels securing "false cocket[s]," or customhouse permits, by bribing foreign merchant house clerks and then proceeding unmolested to ports in the French West Indies. As Cathy Matson explains, although most New York merchant vessels left British West Indian ports "empty," they nonetheless arrived with "large cargoes of sugar . . . at their home ports just months later" (212). Thus practices like false cockets and a ship's losing its identity allowed New York merchants to smuggle contraband—including hundreds of thousands of dollars of sugar, molasses and other West Indian products—into New York in plain view.[16] Equally significant, these commercial strategies of resistance instilled in many U.S. Americans a spirit of patriotic virtue and suggested to them the virtue of pursuing their economic freedom. Figuratively, practices like the losing of a ship's identity reflect the ways in which the Hamiltonian creole merchant could exploit his outlaw status for maximum benefit. If Jefferson's U.S. farmer accrued virtue in proportion to his ability to adapt to the hospitable North American landscape, Hamilton's hemispheric man drew on the tradition of creole-as-rebel-trader to suggest the ways in which "virtue" itself could be made to respond and adapt to an environment rendered hostile by European aggression. Fluidity of identity, even the momentary losing of identity, might be necessary in order to protect the higher virtues of freedom and liberty underwriting the empire for commerce. Hamilton himself in his merchant clerk service, mixing of creole identities, and his patriotic writings embodies the spirit of hemispheric man.

To that end, though not a maritime strategy per se, the tactic of guerrilla warfare captures the innovativeness Hamilton believed infused the "entrepreneurial spirit" of hemispheric man. Months before the U.S. Revolution began, Hamilton encouraged North American colonists to utilize guerrilla warfare as part of their military strategy, something no other North American had advocated, at least not in print. As Hamilton writes in his revolutionary broadside "The Farmer Refuted" (1775), "The circumstances of our country put it in our power to evade a pitched battle. It will be better policy to harass and exhaust the soldiery by frequent skirmishes and incursions than to take the open field with [the British] . . . Americans are better qualified for that kind of fighting, which is most adapted to this country. . . . [By using guerrilla tactics,] we should . . . be at least upon equality with them" (*Works* 1:166–67). One with his environment, Hamilton's guerrilla warrior draws on his unique relationship with the landscape to mount "skirmishes and incursions" so as to "harass and exhaust" a more powerful foe. Hamilton not only advocates guerrilla warfare but suggests it as a more natural form of battle for the North American creole. By adapting to the geographical realities of his environment, the North American creole might be on "equality" with the British. Thus guerrilla strategies of resistance become, Hamilton suggests, integral to the formation of the revolutionary and national character. The maritime high jinks of the smuggler and the guerrilla warfare of the revolutionary patriot: together these figures suggest ways in which European assumptions about North American "creole" inferiority might be manipulated and transformed into ennobling figures in the service of a U.S. empire for commerce.[17]

Despite his inflated rhetoric, Hamilton demonstrates in Federalist 11 his awareness that the United States, prohibited from *legally* trading in the West Indies by Britain at the end of the eighteenth century, cannot meet the powerful British navy on its terms. His guerrilla warfare mindset, however, suggested to him alternate ways in which Europe might be divided and conquered in the Caribbean. More specifically, Hamilton proposes that a provisional merchant marine might be used as a mercenary navy in the West Indies and loaned out to the highest bidder. According to Hamilton, "A few ships of the line, sent opportunely to the reinforcement of either side, would often be sufficient to decide the fate of a campaign . . . in the persecution of military operations in the West Indies, it will readily be perceived that a situation so favorable would enable us to bargain with great advantage for commercial privileges" (87). Thus Hamilton advocates the adoption of ostensibly dishonorable commercial tactics, but he does so in the spirit of the revolutionary smuggler and guerrilla, and in the present spirit of the U.S. empire for commerce. Such improvisational military maneuvers, Hamilton argues, will be transformed over time into the more honorable maneuvers of a well-outfitted U.S. navy. Moreover, mercenary commercial tactics will prompt European empires to negotiate on favorable terms with the United States in order to avoid the decisive blow of the rising empire's hit and run merchant marine. Writes Hamilton, "a price will be set not only upon our friendship, but upon our neutrality. By a steady adherence to the Union, we may hope, ere long, to become the arbiter of Europe in America, and to be able to incline the balance of European competitions in this part of the world as our interest may dictate" (87). Thus "neutrality"—the operating principle of a virtuous U.S. man of empire, and which means in the abstract free trade with all nations, and entangling alliances with none—must be weighed in the context of the present imbalance of power. As Hamilton remarks, "The rights of neutrality will only be respected when they are defended by an adequate power. A nation, despicable by its weakness, forfeits even the privilege of being neutral" (87). Paradoxically, an improvisational merchant marine, the "inevitable offspring of moral and physical necessity," exploits the very notion of neutrality in seeking immediate commercial gratification, albeit in the spirit of preserving the long-term ambition of the upstart empire: "an active commerce, an extensive navigation, and a flourishing marine" (87). This fundamental contradiction would haunt and disturb the New Republic's leading statesmen, intellectuals, and writers into the next century, fomenting pitched battles within and across Federalist and Republican party lines, inducing in them and their would-be powerful nation a profound *creole complex*.

To read Hamilton's writings about empire in *The Federalist* is to have a sense of a United States perpetually at siege inside and outside its borders, and of Hamilton trying to right the ship of progress as the nation's chief steward: Hamilton as manager of the nation's "property," its finances and commercial affairs; as statesman setting the course of a surging empire; as chief commercial officer navigating a U.S. ship of state in the maelstrom of Europe's ongoing aggressions. As he announces to his readers in Federalist 15, "If the road over which you will still have to pass should in some places appear to you tedious or irksome . . . [it] will be my aim to remove the obstacles to your progress" (105). Hamilton's early life had been marked by uprooting and dispossession in an archipelago whose chaotic rhythms responded to European empires perpetually at war. The West Indies in the last half of the eighteenth century were spaces of "lost identities." An island's imperial affiliation might change not once or twice but several times within a matter of years according to ever-shifting alliances between France, Spain, and Britain. And the turbulent and violent plantation economies, the tensions between white creoles and their slaves, and the force of European discourses about West Indian inferiority made forging a coherent sense of self, let alone national belonging, next to unthinkable. Thus his West Indian mercantile experiences and his tutelage under Washington as aide-de-camp provided Hamilton with the "methods and facility" to do now for the independent nation and himself what had been denied under empire: secure a sense of identity and belonging.

Hamilton plotted to accomplish these things by inventing a utopian national subject, the hemispheric man of commerce, who would be motivated by the high principles of honor, liberty, and commercial acquisitiveness—all founding characteristics of the nation's patriotic "virtue." Equipped with these instruments, the hemispheric man of empire might according to his "inexhaustible wealth of national talent" negotiate the turgid waters of empire building. Yet the nation that Hamilton describes on the eve of the ratification of the Constitution in his empire writings seems eerily similar to the West Indian archipelago that he thought he had, fifteen years earlier, escaped. Akin to the West Indies of Hamilton's youth, the states operating under the Articles of Confederation are like "islands" or, in Hamilton's terms, empires unto themselves without direction or a sense of national belonging. The "nation" as well is threatened on all sides: by the British on the north and west, and the Spanish on the west and south. The Atlantic and Caribbean teem with powerful imperial navies wreaking havoc on U.S. commerce.[18]

Hamilton responds to these dire circumstances by drawing on a collectivity of creole experiences and devising the blueprint for a U.S. empire for commerce. According to that vision, the United States and the hemisphere are chaotic places: they have been shattered into fragments by European colonialism. Yet Hamilton urges ironically that they might be reconstituted by harnessing the very imperial energies that have created such chaos. Hamilton as creole cartographer of empire seeks to disentangle the "tropic zones" of the "American" quarter of the globe, climates and tropes that mark him—and West Indians and North Americans alike—as diseased and degenerate. Hamilton aspires to inoculate himself, the nation, and ultimately the hemisphere against the contaminating forces of European colonialism by making of the nation a more "perfect union." Out of the hemisphere's heterodox and dystopic elements, Hamilton chases cohesion: order in disorder, union out of fragmentation. Hamilton urges his New Republic audience to subvert the course of history by erecting a *creole regenerate* U.S. American empire—one marked by U.S. mastery of the Atlantic trade routes and thus the West Indian plantation economies—that will once and for all right the grid of progress and freedom.

Yet far from realizing Hamilton's utopic vision for the United States as an empire for commerce, the United States remained a commercial dystopia in perpetual crisis throughout the 1790s and early 1800s. In *The Age of Federalism*, historians Stanley Elkins and Eric McKitrick chart a series of foreign relations crises in the 1790s that thwarted attempts by the New Republic's leaders to realize what the authors identify as Hamilton's vision for the United States as a "mercantilist utopia." [19] In almost every instance, these crises pivot in crucial ways on the U.S. government's persistent efforts to persuade the British or French to enter into, and abide by, financial and/or military pacts or trade agreements granting the United States more substantial, unfettered access to the West Indian trades. Elkins and McKitrick suggest that Hamilton's sustained efforts to treat with—and favor—the British on matters of foreign, economic, and military policy throughout his political career evidence "a very special attitude toward England," one they provocatively characterize as "ambivalently Anglophilic" (128). In that regard, deft rhetorical maneuvers on the eve of the election of 1800 by Jeffersonian Republicans succeeded in inverting the privileged relationship Hamilton and his fellow Federalists had enjoyed in the minds of a majority of the electorate as the perceived protectors of republican principles and the national character. The practical effects of Hamilton's plan for the United States as an empire for commerce thus become the site for anti-Federalist attacks centered on Hamilton and his allegedly willful desire as British secret agent to provide for the new nation's recolonization by Britain. If, in *The Federalist*, Hamilton boldly portends that the emergent U.S. empire for commerce will once and for all "vindicate the honor of the human race" by defying European charges that the "the human species degenerate in America," by the 1790s Republican opponents of his pro-commerce ideology insist that its utter bankruptcy, coupled with Hamilton's rampant foreign policy abuses, are "Facts" ironically vindicating ongoing European assertions about American creole degeneracy.

As commanding general of the nation's armed forces in the last years of the Adams administration, Hamilton pressed Congress to provide a war bill that included provisions for a fleet of naval vessels and thousands of new soldiers to be used in the increasingly likely event that the nation would have to fight a commercial war against France over ongoing incursions by the French navy against U.S. merchant vessels in the Caribbean. Unbeknown to Hamilton, Adams was simultaneously engaging in secret negotiations with Napoleon to end the so-called Quasi-War peacefully, thereby thwarting Hamilton's aspirations for glory in the West Indian theater, the nodal point for his still unfolding U.S. commercial empire in the hemisphere. Adams's diplomatic resolution to the conflict escalated the series of attacks and counterattacks by Hamilton and Adams on one another treated above, including Adams's execratory remarks about Hamilton's creole degenerate West Indian origins.

Even as Hamilton and his Federalist sympathizers desiring of a war felt betrayed by Adams's double-dealing and perceived weakness toward France, Adams's announcement of a peaceful resolution to the Quasi-War with France was merely the culminating gesture in a series of assaults on Hamilton's war bonds proposal. Notwithstanding French attacks and seizures of U.S. merchant vessels in the West Indian carrying trade, Republicans emphasized instead how Hamilton's "special attitude" toward England on war and trade matters throughout the 1790s, including the granting of concessions not enjoyed by France, had failed to result in the cessation of British seizures of U.S. vessels plying the West Indian trades, or the easing of strict legislative restrictions by the British Parliament on direct commerce between the United States and the British West Indies. The sum effect of these partisan debates was that Republicans succeeded in casting the election of 1800 in the terms of the War for Independence of 1776.[20]

The U.S. Revolution, an act of unprecedented *creole* nationalism in the hemisphere, was accompanied by ongoing discursive efforts by U.S. statesmen and writers—as evidenced in my treatment of Franklin's, Hamilton's, and Jefferson's empire writings—to project back onto Europe via their creolizing strategies of resistance the hierarchical relations of power adhering to such oppressive discourses. Accordingly, as violations of navigation acts and trade pacts by the British mounted in the 1790s, Republicans urged voters to do unto Hamilton and the Federalists, cast as creole *de*generate Tory holdovers, what *true* Americans—creole *re*generate Whigs whose memory and honor Republicans professed to uphold and defend—had done to the British in 1776. Specifically, Republicans insisted that the American people had every reason to be concerned, not about French and Republican intrigue as "Anglicized" Federalists repeatedly insisted, but about secret alliances between the British and the Federalist party—controlled less by the President than by his saber-rattling commanding general, Hamilton.

Based on speeches made in Congress, the crucial essay outlining the terms of Republican opposition to Hamilton's war bonds proposal was authored by Virginia statesman James Madison. Entitled "Foreign Influence" (1799), Madison's essay argues that the British fear exactly two things about the United States: American commerce and U.S. republicanism. In regard to the first, Madison claims, in a feminizing gesture about Britain, "Her spirit, and system of monopoly, must make her particularly dread the policy and prosperity of the United States, in the great articles of which she is most jealous—to wit, *manufactures, commerce, navigation*" (215). In terms of the second, Madison asserts that republicanism threatens to "infect" the British empire, thus causing England to "view with a malignant eye the United States, as the real source of the present revolutionary state of the world, as an example of republicanism more likely than any other . . . to convey its contagion to her" (216). Notwithstanding the partisan motivations underlying Madison's critique, Hamilton would have agreed with Madison's pro-U.S. sentiment here even as he urged a policy of commercial appeasement with the British in the 1790s owing to "her" vastly superior navy. As argued above, Hamilton's plan for the United States as an empire for commerce responds to, and allows for, exactly the sort of hemispheric nervousness Madison acknowledges the United States instills in its former colonizer. Further, having co-authored *The Federalist* in 1787 with his former political ally-turned-enemy, Madison well knew that Hamilton chafed under British restrictions on U.S. trade in the hemisphere and endorsed on symbolic and actual levels U.S. merchant vessels adopting a set of creole strategies of resistance in the West Indian carrying trade in order to outpace the crippling effects of British and French embargoes and assaults.

Madison's censure of Hamilton's economic and foreign policies suggests the importance of understanding the ways in which politico-cultural battles to define and defend the national character manifest an acute sense of anxiety and ambivalence. Madison leaves no doubt as to who he believes is responsible for creating the conditions for such insecurity in the nation's postcolonial psyche: Hamiltonian Federalists, "who are truly British in one or all their characteristics, constitut[ing] a fund of foreign influence that merits very serious attention" (218). Specifically, Madison labels Hamiltonian Federalists colonizers in relation to the U.S. South and the American "people," and colonized in that they allow the United States to slip back into the kind of exploitative political economy that precipitated the Revolution. This is so, Madison believes, owing to the recolonizing tendencies and practical effects of Hamilton's corruptive ideology for the United States as an empire for commerce:

Every shipment, every consignment, every commission, is a channel in which a portion of [British influence] flows. It may be said to make a part of every cargo. Our Sea-port towns are the reservoirs into which it is collected. From these, issue a thousand streams to the inland towns, and country stores. . . . Thus it is, that our country is penetrated to its remotest corners with a foreign poison vitiating American sentiment, *recolonizing the American character,* and duping us into the politics of a foreign nation. (219; emphasis added)

Hamilton's economic agenda and foreign policy thus debase the nation by allowing the U.S. body politic to be violated anew by the former and once more British colonizer. Indeed, Madison rages, the British control not only the nation's commerce, government, and banking industries but also, in their all-encompassing effort to subvert further the national character, U.S. print culture: "How deplorable that this guardian of public rights, this organ of necessary truths, should be tainted with partiality at all. . . . The advertisements for the most part, relate to articles of trade, and are furnished by merchants and traders. In this manner British influence steals into our newspapers, and circulates under their passport" (220). Having conspired with Hamilton to ensure passage of the Constitution by publishing *The Federalist* in that same national media, Madison thus endeavors through the print culture he claims has been largely hijacked by a pro-British faction to recast Hamilton as a British subversive who conspires with fellow Federalists to debase the legacy of the Revolution he only pretends to honor, a charge that anticipates those leveled against the colonial mimic men who figure so prominently in postcolonial Caribbean politics and literature.[21]

The Republican party on whose behalf Madison speaks and writes is clearly not providing a balanced assessment of the U.S. political economy by characterizing it as a recolonizing instrument of a Federalist-led British puppet government. Whatever his successes or failures in achieving it, Hamilton's vision obviously laments the need for such dependency. Yet neither is Madison's estimation of the state of the U.S. political economy and the national character entirely inaccurate. In many ways the U.S. political economy did look and feel like that of the British West Indies in the 1790s. Historian Andrew O'Shaugnessy has argued recently, regarding the condition of the British West Indian political economy incipient to the U.S. Revolution, "The changed circumstances of the postwar years left the planters on the defensive against imperial measures prejudicial to their interests. West Indian demands for a full resumption of trade with the United States clashed with the traditional mercantilist principles of colonial policy, which opposed a trade whose balance did not favor Britain" (239). Had he not specified otherwise, O'Shaugnessy might well have been describing dominant characteristics of the U.S. political economy presided over by Hamiltonian Federalists post-Revolution, which was characterized by a persistent trade imbalance with Britain, repeatedly ignored requests for more unfettered trade access to the British West Indies, and a U.S. government decidedly "on the defensive against imperial measures prejudicial to their interests."

Briefly, Federalists' defense of Hamilton and the Federalist party before and after the election of 1800 against Republican attacks predictably centered on the contradiction of a party espousing the civilizing benefits of Jeffersonian Republican ideology as expressed in the empire for liberty on the one hand, while exploiting black slaves for material gain on the other. That is, Federalists charged that Jefferson's grand notion of America as an agrarian society was in truth the blueprint for the United States as an "enlarged Virginia." Given the prominence of plantation economies in the state, professions by Republicans like Madison and Jefferson to be the true protectors of U.S. republican values rang hollow. Federalists insisted that by failing to recognize their black workforce as human beings, white Southerners remained hostage to undemocratic principles and perverse cultural mores and social practices. Federalist Josiah Quincy characterized such a tautology in satire, quipping that for Jeffersonian Republicans, "democracy" was most accurately defined as "an indian word, signifying '*a great tobacco planter, who had herds of black slaves*'" (qtd. in Kerber 23). Thus Republicans were more than a little hypocritical in charging Hamilton and the Federalist party with plotting with the British to recolonize the national character by pursuing Hamilton's vision for the United States as an empire for commerce.

Such parodies, prominent in anti-Republican writings authored by leading Federalists of the period, gesture to the abolitionist leanings of many Federalists. Yet as Linda Kerber argues persuasively in her important study *Federalists in Dissent* (1970), Federalist "condemnation of slavery enabled Federalists to regard politicians and customs of Southern origin superciliously, but it seldom drove them to abolitionism and still less frequently made them integrationists" (50). Undermining Federalist claims to be themselves the "true" upholders of republican principles is their own complicity in perpetuating slavery not only in the U.S. South but also in the West Indies according to aggressive participation in the West Indian carrying trade by U.S. mercantile interests. Accordingly, anxiety and ambivalence about the precarious state of the national character as expressed in vituperative attacks by each party on the other suggest how fears of creole degeneracy remain operative despite the United States' independent nation status. This results from the complex and somewhat obvious affinities between the plantation economies of the U.S. South and the French and British West Indies. Less transparent but equally important is an understanding of how Northern U.S. social, cultural, economic, and ultimately political prestige pivots on a reliance on Southern slavery *and* a coterminous paracolonial dependency on the West Indian plantation economies. As such, the West Indies become a kind of *metatextual, metaregional, and metanational* creole site through and against which competing versions of the national character are understood and fought for on conscious and unconscious levels by the two parties. Indeed, the West Indies might be said to be the New Republic's creole shadow, a phenomenon embodied in that "other" founding figure, Alexander Hamilton.

Toward a Definition of the New Republic's Creole Complex

The creole complex—defined above in the Introduction but deserving further elaboration here—thus provides a framework for understanding the West Indies as the New Republic's creole shadow. In order to highlight the critical possibilities that such a framework suggests for interpreting anew social and cultural developments in the New Republic, the creole complex might be defined in relation to influential arguments set forth by Edward Kamau Brathwaite in *The Development of Creole Society in Jamaica, 1770–1820*. Since its publication, Brathwaite's work has been evoked frequently in comparative Americas contexts, particularly his foundational paradigm of creolization as a New World process resistant to European colonization. Creolization, Brathwaite suggests, challenges readers to see beyond the binaries informing colonialist discourse's governing structures—black/white; master/slave—so as to apprehend the complex ways in which constituent elements in the Jamaican plantation economy existed less in isolation and more "as contributory parts of a whole" (307). Critics who refuse to recognize such emergent creolizing tendencies, Brathwaite implies, risk reinforcing the illogical binaries that England and white creole Jamaicans employed to justify colonialism. "The failure of Jamaican society," Brathwaite argues, "was that it did not recognize . . . elements of its own creativity. Blinded by the need to justify slavery, white Jamaicans refused to recognize their black labourers as human beings, thus cutting themselves off from the one demographic alliance that might have contributed to the island's economic and (possibly) political independence. What the white Jamaican elite did not, could not, would not, dare accept, was that true autonomy for them could only mean true autonomy for all; that the more unrestricted the creolization, the greater would have been the freedom" (307). Thus white creoles remained largely alienated from creolizing forces that might have effected a more liberating cross-cultural, intercreole understanding with promising social implications for all creoles, regardless of race. In that regard, Brathwaite suggests that in the late 1700s and early 1800s, Jamaica "found itself" after the U.S. Revolution and subsequent "humanitarian" reforms—abolitionism, missionary activity among Jamaican blacks, and the effects of the Haitian Revolution—in a profoundly unstable historical moment replete with revolutionary possibility, "when the island's relationship, to a wider (American) cultural complex was in question . . . [yet] the (white) Jamaicans' ambivalence of attitude and their cultural dependence on the

Mother Country again defeated them. At every step . . . the creatively 'creole' elements of society were being rendered ineffective by the more reactionary 'colonial'" (100).

I cite Brathwaite at length because, with him, I believe *creolization* and *anti-creolization* (what he refers to as colonization) are interrelated processes that are highly productive of, and key to understanding, social and cultural formation in Europe's New World colonies in the eighteenth and nineteenth centuries. Even so, while mindful of the need to attend to the specific material conditions and circumstances producing creole identities across the Americas at the turn of the nineteenth century, this chapter departs from Brathwaite's account in the following way. In a compelling remark that he repeats in slightly altered form several times, Brathwaite suggests that while Jamaican creole society was "part of a wider New World or American culture complex, itself the result of European settlement and exploitation of a new environment" (xiii), it failed to achieve a more liberated society because white Jamaican creoles eschewed the more progressive creolization process developed by their North American creole "cousins": namely, establishing the republican principles that inspired the Revolution, and fostering independent mercantile and proto-industrial economies. Accordingly, Brathwaite contends, "The American Revolution . . . isolated [Jamaica] from any chance of a wider or alternative British American development, possibly leading to constitutional independence, and placed the island *firmly within the mercantilist spider-web operating from the Mother Country*" (306; emphasis added). My analysis, above, of the New Republic's paracolonial practices, however, reveals that the United States' political economy itself, far from being independent, remained to a considerable degree ensnared in the British "mercantilist spider-web" during the nation's first decades of existence. As we have seen, Madison's "Foreign Policy" essay promotes an influential dissenting view to Hamilton's empire for commerce and his Anglocentric foreign policy, which Madison maintained rendered ineffective creolizing elements of post-Revolutionary society, thereby miring the New Republic in a creole complex not wholly unlike that which Brathwaite suggests forestalled the emergence of independence movements and empowered creole identities in the British West Indies.

Thus my departure from Brathwaite argues for the need to challenge influential notions of U.S. hemispheric exceptionalism in regard to New World creolization processes in the wake of the U.S. Revolution. Charged debates over Hamilton's domestic and foreign policy agenda in the 1790s reveal, on the contrary, profound *creole ambivalence* on the part of white U.S. Americans about their still-dependent political economy and imperiled national character despite having arrived at nominal postcolonial nation status. Also, we need to revise received scholarly opinions that suggest that the Revolution and the nation's foundational documents evidence the United States' absolute break from its *creole* colonial condition in favor of a more ennobled, if still flawed, postcolonial *American* nation status. Instead, the early national period is marked by a distinctive because ongoing process of creolization—one that involves a tangled nexus of creolizing and counter-creolizing energies embodied in Hamilton and his empire for commerce.

There is a need to devise as well a more fluid understanding of comparative creole identities in the Americas generally, and specifically a more dynamic (as opposed to static) model for understanding the mutual ways in which West Indian and North American creole societies and cultures influence and shape one another before, during, and after the U.S. Revolution. As such, the West Indies function in the U.S. post-Revolutionary imaginary, I have argued, as a "shadow" double for the nation's still unfulfilled creolization process that the Revolution and the nation's foundational documents have heretofore been thought to inaugurate and ensure—if such a creolization process can be said to stand consistently for a "progressive," anti-colonial identity and cultural formation, something that must be demonstrated rather than assumed. That is, U.S. American creolization processes result in the achievement of independent nation status on the one hand, and the perpetuation of the nation's colonized position vis-à-vis Britain and a paracolonial one vis-à-vis Britain's West Indian colonies on the other. Such an alteration in focus provides us with a way to account for the significance of Hamilton's shadow creole West Indian identity, including Hamilton and his adopted country's shared impulse to repress their West Indian origins in order to promulgate the kind of clean distinction between U.S. and West Indian creole identities, societies, and cultures that scholars have uncritically perpetuated across the centuries.

Finally, we need to recognize and account for anti-creolization tendencies in the New Republic. Such tendencies evidence themselves, for example, in Federalists' debasing parodies in response to Republican attacks on Hamilton and his unfolding empire for commerce. Such stylized investments in stereotypes of New World creole degeneracy reflect the negating impulses of white Federalists and Republicans toward the nation's creolization processes. Accordingly, Brathwaite's admonition about creole Jamaican society seems especially prescient relative to the limitations of creolization in the U.S. American context: "What the white Jamaican"—substitute here "the white U.S. American"—"elite did not, could not, would not, dare accept, was that true autonomy for them could only mean true autonomy for all; that the more unrestricted the creolization, the greater would have been the freedom" (307).

For too long critics have ironically repeated the deft rhetorical maneuver of Hamilton's opponents to brand Hamilton and his plan for U.S. empire as "foreign" and "unAmerican," inconsistent with the "national character" that by default is characterized as Jefferson's vision for the United States as an empire for liberty. Instead, by revisiting the charged political debate over Hamilton's empire for commerce including Federalists' and Republicans' somewhat impenetrable competing assessments of U.S. participation in the West Indian trades, this chapter argues—adapting Brathwaite's provocative phrasing—that the creole complex defies any univocal, triumphant, or stable understanding of national character. Against claims for U.S. exceptionalism, the creole complex highlights the ways in which the early national period is characterized by not so much a departure from, as an ongoing process of refiguring creole conditions in the former North American British colonies.

The question remains as to how viewing the United States in unexceptional terms consequent to the comparative creole Americas framework that has been limned here— specifically by attending to the generative energies of the New Republic's creole complex—alters our perception of literary and cultural production in the early national period. In their creolizing and anti-creolizing tendencies, essays authored by Massachusetts Federalist statesman Fisher Ames suggest the potential rewards awaiting critics willing to submit New Republic writings to examination according to a creole complex matrix, a task undertaken in Part II.

One such essay is "American Literature" (1803), a pioneering work of U.S. literary and cultural criticism. A powerful advocate in Congress for Hamilton's empire for commerce, Ames authored "American Literature" in the aftermath of the Federalist defeat in the election of 1800 and on the eve of the Louisiana Purchase amid fears espoused by secession-minded, "enlightened" New England Federalists that the acquisition of creole New Orleans and the Western Territories by Jeffersonian Republicans might fatally contaminate the white American empire. They worried as well that the proposed expansion might alter the political balance of power, leading to the decline of the commercial North and the ascendance of the slave South and frontier West.[22] According to Ames in "American Literature," the debased condition of the national character in the post-Federalist period of government is attributable to gross excesses in two areas: commerce and republican democracy. Against European intellectuals, Ames explicitly contests the idea that the U.S. nation-space is an inherently degenerate environment: "Nobody will pretend that the Americans are a stupid race" (24). Even so, he suggests throughout the essay that literature and culture produced by, and responsive to, the nation's creole complex creates the conditions sustaining such charges.

The oft-cited opening paragraph of Ames's essay poses a related set of questions framed by a governing conceit—New World creole degeneracy:

> Few speculative subjects have exercised the passions more or the judgment less, than the inquiry, what rank our country is to maintain in the world for genius and literary attainments. Whether in point of intellect we are equal to Europeans, or only a race of degenerate creoles; whether our artists and authors have already performed much and promise every thing; whether the muses, like the nightingales, are too delicate to cross the salt water, or sicken and mope without song if they do, are themes upon which we Americans are privileged to be eloquent and loud. (22)

Neither Ames nor Hamilton supported New England Federalist secessionist schemes, yet in Ames's response to the above questions, he does secede figuratively from what he perceives is the nation's insatiable appetite for wealth, land, and property. Commercial striving—a key tenet of Hamilton's empire for commerce—is perhaps the most powerful evidence to support, Ames asserts, charges of U.S. creole degeneracy. "Of course the single passion that engrosses us," he bemoans, "the only avenue to consideration and importance in our society, is the accumulation of property; our inclinations cling to gold, and are embedded in it, as deeply as that precious ore in the mine. Covered as our genius is in this mineral crust, is it strange that it does not sparkle?" (36). Rather than interrogating, like "American Literature," the causes of national corruption, New Republic intellectuals, in fits "of excessive national vanity" (23), publish writings preoccupied with defending the nation against charges of creole degeneracy that ironically exhibit such tendencies, such remonstrations being "worthless the moment they are found to need asserting" (22). Notable for its *own* anxious assertions about such authors and their works' counter-creole assertions, "American Literature" suggests that texts authored by Franklin, Jefferson, Webster, and others are failed exercises in creole American nationalism, "pretensions to literary fame" full of "mediocrity" masquerading as genius (24). "It will be useless and impertinent to say, a greater proportion of our citizens have had instruction in schools than can be found in any European state" a derisive Ames suggests. "The question is not, what proportion are stone blind, or how many can see, when the sun shines, but what geniuses have arisen among us, like the sun and stars to shed life and splendor on our hemisphere" (23). Accordingly, Ames searches in vain for a U.S. American who might be said to serve as an exemplar of a truly "arisen" genius who transcends such "creole degenerate" hemispheric nervousness.

This chapter remarked at the outset on renewed scholarly interest in Hamilton, much of it centered on the meaning and significance of his traumatic death. In death, Hamilton became—and remains—a signifier of competing national desires. Hamilton's very body, in its creole confusions, functions in the New Republic and beyond as an unstable locus for debates about the national economy, character, and culture. As such, Hamilton emerges as circumatlantic denizen, a ghost in the New Republic ideological machine, defying any tendency to reduce or fix his image or to define with absolute surety his legacy.

Ames nonetheless inaugurates a long tradition of retrospectively accounting for such things by penning a widely disseminated eulogy. Published just six months after "American Literature," Ames's eulogy can be understood as a direct response to that essay, for in the eulogy Ames claims to have located the earlier text's elusive hemispheric genius. In more and less obvious ways, "A Sketch of the Character of Alexander Hamilton" (1804) alerts readers to the intersecting generative energies of Hamilton, the empire for commerce, and the New Republic's creole complex. In the eulogy, Hamilton is said to have loved "his country better than himself, preferring its interest to its favor, and serving it when it was unwilling and unthankful" (511); he accrues genius in inverse proportion to his political adversaries, whose "excessive vanity" places love of self and party over country, dogma over truth, the passions of the multitude over the national interest, all virtues alien to the classical republican ones Ames privileges. Still, Ames's indictment of commercial excess in "American Literature," a logical outcome of a Hamiltonian empire for commerce, would seem to disqualify Hamilton for hagiographic status. Such a contradiction, however, is only seeming rather than actual for Ames. As William Dowling remarks, High Federalist notions of civic virtue, indebted as they are to classical republican antecedents, denounce the pursuit of wealth and popularity to the extent that such pursuits become objects in and of themselves. Dowling usefully explains, "The ideal of otium or 'literary leisure' . . . lies at the heart of Federalist values precisely as it operates to sustain virtue even while a republic is increasing in wealth and populousness. For otium, still carrying associations with Aristotle's theory of leisure as the basis of genuine civilization, is the negation of wealth pursued for the purpose of appetite or ostentation" (40)—the insatiable pursuit and ostentatious display of wealth being perhaps the chief stereotype of European discourse about West Indian creole degeneracy, a charge leveled by Jeffersonian Republicans against Northern U.S. mercantile interests leading up to the election of 1800, and a grave concern in Ames's "American

Literature," we have seen, for the ways in which it tends to confirm charges of U.S. creole degeneracy. Ames's eulogy can therefore be understood as an act of mourning on behalf of not only Hamilton and his empire for commerce ideology and agenda co-opted and transposed in the wake of the Louisiana Purchase by Republicans, but also a Federalist party in decline, no longer able to dictate the terms according to which the nation's increasing affluence is converted into both political and *cultural* capital. Thus we encounter Ames's somewhat despairing suggestion at the end of "American Literature" that only through an active suppression via despotism of the Republic's democratic mob, or by the "restoration" of the Federalist party to national prominence, might the "augmentation of wealth . . . produce some men of genius, who will be admired and imitated" (37).

Ames's deployment of the trope of creole degeneracy in "American Literature" is thus much more than mere rhetorical flourish. Similarly, Ames's commemoration of Hamilton transcends emotional or celebratory gesture. Poised to inspire a literary and cultural renaissance, the recently departed Hamilton in Ames's eulogy emerges as the paragon of civic virtue sorely lacking in the post-Federalist era of government. In a complicated self-reflexive gesture, Ames predicts that Hamilton's genius alone might one day inspire a writer capable of sketching his portrait. Even so, he laments that the New Republic will likely not produce such a writer, for it could only have done so had it "produced two Hamiltons, one of them [who] might then have depicted the other. To delineate genius one must feel its power" (512). This chapter has endeavored to respond to Ames's challenge, to feel Hamilton's "power" and "inspiration," to spy out "two Hamiltons" and to demonstrate the ways in which the West Indian and U.S. American Hamiltons were formed in the crucible of the New Republic's creole complex.

It has also attempted to do what Ames apparently was uninterested in doing or unwilling to do, namely, to "have stretched to the dimensions of his subject" (512). In rendering his verdict, Ames decides Hamilton's "early life we pass over" (514), thereby obscuring—as Hamilton no doubt would have preferred—Hamilton's West Indian origins, emphasizing instead his spectacular rebirth in North America during the Revolution and his subsequent accomplishments as "[u]nparalleled" statesman (516). Accordingly, Ames may be said to repress, in contradistinction to fellow Federalist and Hamilton archenemy John Adams, the potentially contaminative effects of Hamilton's West Indian creole origins on the national character. Further support for such a reading can be found in Ames's repeated lauding of Hamilton as worthy of the memory of "the glory of Greece" (518–19), thereby according Hamilton the kind of glory, coherence, and stability he tirelessly pursued as author and executor of the plan for the United States as a hemispheric empire for commerce. Ames links Hamilton's quest to the epic journeys of Odysseus and to the heroes of Homer's *Iliad*. Like Greece itself, Hamilton's glory is said to be "imperishable . . . it strikes an *everlasting root*, and bears perennial blossoms on its grave" (518; emphasis added). Yet unlike Ames and like Adams, if with contrasting purpose and effect, this chapter has urged that we return to Hamilton's and the New Republic's West Indian roots, productive as they are of the nation's creole unconscious. To evoke Ames's own eloquent phraseology, the West Indies are where we might properly begin "measuring the length of [Hamilton's] shadow" (510) over the formation of national character, literature, and culture.

With Brathwaite, the most recognizable theorist of creolization is perhaps Martinican writer Édouard Glissant. In establishing a roots/ routes matrix of New World writing, Glissant overthrows conservative assessments of classical texts as "rooted," in the process challenging "modern" impulses to view such traditions as stable and fixed, as unencumbered by the processes of creolization or unmarked by the messiness of empire building. Writes Glissant, "[T]he great founding books of communities, the Old Testament, the *Iliad*, the *Odyssey* . . . were all books about exile and often about errantry. This epic literature is amazingly prophetic. It tells of the community, but through relating the community's apparent failure or in any case its being surpassed, it tells of errantry as a temptation (the desire to go against the root) and, frequently, actually experienced. Within the collective books concerning the sacred and the notion of history lies the germ of the exact opposite of what they so loudly proclaim" (15). Inspired in considerable measure by the theories of creolization espoused by Brathwaite and Glissant, the chapters that follow here seek to account for the New Republic's "errantry as temptation," its successes and failures, its creole roots and routes; in treating "the great"—and less great—"founding books" of the New Republic's multiple communities, Part II endeavors to attend to the nuances, paradoxes, and contradictions attending such works' contentious search for power, stability, and personal and national glory. Crucial to such an understanding are the formative influence of Alexander Hamilton, Hamilton's vision for the United States as an empire for commerce, and the countervailing energies of the creole complex.

Part II
Writing the Creole Republic

Chapter 3
Paracolonial Ambivalence in the Poetics of Philip Freneau

On Franklin's death in 1790, Philip Freneau, the so-called Poet of the Revolution, penned an elegy in an act of mythopoetic creole nationalism that credited Franklin with wresting "divine right" from King George III and electrifying a nation to revolt. Franklin's scientific achievements in Freneau's poem emblematize the ways in which the New Republic is poised to fulfill Enlightenment aspirations, rather than monarchical Britain, which has squandered such an opportunity by tyrannically withholding the former colonies' "natural" rights:

When monarchs tumble to the ground
Successors easily are found:
But, matchless Franklin! what a few
Can hope to rival such as you,
Who seized from kings their sceptred pride,
And turned the lightning's darts aside! (*PPF* 3:36)

Less often remembered by scholars is "Epistle: From Dr. Franklin (deceased) to his poetical Panegyrists," a witty prosopopoeia aimed at the cult of Revolutionary hero-worship that the outpouring of Franklin elegies represents. In that poem, Franklin speaks from beyond the grave in dismissive tones about the welter of laudatory verses spawned by his death. Franklin's ghost commands poets to leave off sentimentalizing nature so as to affect grief on his behalf, reminding the sponsors of such tributes of his ironic depreciation of the muse in his lifetime: "'Tis folly to be sad for nought, / From me you never gained a groat" (*PPF* 3:37). In contradistinction to the impulse to ventriloquize nature so as to make "her" speak elegiac claptrap, Franklin recalls the moment in part 1 of the *Autobiography* when he leaves off writing verse in his youth, given his father's command to pursue a more practical trade: "To better trades I turned my views, / And never meddled with the muse," as a result of which decision "Great things I did for rising States" (*PPF* 3:37).[1] Nonetheless, should apostrophized "Poets" feel compelled to persist in writing elegies, Franklin admonishes them,

Let reason be your constant rule,
And Nature, trust me, is no fool—
When to the dust great men she brings,
Make her do—some uncommon things. (*PPF* 3:38)

Freneau believed that writing poetry and laboring in "better trades" were not only not incompatible but mutually formative endeavors.[2] Published alongside "practical" essays he authored on science, commerce, politics, and the arts in leading newspapers and journals of the day, Freneau's occasional lyrics conspire to produce meaning across not only disciplines, genres, and texts but also the circumatlantic geographies of the United States and the West Indies. Moreover, in its vocational commingling, his verse endeavors to accomplish "Great things" on behalf of the "rising [United S]tates." Finally, by submitting "Nature" to not only sentimental and romantic treatment but also rational critique in his poetry, Freneau indeed strives to make "her" do "some uncommon things."

Some of Freneau's best and least-known occasional poems are forged in the crucible of perhaps the New Republic's most vigorous and volatile of "trades"—the West Indian trades that Franklin narrowly avoided plying as a young man and that preoccupied, we have seen, his writings about the future path of empire to be undertaken by the North American British colonies and later the United States. Accordingly, as early national poet as well as trader, captain, and privateer working the West Indian trades in the last decades of the eighteenth century, Freneau was uniquely situated to gauge the attraction and repulsion, and the possibility and danger, of pursuing U.S. empire building in the commercial cross-currents of the West Indian trades through the early 1800s. In many ways Freneau is the poetic complement to Franklin the essayist and pamphleteer on matters of U.S. empire building and related issues like the formation of a national character and culture. Perhaps ironically, given his lifetime of mercantile experiences, Freneau like Franklin urged U.S. westward expansionism on the continent and privileged agriculture on actual and symbolic levels.[3] This was so, this chapter demonstrates, as a result of Freneau's ever-growing distaste for and distrust of commercial empire as a political economy capable of instilling and safeguarding U.S. republican values and principles.[4]

If Freneau greatly admired Franklin as foundational figure for regenerating the national culture and character, no one more embodied the corruption of these things for Freneau than the West Indian immigrant Alexander Hamilton. Thus in the 1790s Freneau became the chief Republican print journalist attacking what he perceived to be the antirepublican excesses of Hamilton's empire for commerce ideology and practice. Yet there are remarkable consanguinities between Freneau and Hamilton. As the chapter discusses in more detail below, Freneau left in 1776, for mysterious reasons, to spend two years in exile living on a plantation on the island of St. Croix. In so doing, Freneau was criss-crossing the circumatlantic ventures of another important figure in the New Republic, Alexander Hamilton. Born in the nearby Dutch-held island of Nevis, Hamilton, as we have seen, spent his teenage years working as a merchant clerk in St. Croix on behalf of North American mercantile interests. Therefore, despite their ideological opposition, both Freneau and Hamilton were formed by U.S. paracolonial relations with the West Indies.

Yet the differences between how Freneau and Hamilton cathect their identities in the context of that relationship are as pronounced as their similarities. Unlike the New Jersey–born Freneau, Hamilton did not flee his adopted country on the eve of the Revolution but wrote a series of important tracts fomenting it. Moreover, while Freneau cruised the Caribbean Sea in West Indian–owned merchant vessels and later U.S. privateers before being unceremoniously captured by the British navy, Hamilton remained on land and fought in the Continental Army, distinguishing himself as Washington's aide-de-camp. After the war, Hamilton would coauthor *The Federalist* (1787) with James Madison and John Jay in order to argue for the strengthening of the executive and the federal government. He would also set forth a plan for the United States as an empire for commerce that privileged commerce over agriculture as the staple political economy of the rising U.S. empire.

Like Madison and Jefferson with whom he worked in intimate relation, Freneau perceived Hamilton to be the most dangerous of an unseemly cast of figures in the ruling Federalist party. Thus he used journalism and poetry as vehicles for indicting Hamilton's character and his pro-commerce economic and foreign policies. Throughout the 1790s, Freneau wrote partisan satirical verse, as in "Ode to the Americans" (1798), that urged his readers to reject Hamilton and the Federalist party's machinations: "And priests, or history much deceives, / Turn'd aide-de-camps to sceptred thieves" (*PPF* 3:204). At once satirizing Hamilton's activities as Washington's aide-de-camp during the Revolution, as Secretary of the Treasury, and as commanding general of the nation's armed forces in the late 1790s, Freneau charges the Federalists with conspiring to return the United States to a state of colonial dependency:

A curse would on your efforts wait
Old british navy to reinstate;
No hireling hosts could force a crown
Nor keep the bold republic down: . . . (*PPF* 3:206)

In another poem, "Reflections on the Mutability of Things" (1798), Freneau anticipates the election of Thomas Jefferson as President, thus ending the reign of Adams as "monarch," Hamilton as Federalist "lawyer," and rival journalist William Cobbett (or perhaps John Fenno) as Federalist "scribe": "When a monarch, new fangled, with lawyer and scribe, / In junto will cease to convene, / Or take from old England a pitiful bribe, / To pamper his 'highness serene'"; then, and only then, Freneau writes, will the moment arise "When virtue and merit will have a fair chance / . . . And Jefferson, you to your station advance, / The man for the president's chair" (*PPF* 3:216). As such lines evince, Freneau's political verse unrelentingly asserts that a corrupt Federalist government, influenced and funded by the British mercantile empire, is the foremost threat to republicanism and the future peace and prosperity of the nation.[5]

This chapter treats Freneau's "West Indies" poems, works that draw on his experiences while living on the island of St. Croix from 1776 to 1778 and then as he sailed the West Indian trades in the last decades of the eighteenth century: first as a sailor and supercargo and later as a captain on U.S. merchant vessels, including privateers licensed by the U.S. government to seize British merchant and naval vessels in the Caribbean should the opportunity present itself. These poems—"The Beauties of Santa Cruz" (1779; revised, 1786) and four poems conceived while Freneau was marooned by a hurricane and an equally unfriendly British navy on the island of Jamaica in 1784—reveal the unique paracolonial tensions and properties attaining to not only Freneau's poetry but also to art and literature across the New Republic period. Thus Freneau is an especially apt figure for foregrounding the central aesthetic and thematic concerns of the literature and culture of U.S. paracolonialism discussed in subsequent chapters. If Franklin and Hamilton emblematize two distinct postures regarding commerce and the formation of a national character, Freneau's West Indies poems, in dialogue with the ideas and precepts advanced by both, manifest a poetics of paracolonial ambivalence.

Like Franklin's empire tracts that Chapter 1 examines, Freneau's West Indies poems transparently indict the tyranny of European colonialism in the West Indies at the end of the eighteenth century. Less understood by readers, however, are the complex ways in which these poems register, albeit ambivalently, the licit and illicit energies and profits stemming from the New Republic's own exploitative relationship to the scene of European colonialism and imperialism in the West Indies and the Caribbean Sea. In my treatment of Freneau's West Indian poems, I suggest the ways in which their denigration of the state of European, especially

British, colonialism in the West Indies—both as it manifests itself on the islands themselves and in the routes of the West Indian carrying trade to and from the West Indies and ports in the United States and Europe—simultaneously operates to negate, mystify, abstract, or otherwise displace the nation's and Freneau's own complicity in exploiting the very practices his poems assail. Thus by treating Freneau's West Indies poetry in the context of his vexed participation as merchant man working the West Indian carrying trade on behalf of a "rising" U.S. empire for commerce, we can better understand the poetics of paracolonial ambivalence shaping his verse.

The chapter follows its treatment of the West Indies poems by measuring Freneau's critique of European commercial empire in the West Indies against several poems set in the United States that focus in explicit terms on the state of the national character at the end of the eighteenth century. In poems like his fittingly fragmentary epic "The Rising Empire" (1790), Freneau is unable to complete a text meant to record the vigor and achievements of the peoples and cultures from the states that were the thirteen original colonies. In veering uneasily between epic and mock-epic strategies, "The Rising Empire" reveals that the "state" of the United States, far from achieving the desired empire for liberty that Franklin and Freneau envision, is not at all unlike the degenerate and debased condition of European commercial empire in the West Indies with which it exists in paracolonial relation, a condition that Freneau's West Indies poems register on conscious and unconscious levels.

Thus treated in the context of one another, Freneau's West Indies poems and his parodically titled "The Rising Empire" suggest not only the mutually entangled relations between the ostensibly descending and rising British and U.S. empires respectively but also, and perhaps more intriguingly, between West Indian and U.S. American creole economies, characters, and cultures. These linkages thereby complicate claims for U.S. American exceptionalism in the hemisphere owing to the nation's putatively superior institutions, values, and achievements, especially its unprecedented military triumph over the British. Such a "revolution" turns out to be inadequate and incomplete according to Freneau's not-so-"Rising Empire" series of poems. Juxtaposing Freneau's various works in this chapter—"Santa Cruz," the "Jamaica" poems, and "The Rising Empire" series—not only illuminates the continuities of his poetic preoccupation with U.S. paracolonialism in the West Indies but also allows us to see anew the ways in which Freneau's artistic investments and achievements are magnified by virtue of his poetics of paracolonial ambivalence.

Paracolonialism's Paradise: Freneau's "The Beauties of Santa Cruz"

Fleeing the scene of the Revolution in 1776 and leaving behind his family and friends for what critics generally agree are mysterious reasons— perhaps pacifism, a spirit of adventure, or to seek a safe haven in which to hone his craft—Freneau only narrowly escaped the pitched violence in the North American colonies. He did so by sailing to the Danish-held West Indian island of St. Croix aboard a ship owned by a Captain Hanson, who held a vast plantation estate there and who traded across the various routes of the West Indian trades. Freneau likely was introduced to Hanson by John Napier, a family relative and St. Croix planter, while Napier was visiting Freneau's family in New Jersey and Hanson was in Philadelphia on a trading mission (Axelrad 76–77). Like Equiano's Quaker master Richard King and Franklin's benefactor Thomas Denham, Hanson and Napier emerge from the margins of American literary history as circumatlantic figures whose multiple holdings, residences, and affiliations in North America and the West Indies owe themselves to the fluid identities, societies, and cultures formed in the commercial cross-currents of the West Indian trades. Freneau would live on Hanson's Santa Cruz plantation until 1778, a period that included a stay in British-held Bermuda. On returning to the United States, Freneau served on U.S. privateers plying the routes of the West Indian trades until his capture in 1780 by the British while on a voyage to the islands of St. Eustacia and Jamaica. His capture and imprisonment are the occasion for one of Freneau's best-known poems, "The Prison Ship."

Such varied experiences, this chapter argues, form the multiple roots and routes of Freneau's unique identity as circumatlantic privateer-poet. Written in the vortex of the West Indian trades during the period of Atlantic revolutionary upheaval in the late eighteenth and early nineteenth centuries, Freneau's "Santa Cruz" reproduces the liminal condition that marks his poetics of paracolonial ambivalence across his West Indies poems. "Santa Cruz" locates itself outside the territorial though certainly not the economic or cultural borders of the United States, was conceived by Freneau during a period of self-imposed exile while sojourning on a "neutral" West Indian island, and was published at a moment when the status of the United States' incipient revolt from an economically and militarily superior British empire was radically in question. "Santa Cruz" evinces the ways in which the West Indies as a metaregional and metanational site in the literature and culture of the early national period provides a space for gauging the failures of European empire in the West Indies and the North American continent on the one hand, and the possibilities—and pitfalls—awaiting the "rising" U.S.

empire as would-be "enlightened" alternative in the hemisphere on the other.[6]

Perhaps Freneau's best-known West Indies poem, "The Beauties of Santa Cruz," was first published in 1778 and revised and expanded substantially in 1786, revisions that Freneau retained in subsequent editions of the poem.[7] Readers of Freneau's West Indies poems cite "Santa Cruz" as characteristic of the "emotional and intellectual confusion of his entire Caribbean adventure"; as emblematic of an oeuvre that manifests a tense dynamic between an investment in fancy and exotic pastoralism, on the one hand, and postromantic rationalism and critique, on the other; as a poem trapped thematically between the West Indies as New World Edenic retreat and as postlapsarian tragedy deriving from the islands' material realities of European slavery and recurring natural disasters that "erode" the unsustainable pastoral edifice that the poet-speaker aspires to construct (Vitzthum 37–38).

Critical understanding of Freneau's poem as marked by, and symptomatic of, a larger Caribbean confusion is tantalizingly suggestive. I aim to provide in my treatment of "Santa Cruz" as well as the Jamaica poems below the routes and roots of such Caribbean confusion, paying special attention to these poems' material surfaces and depths. Scholars have tended to isolate or treat Freneau's West Indian poetry as somehow unconcerned with the political or national issues that more obviously inform his political poetry written before and after the Revolution while Freneau was a journalist living and working in the United States. Such readers view Freneau's West Indies poems as avocations, extranational in scope and personal rather than political in tone. As Mary Bowden states, "No longer a newspaperman who was abreast of all the current events, Freneau was now a trader. . . . His interests were no longer national affairs but local and personal ones. . . . Despite the national and international turmoil of the Revolutionary years, Freneau found in the West Indies a special place that he could transform into his poetic Eden" (47). Such an estimation of Captain Freneau and his West Indies poems tends to obscure the ways in which the "national" is inseparable from the hemispheric in Freneau's poetry. Similarly inseparable are the journalistic from the mercantile, the poetic from the political, and assessments of the national character and the impulse toward expansionism on the continent from U.S. paracolonial involvement in the plantation economies of the West Indies. That is, we might seek to understand the ways in which these poems' paracolonial condition provides for their production less as "pure" fantasy and more as impure co-products of Freneau's ambivalence regarding a proliferating and frequently imperiled U.S. mercantile presence in the West Indies in the late eighteenth century and its consequent effects on national character and the nation's foundational values and institutions.

Freneau's "Santa Cruz" draws on received transatlantic lyrical conventions and themes centered on the West Indies as New World pastoral fantasy or, contrastingly, as postlapsarian site for antislavery critique. Yet "Santa Cruz" is not mere pastoral fantasy or solely antislavery critique but something else altogether as a result of the confounding pressures brought to bear on received themes, forms, and conventions according to Freneau's unique location as U.S. paracolonial poet. The tensions in "Santa Cruz" between baroque or fanciful pastoralism and Enlightenment rationalism, while unresolved and complicated as critics have demonstrated, are evocative of a deep and abiding nostalgia on Freneau's part for a would-be peaceful U.S. expansionism on the North American continent rendered impossible by slavery and the ongoing British military invasion there. Thus "Santa Cruz" deploys competing discursive and rhetorical strategies and registers not simply to contrast a would-be Caribbean Eden with the despotic forces of European empire that invade such a vision, but on progressive levels to call forth New England and Middle Atlantic planters, merchants, and traders alike to inaugurate a new epoch of enlightened, renovated commercial idealism and practice not only in the West Indies but by implication in the hemisphere more generally, including on the North American continent itself. Such ideological underpinnings in "Santa Cruz" are present, too, in Freneau's Jamaica poems in which the rising U.S. empire is set in antithetical relation to a declining and fatally corrupted British mercantile empire.

Yet Freneau's Caribbean confusion ensues where his ostensible critique begins. More precisely, Freneau's West Indies poems struggle to resolve satisfactorily the ways in which U.S. paracolonial participation in West Indian slavery and colonialism, in terms of both the emergent nation's massive investment in exploiting those plantation economies for profit and U.S. Americans' seemingly insatiable desire for products like sugar, rum, coffee, and cocoa, belies the privileged ground of critique that the enlightened West Indian sojourner Freneau endeavors to (re)occupy and from which he writes and speaks. As restorative "fantasy," Freneau's "Santa Cruz" endeavors to repress the paracolonial realities that are its own undoing: namely, the ways in which U.S. commerce within and without the territorial boundaries of the United States perpetuates hemispheric slavery and the exploitative West Indian plantation economies that the poem suggests the poet-speaker and the agents of U.S. commerce who are its addressees might mitigate.

In *Plantations and Paradise: Tourism and Culture in the Anglophone Caribbean*, Ian Gregory Strachan argues that in the late nineteenth-century

British West Indies, "the plantation established a political and economic dependency on the metropolitan centers that tourism merely extends" (9). That is to say, European and U.S. tourism in the West Indies sustains the West Indian plantation economy from which it derives. I evoke Strachan's critique to suggest the ways in which Freneau's "Santa Cruz"—located a century earlier than the texts that Strachan treats—predicts such incestuous relations between tourism and plantation economy over and above the poem's forward-looking abolitionist, antimercantilist critiques. Reversing, or more precisely collapsing, the relation that Strachan sketches above, Freneau in "Santa Cruz" romanticizes U.S. tourism in the West Indies as nostalgic fantasy a priori what the poem ultimately provides for a posteriori, the calling into being of U.S. responsibility for renovating the brutal European plantation economies there. Thus Freneau's manipulation of the time/space continuum of U.S. paracolonialism in the West Indies via a nostalgic island pastoralism corrupted by European imperialism and violence is essential in order to sustain the notion that the Revolutionary United States represents the prospect of an as-yet-to-be-arrived-at more benevolent, more enlightened—in a word, regenerate—commercial ethos in the hemisphere.

Emblematic of the material realities shaping U.S. participation in the West Indian plantation economies and trades that provide the occasion for the poem's innovations of received pastoral conventions, Freneau's poet-speaker does not address "Santa Cruz" to a rustic, isolated shepherd but specifically to "northern . . . shepherd[s]"—by which he means exclusively New England and Middle Atlantic would-be tourists, traders, and planters seeking refuge from the horrors of the Revolution. As such, Freneau not only foregrounds the poem's paracolonial posture but, in seeking to inculcate a desire for Santa Cruz's natural riches, the poem as "tourist brochure" mystifies the already significant role that North American merchants, traders, and planters play in providing for St. Croix's plantation economy, as well as the sale and consumption of its products. Mercantile moguls like the Crugers, the Beekmans, and the Kortrights of New York maintained substantial mercantile operations on St. Croix before, during, and after the Revolution, shaping commercial policy not only in St. Croix but in New York and the emergent Republic. They were mercantile magnates whose "ships, letters, and men shuttled between St. Croix and New York" (J. Thomas 37) throughout the late eighteenth century. Thus Freneau's apostrophe to would-be Northern U.S. "shepherds" not only occludes that reality but raises important questions about the sustainability of the notion that a U.S. presence might actually renovate rather than persist in exploiting parasitically St. Croix's brutal plantation economy. The poem begs the question of what such a U.S.-led mercantile renovation in St. Croix might look like in practice rather than theory, for in many ways the United States' mercantilist agenda and conduct at home and in the West Indies more than a little resembled oppressive European mercantilist practices that the poem urges its U.S. audience to avoid.

From the poem's opening moments when it apostrophizes Northern and Middle Atlantic—crucially *not* U.S. Southern—battle-weary soldiers, it offers up Santa Cruz, both "Santa Cruz" the poem and Santa Cruz/St. Croix the actual island, to soldiers' escapist fantasies and consumptive desires. Save a few archaic word choices, the opening stanzas are eerily anticipatory of the present-day rhetoric of Caribbean tourism. Freneau's poem advertises Santa Cruz as an island of sun and pleasure, an exotic escape from the Northern traveler's infinitely more serious labors— fighting a revolutionary war against Britain—conducted in the harsh winters of the Northeast. In the domains of Freneau's poem, Santa Cruz exists primarily to provide refuge and comfort for his target audience besieged by the tyrannical British empire in North America:

Sick of thy northern glooms, come, shepherd, seek
More equal climes, and a serener sky:
Why shouldst thou toil amid thy frozen ground,
Where half year's snows, a barren prospect, lie,
. . . .
Twice seven days prosperous gales thy barque shall bear
To isles that flourish in perpetual green,
Where richest herbage glads each shady vale,
And ever verdant plants on every hill are seen. (*PPF* 1:249–50)

Elementalizing and primitivizing Santa Cruz in classic (para)colonialist fashion, Freneau thus paves the way for penetrations of Santa Cruz's exoticized, effeminized, and eroticized landscape—"From the vast caverns of old ocean's bed, / Fair Santa Cruz, arising, laves her waist" (251)—by disenchanted Yankee soldiers hoping to exploit the island's "richest" resources for purposes of rest and relaxation, and perhaps for sensual pleasure and material gain. In such a way, the poem actually exploits the trauma (and by 1786, memory) of the U.S. Revolution in order to allow for Freneau's poetics of commercial renovation in the West Indies conducted by "oppressed" agents of the U.S. insurgency. In the process, the poem mitigates the competing reality of ongoing U.S. paracolonial exploitation of Santa Cruz.

In summoning fellow U.S. Americans to join him in self-imposed exile, Freneau moves beyond the rhetorical registers of fantasy and romance, employing widely the discourse of natural history as he catalogues in precise detail just what "richest herbage" and "verdant plants" await the would-be Yankee traveler. The revised 1786 version of "Santa Cruz" greatly expands the original list of items included in Freneau's 1778 inventory, nearly doubling the length of the poem from 52 to 108 stanzas. Like "cluster'd grapes from loaded boughs depend" (*PPF* 1:258), the revised poem itself almost suffocates under the load of Freneau's cluster of recorded items. While on purely aesthetic levels the expanded catalogue seems unnecessarily burdensome, I believe Freneau intends for it to serve multiple purposes according to the poem's ethos of enlightened commerce. First, it is an attempt to make the island more attractive for potential settlement by Northern and Middle Atlantic U.S. Americans. By providing the full array of possible resources available, Freneau suggests such settlers might offset their "loss" resulting from their need to avoid the one item that begets all avarice, brutality, extravagance, and luxury on the island—sugar cane. Second, the revised "Santa Cruz," published a year after Jefferson's *Notes on the State of Virginia* (1785), not only demonstrates Freneau's conversance with circumatlantic natural history writings prominent in Europe and the Americas by the late eighteenth century but also anticipates the admonition of Franklin's ghost to "Make [Nature] do—some uncommon things" on behalf of the "rising [United] States."

Stanza 48, for example, combines fancy and natural history to obscure the need for plantation labor, suggesting that citrus virtually grows itself in the lush Santa Cruz environment:

The plantane and banana flourish here,
Of hasty growth, and love to fix their root
Where some soft stream of ambling water flows,
To yield full moisture to their cluster'd fruit. (*PPF* 1:258)

Similar accounts of the rich natural resources that abound on Santa Cruz form the bulk of the poem's weight, beckoning to those "who first drew breath in northern air" (255) to come and partake of Santa Cruz's "luscious" and "salubrious food" (254). Freneau fastidiously advises the Northern shepherd about items to avoid because of the poisonous or noxious secrets that belie their otherwise beautiful appearances. In other instances, he instructs the would-be harvester about how to properly handle potentially dangerous fruits and nuts, including a pithy account of the cashew fruit and nut in stanza 40:

The conic form'd cashew, of juicy kind,
Which bears at once an apple and a nut;
Whose poisonous coat, indignant to the lip,
Doth in its cell a wholesome kernel shut. (*PPF* 1:257)

The tone of enlightened pastoralism that characterizes the poem's deployment of natural history discourse suggests the ways in which "Santa Cruz" is more than just escapist fantasy but functions, in part, as a screen for Franklin's, Jefferson's, and Freneau's shared vision for the United States as an agricultural empire for liberty. Freneau's Enlightenment critique in "Santa Cruz" dovetails with the poem's indictment of the British invasion of the would-be empire for liberty, a source of melancholy in the poem's revised version for what surely is an imperialist and colonialist fantasy itself, the United States as would-be peaceful *and* expansionist empire for liberty.

In the expanded 1786 version, Freneau, anxious that readers of the poem in its originally published form might not grasp the speaker's self-reflexive recognition of the partial nature of the paradisiacal Santa Cruz he sketches, delineates the ways in which such representations are meant to emphasize rather than minimize the contrasting scene of hardship and sacrifice in more Northern "climes" from whence the poet-speaker has fled:

Sweet orange grove, the fairest of the isle,
In thy soft shade luxuriously reclined,
Where, round my fragrant bed, the flowrets smile,
In sweet delusions I deceive my mind.

But Melancholy's glooms assail my breast,
For potent nature reigns despotic there;—
A nation ruined, and a world oppressed,
Might rob the boldest Stoic of a tear. (*PPF* 1:207)

By establishing a here/there antithesis that recurs across the poem, Freneau suggests that the corruptive British imperial intrusion in the United States' environment actually corrupts and ensnares Santa Cruz as would-be paradise, resulting in the speaker's "Melancholy's glooms" and disrupting his exotic repose amid fragrant, smiling orange blossoms. Freneau thereby inverts the usual trajectory whereby a degenerate West Indies in transatlantic writings of the late eighteenth century threatens to corrupt a putatively civilized metropolitan center.

Yet by drawing an analogy between the despotism on the continent to that occurring on the island and foregrounding the former but not the latter in the preface—perhaps as a consequence of Freneau's own guilt over having fled the Revolution in the first instance—these newly added prefatory stanzas privilege suffering on the continent and provide the grounds for deemphasizing U.S. paracolonial responsibility for despotism "here," meaning Santa Cruz as colony "ruined" by plantation slavery. In the same way, Freneau as roving poet-speaker deflects onto the despotic British "there" the exploitative role he plays "here" as U.S. "sojourner" on a vast plantation estate on behalf of which he conducts periodic trading voyages in the circum-Caribbean rim. Thus Freneau's foregrounding of British commercial and military aggression in the

Americas in the revised "Santa Cruz" occludes the ongoing commercial presence of the United States in the plantation economies of the West Indies, a presence that would seem to make the agents of the U.S. rising empire for "liberty" not especially Adamic figures to oversee Freneau's retooled Santa Cruz "gardens." To the extent that the poem's critique is meant to serve as a "screen" for renovating that potentially contradictory reality, the West Indian black slaves whose plight Freneau takes up in the poem's interior might not have appreciated such an oblique, rather than transparent, criticism.

Nonetheless, in the poem's especially progressive moments Freneau urges his audience to resist repeating European colonialism's mercantile excesses and abuses on arriving from the war-ridden continent to Santa Cruz. The charged figures of the alluring sugar cane and the socially dead West Indian slave are made to facilitate that important work. By avoiding these figures, the Sons of Columbia emerge as exemplary custodians of the island's natural resources and disseminators of republican values across the island, salvaging this one island at least from British tyranny in mutual and reciprocal measure. The figure of sugar cane first surfaces as Freneau relates the deleterious effects of European colonialism on *white* settlers in the West Indies. In the West Indies, the speaker relates, "To sensual souls the climate may fatal prove" (*PPF* 1:255). Yet according to the more progressive paracolonial politics of his poem, rather than suggesting such a fate is endemic to the environment itself—the "degenerate" climate of the West Indies—Freneau insists in his unconventional representation that the island's manmade environment of plantation slavery is what corrupts its otherwise salubrious atmosphere.[8] Freneau is quick to reassure his U.S. listener that degenerate living, not an inherently degenerate West Indies that *almost* seems to transcend the corruptive effects of slavery, is to blame for the high mortality rate among Santa Cruz's white population: "These victims to the banquet and the bowl / Must blame their folly only, not their fate" (*PPF* 1:255). By "bowl," Freneau means drinks made with rum distilled from the island's sugar cane.

According to Freneau's exoticized description of the island's naturally occurring fruit juices and rivulets, the Northerner, in contrast to the degenerate European or West Indian creole planter, might partake in a more salubrious drink that combines lime, water, and "the sweetest syrups of this liquorish clime" (1:255):

This happy beverage, joy inspiring bowl,
Dispelling far the shades of mental night,
Wakes bright ideas on the raptur'd soul,
And sorrow turns to pleasure and delight. (*PPF* 1:255)

A key difference between the degenerate European colonist and the would-be U.S. American one, then, is the latter's presumably more abstemious character, one resistant to the profligate tendencies of the white Europeans and West Indian creoles on the island.

Having alluded earlier in the poem to the noxious properties of sugar cane production, Freneau returns in more precise terms to its corruptive influence several stanzas later:

But chief the glory of these Indian isles
Springs from the sweet, uncloying sugar-cane
Hence comes the planter's wealth, hence commerce sends
Such floating piles to traverse half the main.

Whoe'er thou art that leav'st thy native shore,
And shall to fair West India climates come,
Taste not the enchanting plant—to taste forbear,
If ever thou wouldst reach thy much lov'd home. (*PPF* 1:260–61)

Thus Freneau admonishes those seduced by his lines to sojourn in Santa Cruz to avoid the temptations of the sugar cane plant. Such an avoidance will not be easy—Freneau acknowledges the potentially irresistible pull of sugar cane via an analogy to *Ulysses*, specifically the moment when the eponymous hero and his crew happen upon "Where lotos grew, and, had not strength prevail'd, / They never would have sought their country more" (*PPF* 1:261). Yet moments like this in the poem are when its progressive rhetoric becomes tangled in its multiple discursive registers, given Freneau's vexed location as paracolonial poet. That is, the stanzas' varied rhetorical postures admonishing the Northern shepherd against trafficking in sugar cane obstruct or otherwise cancel each other out. As these distinct discursive registers collapse and overlap here and elsewhere in the poem, Freneau's poetics reveals its deep-seated ambivalence. Specifically, Freneau's inability or unwillingness to confront the complicit scene of U.S. paracolonialism systematically in the ways that he does the debased scene of European colonialism in the West Indies compromises the poem's reformist tendencies. Even so, they provide for, ironically, in their undoing of the ostensibly "pure" motives attending the poet-trader's civilizing mission in St. Croix, the poem's manifest formal and thematic ambivalence—by-products of the intractable paradox marking the emergent democratic Republic's paracolonialist exploitation of the West Indies.

To be clear, the above reading does not deny the poem's forward-looking antimercantilist critique—though as for that, we might recall once more Strachan's remark about the pernicious ways in which tourism extends from the plantation. In whose interest is Freneau's renovated form of colonialism being offered up: the would-be emancipated black population, and/or the U.S. American looking to gain a stronger foothold in the island's political economy? Rather, it is the conflicted paracolonial (im)posture that Freneau occupies (like so many U.S. American writers in the New Republic period, somewhere between colonized and colonizer, neither one but both) that undermines his authority to provide a thoroughgoing critique of U.S. paracolonialism itself in the poem. Even as he gestures in abstract terms to the ways in which the "planter's wealth" and the wealth stemming from "piles" traversing the Caribbean "main" include, by implication, the United States, Freneau never explicitly mentions that U.S. or U.S.-affiliated traders, merchants, and planters already own or control significant portions of Santa Cruz's plantation economy. Further, he abstracts the reality that U.S. merchants and traders represent a substantial portion—some estimates argue a majority—of the West Indian carrying trade that he acknowledges. By abstracting or otherwise negating such U.S. paracolonial presences and practices, it would seem Freneau as paracolonial poet abets rather than undermines them.

Freneau's own culpability manifests at poem's end in a decidedly anxious and ambivalent stanza. Unsurprisingly, this stanza was added to bolster the poem's nationalist tenor in 1786 after Freneau received criticism from readers who perceived "Santa Cruz" in its initial incarnation to be an escapist fantasy:

What, though we bend to a tyrannic crown;
Still Nature's charms in varied beauty shine—
What though we own the proud imperious Dane,
Gold is his sordid care, the Muses mine. (*PPF* 1:267)

Freneau suggests in this stanza that his poem always already—even in its 1779 version—was patriotic, representing the triumph of poetic pastoralism over attempts by the British "tyrannic crown" to silence Freneau as nature's poet. In reality, he makes the feminized island's "varied beauty shine" in order to provide haggard continental soldiers an imaginative, if not an actual, escape to the tropical climes of St. Croix made palpable in the poem.

Freneau's reference to the "imperious Dane" is especially intriguing. What might he mean by "What though we own the proud imperious Dane"? Does he mean: (a) that "we"—his U.S. audience and himself—merely "acknowledge" the Danes, one definition of the verb; (b) that we "own" the Dane's island in practical if not absolute terms as a result of the United States' vast mercantile investments in the island; or (c) that we both acknowledge and in practical terms "own" the Dane? If what Freneau means is option "a" alone, then the reality of options "b" and "c" belie the claim that "Gold is [the Dane's] sordid care, / the

Muses mine." Once more, the point is not to deny the progressive tendencies of Freneau's poem but to reveal its ambivalent rather than unequivocal posture. Freneau's host, should he have read the poem in U.S. newspapers on a trading voyage to Philadelphia, would have presumably been displeased by the poet's indictment of St. Croix's plantation economy, viewing it as a sign of Freneau's ingratitude after enjoying Captain Hanson's West Indian creole hospitality. After all, Freneau—like the U.S. presence on the island he represents and that the poem seeks to augment—lives on Captain Hanson's plantation, participates in the West Indian trades on Hanson's behalf, and thus does not dwell in uncorrupted isolation on the island with "the Muses" as the stanza implies.

We might return briefly to Freneau's admonition above to the Northern traveler to avoid the sugar cane plant, a caution he delivers in alternating fanciful, romantic, rational, and classical discursive registers. Freneau occludes the reality that consumptive desire for sugar and rum on the U.S. mainland itself amounted at the time of his poem's publication in 1786 to a national addiction. It is precisely such an addiction at "home" that causes U.S. traders to journey to the West Indies with lumber, flour, corn, and other products in exchange for sugar and rum. U.S. commerce men's ability to avoid actually having to colonize the West Indies marks the parasitic texture of the U.S. paracolonial relation to the West Indies. That Freneau understood the phenomenon of a U.S. addiction to the "enchanting" sugar cane in his own "much lov'd home" is clear. In a dozen or more works, poems like "The Shop Described, and the Merchant's Outset" and others in the same "Merchant" series, or "Lines Written on a Puncheon of Jamaica Spirits," Freneau urges his U.S. audience time and time again to forbear. Reminiscent of the above-treated moment in "Santa Cruz" when he admonishes the Yankee listener to drink a nonalcoholic lime and water drink, Freneau's speaker in "Lines" advocates avoiding the fiendish "spirit" in favor of "A spring, that never yet grew stale—Such virtue lies in—Adam's Ale!" (*PPF* 3:67). As the satirical bent of Freneau's humorous poem illuminates, U.S. consumers kept their merchants and traders busy plying the Caribbean main in search of rum and sugar and made such journeys worth their while. Since they never had to see firsthand the horrific plantation practices that made such conspicuous consumption possible—a point that Franklin's Richard Saunders persona remarks on, we will recall, in "*Concerning* SWEETS"—they were able to nurture their addiction on the one hand while avoiding forbearance on the other. Significantly, such practices were possible and enjoyable because U.S. consumers never had to leave their rum-filled and "much lov'd home," unlike the degenerate European and creole West Indian planters critiqued in "Santa Cruz" or the African slaves whom North American traders secured for the West Indian plantation economies by trading rum.[9]

As mentioned above, Freneau exploits the reality of ongoing military conflict between the United States and Britain—which was not ongoing when he overhauled and expanded the poem in 1786—to legitimate the always already dubious proposition that U.S. Americans have the moral standing to renovate the violent practices of European colonialism in the West Indies in which they are implicated:

> There, triumphs to enjoy, are, Britain, thine;
> There, thy proud navy awes the pillag'd shore;
> Nor sees the day when nations shall combine
> That pride to humble and our rights restore. (*PPF* 1:266)

Accordingly, Freneau's vision of a restorative U.S. commercial presence depends a Northern U.S. American addressee who, situated in relation to the enslaved West Indian black, seems to achieve moral authority based on a putative future U.S. "republican" victory according to which he might spread the principles that inspired it across the hemisphere in cooperation with like-minded nations. Thus in "Santa Cruz" Freneau in a sense previsions as moral representative the day when a triumphant and rising U.S. empire might not only displace Europe's empires in the hemisphere but inspire the demise of the slave trade and the emancipation of West Indian slaves.

Yet elsewhere Freneau's use of the first-person plural implicates himself and fellow U.S. Americans in the slave trade and would seem in advance to undo such prospective reformism. Reflection existing in uneasy tension with Freneau's poetic revisionings, such a contradiction redounds across time and textual *and* metatextual space: "O gold accurst! for thee we madly run / With murderous hearts across the briny flood, / Seek foreign climes beneath a foreign sun, / And there exult to shed a brother's blood" (*PPF* 1:263). Freneau's "we" thereby acknowledges in progressive ways his and his nation's culpability for denying to Africans the "rights" that the tyrannical British have denied U.S. revolutionaries.

But in the stanza that follows, the "I/thou" division reasserts itself when he apostrophizes West Indian plantation owners:

> But thou, who own'st this sugar-bearing soil,
> To whom no good the great First Cause denies,
> Let freeborn hands attend thy sultry toil,
> And fairer harvests to thy view shall rise. (*PPF* 1:263)

Setting aside for the moment the question of how emancipation will in and of itself allow for the more humane working conditions that Freneau strives for, this is an especially progressive colonial policy that calls on plantation owners to employ wage labor rather than rely on chattel slavery. Even so, Freneau here does not specifically call on the "I," U.S. Northern shepherds, to give up trading with the "thou" who owns "sugar-bearing soil" in the West Indies. Neither does he call on his Northern reader to avoid consuming sugar and rum—as did Franklin, and as does Freneau himself in other "commodities" poems such as the "sugar" and "rum" ones gestured to above—in such vast quantities that they provide the market for the "thou" to trade the cheap luxury products from his sugar cane plantation worked by slave labor. In other words, for Freneau's abolitionist and antimercantilist critique to be wholly efficacious, he must systematically critique—rather than abstract, mystify, displace, or deny—the vertical and horizontal ways in which U.S. paracolonialism perpetuates the European colonial system that he excoriates in the poem.

Underscoring the conflicted economy of meaning in the poem ultimately is the unsteady structural analogy it draws between enslaved black West Indians on Santa Cruz and the (self-)exiled North American poet-speaker and his white audience of would-be North American tourists and future planters oppressed by the tyrannical British. Freneau treats the African and Afro-Creole slave population in a notably expanded section of the revised 1786 version of the poem. While his call for their emancipation is laudable, by privileging his Northern U.S. shepherd's suffering as a key factor in inducing the poet-speaker's "Melancholy's glooms" he reproduces the poem's less progressive paracolonial tendencies. He stylizes, appropriates, and ventriloquizes in a nifty act of paracolonial appropriation West Indian slave suffering while simultaneously distancing U.S. complicity for perpetuating it:

See yonder slave that slowly bends this way,
With years, and pain, and ceaseless toil opprest,
Though no complaining words his woes betray,
The eye dejected proves the heart distrest. (*PPF* 1:262)

Might the sentimentalized St. Croix slave whose voice—as well as eye/ I—Freneau appropriates in the poem from a position of paracolonialist surveillance be uplifted by the prospect of emancipation at the urging of a newly enlightened U.S. presence? Or would s/he be "dejected" by the reality that the same presence *in actuality*, as opposed to the realm of pastoral fantasy, brutally enslaves his brethren on the continent all the while exploiting his own "ceaseless toil" in the sugar plantations of

Santa Cruz according to the white continental revolutionaries' addictions to profits stemming from the West Indian carrying trade?

Notes on the (Colonial) State of Jamaica: Freneau's Jamaica Poems

In "The Beauties of Santa Cruz," the West Indies emerge as the scene of degenerate European commercial practices, practices that the New Republic as rising empire might avoid repeating and by so doing displace, even as the poem gestures—albeit obliquely—to U.S. complicity in perpetuating such oppression. Similarly, Freneau's Jamaica poems, like "Santa Cruz" literal by-products of U.S. participation in the West Indian plantation economies during and after the Revolution, in their unrelentingly negative critique of British West Indian colonialism on the island bear traces of the unstable and vexed relation of the United States to such conditions. The Jamaica poems thus position themselves somewhere between the postcolonial and the colonial, empire and colony, and colonizer and colonized; between master and slave, the hegemonic and the oppressed, and European and creole West Indian. In short, these poems occupy the interstitial location of U.S. paracolonialism, thereby rendering received binaries from postcolonial thought inadequate as a way of apprehending the intricate economies of meaning that shape and structure such works. Likewise, as privateer-poet plying the West Indian trades, Freneau embodies the antipodal postures, tendencies, and energies of the considerable body of literature and culture responsive to U.S. paracolonialism in the West Indies in the late eighteenth and early nineteenth centuries.

Freneau's Jamaica poems were conceived a decade after Edward Long published *History of Jamaica* (1774). As I discussed in the previous chapter, Long's *History* is a scathing critique of the British empire's most valuable West Indian colony and its "degenerate" peoples—white, black, and mulatto. In addition, the Jamaica poems were written contemporaneously with the publication of Thomas Jefferson's *Notes on the State of Virginia* (1785), a tract that inventories the manners, customs, laws, institutions, population, climate, and resources of Virginia so as to confront and challenge European notions that North American creoles had degenerated. Written in the aftermath of a near-fatal trading voyage to Jamaica in 1784, the Jamaica poems should be read collectively as well as individually. That is, I believe they are meant to produce meaning intertextually. By treating the Jamaica poems in relation to one another, we can better grasp the intricate ways in which Freneau within and across these poems expands the genre of eighteenth-century occasional lyric in order to accommodate the influence of natural history prose writings by figures like Bryan Edwards, Jefferson, and particularly Long. Freneau's Jamaica poems are not eclectic pieces as critics have frequently understood them, occasional poems written about Jamaica and thus somehow unconcerned "with national events" or the "national interest" as a result of journalist Freneau's decision to resume a trading career in the West Indies (Bowden 47). Rather, we need to consider Freneau's *collected* Jamaica poems—equal parts travelogue, ship's journal, captivity narrative, antislavery tract, occasional lyric, and natural history account of Jamaica's flora, fauna, peoples, climate, laws, manners, economy, politics, and prospects—as improvising on the form and themes of natural history prose writings of the period. They operate simultaneously as U.S. empire for liberty propaganda and critique, Jamaica functioning as a screen through and against which Freneau implicitly inventories, like Jefferson, the state(s) of the union.

Perhaps the most significant context for understanding the anticolonial, nationalist sentiment of these poems is one already treated in previous chapters: the unsuccessful efforts by U.S. diplomats and not a few British ministers sympathetic to their cause to push through full and reciprocal trade relations between the British West Indies and the United States in the commercial articles of the treaty of peace (1783). This failure was a major blow to triumphal notions of national character. Despite having arrived at nominal independence, the United States remained subject to militarily enforced British prohibitions against U.S. mercantile vessels trading legally with the British West Indies. Coupled with the new nation's limited successes in establishing commercial treaties with Spain and France that would open their West Indian colonies' ports to U.S. commerce, that commerce found itself in an unstable and uncertain predicament vis-à-vis the West Indian trades. For the remainder of the century and well into the next one, U.S. commerce in the West Indies would be subject to the whims and fancy of European legislative bodies and armed conflict between empires. Wars occurring between France, Britain, and Spain alternately opened or closed ports on a limited-time basis to U.S. ships, forcing U.S. merchants to trade almost indiscriminately with the various empires' West Indian colonies at the risk of seizure and forfeiture of their merchandise and ships should they be captured by British or French navies or privateers.

Historian Lawrence Kaplan remarks, "[E]ven in areas proscribed by British Orders in Council, there were sufficient caveats to enable enterprising American shippers to operate with relative freedom in Caribbean ports, usually with the active collaboration of the islanders themselves. Clandestine American–West Indian connections in the 1780s were reminiscent of the relations between the Spanish West Indies and British 'pirates' of the seventeenth century in which mutually profitable trade relations were conducted in the face of the express displeasure of the Spanish crown" (*Colonies* 163). Such illicit trading activities, although substantial, lucrative, and important to the survival of the New Republic's political economy in the ways that Kaplan suggests, were decidedly paracolonial in the worst sense possible. Their clandestine, piratical, and parasitical nature made them far more dangerous than Kaplan's notion of "relative freedom" might indicate. Moreover, such illicit trading operations would become increasingly dangerous in the 1790s and first decades of the eighteenth century, given the United States' inability to persuade Britain and France to enter into, and abide by, more favorable trade agreements in relation to their West Indian colonies. As *Creole America* has been suggesting across its chapters, the precarious role of the United States in the West Indian trades in the 1780s and 1790s proved ambivalent in its effect on national character, inducing in the United States a creole complex. On the one hand, the proliferation of illicit trading ventures undertaken by U.S. commercial interests was viewed by many in the mercantile community and by leaders in the Federalist party as a triumph over more powerful European empires seeking to exclude the United States from the lucrative West Indian trades. On the other hand, such maneuvers laid bare the still hegemonic situation of the British mercantile empire in relation to the United States as paracolonial presence in the West Indies. As such, the United States remained helpless to protect its commercial interests in formal or conventional ways, whatever the extent of hemispheric nervousness experienced by European empires anxious about the potentially deleterious effects on their West Indian colonies of liberal trading practices undertaken by the newly independent Republic. Thus in treating Freneau's Jamaica poems, we need crucially to consider their production in relation to the unstable balance of power between U.S. and British commercial and naval forces in the West Indies. If U.S. Americans had fought a revolution in considerable measure to defy increasingly harsh restrictions on North American colonial trade with the West Indies—both foreign and British—the new nation, despite winning that battle, was still in a sense losing the war when it came to being able to dictate the terms of trade relations between the United States and the West Indies.

On its surface, "The Hurricane" (1785) is a poem universal in meaning about the dangers sailors in the Caribbean face when set upon by such a violent storm. Yet even as the poem eschews any mention of the national origin of the sailors or vessel in question, by recalling the precise occasion for Freneau's being in Jamaica we can avoid the critical tendency to elide Freneau's paracolonial presence there by isolating it

from Freneau's seemingly abstract occasional poem. Headnotes to other
Jamaica poems make clear that Freneau composed "The Hurricane"
while he was on what was very likely an illicit trading run to Jamaica on
July 20, 1784. Freneau was supercargo aboard a U.S. vessel struck by a
hurricane in the middle of the night while exposed off the coast of
Jamaica:

While death and darkness both surround,
And tempests rage with lawless power,
Of friendship's voice I hear no sound,
No comfort in this dreadful hour—
What friendship can in tempests be,
What comfort on this raging sea? (*PPF* 2:251–52)

The poem's gothic strains eloquently recount the physical and psychic
trauma of such an experience from Freneau's unique vantage point as
trader-poet. As readers of colonial literature about the West Indies and
postcolonial Caribbean writing well know, the figure of the hurricane is
almost always deployed with multilayered significance. With that in
mind, on transparent levels Freneau's poem is about the treacherous
condition of sailors stranded at sea during a hurricane. Accordingly, the
poem suggests metaphysical "man vs. nature" thematics in its closing
stanza: "The barque, accustomed to obey, / No more the trembling
pilots guide: / Alone she gropes her trackless way, / While mountains
burst on either side—/ Thus, skill and science both must fall; / And
ruin is the lot of all" (*PPF* 2:252). However, the final stanzas of "The
Hurricane" also critique on metatextual levels the dangers that U.S.
Americans faced not solely from natural disasters alone, but from manmade ones at the hands of the powerful and predatory British navy.
Thus the hurricane's "lawless power" is meant to suggest figural associations with British tyranny over U.S. commerce in the Caribbean. In
richly allusive terms, the poem sets forth the profound sense of alienation, anxiety, and ambivalence U.S. mercantile men felt on experienc-
ing not only an actual hurricane in the Caribbean Sea but a metaphoric
one as well. Unprotected by a meager U.S. navy, traders like Freneau
encountered the powerful British navy according to the decidedly
unfriendly terms of the peace at Versailles and subsequent Orders of
Parliament, which prohibited U.S. commercial interests from lawfully
trading in the British West Indies except under very limited circumstances and forbade them from trading with the colonial possessions of
countries with whom Britain was at war, most typically the French.

If such an interpretation of the poem seems farfetched, we might
examine a companion text—an occasional poem written in 1784 but not
published until 1792 in Freneau's *National Gazette*—about the trying

experiences in Jamaica during and subsequent to the destruction of Freneau's vessel. In the intermediate eight-year period, British predations on U.S. commerce had escalated, the "rising empire" seemingly powerless against such outrages despite threatening embargoes, nonimportation acts, and other measures, all of which Freneau aggressively urged in anti-Federalist propaganda written in the 1790s and published in the *National Gazette* alongside his lyrics. "To the Keeper of the King's Water Works" (*PPF* 2:252–53) is a five-stanza poem characterized by pronounced irritation and anger over a seemingly local offense. Freneau appended a prefatory remark to the poem indicating that it was inspired by the British navy's refusal to provide necessary refreshment in the aftermath of the 1784 hurricane that ravaged his ship.[10] Thus the poem begins with a series of charged questions posed to the Royal Navy's keeper of the Kingston harbor reservoir that seek to magnify the gross outrage of the decision to withhold water from Freneau's storm-weary and battered crew.

Yet the withholding of the reservoir's water resonates on levels far beyond the quotidian offense the poem ostensibly addresses. Indeed, the British empire's force and sway over the Caribbean Sea as "reservoir" is foregrounded in the initial stanza: "Can he, who o'er the two Indies holds the sway, / Where'er the ocean flows, whose fleets patrole . . . / Of worth untold—can he, so rich, deny / One wretched puncheon from this ample waste, / Begg'd by his quondam subject—very dry?" (*PPF* 2:252). Contemporary readers of Freneau's poem—published in the midst of national outrage over the British navy's mounting seizures of U.S. merchant vessels plying the West Indian trades and the impressment of U.S. merchant men into British naval service in violation of international agreements—would have understood these lines as metapoetic critique of atrocities perpetrated by the British in the West Indies generally and on the Caribbean Sea in particular: "Keeper!—must we with empty cask return! / . . . Denied the stream that flows from Nature's urn, / By locks and bolts secur'd from rebel taste?" (*PPF* 2:253). According to such a reading, the poem functions as a barely veiled protest, insisting that monarchy and Parliament not only unlock the "locks and bolts" of the Kingston harbor reservoir in order to provide refreshment for storm-ragged U.S. sailors, but also throw open the waterways of the West Indian trades to the British empire's "quondam subject" and its "rebel taste." While such a sentiment is one that many British West Indians themselves in 1784 and less stridently so in 1792 agreed with, Parliament declined to do so. The British refusal is attributable in part to mercantile greed, but it also stemmed from fear over the liberal and liberalizing effect that republican-minded "Sons of Columbia" might have on its colonies. Such prohibitions, too, were intended to punish the former colonists, who, according to British mercantile policy, must suffer under a distinct commercial disadvantage in the West Indian trades until such a time when the upstart United States could defend its boldly worded principles with more than a sparsely equipped navy—something the British felt might never come to pass.

"Lines Written at Port-Royal, in the Island of Jamaica" (1788; alternately titled "Port Royal") is a third poem written in response to the same ill-fated voyage to Jamaica in 1784, a work whose formal and thematic sophistication has been underestimated by readers.[11] In "Hurricane" the "tempests rage . . . with lawless power," leaving Captain Freneau and the crew of the *Dromilly* "grop[ing their] trackless way"; and in "To the Keeper of the King's Water Works," the hurricane and reservoir are images yoked to British imperialism toward U.S. commerce in the West Indies. In "Lines," natural imagery is evoked once more not so much to allude to British dominance over U.S. mercantile interests in the West Indies as to signal the degenerate, debased, and crumbling edifices of British colonial might in the New World. Specifically, Freneau recalls the roughly centennial memory of an unprecedented late seventeenth-century earthquake that literally dropped Port Royal, Jamaica, into the ocean, a recollection he deploys to indict the state of the British mercantile empire in the present and future. In a headnote accompanying the poem's publication in 1788, Freneau notes that "Old Port-Royal contained more than 1500 buildings, and these for the most part large and elegant. This unfortunate town was for a long time reckoned the most considerable mart of trade in the West Indies. It was destroyed on the 17th of June, 1692, by an earthquake which in two minutes sunk the far greater part of the buildings; in which disaster near 3000 people lost their lives" (*PPF* 2:254). Just as the poem proleptically demythologizes this seismic trauma in British and New World colonial history to foreordain the demise of the British empire in the West Indies, so the thickly figured Port Royal earthquake operates as a chronotope that collapses time and space: the U.S. Revolution of 1776–84 is yoked to the 1692 natural disaster. Such a conflation is engineered in discrete ways, the twin "seismic" traumas—one natural, one manmade—haunting the British mercantile empire in the New World. If Port Royal, Jamaica, stands as the grand "mart" of elegance in British colonial history, it also serves as a figure for British colonial and mercantile excess according to Freneau's poetics of creole resistant countermemory.

Bryan Edwards's pamphlet *Thoughts on the Late Proceedings of Government Respecting the Trade of the West India Islands with the United States of North America* (1784), in its remarkable figural and thematic overlaps with Freneau's poem, points to the ways in which Freneau's poetics in "Lines" operates as a progressive act of inter-creole resistance on behalf of U.S. Americans and West Indian creoles alike against a tyrannical London. Best known for his ambitious, five-volume natural history work *The History, Civil and Commercial, of the British West Indies* (1798), Edwards in *Thoughts* indicts, like Freneau, the dim-sightedness and utter inhumanity of Parliament's ultimate decision to restrict U.S. trade access to the British West Indies. For Edwards, such a proclamation is but a continuation of the wrong-minded mercantilist policies that provoked the U.S. Revolution:

what a dreadful monument of infirmity does Great Britain exhibit to the world! And what have we to console ourselves with, for the millions we have expended, and the blood we have spilt? We have dismembered the noblest empire in the universe;—and for what? *To make assurance sure!*—to possess ourselves of an object already our own, and of which nothing it seems could have deprived us! (7)

Rather than follow the policy recommendations of men with more "comprehensive discernment" (8) like Edmund Burke, who advocated reformist mercantile principles based on *"mutual advantage, founded in mutual confidence"* (6) between nations, the current British "administration" regretfully, Edwards maintains, chose instead to reinstate harsh, oppressive restrictions on commerce between the islands and the United States, a decision characterized by "the grossest misinformation, and . . . fraught with the most serious consequences" (9).

In the text's body, Edwards foregrounds his firsthand experience living in the West Indies to debunk such "misinformation" used to advocate the imposition of the trading ban. For instance, even as Edwards acknowledges the legitimacy of British mercantilists' concerns about a potential "American" rivalry in the carrying trade to and from London and the West Indies should the Americans be granted access there, he insists that such trepidation might be handled in a way "less dangerous in its effects than the project of starving her sugar colonies . . . the disease, in this case, is, indeed, by far the lesser evil" (27). In that regard, Edwards refutes the notion that trade between the United States and the islands is about promoting "vanity," "vice," or "luxury." On the contrary, he submits that the United States supplies the islands with commodities necessary for their very survival: "The commerce of America . . . is beyond all equivalent more necessary to the British West India islands, than that of the islands to her," Edwards argues, for what the Americans take away from the islands—rum, sugar, molasses, and coffee—is not, like the goods they carry southward from the continent's forests and farms, "absolutely necessary to the preservation of life" (12). In a gesture reminiscent of Freneau's "Hurricane" poem, Edwards evokes the specter of recent "dreadful hurricanes" in the islands for sentimental effect. Such storms are said to have caused "suffering inhabitants" to reside "in miserable hovels"—a figure Freneau mobilizes, as shown below, in "Lines"—until "America, in the very first moment of reconciliation, hastened to their relief"; yet now, as a result of Lord Sheffield's 1783 proclamation that operates to deny them such aid, British West Indians suffer once more, hardships that are compounded by West Indians' intense feelings of being betrayed not by the Americans but by their own government: "How grievous then is their disappointment!" (30).

If Edwards's appeals to his audience's sentiments and sensibility fail to persuade, he appeals instead to their accounting ledgers. Confessing his own hypocrisy as professed abolitionist on the one hand, and merchant and stockholder in the plantations and the slave trade on the other, Edwards insists that the trade restrictions will lead to the collapse of not only the West Indian plantation economies but likewise the slave trade: "Deprived of the means of procuring sustenance for the slaves they already possess, it can hardly be supposed that the planters will think of purchasing others" (31). Thus such ill-considered, unprovoked, and "premeditated mischief" by Parliament marks not so much the corruption of the creoles in America as that of the white politicians who support such legislation in the metropolitan center: "When unretracted error hardens into obstinacy, and disappointed ambition is degraded into malice—these are signs of a fatal degeneracy" (32). Edwards thereby inverts the conventional valuation of an "enlightened" metropolitan center in binary opposition to a "degenerate" creole periphery.

Freneau's West Indies poems, perhaps especially "Lines," deploy many of the very figures and themes that structure Edwards's tirade against a hopelessly "degenerate" British government—devastating hurricanes, unfeeling government agents, starving planters and their slaves, a pathological investment in failed mercantile policies. As such, Edwards's "Thoughts," published at the time of Freneau's 1784 "captivity" in Jamaica, might well have emboldened, and perhaps even informed, Freneau's retrospectively written poems about that unpleasant experience. At a minimum, Edwards, who speaks on behalf of desperate island planters now opposed to the mercantile interests in Parliament who had so often supported them before the Revolution, predicts in his charged dissent and in such a way confirms the sophisticated reformist principles shaping Freneau's anti-British mercantilist poetics.

After surviving the hurricane and securing water from Jamaican "beggars"—sympathetic white and/or black creoles—who give what "kings that now in Britain live . . . withhold" (*PPF* 2:253), Freneau becomes something of a beachcomber in the harbors of Kingston while awaiting safe passage on a U.S. vessel other than his now-scuttled *Dromilly*. As he looks out from the shore to the city under the sea, he remarks, "Of all the towns that grac'd Jamaica's isle, / This was her glory, and the proudest pile, / Where toils on toils bade wealth's gay structures rise, / And commerce swell'd her glory to the skies" (*PPF* 2:253). The poet-speaker as surveyor of Port Royal's ghostly landscape of memory employs anaphora with haunting effect to simulate the panorama of trauma occurring across multiple locations in the city when the earthquake struck:

> While o're these wastes with wearied step I go,
> Past scenes of death return, in all their woe,
> Here, opening gulphs confess'd the almighty hand,
> Here, the dark ocean roll'd across the land,
> Here, piles on piles an instant tore away,
> Here, crowds on crowds in mingled ruin lay,
> Whom fate scarce gave to end their noon-day feast,
> Or time to call the sexton, or the priest. (*PPF* 2:254)

Freneau connects Jamaica's submerged past with its present commercial condition, remarking how "yond' tall barque, with all her ponderous load, / Commits her anchor to [Port Royal's] dark abode" (*PPF* 2:254). Lest the listener misapprehend any mournful note of nostalgia or "Santa Cruz"-esque "Melancholy's glooms" in what the speaker says about the now-vanished world of luxury and pomp that marked Port Royal's character, such an impression is dashed in a note of exclamatory derision leveled by the speaker to an apostrophized Port Royal/British empire: "What now is left of all thy boasted pride! / Lost are thy glories that were spread so wide, / A spit of sand is thine, by heaven's decree, / . . . Is this Port-Royal on Jamaica's coast, / The Spaniard's envy, and the Briton's Boast!" (*PPF* 2:255). Such figuration recalls in nostalgic terms the contrasting late seventeenth-century moment when British North American and West Indian creole colonists commingled bodies, commodities, and cultures along the West Indian trade routes in the ports of the then rising British mercantile empire in the New World, rather than being separated by the degenerate mercantilist policies and excesses of the late eighteenth century.

Freneau strategically juxtaposes the romanticized residents of Port Royal's colonial past with the degenerate and debased remnant populations of the present:

> A negro tribe, but ill their place supply,
> With *bending back, short hair*—and *vengeful* eye—
> That gloomy race lead up the evening dance,
> Skip on the sands, or dart the *alluring* glance:
> Sincere are they?—no—on your gold they doat—

And in one hour—for that would cut your throat.
All is deceit—half hell is in their song
And from the silent thought?—You *have done us wrong!* (*PWD* 196)[12]

Freneau provides a gothic caricature of contemporary Jamaican society, one that pivots on primitivized black creoles watching over now-vanished Port Royal and seething with pent-up rebellion, corrupted by generations of bondage and violence that they yearn to revisit on their white oppressors.[13] Alongside them, no less, are the pathetic Tories "banish'd" from the United States "come to seek renown." In short, the once grand Port Royal has been replaced in the late eighteenth century by an inglorious Kingston, a place "Where hungry slaves their little stores retail, / And *worn out veterans* watch the approaching sail" (*PWD* 196).[14]

Even as nature in Jamaica almost "herself transcends," the corrosive scene of aging British imperial power ultimately overtakes her:

Who would be sad, to leave a sultry clime,
Where *true Columbian virtue* is a crime:
Where parching sands are driven by every blast,
And pearl to swine are by the muses cast—
Where *want* and *death*, and *care*, and grief, reside
And boisterous gales impel the imperious tide. (*PWD* 197)

Freneau's reference to an italicized "*true Columbian virtue*" as "crime" is powerful in its layered significance according to the poem's complex paracolonial poetics. Columbian virtue is a "crime" because the Sons of Columbia are banned from trading in the British West Indies. Yet as poet-trader—according to his dual role as mercantile representative of the rising U.S. empire in Jamaica and as artist penning verses in the spirit of true Columbian virtue—Freneau aims to indict and subvert those policies. Ultimately such activities belie the poet's mystifying note of pathos at the poem's end: "Why came I here to plan some future page—" (*PWD* 196). Freneau "came" to Jamaica as an agent of U.S. paracolonialism and cast himself in binary relief to debased black creoles and Tory refugees fled from the scene of Revolution in the now-independent United States. Such a flight exists in ironic relation to Freneau's own flight *pre*-Revolution to Santa Cruz.

Yet the inability of the weak U.S. navy to protect Freneau in the Caribbean "Main" from search and seizure, analogized across the Jamaica poems by the desperate condition of Captain Freneau and the *Dromilly*, raises compelling questions about whether it is so easy to draw distinctions between the degenerate creole slaves and Tory refugees in Jamaica and the paracolonial Sons of Columbia for whom Freneau functions as moral exemplar within and without the borders of his poem.[15] Is Freneau on the side of the disturbingly drawn creole slaves, and/or the white West Indian creoles and Tory refugees with whom he ostensibly trades, thereby perpetuating the *"wrong"* done the slave?[16] If wrongs done unto the slaves are indices of the debased and degenerate condition of Jamaica and the British West Indies, then what of like wrongs committed against black slaves in the United States where true Columbian virtue sustains the crime of slavery, thereby undermining the linkages that Freneau's poet-speaker draws across poems between the abused Sons of Columbia and the enslaved son of Africa in Jamaica as like victims of British mercantile tyranny in the West Indies?

Although Freneau's starkly primitive representations of Jamaican slaves prepossessed with pent-up rebellion are, in a backhanded sense, antislavery-like in sentiment in "Lines Written at Port-Royal," the most explicit and conventional antislavery poem in Freneau's Jamaica series and arguably his entire oeuvre is "To Sir Toby" (1792), originally titled "The Island Field Hand." With "Sir Toby" Freneau completes the poetic retelling of his ill-fated commercial, though artistically fruitful, 1784 journey, the sort of fractured epic characteristic of what Glissant terms a New World poetics of relation as creolization. Beginning his poetic act of re-memory somewhere off the coast of Jamaica in "Hurricane," then proceeding, as he would have in 1784, to the harbor of Kingston in "To the Keeper of the King's Water Works" and from thence to the shoreline in "Lines Written at Port-Royal," Freneau ultimately takes his audience to the interior of Jamaica, specifically to its vast sugar plantations, in "Sir Toby." The gothic strain of the poem is apparent from its diction at the outset: "If there exists a hell—the case is clear—Sir Toby's slaves enjoy that portion here" (*PPF* 2:258). Told in heroic couplets, the poem proceeds according to antislavery convention to catalogue the implements of torture that Sir Toby as monstrous planter uses on his helpless victims: in seriatim, the master's *"brand . . . that marks poor Cudjoe's breast,"* and the whip that "cracks, like pistols, from the fields of CANE" and thus "excite[s] perpetual fears, / And mingled howlings [that] vibrate on my ears" (*PPF* 2:258); also described in horrifying detail are devices like the gibbet, the windmill, iron collars, and so on.

The speaker connects the implements of torture to the "avarice of A TYRANT" on whose behalf his "black herd" are made to "toil" (*PPF* 2:258). Once more in "Sir Toby," however, consistent with the poetics of paracolonial negation across his West Indies poems, Freneau neglects to include any systematic, sustained account of U.S. complicity in the scene he describes or any reference to slavery in the United States, thus displacing onto the British West Indies responsibility for slavery at home. At moments like this, Freneau's poetics of relation as creolization tends toward one of creoleness—or U.S. Americanness, more exactly. Yet as Philip Gould argues in a recent reading of the poem, the "poet's consideration of the plantation's larger commercial connections makes this localizing strategy untenable" (55). Even so, Gould suggests Freneau deploys classical imagery from the underworld in book 6 of Virgil's *Aeneid* to abstract and mystify U.S. responsibility for the slave trade:

> Here Stygian paintings light and shade renew,
> Pictures of hell, that Virgil's pencil drew:
> Here, surly Charons make their annual trip,
> And ghosts arrive in every Guinea ship,
> To find what beasts these western isles afford,
> Plutonian scourges, and despotic lords:— . . . . (*PPF* 2:259–60)

Thus, Gould maintains, "Sir Toby" in a sense romanticizes the slave trade by failing to list actual ports along its routes such as "Bristol, Liverpool, and Newport, Rhode Island" (56) or to identify any specific slave ships.

However, a great many U.S. vessels—like the *Dromilly* that Freneau captained—did not originate in Newport as slave ships. Thus Gould's focus on ships directly responsible for the Middle Passage itself ironically ignores the far more prevalent trade routes plied by U.S. traders involved only indirectly in the slave trade. Such an understanding becomes vivid by treating "Sir Toby" in the context of Freneau's other Jamaica poems rather than in isolation as Gould does. This is important to note because by not actually transporting *slaves* across the Middle Passage, mercantile abolitionists like Freneau were able to mitigate their own sense of culpability in perpetuating the plantation economies of Jamaica. Thus, when Freneau writes of "Angola's natives scourged by ruffian hands, / And toil's hard product shipp'd to foreign lands" (*PPF* 2:259), the "foreign lands" to which Jamaica's "hard product" of sugar is shipped include Philadelphia, from whence Freneau steered the *Dromilly* in order to exchange products like flour and staves. By privileging U.S. commerce in relation to the slave trade exclusively, we neglect attending to the much more layered and complex routes of the West Indian trades according to which vessels from Boston, New York, Philadelphia, Baltimore, Charleston, and other U.S. port cities carried on their return voyages hard products such as sugar, coffee, and cocoa—as well as much needed specie—from Europe's West Indian colonies.

In truth, "Sir Toby" is something of an anomaly; in his other West Indies poems, we have seen, Freneau does foreground a U.S. mercantile presence in the scene of corrupted West Indian plantation economies. Indeed, each of these poems is told from the unique point of view of surveillance occupied by Freneau as U.S. poet-trader. Yet Freneau and his fellow citizens' shared outrage over British restrictions and depredations on U.S. commerce in the West Indies often trumps Freneau's repressed awareness that the United States' insatiable appetite for the "hard goods" of St. Croix, Jamaica, and other West Indian islands complicates his recurring impulse to analogize the ongoing victimization of U.S. commerce in the West Indies and its agents post-Revolution with the outrages perpetrated against African and black creole slaves there, a flaw in analogy predicted by "The Beauties of Santa Cruz." Such are the contradictions that inform Freneau's profoundly productive poetics of paracolonial ambivalence in "Santa Cruz" and the later-published Jamaica poems.[17]

Freneau's Rising and Not-So-Rising U.S. Empire

Freneau's West Indies poems thus reproduce in their multiple acts of paracolonial negation, abstraction, and displacement the sort of mysterious, illicit, and parasitic practices that U.S. traders plying the West Indian trades engaged in during the last decades of the eighteenth century. By so doing Freneau, like Franklin, is (almost) able to negate not only the ways in which the United States perpetuates the plantation economies of the ostensibly degenerate West Indies through U.S. paracolonialism but also how such debasing and degenerate conditions always already exist in the U.S. South, Middle Atlantic, and North. Such intersections become especially palpable in Freneau's West Indies poems when his dual occupations as U.S. poet and trader converge in their ambivalent acknowledgment and treatment of the New Republic's rampant consumption of West Indian plantation economies' "hard product[s]."

Freneau systematically critiques such contradictions in a series of poems set in the United States, unable to deflect them onto a tyrannical British empire according to the negating tendencies of his West Indies texts. Concurrent with the publication of his Jamaica poems (1785–92), Freneau published in various newspapers and periodicals on the eastern seaboard a set of "state" poems that were to constitute an epic poem known as "The Rising Empire." He also published a significant number of "commodities" poems, many of them humorous but with a distinctly indicting undertone. Such poems often focus explicitly on "Jamaica," not the actual colony but a figure connected to the island by Freneau and his contemporaries according to its commonly used name, "Jamaica" meaning rum distilled from cane sugar. In both "The Rising Empire" and his commodities poems, Freneau in explicit and implicit terms identifies the systemic intersections between U.S. and West Indian economies, societies, and cultures that he ambivalently treats in his West

Indies poems. In its trafficking in "Jamaica" and other hard and luxury goods from the West Indies and Europe, the ostensibly rising U.S. empire seems less like in character, manners, tastes, and ambitions the idealized empire for liberty that Franklin and Freneau mythologize and aspire to, and more like the degenerate and debased British empire and West Indian slave colonies against which such a vision defines itself.[18]

Before treating Freneau's fragmentary epic about an actual U.S. commercial empire gone badly awry, it would be useful to foreground Freneau's privileged empire for liberty ideology as it manifests itself in the revised version of one of his best-known poetic statements about U.S. national character. Freneau and fellow graduate Hugh Henry Brackenridge install the New Republic as a rising empire in explicit terms in the revised version of a poem originally delivered as the graduating address at Princeton in 1772. Although in 1786 and subsequent editions Freneau claims only to have "a little altered" the poem from its original form, the revised version of "The Rising Glory of America" is substantially modified. In the space/time continuum of empire building in the pre-Revolutionary version of the poem, the Spanish "Black Legend" is contrasted with the decidedly more enlightened project of British empire building in the New World: the North American colonies, inheritors of those same Enlightenment values, serve in the poem as particular evidence of Anglo-American "Rising Glory" in the hemisphere. Accordingly, white North American British colonists are linked with the oxymoronic project of British colonialist benevolence: "And we the sons of Britain learn like them / To conquer and to spare," which is to say they renounce degenerate "Spain's rapacious mind, [from] hence rose the wars / From Chili to the Caribbean Sea."[19] North American British colonists—in a moment of gross paracolonial negation—are "more happy" because they "boast / No golden metals in our peaceful land" and thus pursue "agriculture . . . a safe, humble life" (*PPF* 1:65).

Even as Freneau in the 1772 version of "The Rising Glory of America" gestures to agriculture as a main pursuit of Anglo-American colonists on the continent, he emphasizes the crucial role that commerce and mercantilism play in expanding empire's wealth and power and in forming the character of British North America. Indeed, in the initial version of "The Rising Glory of America," commerce is the site of an incipient creole nationalism, New York emerging as a rival port city to the metropolitan center of London: "New-York emerging rears her lofty domes, / And hails from far her num'rous ships of trade, / . . . From Europe's shores or from the Caribbees, / Homeward returning annually they bring / The richest produce of the various climes . . ." (*PPF* 1:69). Nowhere present is the derisive critique of British New World excess that marks

Freneau's West Indies poems, or the note of paracolonial ambivalence regarding North American complicity in extorting the "riches" of West Indian "climes" that informs the tone, shape, and structure of those texts. Instead, according to the crucial roles played by the Northern and Middle Atlantic colonies in expanding Britain's mercantile empire as merchants and traders in the West Indian trades, "The Rising Glory of America," even as it mentions "peaceful" agrarian expansionism on the continent, affords commerce far greater space than agriculture. Nor is commerce said to detract from but instead enhances the manners, character, and customs of British North Americans who, in return, redound glory onto the greater British empire through their devotion to its defense of liberty.

In the thoroughly revised 1786 version of the poem, the United States unsurprisingly is said to have inherited the mantle of peaceful and prosperous empire building from the now declining and debased British, demoted as it were to Spanish Black Legend status. Published the year after Jefferson's *Notes*, Freneau's revisions to the poem dramatically invert the hierarchy of value accorded commerce and agriculture. Although the speaker grants, "Great is the praise of Commerce, and the men / Deserve our praise, who spread the undaunted sail" (*PPF* 1:72), the revised "Rising Glory" stresses, both in terms of the disproportionate space accorded it and the celebratory tone with which it is treated, that agriculture—not commerce—will be the core political economy of the rising U.S. empire for liberty. As the speaker remarks, "Better these northern realms demand our song, / Designed by nature for the rural reign, / For agriculture's toil.—No blood we shed / For metals buried in a rocky waste.—" (*PPF* 1:50). In expressing such sentiment, Freneau mystifies the gross acts of violence perpetrated against Native Americans and enslaved blacks in order to provide for the expansion of "agriculture" west and south on the continent. Consistent with the reduced emphasis placed on commerce as formative of a national character, the poem downplays the still-prominent place of mercantilism in the new nation's political economy. In such a way, Freneau's revised poem ironically suggests his—and many other U.S. Americans'—deeply held ambivalence toward the ways in which commercial expansionism intersects with the nation's foundational republican values and institutions.

In accordance with such a reading, Freneau's speaker touts the nation's laws as responsible in part for helping its citizens avoid repeating the tyrannical form of government that oppressed them. "Say, shall we ask what empires yet must rise[?]" (*PPF* 1:75), the speaker apostrophizes the reader, "Here independent power shall hold her sway, / And public virtue warm the patriot breast: / No traces shall remain of tyranny, / And laws, a pattern to the world beside, / Be here enacted first.—" (*PPF* 1:81–82). Yet "laws" alone do not allow the United States to emerge in the space of Freneau's revised poem as "pattern to the world." Rather, Freneau's text must actively negate the powerful and still-prominent place that commerce and mercantilism occupy in the formation of the new nation's political economy and *actual*, rather than Freneau's utopic, national character. Having already stressed that U.S. Americans are an agricultural people, Freneau occludes the critical part that commerce men and women played—particularly in their charged response to the Intolerable Acts and their insistence on an increased role for North American traders and merchants in the West Indian trades—in fomenting revolution by engaging in subversive trading practices and acts of violence and counterviolence against British mercantile oppression. Thus Freneau's acts of paracolonial negation allow for Britain to join Spain as the antithesis to the United States as enlightened exemplar. Ultimately, we are left as readers of the revised "Rising Glory" to wonder where, in fact, the agents of U.S. commerce now work and how it is that they are able to avoid repeating the acts of commercial violence and tyranny that the poem argues undo first the Spanish and then the British empires.

For Freneau, any North American complicity in perpetuating acts of European colonial violence in the hemisphere as a result of U.S. participation in the West Indian trades is somehow rendered moot by the superior power of the British empire, which is said to control the "main" with overwhelming naval and mercantile forces and to administer colonialism *directly*, which is to say, other than *paracolonially*, in the West Indies and elsewhere. This precarious distinction is not only implied in the revised version of "The Rising Glory of America" but explicitly foregrounded in Freneau's West Indies poems, as we have seen. Paracolonialism is that which, given the in-between status of its beneficiaries—not quite colonizer, not quite colonized, but both—provides the liminal territory within and without the domains of Freneau's West Indies poems and the revised "Rising Glory of America" from which to mount a critique of British colonial and mercantile abuses. Such a critique operates by emphasizing one's affinities with colonialism's oppressed and simultaneously de-emphasizing one's complicity with the colonial oppressor in perpetuating European colonialism in the West Indies on the one hand while fostering internal forms of colonialism on the continent for purposes of economic and territorial "conquest" on the other. In the revised "Rising Glory," for example, Freneau attempts to claim that the Revolution was solely a product of British avarice for North American natural resources rather than an effort to enforce, according to British mercantile policy, restrictive laws on U.S. merchants and traders plying the West Indian trades in subversion of those laws. U.S. Americans, in other words, emerge as agricultural purists and isolationists. That duplicity provides an opportunity for the displacement of imperial and colonial violence perpetrated in the ostensibly Edenic agrarian fields of the rising empire for liberty, both in the slave plantations of the U.S. South and in the Western territories according to the federally sponsored project of ongoing removal and genocide of Native Americans. Such paracolonial acts of negation, displacement, and ambivalence are not only what provide the occasion to produce the occasional West Indies poems that Freneau writes but also the energies constituting the poems' forms and meanings designed to set forth the notion of the United States as exceptional nation-state, a regenerative and "rising" hemispheric empire.

Yet Freneau's agrarian utopianism in the revised "The Rising Glory of America" is profoundly undone in his mock-epic "The Rising Empire." In this series of "state" poems, Freneau actively draws on his experiences in the West Indies as trader-captain to emphasize the material relations between European colonialism in the West Indies and the United States as rising commercial empire in the 1790s. "The Rising Empire" was meant to be an epic consisting of a series of individual poems on the thirteen states that were the original fourteen North American British colonies, minus Nova Scotia. Freneau never finished the series; indeed, he only provided poems for seven of the thirteen states, leaving critics puzzled about why he did not complete "The Rising Empire" and unclear as to how to interpret the peculiar cross-currents of meaning that shape the extant seven state poems, many of which are fragments themselves of what Freneau seems to have intended to be longer individual poems. Close reading of the text suggests its satirical undertones begin to overwhelm and overtake the nationalist sentiment "to honor each state of the union as it contributed to the consummation of liberty" (Axelrad 195) that Freneau seems to have intended to prevail—as, indeed, it does in certain individual poems. In more specific terms, the effects of commercial avarice and the tyranny of consumptive desire and luxury that the "Rising Empire" obsesses over make the United States as rising empire seem much more like than unlike the ostensibly declining British empire it is defined against in both the West Indies poems and the revised "Rising Glory." As such, the practical effects of commercial empire invade and corrupt the romanticized agrarian landscape and ideology characteristic of the United States as an empire for liberty. Thus, by treating Freneau's West Indies poems alongside his mock-epic fragment "The Rising Empire" and his Jamaica [rum] commodities poems, we can begin to coordinate and fully appreciate the full extent of the rising U.S. empire for *commerce*. Ultimately, unable to sustain the project of paracolonial negation whereby the corruption and debasement of republican values and principles are projected elsewhere onto Europe and Europe's West Indian colonies, Freneau finds a new villain: the Anglicized Federalist party ruled by the corrupted West Indian immigrant and mercantilist Alexander Hamilton.

Of the seven states represented—Massachusetts, Connecticut, Rhode Island, New York, Pennsylvania, Maryland, and Virginia—the only one that escapes unscathed in "The Rising Empire" is Pennsylvania. In "Pennsylvania," Freneau's romantic pastoralism situates nature in perfect and peaceful coexistence with merchants, farmers, and more "polished men": "She, famed for science, arts, and polished men, / Admires her Franklin, but adores her Penn, / Who, wandering here, made barren forests bloom, / And the new soil a happier robe assume" (*PPF* 3:14). Penn is notable, according to the speaker's celebratory cant, for not committing any unvirtuous "schemes"; on the contrary, Penn's Quakerism caused the populations of Pennsylvania to expand, the soil to yield, and peace to flourish, all the while "robb[ing] no Indian of his native groves" (*PPF* 3:14). Pennsylvania's towns thus remain "gay," her ships built of exact "proportions," her hills "stupendous," her agriculture bountiful: "Fair Pennsylvania holds her golden rein, / In fertile fields her wheaten harvest grows . . ." (*PPF* 3:13). In this way, Pennsylvania serves as exemplar, part for the whole, for what the "rising empire" *ought* to be: an effeminized land of fertile farms and fields and ever-expanding populations all dependent on Freneau's euphemistic mystifications of past and ongoing violence against, among other groups, Native Americans and black slaves. Moreover, by summoning up Pennsylvania's sentimentalized past in the poem, Freneau eschews the reality that by the 1790s Philadelphia had emerged as perhaps the single most important U.S. port of trade with Europe and the West Indies. Rather, Pennsylvania is portrayed as a land of modest means where virtue—liberty, learning, and achievement—tends to the peaceful origins of "her" Quaker founders.

To the north, what corrupts Freneau's idyllic empire is unchecked commerce manifested as mercantile avarice and prideful consumption. In "Rhode Island," "grateful soil" provides land that should be incomparable: "Nature has strove to make her native blest / And owns no fairer Eden in the west" (*PPF* 3:7). According to Freneau's patriarchal poetics, Rhode Island's "lovliest dames" who need not "art's false colours" to seduce the "traveller's . . . wandering heart" are prominent, as are farms that raise cattle "the staunchest of the kind" (*PPF* 3:7). Yet rather than inculcate greater freedom and contentment, Rhode Island's natural gifts are transmuted by its inhabitants into widespread corruption, greed, and extravagance as a result of international commerce:

Half that the lands produce or seas contain
To other shores transported o'er the main
Returns in coin, to cheer the miser's eye,
In foreign *sweets,* that fancied wants supply,
Or tawdry stuffs, to deck the limbs of pride,
That thus expands what avarice strove to hide. (*PPF* 3:7)

Freneau doesn't explicitly condemn Rhode Island for participating in the slave trade, but he does locate its crucial part in perpetuating that trade by trafficking in sugar from the West Indies, and he gestures to other "tawdry stuffs" purchased with profits from the triangular trade. Rhode Island is a land of the avaricious speculator "bold in wrong" and greedy lawyer who "paper fabric rears / And steels his bosom to the orphan's tears / To those he ruin'd grants no late relief!" (*PPF* 3:8). Freneau might have mentioned the orphans Rhode Island's "sons" create via their participation in the African slave trade, but there is so little redeeming about his characterization of Rhode Islanders that such connections seem almost beside the point, or always already implied. In Freneau's "Rhode Island," the ostensibly "Rising Empire" seems an empire always already degenerate, debased, and in decline, not dissimilar to those European empires that colonize Jamaica or the French West Indies from whence Rhode Island's "foreign *sweets*" derive. Similarly, Newport seems quite like the decadent "mart" of the once great but now submerged city of Port Royal, merely waiting for the quake that Freneau's "commercial jeremiad," to evoke Gould's keen term for such antimercantile works, delivers. "Hurt at the view" of Rhode Island, Freneau writes, "I leave the ungrateful shore / And thy rough soil, Connecticut, explore" (*PPF* 3:9). Yet Connecticut proves equally disconcerting: "Eternal squabblings grease the lawyer's paw, / All have their suits, and all have studied Law" (*PPF* 3:9). Connecticut's famed poets, the "Wits," are the rival of their smooth-tongue deceivers at the bar in Freneau's mocking note of praise: "Even beardless lads a rhyming knack display— Iliads begun, and finished in a day!" (*PPF* 3:9). Once more, fraud, corruption, and duplicity reign supreme: "Honest through fear, religious by constraint, / How hard to tell the sharper from the saint!—" (*PPF* 3:9).

"Massachusetts" is more complimentary and balanced in tenor and tone, yet as commerce once more tends to predominate over agriculture, such praise seems almost backhanded. That is, Freneau can tolerate and to some extent celebrate Massachusetts' merchants for forsaking "her" pastoral meadows and blooming fields—"Were this thy all, what happier state could be!"—for commercial pursuits. For Massachusetts' commerce men, Freneau acknowledges—a detail he strategically occludes in the revised "Rising Glory"—first rebuffed the tyrannical

British empire: "Here, first, to quench her once loved Freedom's flame, / With their proud fleets, Britannia's warriors came" (*PPF* 3:11). The speaker begrudgingly grants that in Massachusetts, "avarice lends new vigour to mankind . . . / With her, Ambition linked, they proudly drive, / Rule all our race, and keep the world alive" (*PPF* 3:11), just as they rebuffed Britain's tyrannical navy. Still, as the poem's opening antithesis suggests, Massachusetts' "independence" and acquisitiveness are ambivalently regarded by the poet-speaker for their inevitably corrupting tendencies: "But avarice drives the native to the sea, / Fictitious wants all thoughts of ease controul . . . / Then to some distant clime explores his way, / Bold avarice spurs him on—he must obey" (*PPF* 3:10). Massachusetts, then, is a figure for an empire at once in ascendance and decline, paradoxically proud of its role in defending liberty and freedom against British tyranny, and enslaved and governed by the same ambition and avarice that drove it to repel the British in the first place. Ironically, Massachusetts' compulsive mercantilism and consumerism suggest that beneath the veneer of the rhetoric of values adhering to the U.S. empire for liberty, corruptive British mercantilist tendencies still hold sway, at least over Massachusetts' political economy and manners.

After passing through New York and Pennsylvania, Freneau travels to Maryland and then Virginia. Once more, his would-be pleasing agrarian view is occluded by the reign of unenlightened commerce—by the excesses of liberty and individualism on the part of whites, and by the enslaved condition of blacks. These poems are crucial in that, coupled with "Massachusetts," "Rhode Island," and "Connecticut," they indict the "rising empire" for becoming less "an empire for liberty" and more an empire for commerce that must inevitably—for Freneau—subsume and overwhelm the nation's foundational values, virtues, and principles, its democratic manners, customs, and laws. In "Maryland" and "Virginia," Freneau excoriates gross excesses of consumptive desire that drive the nation's paracolonial investments in the plantation economies abroad and, crucially, at home. In "The Rising Empire," the United States is to the plantation economies of the West Indies as its urban centers are to the exploitative plantations of its own rural countryside.

In "Maryland," Freneau begins by marking the relatively short time span in which Baltimore has arisen from a coastal area inhabited by the "sloth[ful]" and "thoughtless native" in "wretched huts" to a city "High in renown" that "envied commerce draws" (*PPF* 3:15). Maybe so, but once more Freneau's antimercantile themes intrude on the would-be encomium turned satire; a string of mock-heroic couplets begin the poem's shift in tone by chastising Maryland for trading away like Rhode

Island its natural resources to acquire foreign hard goods—European and West Indian among them—and by so doing incurring not only a trade but a *morals* deficit. "[E]nvied commerce" thereby corrupts republican values by conveying to U.S. shores degenerate European empires' tastes and manners:

> Though rich at home, to foreign lands they stray,
> For foreign trappings trade the wealth away.
> Politest manners through their towns prevail,
> And pleasure revels, though their funds should fail. . . . (*PPF* 3:15)

Such foppish extravagance marking Baltimore genteel living only seemingly exists in unrelated relationship to its own slave "colonies" in rural Maryland. There, "The sad master strays amidst his grounds, / Directs his negroes, or reviews his hounds" (*PPF* 3:56). Plantation slavery, from which Maryland's "natural wealth"—tobacco and cotton— derives, creates in the state's "rural scene" a kind of monstrous rustic. Recalling famous critiques by Bryan Edwards regarding the perverse reasons for excessive West Indian hospitality, the speaker notes, "If some chance guest arrives in weary plight, / [The master] more than bids him welcome for the night; Kind to profusion, he spares no pains to please, / Gives him the products of his fields and trees" (*PPF* 3:16). Thus Freneau's Maryland poem brilliantly connects the corruption of goods and commerce of urban port cities like Baltimore to plantation economies both within and without the rising U.S. empire. The emporium of hard goods pouring in and out of Baltimore and into the Maryland countryside stems from participation in chattel slavery at home and paracolonial activity abroad. Baltimore and London exist in exploitative relation to rural Maryland, then, as they do to the colonial West Indian "periphery."[20] Before leaving "Maryland," the speaker delivers a final indictment of how the master's silver shelf evokes the perversions and corruptions of U.S. commerce: "On his rich board shines plenty from her source, /—The meanest dish of all his own discourse" (*PPF* 3:16), which is to say, silverware (perhaps derived from West Indian specie) and stores with which Maryland's rural masters host their visitors "to profusion" in a grotesque economy of manners descended from the sordid discourse of slavery marking Maryland's rural plantation economy.

If in Virginia Freneau seeks a reprieve, he is sorely disappointed. Freneau doesn't wait beyond the opening couplets of this poem to launch into his condemnation of Virginia's plantation economy, suggesting that by the time he wrote "Virginia," his mock-epic tone had so consumed his project that it became necessary for him to leave it off. After all, Jefferson, Freneau's Republican party hero, had declared Virginia to be the seat of the rising empire for liberty in *Notes* several years earlier and thus Freneau's poetic encounter with the manners, laws, and customs of Jefferson's homeland suggests deeply sedimented feelings of resentment on Freneau's part about Southern Republicans' duplicity and betrayal of the nation's putative democratic values. Freneau dismisses any notion that Virginia's corruption can be overlooked merely because Virginia is rich in natural resources, or by recalling that Jamestown was the first settlement built by pioneering British colonists: "This was her praise— but what can years avail, / When times succeeding see her efforts fail!" (*PPF* 3:17). Instead, Virginia in the 1790s is characterized by luxury and extravagance at the expense of producing serious "art" or respectable living. In Virginia, "herds of slaves parade their sooty band / From the rough plough to save the fopling's hand" (*PPF* 3:17); white Virginians, West Indian creole-like "foplings," are said to be "Averse to toil," and addicted to a degenerate lifestyle. The "native . . . / heaps up wealth from luxury and pride, / Exports the produce of a thousand plains, / Nor fears a rival, to divide his gains" (*PPF* 3:18), thereby embodying the precise degeneration and debasement said to mark the stereotypical West Indian creole featured in eighteenth-century transatlantic writings like Long's and Edwards's. As in Maryland, the degenerate condition of urban and rural life in Virginia are inextricably bound to the exploitation of the stylized black slave, who each day from the fields "Bind[s] up the recent wound, with many a groan" (*PPF* 3:18). Freneau, who frequently traded at the mouth of the Potomac, employs in the text's final stanza his characteristic U.S. poet-trader viewpoint of surveillance that I have stressed marks the unique speakerly location of his West Indies poems: "Yet here the sailor views with wondering eye / Impoverished fields that near their margins lie, / Mercantile towns, where languor holds her reign, / And boors inactive, on the exhausted plain" (*PPF* 3:18). The "fops" of the city thereby function as a more urbane and vain version of the white boors who rule the rural plantations.

Freneau in "Santa Cruz" draws an analogy between the slaves of the West Indies and the patriots in the Continental Army as communities similarly oppressed by European violence and commercial greed. If he calls into being in that poem a "Northern" shepherd who might somehow rescue the plantation economies of the West Indies from European tyranny by instead founding a less exploitative economy that relies for its subsistence on commodities other than the monstrous sugar cane, he despairs in 1792 in "The Rising Empire"—particularly in *his* notes on the state of Virginia—that U.S. planters and mercantilists ironically reproduce the very tyrannical tendencies of European and West Indian planters, merchants, and lawgivers.[21] The corruptive political economies of the West Indies thus overlap with and collapse into those of the U.S. North, Middle Atlantic, and South. As such, Freneau's Jamaica poems, even as they focus in their indictments on British mercantile degeneracy in the West Indies, seem ironically on both conscious and unconscious levels to recognize the unsustainable strategies of paracolonial containment—negation, abstraction, and displacement—that provide for their contrasting affirmation of the would-be regenerative rising U.S. empire for liberty. Put differently, Freneau's scathing indictment of the already descending would-be rising empire in his fractured epic of the same name renders transparent the undercurrent of paracolonial ambivalence informing his West Indies poems.

Perhaps unsurprisingly, Freneau wrote a poem—"Commerce" (1797)—suggesting that only by avoiding "foreign" commerce altogether might the United States preserve its republican virtues. The poem's headnote states, "That internal commerce only, promotes the morals of a country situated like America, and prevents its growth of luxury, and its consequent vices" (*PPF* 3:220):

The product of the furrow'd plain—
Transferr'd to foreign shores,
To pamper pride and please the vain
The reign of kings restores:
Hence, every vice the sail imports,
The glare of crowns, the pomp of courts,
And War, with all his crimson train!
Thus man design'd to till the ground,
A stranger to himself is found—
Is sent to toil on yonder wave,
Is made the dreary ocean's sport,
Since commerce first to avarice gave
To sail the ocean round. (*PPF* 3:220)

Perhaps embedded within such a critique, or even inspiring it, is Freneau's own guilt at having participated in paracolonialism by sailing vessels destined for the West Indian trades that specifically sought in the post-Revolutionary period to exploit ongoing European warfare in the Caribbean theater for purposes of U.S. economic benefit. Yet Freneau chooses to deemphasize such agency in the poem's final stanza, emphasizing instead how in the Caribbean Sea "hostile navies . . . bend [Americans] to their will" (*PPF* 3:221). Likewise, even as Freneau indicts the United States for participating in international commerce, he does so by deflecting chief responsibility for the corruption of the nation's foundational values and institutions onto outside forces that invade inward—"every vice the sail imports." Nowhere in the poem does he acknowledge, according to the reciprocal exchanges attending to trade between nations and their colonies (and paracolonies), how the Republic itself exports "vice" outward. Such exportation occurs not only to the Western territories where, according to Freneau's preferred course of U.S. empire building, his readers might "find their wants supplied" (*PPF* 3:221), but also to Europe, Africa, and the West Indies.

By juxtaposing Freneau's West Indies poems with his mock-epic "The Rising Empire," we can better see how as Freneau travels North and South along the eastern seaboard of the United States and from thence into the Caribbean, he becomes less and less sure that, indeed, the rising U.S. empire is in any significant measure distinct from the British empire whose corruption his West Indies poems seek to expose. Accordingly, the economic, cultural, and social cross-currents between the one-time British North American colonies and the still-British colonies in the West Indies seem more and more mutually formative, U.S. paracolonialism abroad and internal colonialism at home eroding the boundaries between a would-be regenerate rising U.S. empire on the one hand, and a degenerate and descending British one on the other.

Chapter 4

The West Indies, Commerce, and a Play for U.S. Empire

Recovering J. Robinson's The Yorker's Stratagem *(1792)*

Hamilton's bold design of empire depends on a U.S. man of commerce who, backed by a strong union, a powerful federal government, and a crafty corps of diplomatic negotiators, would become a central actor in the drama for U.S. hemispheric ascendance. Citizens and noncitizens reading his revolutionary ideas in rural and urban North America were no doubt asking one another how a *virtuous* man of empire might look, think, feel, and behave. How might he be made to perform the ideals of the proposed Constitution? Clearly U.S. mercantile men existed in the literal sense, yet how might they be transformed into an emblem of the emerging national culture, a model of republicanism, and a symbol of national pride and hemispheric superiority? For a time, Hamilton himself came to embody the answer to these questions in the national imaginary. The fate of the Constitution hanging in the balance, Hamilton rushed to the New York state ratifying convention floor in 1787 and recited from memory the bulk of the arguments he set forth in *The Federalist*, it always having been his intention that these writings be read aloud and performed (Schachner 221). As Clinton Rossiter remarks, "The story of how Hamilton persuaded and plotted and bullied his way over the months to the narrowest of victories in the New York convention is an epic of American politics that deserves to be better known" (ix). Rossiter's account of Hamilton's statesmanship—the persuading, the plotting, and the bullying—gestures to the ways in which Hamilton seized on multiple and at times conflicting modes of performance in order to effect his vision of American governance.

His exertions on behalf of the Constitution did not go unrecognized by the nation's citizens. They lauded his eleventh-hour heroics, memorialized his patriotism, and anointed him a "founding father." Through public ceremony his very likeness became a surrogate for federalism and the rising U.S. empire of commerce. Between the fall of 1787, when the Constitution was adopted, and 1789, when it officially became the law of

the land, Hamilton was treated as a national hero like no other statesman save Washington, who largely endorsed Hamilton's views on
empire. Merchants sold busts of Hamilton and affixed his visage alongside the "American eagle" on shop windows and doors. Even more dramatic, parades were held in Hamilton's honor. New York traders and
merchants erected floats in the shape of merchant and military vessels
and placed likenesses of Hamilton at the helm (Rogow 126).[1] When they
were advised by more solemn minds that Washington, not Hamilton, was
President, they allowed Washington's likeness to ride alongside that of
his Treasury Secretary. Hamilton even had a battleship named after him
in the 1790s as a tribute to his role in securing the ratification of the
Constitution, the only founding father to be so honored (Ferling 375).
His appetite for glory notoriously omnivorous, Hamilton must have
been gratified that his name had become synonymous with the commercial empire he had fashioned, the public trade in his image serving as
an especially prepossessing endorsement of his policies. Such pomp and
recognition would have been further reassuring given his tenuous status
in the national imaginary as a "Creole Bastard."

This chapter focuses on the resituation of performances on behalf of
Hamilton and his commercial view of empire in a specific performative
space, the theater, and in a particular play, J. Robinson's *The Yorker's
Stratagem; or, Banana's Wedding*. In a 1794 letter to his family, trader
James Brown, brother of famous Philadelphia novelist Charles Brockden
Brown, urged, "It is time to decide what we ought to think of the real
utility of theatres. A patriot had said . . . that theatres are a kind of priest-
hood exercised over thoughts. We should examine whether our theatres
should not in future be set aside for mercantile purposes. This question
is of greatest importance and I move that it may be referred to the [Phil-
adelphia] Committee of Public Instruction" (qtd. in Bingham 150–51).
Set on a remote, unnamed West Indian island, *The Yorker's Stratagem*
appears on its surface to have little to do with James Brown's imperative
about the theater as a space for "public instruction" in U.S. commercial
policy. First performed three years into Alexander Hamilton's tenure as
Washington's aggressively procommerce Secretary of the Treasury, Robinson's drama has remained obscure since its publication in 1792. It has
gone virtually unremarked by literary scholars and is alluded to but a
handful of times, often imprecisely, by historians of U.S. drama.[2]

Still, these fleeting references to Robinson and his play are telling.
Famed playwright and drama historian William Dunlap, the "Father of
American Drama," accords Robinson considerable praise in the few sentences he devotes to Robinson's play. He notes that *The Yorker's Stratagem*
evinces "much dramatic skill" and an inventive use of dialogue "well
suited to the characters" (221). Further, having viewed a live perform-

ance of the play in New York, Dunlap indicates that *The Yorker's Stratagem* met with "universal applause" by theater audiences there and in Philadelphia (221–22). An anonymous reviewer with the New York *Daily Advertiser* corroborates Dunlap's observations, remarking that "the public have not been better entertaind by a dramatic piece" in some time, stressing how the play features "a variety of very striking characters . . . [with] novelty to commend them" and "a very good imitation of the Creole dialect" owing to many members of the cast, including perhaps Robinson, having resided for "some time in the West Indies" (qtd. in Odell 1:306). Citing Dunlap as a source, late nineteenth-century drama historian George O. Seilhamer lauds *The Yorker's Stratagem* for its "originality," suggesting that Robinson "was a better playwright than player" (2:345, 364).[3]

If briefly and in abstract terms, these accounts gesture to some of Robinson's formal achievements—his inventiveness, his originality, his compelling use of dialogue. *The Yorker's Stratagem* is far more significant than they acknowledge, however, not only formally but historically and thematically as well. By measuring the play against relevant historical contexts and interpretive paradigms, I wish to rescue *The Yorker's Stratagem* from obscurity by pointing out the play's artistic achievements, as well as its significance as a theatrical corollary to Hamilton's ambitious plan for U.S. dominance in the West Indian trades. The warm reception to Robinson's linguistic innovations suggests the intriguing polyglossic affinities of urban theater audiences during the early national period, and Robinson's appropriation of conventions and figures from Renaissance and eighteenth-century literature set in and against the "New World" gestures to the play's manifold "creole" properties. Robinson's play also provides a cultural window into the ways in which Hamilton's imperial designs were shaped by, and responded to, an especially turbulent period of mercantile expansion and contraction in the Western Hemisphere. Robinson wrote his plays in response to a notice posted in the *Federal Gazette*, "in which dramatic writing in this country was advocated" (Seilhamer 2:324).[4] Dedicated "[t]o the generous Patrons of the Drama, and to the worthy Sons of Columbia who feel an interest in the American Stage," *The Yorker's Stratagem*, this chapter reveals, evokes a triumphant political, commercial, and cultural expansionism while simultaneously mystifying by means of devices like imposture and blackface the ways in which U.S. rhetoric about a budding commercial empire relied on paradoxical postcolonial *and* imperialist tendencies.[5]

Yankees, Creoles, and Slaves: Robinson's Circumatlantic Artifices

A two-act afterpiece or farce set in the West Indies, *The Yorker's Stratagem* centers on the heroic actions of the "Yorker," Amant, an Anglo-American businessman. Amant seeks to win the hand of Sophia Bellange, a West Indian "Creole girl of fortune" (12) with whom he fell in love during their boarding school days together in New York. Amant's voyage to the West Indies aboard a U.S. merchant vessel has been prompted, we are told, by a frantic letter he has received from Sophia in which she informs him of her guardian's tyranny. So named owing to his unscrupulous practices as proprietor of a West Indian trading house, Fingercash refuses Sophia access to the inheritance that her parents have left her, which he stores with other monies and pilfered goods in his miser's strongbox. Shortly after his arrival on the island, Amant learns that Sophia is not Fingercash's only victim. Fingercash intends to ruin his daughter Louisa's life and future as well by marrying her off to a black planter named Banana in exchange for a tidy sum. By means of a superior "stratagem" and an ever-widening circle of collaborators, Amant eventually thwarts Fingercash's evil designs against the acceptable boundaries of sentiment. With the cooperation of the ship's captain, his stratagem entails disguising himself as a "Yankee" trader with a lucrative cargo of lumber, livestock, and other items. By proffering his phony stock of goods, Amant plans to seduce the avaricious Fingercash into "exchanging" Miss Bellange and her tidy inheritance.

Although the play's character types and stage devices might seem conventional, Robinson's use of the stage Yankee is highly inventive and relates in powerful ways to the "superior entrepreneurial spirit" that Hamilton identifies as characteristic of the rapidly emerging (and performative) U.S. man of commerce in his writings, a figure he elaborates on, we have seen, in *The Federalist* (1787–88). Far from being unrelated to the formation of a national character and culture, Robinson's play is the cultural analogue par excellence to the push for U.S. commercial empire in the West Indies during the last decades of the eighteenth century espoused by Hamilton. Toward that end, a fascinating part of Amant's artifice involves "trading" on his "Yankee" ignorance. When asked by the captain how he plans to secure a meeting with Fingercash, Amant replies ironically, "With his own weapons, artifice and chicane" (6). He then unveils the disguise he will adopt:

You must introduce me as supercargo, a true Yankey, sent out by daddy with a cargo of lumber, hog and poultry, to make daddy's son a squire. My apparent simplicity will ensure him a gull, and me an opportunity of seeing my mistresse, and contriving some means to get her and her fortune out of his hands. (6)

According to his statement, Amant intends to embrace the West Indian proclivity for artifice so as to gain access to the island's mercantile culture in the furtherance of his stratagem to secure Sophia and her inheritance. His challenge of keeping proliferating identities distinct—the virtuous "real" self from the tainted, corrupt artificer—is the burden of the chiaroscuric agent of U.S. empire building. As the ship's captain remarks on seeing Amant as Jonathan for the first time, "your coming ashore in this disguise has something the appearance of a spy" (5). The captain's observation ironically captures the role of counterintelligence Amant fulfills in Robinson's play—actor as agent, agent as spy, and spy as (model) subject for U.S. empire.

As part of his complex "Jonathan" characterization, Robinson includes traits of the "Jonathan" type inaugurated in Royall Tyler's foundational U.S. drama *The Contrast* (1787).[6] Readers of Tyler's play will recognize affinities between Amant's "Jonathan Norrard" disguise and Tyler's character. Like Tyler's Jonathan, Jonathan Norrard speaks in a thickly accented rural dialect, carries himself in an uncouth way, and is prideful about U.S. democratic and republican principles. For example, when a duplicitous innkeeper named Acid asks "Jonathan" about his father's name, Amant responds indignantly, "What! do'nt you know he? I did'nt think there was a dog in the parish but knew Old Caleb at the saw-mill" (8). Later in the exchange, as Jonathan is blathering on about the democratic virtues of his hometown of "Stony-Brook," he unwittingly reveals his father's name to be "Epram Norrard." Amant then feigns surprise when Acid refers to him as "Mr. Norrard," exclaiming, "But how the plague did you make out to know my name? I'll swear you must be a witch" (8). Amant's artifice has the desired effect. As Acid directs the Yankee "jack-ass!" to his friend Fingercash's counting house, he jokes to the audience in an aside how Fingercash "will make it [his] study to profit by so valuable an acquaintance" (8). Amant exploits their perception of him as an exploitable bumpkin on his first mission as a supercargo by mimicking his approach as Jonathan to Fingercash's mercantile house in a highly absurd manner. When a slave reports Amant's arrival to Fingercash, he tells his master in a stylized creole dialect that he knows the visitor is a Yankee because "Dem tan so, dem hab salt fish in one hand, and trokey in todder" (9),[7] referring to Amant's clumsy posture and the cargo samples he carries as "bait" for Fingercash.[8]

Tyler's rustic, uncomplicated Jonathan is not the only character shaping Robinson's circumatlantic Jonathan. Also influential is the titular figure of *Jonathan Corncob, Loyal American Refugee*, published contemporaneously with *The Contrast* in 1787 and authored by a British West Indian who had extensive firsthand knowledge of the United States. The setting of the novel alternates between New York, Massachusetts, and the West Indies and features a New England loyalist during the Revolution who fancies himself a sophisticate and who endures a series of Atlantic adventures and unrealized romances. Egotistical and inevitably disappointed in his schemes, Jonathan Corncob nonetheless displays a talent for daring escapes from would-be pursuers, including U.S. revolutionaries. As Robert Heilman remarks, "Jonathan [Corncob] is a New Englander who can take care of himself by hook or by crook, who can take advantage of what the situation offers. . . . He is an itinerant rather than a true Yankee. He is undependable, superficial; some basic stability is lacking. He is on the fence between the picaresque hero and the real Yankee" (73–74). Robinson's text's action and allusions reveal that his composite Jonathan is as indebted to Jonathan Corncob as it is to Tyler's Jonathan. For instance, when Acid serves Amant and the captain a bottle of wine, Amant says to him, "Come, landlord, won't you take a glass? Come, be bold, I don't value a glass of wine a corn-cob, not I" (7). Robinson's reference to Jonathan Corncob is more than a comical allusion. Many in the audience would have been as aware of Corncob as of Tyler's character. They would have understood Jonathan Norrard's fabricated urbanity, his picaresque adventure throughout the Atlantic and the Caribbean, and his amorous delusions, to derive from the former rather than the latter Jonathan. Robinson's decision to conjoin the two Jonathans suggests that he intends for Jonathan Norrard to function as a hybrid caricature of the adaptable U.S. man of commerce that Hamilton describes. By developing the stage Yankee in such a provocative and ingenious way, Robinson invented, to the certain delight of his audience, one of the first fictional confidence men, and certainly the first Yankee confidence man—Amant.[9] The *real* man behind the Yankee mask, the shrewd U.S. businessman who seems despite or *because* of his mask instinctively to comprehend and control the West Indian commercial and colonial scene, is a match for any merchant man. When the soon-to-be upbraided Fingercash, alluding to the received "Yankee" stereotypes described above, exclaims in an aside to the audience, "How I do long to pray upon a bacon-fed Yankey, or porgy-headed Bermudian!" (9), he knows not of—or to whom—he speaks: the Hamiltonian man of empire and a largely pro-Federalist audience.

Amant's willingness to don a Yankee mask in the furtherance of his stratagem is significant on textual and metatextual levels. Amant, like his creator, demonstrates a facility for manipulating "creole" traits that mark him according to the terms of European colonialist discourse as stereotypically primitive. Thus the actions of playwright and character alike betray the seductiveness of trading simultaneously in multiple realms—goods, values, identities—and the exertion required to discern the authentic from the counterfeit, the virtuous from the scandalous, and the pure from the tainted. How does one positioned beyond the idealized stage of Robinson's play, in the urban spaces of the United States, tell the "real" or "virtuous" U.S. man of commerce from his West

Indian impostor if the West Indian impostor is but another version of oneself?

Amant's storyline is but one of many that converge as Robinson's drama unfolds. The play's subtitle, "Banana's Wedding," denotes a subplot that causes Amant to redraw the boundaries of his stratagem. In addition, the subplot suggests ways in which the Hamiltonian man of empire depends on a second term for the successful dissemination at home and abroad of his professedly "pure" political and economic values. That term is not, as U.S. nationalist rhetoric suggests, its opposite but its constitutive double, a shadow plot of the U.S. hemispheric dream of empire: hemispheric slavery. What Robinson's play reveals is how a budding U.S. nationalism imagined itself through and against the West Indies. West Indian creole culture and European colonialism in the West Indies functioned in the U.S. imagination as oppositional and thus legitimating figures for empire, and simultaneously provided Northern Federalists a means of displacing domestic anxieties about racial contagion and slavery. This West Indian–centered discourse justified the commercial and geographical expansion of the United States across national borders. Yet these expansionist impulses shaped, and were shaped by, a highly ambivalent discursive stance toward an emergent series of crises within the nation's borders. Robinson's shadow plot to Amant's triumphal quest for West Indian women, wealth, and commodities raises the specter of such discursive ambivalence.

The specific figure that concretizes these tensions in *The Yorker's Stratagem*, West Indian miscegenation, signals the widespread contamination of the play's West Indian society by European colonialism and highlights the contrasting purity of the United States, its culture, and its institutions. The unscrupulous West Indian merchant Fingercash emblematizes the island's abandonment of the Constitutional principles upholding the rising U.S. empire. Although he schemes to fleece Amant of his ship's cargo, in the process abandoning all sense of economic and legal fairness, Fingercash's foremost crime is his plot to marry his white creole daughter by a previous marriage to a black planter. He justifies his decision solely on the basis of material gain: "[Banana] has got a fine estate, and however defective he may be with regard to education, and that bauble sentiment, it will be amply made up for by his cash and canefields" (9). Fingercash's exchange of his daughter's virtue for hard cash, and his unwillingness to listen to Louisa's entreaties about "breaking *the laws* of delicacy and society, by joining two persons whose souls are so very opposite" (20; emphasis added), signify the corruption of "blood"—the delicate boundaries between "black" and "white" established by U.S. cultural mores. They also predict a U.S. intervention under the pretext of fostering within the island "pure" moral and ethical Constitutional values that "blood" is made to figure in U.S. jurisprudence. In 1786, Thomas Jefferson had drafted a bill forbidding interracial marriage, and the same year Massachusetts passed a law prohibiting "a marriage between a person of free condition and a slave, or between a white person and a negro, or between a white person and a mulatto" (Sollors 398). Between 1800 and 1900, thirty-eight U.S. states would act accordingly. Thus the play's central metaphor—miscegenation—exposes the contaminated character of the West Indies on the one hand and divulges the island's need for the "purifying" effects of U.S. republican democracy on the other. Moreover, Amant's "heroic" act of "purification" on behalf of the island's vulnerable West Indian (white) women anticipates the parallel legal cleansing of U.S. "blood" in the nineteenth century by the proliferation of antimiscegenation statutes.[10]

The hemispheric cleansing of European colonialism's miscegenetic tendencies and effects in the West Indies by the United States in Robinson's drama is undertaken not only by Amant but also by a second U.S. mercantile man who likewise proves an able impersonator. Amant's compatriot, Ledger, plots to thwart the unholy marriage of Louisa to Banana for two reasons. The first is obvious enough: Louisa has promised herself to Ledger, and thus her impending marriage to Banana offends both sensibility and sentiment. The second reason is somewhat more complicated and concerns how Ledger came "to be" on this West Indian island in the first place, a tale that the text's dialogue only alludes to but which the play's contemporary audience would have fully understood. Throughout most of the 1790s, England and France were at war, and their conflicts always spilled over into the two nations' colonial peripheries, especially the West Indies. Meanwhile, the United States under Washington's leadership and at Hamilton's prompting had declared itself a neutral party to the conflict. By doing so, the United States hoped to benefit economically by becoming carriers of commercial goods for both England and France in the West Indies. Yet the two European empires ignored Hamilton's machinations and proceeded to seize U.S. ships and cargo and imprison U.S. mercantile men in West Indian jails, often without trial. In short, trading in the West Indies became a truly treacherous enterprise. The imprisoned sailors and lost commerce became symbols of the United States' inability to "back up" its bold talk about a burgeoning U.S. commercial empire.

The predation of British naval and pirate ships on U.S. merchant vessels is the cause for Ledger's being stranded on Robinson's textual island.[11] Labeled a "beggarly adventurer" (21) by his "master" and threatened with re-imprisonment, Ledger toils like a slave for Fingercash, who has bailed him out of jail in order to exploit his considerable talents as a merchant clerk.[12] His chances of securing his release from captivity initially appear at least as remote as Louisa's prospects for avoiding bondage to Banana. When Louisa drops to her knees, begging her father to reconsider selling his "child to a being that the most abandoned of our sex would loath and spurn at" and protesting that "the very thought strikes me with madness," her father derides her performance. He quips that perhaps her "knight-errant" might rescue her with his "quiver of quills and a shield of parchment? Ha, ha, ha" (20). Louisa's plea indicates that she has become infected by Euro-American colonialist notions that link miscegenation with insanity. For her, the mere prospect of building a home with a black man amid West Indian black culture affronts her domestic sensibility to the point of "madness." In order to alleviate her distressed mental condition, Ledger plants seeds of rebellion that unsettle Fingercash's own mind. Invoking the Hegelian dialectic of the "enslaved master, the unmastered slave," Ledger warns Fingercash, "Take care, Sir, how you threaten: recollect your villainous practices have put you in my power, not me in yours" (21). Fingercash's jest about Ledger's "quills" and "parchment" ultimately proves indi(c)ting. Ledger, as his name denotes, possesses islands of evidence concerning his oppressor's illegal business transactions. A "ledger" also refers variously to fishing bait, line, or tackle; the horizontal timber attached to the uprights of a scaffold; and a stone slab placed over a grave. Why one would want to scheme against a man whose very name denotes lynching and burial (the line, the scaffold, the grave) is mystifying enough. What ultimately undoes Fingercash is the most unlikely le(d)gerdemain. Ledger proposes saving face by performing that which he is determined to avert: Louisa's miscegenetic marriage.

As I hope is already evident, Robinson's drama relies on a series of binaries for meaning, including virtue and immorality, industry and exploitation, freedom and slavery, and justice and illegitimacy. Yet as I have also been suggesting, the play's meaning pivots on a series of interrelated devices that threaten to blur its distinctions, among them stratagem, mimicry, and imposture. Ultimately all these things circulate within an economy of values pitting U.S. racial purity and hemispheric ascendance on the one hand against West Indian racial contamination and European colonial degeneracy on the other. At once metonym and metaphor for West Indian degeneracy, the play's black culture and characters provide for, provoke, and sustain multiple revolutions that upset the balance and character of power by play's end, ironically without ever having rebelled themselves. Robinson, in turn, exploits the specter of black slave rebellion for purposes of theatrical recognition and prestige, fomenting a series of dazzling tropes that depend for effect on the accrual of "value" that attains to "blackness" in relation to "whiteness" in theaters throughout the hemisphere and Europe—in England,

France, the United States, and the West Indies. Before revealing the winners and losers in the play's final scene of virtual rebellion, we might first consider how the always already changing face of West Indian "blackness" managed to perform so much cultural work on and off Robinson's stage.

Revolutionary Performances, (Un)Performing Revolutions

What significance should we attach to the fact that *The Yorker's Stratagem* is a play written by a U.S. writer set amid the plantation economies of the West Indies featuring characters performing in blackface? Judging from the prohibitions against such performances in many Southern U.S. cities at the time of Robinson's production of his play, quite a lot. Because of Robinson's blackface casting, his play could not have been produced in many places in the South in the way it was performed on New York and Philadelphia stages. Thus the play could not have been performed at all, or at least it is difficult to conceive how it might be performed in whiteface. The material realities at the turn of the nineteenth century surrounding this unusual theatrical phenomenon are revealing and important. They produce a set of issues regarding regional and national identity that are dependent on pairs of mutually constitutive terms such as empire and nation building, North and South, abolition and slavery, black and white, stage and society, and actor, slave, and citizen subject. If we consider these terms according to the multilayered trope of miscege[-]nation so crucial to Robinson's play, the issues become even more palpable.

Charleston's theaters at the turn of the century are singular for the ways in which they regulated relations between race and drama. John Lambert, a British visitor to North America in the first decade of the nineteenth century, writes in his popular and widely read travelogue with equal amounts of dismay and disgust about the adaptation and appropriation of European dramas by U.S. theater companies. Lambert remarks that entire acts of canonical English plays are "converted wholly in an *American scene*" and that "allusions and claptraps" intended for British characters are "transferred" to American ones. Writes Lambert, "In this manner most of our dramatic pieces are obliged to be pruned of all their luxuriant compliments to *John Bull*, before they can be rendered palatable to American republicans" (374). Lambert's comments on the widespread creolization of British drama by U.S. theater directors, and his implication that American mongrelization of British drama detracts from a play's value, reflect the paternalistic, condescending attitudes characterizing much of his *Travels* (1810). Yet his comment is compelling for what it suggests about U.S. theater during the early national period. Many scholars have treated early U.S. drama as a genre scarcely worth examining in light of its derivative nature and the alleged inferiority of the U.S.-authored plays to European ones.[13] Lambert's comment suggests that we may not be asking the right questions about drama in the early national period. His diatribe against the cultural hybridity of U.S. theater productions ironically indicates the importance of examining scripts, theater reviews, contemporary drama histories, and other sources in order to assess how extensive U.S. postcolonial adaptation and appropriation of European drama was, and with what material consequences for the early national culture.[14]

In his extended discussion of the Charleston theater, Lambert gestures to one material consequence:

I expected to find the Charleston stage well supplied with *sooty negroes*, who would have performed the *African* and *Savage* characters in the dramatic pieces, to the life; instead of which, the delusion was even worse than on our own stage; for so far from employing *real negroes*, the performers would not even condescend to *blacken* their faces, or dress in any manner resembling an African. This I afterwards learnt was occasioned by motives of *policy*, lest the negroes in Charleston should conceive, from being represented on the stage, and having their colour, dress, manners, and customs imitated by the white people, that they were very important personages; and might take improper liberties in consequence of it. For this reason also, Othello, and other plays, are not allowed to be performed, nor are any of the negroes, or people of colour permitted to visit the theatre. (374)

Lambert describes a form of U.S. appropriation of British drama that is not a postcolonial transformation of authoritative English roles into American ones. Nor is it a performance of blackface asserting an anxious superiority over black slaves. Instead, it is a neocolonial act of white-face, a parody of the postmodern enthusiasm for race-blind casting.[15] Lambert keenly observes how the steadfast refusal by Charlestonians to use "sooty negroes" in the performance of "black" character roles does not evince a more humanistic orientation by white Southerners toward blackness and slavery than by their British counterparts. Instead, Lambert suggests such proscriptions involving racial casting indicate that the South's racial "delusion was even worse" than Europe's. As described by Lambert, Charleston theater practices signal an involuted, prismatic racial pathology marked by the manic obsession of preventing "*African and Savage* characters" from being performed "to the life." Lambert's observations, confirmed by extant newspaper accounts and theater records, suggest that theater companies were engaged in a systematic washing of heroic black characters white.[16] Black mannerisms, speech patterns, gestures, and costumes were cleansed white so as to prevent blacks from getting any ideas "that they were very important personages." Denied access to the theater, many members of Charleston's diasporic black population, including significant numbers of well-educated mulattos recently arrived from the French West Indies, may well have had the impression that white society's impulse to exorcise blackness from its stages had more to do with white obsession with its fetishized "others," and less to do with blacks themselves taking "improper liberties" as a result of being "represented" and "imitated" on stage. They might have surmised, accordingly, that the reversal of attitudes by whites toward imitating "blacks" in public evinced a metastasizing fear about the unstable boundaries between whiteness and blackness, self and other. Whites were not banishing *blacks* from the stage in Charleston. They were newly banishing representations of themselves representing a black other. Some whites may have even been unconsciously recoiling from the moment that Michael Taussig identifies in *Mimesis and Alterity* as "mimesis turned on itself": "the self is inscribed in the Alter that the self needs to define itself against" creating "mimetic excess—mimetic self-awareness, mimesis turned on itself" (252). Whatever the verdict of blacks themselves, the decision to whitewash black character roles stands as an especially anxious statement about the tautological specularity surrounding race and performance in antebellum Southern culture.

Yet South Carolinians were not alone in their paranoia. Many West Indian colonialists came to proscribe the acts of countermimesis—of blacks imitating whites—that were a widespread phenomenon in the West Indies. Such performances contributed on more than one occasion to creating the very insurrectionary atmosphere Charleston's white residents feared, moments when blacks became the imitators of savage whites. Such imitative acts usually occurred during festivals known as Jonkunnu (John Canoe), present-day manifestations of which include "carnival." Jonkunnu was part of the retinue of Christmas holiday activities wherein blacks, with their masters' permission, devised performances that mocked their white masters by imitating, in hyperbolic form, white fashion, language usage, and bodily expression. Although masters usually found these performances amusing, laughter turned to shrieks of horror on several occasions: West Indian slave rebellions were often orchestrated to coincide with Jonkunnu and related performances.[17] Moreover, by 1792 a slave revolution that patterned itself after the U.S. Revolution of twenty years earlier, and in which the Haitian revolutionary Henri Christophe had fought, had been underway for several years and would eventually result in Haitian independence in 1804. The revolution led to thousands of West Indians and their slaves resettling in cities up and down the Atlantic seaboard, including Savannah, Charleston, Newport News (Virginia), Baltimore, New York, and Philadelphia, as well as New Orleans on the Gulf Coast. After the Haitian Revolution began, and the creole and African refugees began pouring in by the thousands to lucrative U.S. ports, both Southern and Northern leaders took fewer and fewer chances with hemispheric influences on their black slave culture. Their precautions led to perhaps the most repressive half-century in U.S. slave history. Lambert was witness to its unfolding. Whites at once imitating and not imitating blacks; blacks at once imitating and not imitating whites: the circumatlantic "theater" of mimicry and mockery, of indelibly stained "blood" lines, of alterity's violent excesses, of "mimesis turned on itself." These are the things that Robinson stylizes in his comic drama about a virtuous United States and a degenerate West Indies.

White West Indians were known to be especially keen imitators of black culture—of black speech patterns, cultural forms of expression like dance, black fashion, and so on. Thus Robinson's inclusion of performances in blackface and of black cultural forms of communication, including dialect and signifying, should be considered in that context and compared with what was occurring on the Charleston stage in order to appreciate fully the significance of his cross-cultural achievement. Also, theater had many detractors in the North as well as the South during the first decades of the nation's existence. Undoubtedly such widespread opposition to drama contributed to the relatively modest output of original, U.S.-written plays during the period. The theater's most vitriolic critics included ministers, politicians, leaders of women's groups, and other concerned citizens who felt that rather than inculcating national values, theater polluted an already depraved urban citizenry. Theater, according to them, was democracy run amuck; as in Charleston, mimesis was the trope on which crisis centered. While playwrights and theater managers insisted that portraying vice and buffoonery on stage in the context of sentimentally sound dramas had the effect of inculcating virtue, theater's adversaries categorically denied that drama had any ameliorative effect. For them, not only did theater promote immorality but it portrayed contrary behavior in such grotesque proportions that the clowns, seducers, and thieves seen on stage surpassed in their vileness anything one confronted in the street. Opponents of the theater were also convinced that theater fostered criminality: seduced by the abominations they had witnessed on stage, audiences were highly likely to mimic them once outside the theater.[18] The Foucauldian implications of the work being performed by the theater police in early national culture are, I hope, obvious. Imagine these critics' reactions on being confronted with the actors in Robinson's play, who performed and imitated a people whom such critics would have felt utterly incapable of sense or sensibility: West Indian blacks. Although his version of

creole dialect is remarkably faithful compared to others published contemporaneously in England and the West Indies, Robinson exploits
black culture for comic effect in his play. It is precisely the metonymic
relationship of black West Indian culture to the figures representing the
rising U.S. empire of commerce that shapes and inspires their successful
rebellions. Ultimately Banana, his mother, his mistress Priscilla, and the
other nameless black characters function as the antidomestic and anti-
sentimental models providing the pretext for the marrying of a heroic,
hemispheric, white U.S. masculinity to a wealthy, vulnerable, white West
Indian femininity. Mimesis enchants, but resists possessing the spirit of
the U.S. empire for commerce in Robinson's play.

A wealthy planter, Banana is nonetheless illiterate, speaks in a stylized
black West Indian dialect, and is portrayed in stereotypically primitive
ways.[19] Just as the play's sentimental plot about race and empire depends
to a great extent on Louisa's rescue from a racially mixed marriage, an
important component part of that plot, and much of the play's comic
effect, derive from Banana's profound insecurities about marrying a
more socially elevated white woman.[20] Unlike Shakespeare's Caliban,
Banana does not dream of besmirching Louisa's virtue and populating
the island with more mixed raced children in a violent act of colonial
resistance. Such widespread racial mixing had already been accom-
plished during the nearly three centuries of miscegenetic encounters
since a racially ambiguous Caliban (Carib, African, or both?) occupied
a fictional West Indian island. Indeed, the relationship between the
racially ambiguous Banana (free black, mulatto, quadroon?) and his
light-skinned mulatto or, in the discourse of the play, "coloured" (18)
slave mistress Priscilla with whom he has a child operates for Robinson's
audience as a signifier of the ongoing racial perversions being perpetrated across a bewildering range of racial classifications in the West
Indies. Although Banana's proposed marriage to Louisa inspires an
uprising in the colony, he is a passive, unwilling participant. Banana
wishes to remain in his present relationship, preferring the love he
shares with Priscilla to the improved social status his mother hopes the
family will achieve through his marriage to a respectable white creole.

Banana is cast as a plainly stereotypical character. Yet Mrs. Banana and
Priscilla challenge in limited ways the absolute categorization of Robinson's black characters as "stereotypical"—unintelligent, two-dimensional, lacking in sympathy, without strength of purpose, and so
on—though their behavior is admittedly minstrel-like much of the time.
When Priscilla learns that Banana is to marry Louisa, she berates him
for violating her trust—"You no hab shame, for use somebody?"—and
for threatening the well-being of their child—"When you marry de lady,
dem will bang poor little Quaka. . . . Worka like a horse; hungry da kill.

. . . If he speak, obaseer, da bang he" (17).²¹ Like Priscilla, Mrs. Banana is sensitive to white dominance on the island, and although leery of Fingercash's double-dealings, she seeks to capitalize on her status as a plantation owner and infiltrate white society by marrying her son to Louisa. The argument that ensues between Mrs. Banana and Priscilla over their conflicting desires quickly veers into a carnivalesque shouting match. Still, before the nineteenth century we have relatively few published examples of West Indian creole vernacular, and Robinson's play contains the first extended passages of black dialect to be written, produced, and published on behalf of the U.S. theater. Readers familiar with contemporary Caribbean dialects will recognize in the following excerpt many features of creole languages spoken today, including the use of improvisation:

MRS. BANANA:	You, Priscilla, you no hab de imperence of de dibel, to make such a noise in a my house?
PRISCILLA:	I no hab right for come see my husband?
MRS. BANANA:	Who da you husband?
PRISCILLA:	Banana da my husband.
MRS. BANANA:	Who tell you so?
PRISCILLA:	Da, me tell myself so.
MRS. BANANA:	Who, you, you?
PRISCILLA:	Me, me, me, me, Priscilla.
MRS. BANANA:	You mullatto Seasar [a house slave], go tell de obaseer for come turn dis imperence hussy out of doors.
PRISCILLA:	Lard a mighty in a tap, me poor one in a buckra country; you eber been hear da like of dat—me da imperence hussy—eh—who da you?
MRS. BANANA:	Me da lady.
PRISCILLA:	You da dible, look a like a lady; tigh, dirty no come dab me.
MRS. BANANA:	Me hab plantation.
PRISICILLA:	You, ye lookee like a mumu; you mout like a bull-frog.
MRS. BANANA:	Me hab nega like a you.
PRISCILLA:	You lye, you sesy yi, you mumu nose, you daddy mout chew tobacco, sire gun beem; me no care dat for you. [Snaps her teeth with her fingers.]
MRS. BANANA:	Cato, Quamina [house slaves], somebody come and carry dis yere dibel to de justice, for de tie up her mout. [Enter Negroes, who take hold of Prissey and carry her off.]²²

Clearly this exchange between Mrs. Banana and Priscilla operates primarily to amuse white Northern audiences at the expense of black West Indian culture.[23] Yet it evinces the actual speech patterns of West Indian creole. Moreover, the dialogue captures the verbal dexterity and wit that characterize contemporary creole dialects, but in a late eighteenth-century context.[24] What this "corrupt" dialogue reveals is a highly constructed scene of corrupted and corrupting domesticity: the enslavement of one's own race, the internalization of oppressive racial hierarchies and of white violence against slave families, and the debasement of "blackness" through bestial figures and metaphors. It is precisely the threat these things pose to the virtues of their West Indian lovers that motivates Robinson's U.S. men of commerce, Amant and Ledger, to scheme on Louisa's and Sophia's behalf against Fingercash and Banana.[25]

Before Amant's counterplot to dupe Fingercash by means of his phony cargo of goods into exchanging Sophia and her fortune reaches fruition, Robinson makes it twist and turn and twist again. "Disconcerted" at seeing Sophia for the first time (10), Amant unmasks himself to her by unwittingly displaying the promise ring that she gave him before returning home to the West Indies on the completion of her schooling in the United States (10). Overcome by the "strong power of sympathetic love" (13) that exists between her step-sister and her beloved, a virtue in short supply on the distinctly immoral island, Louisa vows to keep Amant's designs against her father secret and solicits his support on her behalf. As the curtain falls on the play's first act, she entreats Amant to

lay aside your love and sentiment for a period . . . and re-assume your character of Jonathan, which you perform so well; a thought has struck me, that with the assistance of a dying swain . . . we may all of us be enabled to set sail for your country, where Virtue gives distinction, Industry wealth; and where, like Majesty Divine, the hand that can deal thunder to usurping foes, distributes the blessings of Liberty and Concord to his fellow citizens, by the justice and wisdom of his laws. (14–15)

Louisa's "dying swain," Ledger, turns out miraculously to be Amant's long "lost friend" whom he and others of their acquaintance presumed to have "died in a [West Indian] prison" (23), the victim of European colonial violence. Along with the play's audience, the two Americans are spurred into the forthcoming "act" of liberation by Louisa's litany about an ethically superior code of U.S. republican values.[26] Such staunchly pro-Federalist, expansionist rhetoric—voiced, crucially, in triumphant tones by a West Indian woman threatened with an unwanted interracial marriage devised by parental betrayal—demonstrates in precise terms the ways in which U.S. republican values inspire the ideological pretext for, and comic resolution to, Robinson's play. Amant and Ledger function not only as the West Indian sisters' lovers but as their adopted "father[s]" according to Amant (13). Like their native United States, Amant and Ledger exude a masculinist sensibility that contrasts favorably in the play to the unheroic nature of Europe's colonial "others," thus prompting the creole West Indian women to announce their intent to "set sail" for the United States in order to preserve their valuable maidenhood against unspeakable acts of patriarchal violence and colonialist exploitation. Louisa anticipates living her life out as a virtuous wife in a virtuous land, rather than as a sullied woman on a corrupt island, the victim of a predatory father's heartlessness and rapacious greed. The "worthy Sons of Columbia," to whom *The Yorker's Stratagem* "is most respectfully dedicated" (2), have "deal[t] thunder to usurping [colonialist] foes" before. According to Louisa's patriotic encomium, they may be depended on to do so again on behalf of those pinched in the "vice" of European colonialism and imperialism within *and* without U.S. territorial borders, especially their British West Indian cousins.[27]

Indeed, Robinson's play culminates with several acts of "slave" rebellion orchestrated by the agents and allies of the U.S. empire for commerce. One is fomented by a West Indian daughter, Louisa, against an oppressive father who has threatened to "sell" her into black bondage. Another is devised by her soon-to-be husband, Ledger, who seizes on his meticulous records of Fingercash's dishonest business dealings while leading a black-faced rebellion for freedom. When Banana fails in his farcical efforts to imitate the manners of a white dandy so as to win Louisa's heart ("I will tell you one tory; I lobe a you, I lobe a you, like peppa pot my heart da burn, a burn like a fire coal" [25]),[28] he suddenly finds himself on his knees staring up at the cold barrel of Ledger's pistol. Considering that Banana, too, is looking for a way out of the marriage arrangement, the pistol seems an excessive gesture. Yet it becomes apparent that the confrontation is intended as yet another comic moment at Banana's expense. His reaction to Ledger's pointed pistol— "Da something you hab dere look angry so . . . shut up he mout, no let he talk, and I will tell you one tory" (26)—is a parodic version of Olaudah Equiano's simultaneous wonderment and fear of surveillance on seeing the "faces" of a Western clock and portrait for the first time.[29] Banana reveals that, like Louisa, he has been coerced by an artful parent into accepting the terms of their unlikely marriage, and he suggests that he will do anything Ledger requests so long as he can "see Prissey's face again" (26). Further, in exchange for his cooperation with Ledger's scheme against Fingercash, Banana begs Ledger to shoot and kill his mother, a grotesque version of Louisa's plot against her father. Dismissing his absurd request, Ledger orders Banana to strip off his clothes and to get into a closet. Ledger then blackens his face, "put[s] on Banana's clothes" (27), and departs for the church with Louisa, where they are to be married in the guise of a loving and happy interracial couple. [30]

Peter Stallybrass and Allon White have demonstrated the ways in which discourses of the high and low structure our notions of mental and physical forms, geographical space, and an ordered society. Further, they suggest that "transgressing the rules of hierarchy and order in any one of the domains may have major consequences in the others" (3). Robinson's play represents the West Indies as an environment particularly vulnerable to the sorts of consequential disruptions of power and society White and Stallybrass identify. One might suspect that the boundaries between purity and danger, to borrow Mary Douglas's famous phrase, would be especially attenuated when popular eighteenth-century devices like blackface, imposture, and artifice are appropriated for U.S. nationalist purposes in an American play set on an anonymous West Indian island. The play asks us to consider within its strictly regulated comic frame how one polices the borders between ignorant bumpkin and sly businessman, hero and villain, master and slave, and imitation white and imitation black when items in each pairing are mutually constitutive and function in a society hobbled by fraud and deception. Indeed, by transgressing the "rules of identity" in the West Indies and assuming the guise of a composite Yankee, Amant *does* trigger a revolution by means of dissemblance. [31]

Robinson includes tantalizing details that raise the prospect that Amant's stratagem may perhaps be doomed, however, precisely because of his elaborate disguise. The potential culprit of that undoing is not the villainous Fingercash but the faceless black characters who drift on and off the stage as extras, slaves upon whom the island (and theater) depend for profitability. Another indicator of the hemispheric cultural sensibilities of the play's contemporary audience, signs of the West Indian slave religion obeah slip in and out of the play's background and are explicitly linked to Amant's "Jonathan Norrard" mask. Performing Jonathan, Amant loses hold of a prize hen and it scurries out of Fingercash's counting house. Aping duress, Amant exclaims, "I must never look daddy in the face again, for loosing sister Tabithy's black hen" (11). Sophia, who is amused by Amant's "simplicity" and has not yet learned his "true" identity, says to him, "Be not afraid, Sir, the Negroes will take care of it" (11). Her sly allusion here is to the use of black hens in obeah rituals for sacrificial purposes.[32] Ironically, the only black "hen" that ever reappears in the play is a tarred and feathered Frenchman Amant accosts at the end of the play.

The linking of Sophia, obeah, and Amant recurs later when Amant

attempts to plant the seeds of his desire for Sophia as part of his stratagem. Yet the only obeah performed in that context is by Amant on a
gullible Fingercash. When Amant exclaims that he is "bewitched" (21),
Fingercash strikes a note of concern and inquires whether "any of the
Negroes been practicing their obeo" (23) on him, to which Amant jests,
"No it's neither obeo nor o.b.o.e., but the tarnish roguish looks of that
satin's imp, Miss Bellange" (23). Fingercash responds by reminding
"Jonathan" that he had predicted he "would carry off some of our Creole girls!" (23), but not wishing to appear overanxious to make a deal,
Amant suggests "Yankee" fears about contaminated West Indian creole
women will prevent him from "carrying" her home:

Ay, she may be fine enough for these parts, but she would not suit our markets;
I would give all I am worth in the world, and mammy's hogs in the bargain, that
I had never seen her face, for when I do go home to daddy's, *she'll haunt me like
a ghost.* (23; emphasis added)

Amant's artifice involves suggesting to Fingercash the very possibility of
securing the exchange of commodities to which Amant pretends he is
least at liberty to assent: his (fabricated) cargo of goods for "satin's
imp," an exchange to which the covetous Fingercash will surely assent.
Especially intriguing are Amant's suggestions that Sophia might not be
"suited" for U.S. markets, that somehow Jonathan's daddy will censure
the exchange, and that despite her negative "worth" in the Yankee
"market," a West Indian woman possesses others by means of an *other*
worldly market worth, a spectral, otherworldly surplus value: despite all
these things, she can "haunt . . . like a ghost." The figure of a fetishized
West Indies "haunting" the U.S. dream of empire is an appropriated
one. The related image of the West Indian woman infected by her West
Indian "creoleness" was strategically deployed by European colonialist
discourse about the "periphery" in order to suggest a contrastingly pure
metropolitan center, and to discourage potential threats to established
racial, gender, and class hierarchies. Yet while Robinson entertains the
specter of a contaminated, infectious West Indies, its "haunting" effects
are exorcised by Robinson's authorial ideology and the text's agents of
the U.S. empire for commerce. The play's comic resolution does not
pivot on the contagion of mysterious West Indian commodities, features
of slave culture, or creole women, but on the possession of these things
by an expanding U.S. hemispheric presence driven by republican values
like freedom, industry, and social mobility.

By injecting U.S. republican values into an otherwise ethically bank-
rupt society, Amant proves to be what he quips, Fingercash's "match . . .
[in] every way" (33). Fittingly, the heading off of rival stratagems occurs
at Amant's cargo ship. On intercepting a note Ledger has forged indi-

cating that Ledger intends to abscond to the United States with Louisa *before* "Banana's Wedding" can occur, Fingercash hires Amant to bind and gag him, stow him below decks on his ship, and transport him like a slave to New York in order that the wedding may proceed as planned. A "resourceful" Amant then accepts a separate bribe from a French rogue who takes advantage of Mrs. Fingercash's disillusionment with her miserly husband by seducing her and encouraging her to secure her husband's "strongbox" of cash and goods. In return, he promises to hustle her off to the neighboring French colony of Martinique aboard Amant's ship, "where [they] vel live upon l'amour" (16).

Were Amant not the honorable republican that he is, he might depart the island with a motley crew indeed. Yet his stratagem to secure Sophia and her fortune and to ensure the safety and happiness of Louisa and Ledger dictates otherwise. In the process of manipulating the multiple stratagems that have taken hold of the island, Amant lures Fingercash to his ship's dock, whereupon Fingercash proceeds to cane none other than the Frenchman, whom Amant has directed to disguise himself as Ledger. As he beats the howling Frenchman ("Oh des voleurs! Des voleurs!"), Fingercash yells out, "Changing your language won't do; we are prepared for you, altho' the lady was'n't" (29). Of course, the cuck-olded Fingercash is only half right: his wife (not Louisa) was indeed "not ready" for the Frenchman, though the rebellious Louisa *was* ready for Ledger. He is wrong, too, about changing one's language. Amant proves it *will do.* By adopting a Yankee dialect, Amant has shown the audience that the unprincipled West Indian merchant is not "pre-pared" to stem the rising tide of the U.S. empire for commerce.

Confident that Ledger is secured aboard Amant's merchant vessel and his stratagem a success, Fingercash returns to his counting house, where he learns he has been had by an elaborate countermasquerade. The colony's governor holds the accounting sheet Ledger has sent him detailing Fingercash's frauds and schemes, and Ledger, stripping away his black mask in dramatic fashion, reveals that he, not Banana, has just been married to Louisa.[33] While moaning about having been done in by a "wicked black plot" (31)—or more precisely a wicked white one in blackface—Fingercash is further undone when Amant presses his claim on Sophia and her fortune in the voice of an educated, urbane business-man and not a clownish Jonathan. Banana and Priscilla embracing in the wings, Fingercash utters aloud, "Well this makes good the old saying, that true bred Yankey is a match for the devil" (33). U.S. participation in hemispheric empire will not erode the bonds between family and community, or diminish the values and institutions of the United States, Robinson's play suggests. Rather, it is precisely the values and institu-tions of the United States that will renovate the hemisphere's villages, including the colonies of the West Indies, uniting them against the European colonial menace in the service of a new (imperial) U.S. empire with a political, social, and economic network all its own.

Most stunning of all is the ameliorative effect the "Sons of Columbia" have on Fingercash himself. Acknowledging the governor's judgment that he has obliged everyone around him "to descend to the lowest arts, to defeat you in your villainy" (33), Fingercash vows to refashion himself in the mold of the "sons of liberty, from the land of freedom" (11) that he had once mocked. In his newfound pursuit of "honour and honesty," he promises in "the future only [to] exist in meriting your—no—(to the audience) their approbation" (33). His apology signals a reorientation in the dreamscape of Robinson's play of the hierarchical structures of dominance in the hemisphere. Having cleansed the island of its impurities, rescued its women from besmirchment, and pocketed their fiancees' fortunes, Amant and Ledger prepare to set sail for the United States with assurance that on this island at least they have secured a hospitable port of call for merchant men plying their trades on behalf of the U.S. empire for commerce. In *The Yorker's Stratagem*, Robinson summons forth a utopian empire, but he does so by displacing onto the West Indies real conflicts that exist at home. In Robinson's play, the West Indies, its inhabitants, and its cultural effects are cast as the very anxieties they are meant to signify—corruptions of ostensibly pure blood lines and codes of conduct.[34]

This chapter has argued that Robinson's impressive play gives cultural credence to the political economy on which the Hamiltonian empire for commerce was based. Yet underpinning the ideological assumptions of the two immigrants' shared vision of U.S. commercial and cultural ascendance in the hemisphere are issues of mastery and control the Constitution ostensibly resists.[35] Moreover, as discussed in Chapters 2 and 3, a series of foreign relations crises in the 1790s thwarted attempts by the New Republic's leaders to realize Hamilton's vision of the United States as a "mercantile utopia" (Elkins and McKitrick 92). I would emphasize once more the crucial ways in which those crises pivot on the U.S. government's persistent efforts to persuade the British (and French) to enter into, and abide by, financial and/or military pacts or treaty relations granting the United States more substantial, unfettered access to the West Indian trades.

The chapter began by citing a 1794 letter authored by James Brown urging that U.S. theaters be "set aside" for the "real utility" of furthering the New Republic's commercial interests in the hemisphere, a suggestion predicted—and demonstrated—by Robinson's play two years earlier. Yet if Robinson's celebratory play augurs the triumph of the

United States over European empires in the battle for the West Indian trades, James's more famous brother Charles reveals in fiction and non-fiction alike that, at the turn of the century, control over not only the hemisphere's tradeways but also the mainland is largely illusory. In his novel *Arthur Mervyn* (1799–1800), the next chapter argues, Brown transforms the Hamiltonian empire for commerce into a chronotopic zone of instability wherein West Indian and Anglo-American cultures and commodities circulate in ways that resist U.S. attempts to sustain hierarchical distinctions between them. Thus Robinson's play might be reclaimed by scholars of early U.S. drama and literature by resituating it alongside other works produced in the New Republic era such as Brown's highly theatrical novels, texts that alternately celebrate—in the case of Robinson's utopian drama—or interrogate, in the case of Brown's profoundly dystopian novel, U.S. aspirations for commercial empire. In such works, West Indian creole societies and cultures function as simultaneously the most attractive sites for—and threats to—U.S. commercial ambitions in the hemisphere and "pure" notions of national character and culture.

Chapter 5

Charles Brockden Brown's West Indian Specie(s)

Hundreds of miles away from the fictional island of Robinson's drama, or from the St. Croix of Hamilton's youth, the eponymous hero of Charles Brockden Brown's novel *Arthur Mervyn: or, Memoirs of the Year 1793* (1799–1800) nonetheless finds himself marooned on a virtual West Indian island, subject to the creole contaminations of Philadelphia's diseased and infectious commercial economy.[1] His urban existence but a few hours old, Mervyn falls prey to a young merchant clerk's game of confidence. Recognizing Mervyn's greenness from his rustic clothing and pretty face, Wallace offers the penniless migrant shelter. Mervyn gladly accepts, believing Wallace's generosity a token of his future commercial prosperity. Instead, Wallace locks Mervyn in the recesses of an unlighted chamber. Wallace's prank emblematizes Mervyn's immersion in the entanglements, corruptions, and hermeneutic mysteries of U.S. paracolonialism.

"Immersed in palpable darkness" (38), Mervyn cannot orient himself. While Mervyn is literally "in the dark," a disembodied voice announces a plan to defraud an anonymous "nabob . . . [who] artfully encourages his poverty" but who is said to be a "grand imposter . . . [who] has found his way, by some means, to the Portuguese treasury" (40–41). Only when Mervyn delivers several weeks later a billet from his employer Welbeck to the unscrupulous Philadelphia merchant mogul Thetford are the perpetrator and target of the above scheme revealed. Scanning Welbeck's cryptic message, Thetford utters, "Lo! . . . this from the *Nabob!*" (77). "This little word, half whispered," Mervyn confesses to his audience, "was a key to unlock an extensive cabinet of secrets" (77–78). Mervyn's remark points to interpretive mysteries at the core of his various "creole" encounters in the narrative and his formation as a "virtuous" agent of a renovated U.S. empire for commerce. To "detect and to counterwork this plot was obviously my duty," Mervyn remarks (78), yet his countersubversive activities prove highly suspect and result in the reader having to sort through repeated acts of imposture and layers of interpretive ambiguity.

Welbeck is the quintessence of imposture and mystery. Like the figure of the West Indian nabob he masquerades as, Welbeck frivolously spends most of the money he has purloined from a Guadeloupean slave-holding family. Thus he desperately invests in Thetford's scheme to purchase and lade a ship with cargo for the West Indies. The ship insured against "storms and enemies"—costs in the hostile commercial climate of the 1790s that ran to half the total value of a ship's cargo—Welbeck agrees to have Thetford's "brother, a wary and experienced trader" (97) be the ship's supercargo. Yet despite the younger Thetford's seasoning, the vessel is intercepted and condemned by a British privateer on its return voyage from Saint-Domingue:

Two French mulattos had, after much solicitation, and the most solemn promises to carry with them no articles which the laws of war decreed to be contraband, obtained a passage in the vessel. She was speedily encountered by a privateer, by whom every receptacle was ransacked. In a chest, belonging to the Frenchmen, and which they had affirmed to contain nothing but their clothes, were found two sabres, and other accoutrements of an officer of cavalry. Under this pretence, the vessel was captured and condemned, and this was a cause of forfeiture which had not been provided against in the contract of insurance. (101–2)

Ruined by the loss of his investment, Welbeck absconds from his creditors with Mervyn's assistance. As they row across the Delaware River in the middle of the night, Mervyn sees as if through a glass darkly his own precarious predicament. "I found myself entangled among boats and shipping" (114), and as he looks back on Philadelphia, he remarks, in perhaps the most eloquent description in the entire novel, "Lights . . . were perpetually fluctuating, as masts, yards, and hulls were interposed, and passed before them. In proportion as we receded from the shore, the clamours seemed to multiply and the suggestion that the city was involved in confusion and uproar did not easily give way to maturer thoughts" (115). Mervyn's beautifully rendered impression of Philadelphia's heterotopic waterfront signals the coming of the yellow fever epidemic, as well as the corruption of Mervyn's and the nation's "immature" republican virtues by their participation in the West Indian trades.

Key to the corruption heralded by the West Indian trades is the mystery of the condemned ship. "Had the cause of [the] forfeiture been truly or thoroughly explained?," Mervyn wonders aloud. "Might not contraband articles have been admitted through the management or under the connivance of the brothers? And might not the younger Thetford be furnished with the means of purchasing the captured vessel and her cargo—which, as usual, would be sold by auction at a fifth or tenth of its real value?" (137). As Teresa Goddu has sharply observed, Brown refuses to satisfy our hermeneutic desires to have these commercial ambiguities resolved (169, note 8). In Thetford's densely metaphoric ship, we become ensnared in the vagaries of the U.S. empire for commerce. Has the unscrupulous Thetford, his tentacles seemingly reaching every hemispheric port, hustled the Saint-Dominguan mulattos aboard his vessel and planted regalia and sabers in the ship's cargo so as to cause the ship to be condemned, thereby providing himself the opportunity to repurchase the ship and its cargo, once towed to Jamaica, at a fraction of its worth?[2] If so, we might ask why the nation should even attempt to defend a mercantile community that operates according to such a mentality. A second possibility, however, is that for all their combined experience at games of confidence, Thetford and Welbeck are victims here of conspiratorial mulattos who not only cause the ship to be sacrificed to the British, with whom France is at war, but also raise the specter of servile war being "carried" like fever to the United States from the West Indies by the nation's diseased paracolonial commerce.

Ultimately, we are left, like Mervyn, to discern what secrets have been unlocked—or left undisclosed—by the half-whispered word "Nabob." A term of identity consistently defiled in the discourse of creole degeneracy, it opposes the renovated creole identity of the "American" as described by U.S. nationalist ideology. The nabob's ill-begotten wealth, his liminal status between center and periphery, his contagion by slavery, his threat to the purity of national character owing to his libertine, scheming, and reckless conduct are all traits that contradict republican codes of conduct. Yet the novel suggests uneasy affinities between agents of U.S. empire and the West Indian nabob, and thus between the status of virtue in the United States and in the ostensibly degenerate empires of Europe and their creole West Indian colonies. If the nation argued for free trade, neutrality, and non-entanglement, its paracolonial conduct often belied these things. If the Constitution promoted values like freedom and liberty, the political economy of the nation remained tied to slavery in the South and in the West Indies. Accordingly, the impostures and duplicities surrounding the scuttling of Thetford's West Indian trader—a foundational moment in early U.S. American literature and culture of paracolonial ambivalence—sharply define Brown's recurring interest across his fiction and nonfiction alike in threats posed to national character deriving from the chaotic circumstances surrounding U.S. involvement in the West Indian trades in the late eighteenth and early nineteenth centuries.[3]

In Chapter 2, I treated Fisher Ames's important essay "American Literature" (1803) on the state of national character and culture, which begins by asking its audience "Whether in point of intellect we are equal to Europeans, or only a race of degenerate creoles[?]" (22). Contemporaneous to the publication of Ames's essay a faction of New England Federalists threatened to hatch a secessionist plot over concerns that the acquisition of the Louisiana territories might indelibly corrupt the "Anglo-American" Republic by expanding the territory and influence of the Southern slave states while diminishing the importance of the commercial North. Yet Ames suggests that democratic abuses and commercial extravagance may be the most powerful evidence to support charges of U.S. creole degeneracy at home and abroad: "Of course the single passion that engrosses us, the only avenue to consideration and importance in our society, is the accumulation of property; our inclinations cling to gold, are embedded in it, as deeply as that precious ore in the mine" (35–36).[4]

The question of creole degeneracy that motivates Ames's essay, and the anxieties about empire's excesses displayed by xenophobic New England Federalists, guide my examinations of Brown's novel in this chapter. Like Ames, Brown mobilizes the figure of "creole degeneracy" as a trope through and against which to inventory the state of the nation's character and culture. Unlike Northern secessionists, however, Brown exploits that disruptive figure not to critique the potentially deleterious effects of U.S. Western expansionism but rather the ways in which the nation's rampant participation in the West Indian trades undermines the would-be model Republic's claims to hemispheric exceptionalism. In *Arthur Mervyn*, Brown pursues a novelistic trafficking in West Indian "species" so as to check the New Republic's race for West Indian "specie."

In the first section, I maintain that the novel is structured formally and thematically by a series of dramatic—and frequently traumatic—encounters between the besieged Republic and a volatile West Indies. Such confrontations prove profoundly consequential in their effects on the title character's emergent impulse to demarcate that which he himself comes to embody: namely urgent and exceptional, and exclusive and racially inflected, ways of classifying legitimate terms of identification for the national citizen, character, and culture, albeit in strict relation to West Indian presences within and without the nation's borders. In that regard, arguably no event in the novel is more traumatic for Mervyn than an ethnically and racially coded encounter he experiences during the yellow fever epidemic, and no development more disturbing to the reader than Mervyn's subsequent awakening to a racially supremacist consciousness. More precisely, the titular character is struck by a ghostly, renegade West Indian "servant" at the height of the yellow fever epidemic. What transpires in the wake of the assault, however, is not a black slave revolution against the white citizens of the United States. Instead, a far more subtle, insidious *evolution* occurs as Mervyn adapts to negate the metastasizing effects of racial trauma. Fascinated with "classifying" species in the natural world as a precocious, eccentric youth, he redirects his scientific gaze away from the plants and animals of the countryside and toward America's urban spaces and racial others. Ultimately, Arthur Mervyn's specular transformation in response to the West Indian specters haunting his mind and the American landscape parallels the evolution of racial discourse at the turn of the nineteenth century in the United States. Such discourse evolved in large measure to discipline the effects of increasingly democratic, creolized, and fractious French and British West Indian colonies on the stability of the national character.

The chapter's second section examines Arthur Mervyn's fascinating journey "South." In part 2 of the novel, Mervyn departs from Philadelphia for Baltimore, charged with restoring purloined West Indian specie rightfully belonging to slave-holding families from Jamaica and Charleston. Along the way, he is determined to define clear distinctions between himself as benevolent representative of the U.S. empire for commerce and "degenerate" West Indians alongside whom he travels south in a highly stylized "stage" coach and with whom he seeks to conduct business on his arrival in Baltimore. According to Mervyn's charged ocular politics, such figures are eyesores, albeit curious ones, on the otherwise decolonized (and highly sentimentalized) U.S. nation space. Yet the West Indies, and West Indian characters and cultures, operate in excess of Mervyn's impulse to strictly regulate them; they emerge as surrogates, monstrous doubles for urgent national crises. By deftly transposing the scene of West Indian slavery and the profits of U.S. paracolonialism onto the geographically liminal port city of Baltimore, Brown's novel lays bare the ways in which the West Indies as extracontinental site bind mutually constitutive regional and national issues, foremost among them race and slavery.

Figuring the Not-So-Pretty Face of Race, Commerce, and National Character in *Arthur Mervyn*: The West Indies as U.S. "Phantom Limb"

In *Notes on the State of Virginia* (1785), Thomas Jefferson attempts to refute claims made by European natural historians and philosophers about the degenerate condition of the New World, its plants and animals, and its human inhabitants. Georges-Louis Buffon, for example, in his voluminous natural history writings about the New World, argued that New World species were inferior because of the intemperate, humid environment. Buffon and others maintained that when one compared like species from the two hemispheres, inevitably the European varieties were bigger and more vital. In their assessments of the New World, philosophers, natural historians, and travel writers relied on the revolutionary taxonomies of Carolus Linnaeus, who in *Systema Naturae* provided a method for classifying the world's plants, animals, and peoples according to genus, species, varieties, and so on. For Linnaeus, the study of nature by means of his principles of "natural classification" would reveal that there was indeed "order" in the universe. If Linnaeus, Buffon, and their disciples employed such systems of classification in the service of empire, the last decades of the eighteenth century saw the colonies resisting the values Europe assigned them. As we have seen, Jefferson, Adams, Franklin, Hamilton—virtually all the founding fathers— responded in charged ways to the increasingly virulent attempts by prominent European natural historians to reassert European superiority at a time when such superiority seemed most threatened. In Jefferson's case, he seized on the very classification discourse that such philosophers had used to systematize and expand empire in the eighteenth century to show the illogical nature of charges about the degeneracy of America.

In 1787, Samuel Stanhope Smith, a professor of moral philosophy and a future president of Princeton, published a lecture that, like Jefferson's *Notes*, celebrated the ameliorative effects of the U.S. climate and foundational institutions on the physical and moral development of the American species. Smith railed against Jefferson, however, for suggesting that, unlike whites, blacks did not improve in the American climate. Arguing that Jefferson bordered on heresy by maintaining that blacks were a "naturally" inferior race and by implication a separate "species," Smith set out to prove otherwise by arguing that any variation in the human species could be attributed to environment and social conditioning. If perceived inferiorities were solely an effect of the environment, as Smith insisted, then slavery was a crime against humanity, an assault on the "children" of God.

Drawing on climatological arguments such as those Smith devised, abolitionist groups in the United States and Europe denounced the utter inhumanity of slavery in the 1780s. If the science backing the abolitionist position was sketchy, the moral suasion of the argument was powerful nonetheless and undoubtedly contributed to the outbreak of a series of slave rebellions in the West Indies in the 1780s and 1790s. The most serious transpired in the French colony of Saint-Domingue and led to the formation of Haiti, the second independent nation-state in the Western Hemisphere in 1804. For Jefferson and Anglo-Americans who believed blacks to be "naturally" inferior, the Haitian Revolution was a trauma of seismic proportions. More significantly for purposes of my arguments in this chapter, the rash of rebellions, and the attendant flow of West Indian creoles, their slaves, and commodities into the United

States, caused many U.S. citizens to become anxious about possible slave rebellions breaking out in the United States, and about the cohesion of their national culture and character. Northern whites, including many avowed abolitionists, suddenly began to balk at the idea of a general, or even a gradual, emancipation of blacks, even as freed blacks in the North had made significant contributions to society and had thus proven the efficacy of the abolition movement.[5]

Crucially, white supremacists—particularly in the North—cited Jefferson's statements about innate black inferiority, as well as arguments being put forth by a new breed of racial scientists, to justify the shift in their mood away from abolition in favor of the status quo, or toward a policy of colonizing blacks to the Western territories or to lands outside the United States. Jefferson's *Notes* and Edward Long's *History of Jamaica* were often cross-referenced in print, unsurprisingly given that Jefferson had based his claims of black inferiority in part on Long's studies of the West Indies. Ethnologists began to assert confidently, too, that there had indeed been separate creations, and that whites and blacks were different species, or at a minimum wholly different "races," the two terms often being used interchangeably. The aptly named Charles White, for example, compared the skulls of the European, the Asiatic, the American Indian, the Negro, the orangutan, and the monkey and concluded in *The Regular Gradation of Man* (1799) that there existed a human chain of being, with the white European being superior to all others in the great chain. As racial science and social and political policy in the United States converged, and as the Haitian Revolution neared its conclusion, the West Indies and West Indians within and without the United States became vehicles for registering the extreme dangers that abolition and emancipation posed to the future of the Republic.[6] Thus, by the time Jefferson became President in 1800, many of the nation's citizens had come to perceive themselves, their culture, their government, and their identities through and against the democratic upheavals and proliferating identities in the West Indies.

Acutely aware of the potentially devastating effects of both colonization and slavery, African American ministers Absalom Jones and Richard Allen addressed these concerns in *A Narrative on the Proceedings of the Black People, during the late Awful Calamity in Philadelphia in the Year 1793* (1794). The document responds to slanderous accounts of black activities during the 1793 Philadelphia yellow fever epidemic set forth by prominent white publisher Matthew Carey. In *A Narrative*, Allen and Jones invoke the specter of West Indian rebellion, but in unconventional ways. They do so in order to justify urgent appeals to their white audience for the emancipation and full integration of black slaves according to single-creation, environmental arguments, in contradistinction to the ways in which images of West Indian uprisings were being used to justify polygenetic, separate-creation theories shaping ethnographies disseminated throughout the Atlantic world by the beginning of the nineteenth century. As Jones and Allen remark, "Were we to plead with our masters [for freedom], it would be deemed insolence, for which cause [blacks] appear as contented as they can in your sight, but the dreadful insurrections is enough to convince a reasonable man, that great uneasiness and not contentment, is the inhabitant of their hearts" (26–27).

Arthur Mervyn needs to be weighed in the context of these developments in the United States and West Indies during the 1790s. Until Bill Christophersen's keen, if undeveloped, observation in *Apparition in the Glass* (1993) that blackness and the fear of black insurrection are urgent issues in the novel, Brown scholars had paid scant attention to these things. Since the publication of Christophersen's book, critical estimation of the function of race and rebellion has been slow to extend or depart from his insights.[7] What I argue here is that the novel and its eponymous figure are shaped in complex ways by encounters between the white American republic and a fragmenting West Indies, encounters that precipitate the ascension of proslavery and colonization movements in the 1790s and the dramatic evolution of racial science to justify such a trend. By marking the emergence of racist modes of classifying the human species in reaction to the turbulent West Indies, Brown's novel exposes in unflattering ways the classificatory mechanisms used by the budding empire to constitute national character, to establish the boundaries between acceptable and unacceptable terms of identity for the nation and national citizen, and to devise frameworks for belonging and removal.[8]

In the opening moments of *Arthur Mervyn*, Dr. Stevens, the novel's frame narrator until Mervyn takes over during the story's later stages, characterizes his protégé as a Jeffersonian husbandman. For him, Mervyn is the Jeffersonian ideal become real, an embodiment of the "American Farmer" type that Crèvecoeur inaugurates in his fictionalized travel account *Letters from an American Farmer* (1782), and which Jefferson codifies as the figure of national belonging in *Notes on the State of Virginia* and other writings. Although Stevens risks the danger of nursing the fever-stricken Mervyn back to health, he implies that his munificence has, to a considerable degree, been an involuntary reaction to the irrepressible features of Mervyn's (white) face. Believing men's faces to be indexes to their characters, Stevens places supreme value on Mervyn's Adamic guise, claiming he "scarcely ever beheld an object which laid so powerful and sudden a claim to [his] affection and succour" (6). Stevens's iconic portrait suggests that Mervyn possesses the *face* of someone in whom God "has made his peculiar deposit for substantial and genuine virtue" (Jefferson 165). Although the fever metaphorizes Philadelphia's pockmarked condition under Federalism, not even it can tarnish Mervyn's uncommon, countrified good looks: unlike the monstrously scarred visage of the West Indian mulatto who assaults him on the eve of his infection, his resplendent face emerges unscarred after his illness.

Despite Stevens's nomination of Mervyn's face as an indicator of his inner virtue, evidence gathered by others suggests a wholly different view of things. Most prominent among Mervyn's detractors is Stevens's merchant friend Wortley, who accuses Mervyn of conspiring to defraud him and devising elaborate plots to conceal his misdeeds. For Wortley, Mervyn's visage is a republican façade that conceals his treacherous conduct. While Stevens entertains the possibility of Mervyn's imposture, his faith in him never wavers significantly. Stevens insists that "the face of Mervyn is the index of an honest mind. . . . He that listens to his words may question their truth, but he that looks upon his countenance when speaking, cannot withhold his faith" (229–30). In the commercial atmosphere of plague-ridden Philadelphia, where virtue rather than corruption and wellness rather than sickness are in short supply, Stevens is willing to bet the survival of the American democratic experiment on not just the plausible relation, but the actual identification, of virtue with Mervyn's white face.

These attempts to classify relations between faces and language in the novel are crucial because they are symptomatic of a much more systematic effort to put a pretty face on the illogical structures underpinning the nation's foundational discourses and institutions. Paradoxically, the "alien" forces that threaten disorder belie the violence that lends order—particularly classifications centered on race and ethnicity—to U.S. republican ideology in the New Republic. Even so, Stevens's faith in Mervyn's face ultimately *seems* validated by novel's end. Such vindication suggests there is something simultaneously mystical and mystifying about the interrelations between Mervyn's face, the magic of U.S. republican ideology, and the kindly physician Stevens's physiognomic successes despite his illogical reasoning. In Mervyn's face and Stevens's physiognomic gifts, national character and racial science are happily married and confidence restored in the wake of the horrific epidemic. Yet even as we appreciate the good doctor's urgent protests that he would not nominate just any pretty face as the embodiment of virtue, we ought to scrutinize more carefully the structures of belief that escape nomination in Mervyn's face. In what follows, I attempt to declassify Mervyn's and the young nation's secrets. Recognizing that the critical question in *Arthur Mervyn* is only partly about how Mervyn's face should be read, but also about the ways in which Mervyn reads the faces of others,

I demonstrate that, confronted with real and imagined disorder, there is something considerably more violent, and less natural, about the ways in which Mervyn arranges and orders things.

What critics of the novel have failed to remark on is that Mervyn is more natural historian than farmer.[9] Although familiar with the foundational values of Jeffersonian political economy, Mervyn derives satisfaction from the *rhetoric* of such values rather than their practice. Having fled the commercial horrors of urban America for the country, Mervyn contemplates a life of farming with a newfound love interest, Eliza Hadwin. Rather than assisting with the many chores involved in running the Hadwin farm, however, Mervyn retreats to the edge of the forest to translate the manuscript of an Italian novel he surreptitiously comes to possess. Although Mervyn confesses that he has "no grammar or vocabulary to explain how far the meanings and inflections of Tuscan words varied from the Roman dialect," he scrutinizes "each sentence and phrase . . . to select among different conjectures the most plausible interpretation" (126) and professes a special talent for "tracing distinct characters . . . [so as] to give form to my own conceptions" (21–22). Mervyn's talent for tracing or giving shape to "characters" relates to *his* evolution as a character and the narratological intricacies of his testimony and the novel. "Tracing" words, phrases, and sentences in order to deduce "among different conjectures the most plausible interpretation"—a semblance of meaning that more often relies on compulsive serial induction rather than sustained deductive reasoning—also signifies Mervyn's proclivity for objectifying the people he encounters, and who encounter him. The semblances that Mervyn traces in the novel are both contextual, as evidenced by his passion for classifying things and people by measuring them against others they do or do not resemble, and actual, as with his tracing of linguistic characters, or the spinning of his narratives through situated languages. Like his reticulated web of justifications and counterjustifications of his actions, Mervyn's "talent" for tracing people and linguistic "characters" depends on their actual and contextual likenesses. This methodological paradigm on which he depends for meaning proliferates over the course of the novel in crucial ways, and his classifications mark the formation of his character, his attitudes toward race, and his intellectual proclivities for the future, all of which I trace below.[10]

Occurring in real time well before the harrowing events that transpire during the Philadelphia yellow fever epidemic described in the novel's first volume, Mervyn's dictation of details concerning his rural upbringing well into the second volume casts considerable light on what he and Stevens have previously narrated. He confesses that it "is true that I took up the spade and the hoe as rarely, and for as short a time, as possible"

(341), thus contradicting his earlier testimony that farming allows for the sorts of intellectual pursuits that interest him. A mobile explorer type who seeks to apply his bookish knowledge about the "natural" order of things, Mervyn suggests he "preferred to ramble in the forest and loiter on the hill" (341). While doing so, he tried "perpetually to change the scene; to scrutinize the endless variety of objects; to compare one leaf and pebble with another; to pursue those trains of thought which their resemblances suggested; to inquire what it was that gave them this place, structure, and form, were more agreeable employments than ploughing and threshing" (341–42). In embryonic form, these activities demonstrate the classificatory structures that Mervyn relies on for his worldview, and which Jefferson and other U.S. racial scientists exploit in order to nominate, identify, and differentiate between the various species and "races" in the United States.

Even as Mervyn trains himself in the logical structures of classification, he finds himself inconvenienced by the classificatory gaze wielded by others. He withdraws from school because he "hated to be *classed*, cribbed, rebuked" (341) and suggests that his neighbors not only misjudge his character but judge the character of another, a semblance of himself, "the *phantom that passed under my name*, which existed only in their imagination" (340; emphasis mine). What Mervyn describes is a war of classification and counterclassification, of identities defined by oneself, and of "phantom" identities that pass as truth and thus have material force. Such phantom nominations exert their sway not only in the communities in which they are devised but also to the extent that they shadow the person/object who is made a "phantom"—Mervyn/ "Mervyn"—by scurrilous taxonomies that circulate as semblances of the actual person.

Of course, such essentializing tendencies distinguish Mervyn's own characterizations of his persecutors: he scrutinizes, classifies, and assigns traits, and the picture he portrays bears no resemblance to his expressions of rural longing that condition the ways in which Stevens—and we—initially come to classify his "rustic" face. Mervyn's "experiments" with his stepmother Betty Lawrence, for example, are characterized by his condescending assessment of her as an "*animal salax ignavumque* who inhabits the stye" (346). Like Jefferson and Prospero before him, Mervyn relishes the power to name and classify, to study the structures and forms of things, and to make "phantoms" of them according to his classificatory genius.[11] As Mervyn is but an urban trauma or two, and the nation a rebellion or epidemic, away from training their collective classificatory regime on matters of race and ethnicity, Brown's carefully structured examination of the impulse toward such classification lays bare the logical inconsistencies and infinitely mutable nature of such impulses.

As noted above, the revolution in Saint-Domingue resulted in thousands of white and mulatto creole refugees and their slaves immigrating to port cities of the United States and New Orleans. With their arrival, and outbreaks of yellow fever throughout the nation, Americans who had repressed unpleasant thoughts about slavery, rebellion, and the nation's foundational institutions found it necessary to reexamine these things. Accordingly, the refugees made transparent to all Americans the ways in which the United States depended on the plantation economies of the West Indies for its fiscal survival. Moreover, macabre accounts in the national media throughout the 1790s of the alleged traumas creoles and Europeans were enduring at the hands of "raping and pillaging" black banditti reflect the ways in which the Haitian Revolution and slave uprisings elsewhere in the French West Indies functioned as an assault on the deep racial structures upholding the U.S. nation-state and dominant notions of national character. Typical is an anonymously published account in the New York *Daily Advertiser*, which bemoans the ways in which West Indian "planters . . . suffer greatly from the frequent excursions of Negroes and Molattoes, who are continually going about the country, murdering, and committing every species of depredation" ("French West-Indies" 2). Instability in the West Indies further disturbed already unstable racial, ethnic, and class divisions at home, as symbolized by the passing of the Naturalization Law of 1790, the Fugitive Slave Act of 1793, and the Alien and Naturalization Acts of 1798. The material realities of the West Indies contributed in direct ways, too, to the silencing of any significant discussion of abolitionism and emancipation in the North and South alike, and the simultaneous formation of new paradigms for addressing the slavery crisis, such as the discourses of colonization and black removal. The emergence of these national policies for dealing with slavery according to the terms of a rapidly proliferating regime of racial discourse in the 1780s and 1790s evinces the intricate ways in which the West Indies impinged on relations between race, power, and national identity in the United States at the turn of the century. Significantly, racial anxieties do not manifest themselves in Arthur Mervyn until his self-insertion into the rebellious and feverish climate of Philadelphia in 1793. Thus his transformation as a result of a series of racial and ethnic traumas he endures mirrors in many ways the ideological evolution that marks the transformation of many white U.S. Americans' identities in response to traumas stemming from unstable political and commercial relations between the United States and the French and British West Indies and the emerging nation-state of Haiti.

Shortly after arriving in Philadelphia Mervyn is adopted into the family of a West Indian "nabob," Welbeck, who turns out to be an imposter and a villain. Indeed, the West Indian specie Welbeck uses to effect his disguise, and through which he hopes to secure even greater wealth, has been entrusted to him by Lodi, a young Guadeloupean immigrant who before dying of yellow fever begs Welbeck to deliver the money to his sister. Dressed in the foppish fashions of the French West Indies, Mervyn bears "a remarkable resemblance" (57) to the deceased man. That Mervyn bears an uncanny resemblance to a French West Indian is complex in its figural significance: fever, rebellion, and commercial extravagance become affiliated with his culturally coded West Indian clothes, and his uncanny resemblance to the now deceased Lodi. Thus Mervyn's character, and by association the character of the young nation, are imperiled by their affiliations with the West Indies.

Although Mervyn does free himself from his entanglements with Welbeck and escapes to the bucolic atmosphere of the Hadwin farm, his stay is short-lived and he impulsively returns to Philadelphia. His return to a city reeling from the outbreak of yellow fever seems a semivoluntary effort to inoculate himself against the contaminative effects of the West Indies.[12] It is while in the city searching for Sarah Hadwin's fiancé, Wallace, that Mervyn is assaulted. Having arrived in the mansion in which he believes Wallace resides, Mervyn stumbles on not Wallace but another expiring yellow fever victim. He remarks how the man's visage, "[t]hough ghastly and livid . . . [possessed] traces of intelligence and beauty [that] were undefaced" (147). Thus Maravegli joins a growing list of international agents of empire whose faces are said to resemble Mervyn's own, although it turns out that such associations prove fatal, not for Mervyn but for his many likenesses: their deaths from fever or rebellion conveniently leave the redeemed Mervyn and the young American empire solely in charge of administering empire's riches, including wealthy heiresses and valuable commodities. Such a role, however, can only be performed by an agent hardened through exposure. As the practice of inoculation suggests, Mervyn can contain the potential contagion signified by the West Indies only after being exposed to the pervasive presence of West Indian figures circulating through the American urban landscape.

When Mervyn momentarily turns his gaze away from Maravegli in order to contemplate "the train of horrors and disasters that pursue the race of man" (147), he suddenly apprehends "some appearance in the mirror . . . a human figure" (148):

One eye, a scar upon his cheek, a tawny skin, a form grotesquely misproportioned, brawny as Hercules, and habited in livery, composed, as it were, the parts of one view. To perceive, to fear and to confront this apparition were blended into one sentiment. I turned towards him with the swiftness of lightning, but my speed was useless to my safety. A blow upon my temple was succeeded by an utter oblivion of thought and feeling. I sunk upon the floor prostrate and senseless. (148)

Insensible, he nonetheless afterward recalls being "haunted by a fearful dream . . . hands and legs . . . fettered . . . My terrors were unspeakable, and I struggled with such force, that my bonds snapt and I found myself at liberty" (148). The interplay in Mervyn's nightmare between restricted limbs, bondage, and uncommon liberation so as to avoid, it turns out, being nailed shut in a coffin by three undertakers who have supposed him yet another yellow fever victim represents Mervyn's momentary loss of identity. Paralyzed or "phantom" limbs are, from this point forward, recurring figures for Mervyn and others in the novel, particularly during the plague that fills out the first volume. On carrying other fever victims to safety, Mervyn remarks how his "limbs were scarcely less weak" (177), and a few pages later he suddenly is stricken with fever. Echoing his assault by his "phantom" mulatto attacker, he states, "My brain was usurped by some benumbing power, and my limbs refused to support me" (180). For Mervyn—and the United States— such phantom limbs represent their inability to control their fractious relationship to the West Indies on multiple levels: psychic, epistemological, territorial, and economic.

The psychological significance of the "phantom limb" as it manifests itself in the psychic depths of those who have lost a limb because of trauma, Elizabeth Grosz maintains, signifies paradoxically desire and disavowal, loss and remembrance, and trauma and the illusion of wholeness. According to Grosz, "The phantom limb is a libidinally invested part of the body phantom, the image of *Doppleganger* of the body the subject must develop if it is to be able to conceive of itself as an object and a body, and if it is to take on voluntary action in conceiving of itself as a subject" (41). On the national level, the father of American geography, Jedidiah Morse, and a cast of other figures romanticized that sometime in the past the West Indies had been attached to the southern tip of Florida (Morse 475). The imperial overtones of such fantasies— especially as they become figured in Jefferson's lifelong desire to annex Cuba—reflect the unconscious imperial desires to make the hemispheric body "whole" again. As Charles Thomson, secretary of the Continental Congress, mused: "I have often been hurried away by fancy, and led to imagine . . . that from the point or cape of Florida, there was a continued range of mountains through Cuba, Hispaniola, Porto rico, Martinique, Guadaloupe, Barbadoes, and Trinidad, till it reached the coast of America, and formed the shores which bounded the ocean, and guarded the country behind" (qtd. in Jefferson 199).

A little over a decade later, reattachment fantasies had transformed themselves into the fear that the "contagion" of the West Indies might ultimately dismember the United States itself. The West Indies came to be referred to as "vectors" of rebellion, or a "plague" on the orderly arrangement of the United States. Laws against the entry of West Indian mulattos and freed blacks proliferated in the South, and when Gabriel Posser's rebellion plot was uncovered in 1800, the nation turned firmly away from abolition and emancipation as viable solutions to the slave problem, and toward the possibility of relocation and colonization of blacks—to the Western territories, ironically enough to Haiti, or to Africa. Almost inevitably, such pathological impulses were registered according to the classificatory structures of racial science. For example, in 1795, Virginian St. George Tucker, in suggesting the ways in which colonization schemes proposed to that point were impractical, expressed profound anxieties about any viable solution being found to address the phantoms of hemispheric slavery haunting national efforts to sustain the dreams of the white American empire: "The objections to the [gradual emancipation and colonization of blacks in the Western territories] are drawn from deep-rooted prejudices in the minds of the whites against blacks, the general opinion of their mental inferiority, and an aversion to their corporeal distinctions from us, both which considerations militate against a general *incorporation* of them with us" (qtd. Jordan 556). Tucker leaned uneasily toward keeping blacks in bondage, though he urged slaveholders to improve the slave's condition or else face certain rebellion. As he admonished, "The calamities which have lately spread like a contagion through the West India Islands afford a solemn warning to us of the dangerous predicament in which we stand" (qtd. Jordan 555–56). Tucker's distressed confessions illustrate the nexus that emerged in the 1790s between racial science, the "contagious" West Indies, and rampant anxieties stemming from the intractable problem of U.S. slavery.[13]

Mervyn's trauma induced by slave rebellion—actual or imagined—parallels the anxieties surrounding West Indian contagion on the national level. His consanguinity with the young Lodi, whom he resembles, is registered in his "dream" of terror on being assaulted by the mulatto servant. Genealogically he is associated as well with Lodi's father, who was murdered by an enraged slave. Like the transplanted senior Lodi, who emigrated to Guadeloupe from Italy some years prior to his fatal encounter with his slave, Maravegli is an Italian nobleman. Mervyn is said to look like Maravegli as well, and thus his assault by Maravegli's mulatto servant—especially given that Mervyn has been frolicking as Lodi's likeness while living with the "West Indian" nabob Welbeck—denotes the thick figural associations across time and space that converge in fever-ridden Philadelphia's chronotopic zone of instability.

Convulsions in empires past and present, and volatile paracolonial relations between the West Indies and the United States, become embodied in the maze of relations heaped on Arthur Mervyn's besieged though still pretty face. Through the facial transmutations of Arthur, Lodi, Maravegli, and others—especially the horrifying guise of the rebelling mulatto slave—the novel figures the ways in which the West Indies, particularly West Indian "blackness," resist the hemispheric dominance of the rising, and resolutely white, American empire and suggests the dramatic effect the West Indies had on the beliefs, fears, and desires of the United States in the 1790s and beyond.[14]

Arthur Mervyn's Travel Narrative "South": The West Indies as U.S. Metanation

After repeated and, on the level of the novel, systematic exposure to the contaminative effects of the West Indies, Mervyn dreams of spending the next "five to eight years" of his life traveling the world, joining the ranks of those "who have tried all scenes; who have mixed with all classes and ranks; who have partaken of all conditions; and who have visited different hemispheres and climates and nations" (293). Such desires were the rallying cry of the natural historians and travel writers who blanketed the globe throughout the eighteenth century in the service of "masters" like Linnaeus, Lamarck, Buffon, and Haller. A willing disciple, Mervyn soon gets his chance to test his training in unfamiliar environs. Yet before he can travel to Europe, the seat of great and receding empires, he must first familiarize himself with the extent of his own nation. With an eye toward renovating commerce and adopting the role of the virtuous American man of empire, Mervyn departs Philadelphia for Baltimore, an admittedly minor expedition, though, it turns out, an "exotic" one nonetheless. Carefully structured by Brown to provide a panoramic view of hemispheric trade and slavery, Mervyn's modest travel narrative south to another of the United States' heterotopic commercial ports exposes his evolving ability to classify "race" and "ethnicity" according to the hierarchical structures of his classificatory gaze.

Before I turn to Mervyn's Baltimore adventures, there are several aspects of Brown's narrative structure that deserve mention. First, Mervyn has taken over the writing of his own narrative from Stevens a chapter before his narration of his journey. Moreover, only a single chapter in the text's narrative chronology separates the chapter in which Mervyn strenuously defends the "labors" and actions of his youth discussed above, in which classificatory discourse is so pervasive, and the several chapters that chronicle his travels south. Such careful juxtapositions denote Brown's own investments in the positionality and ordering of the novel's genealogy of classification. We are meant, I believe, to compare and contrast the young Mervyn as natural historian/ethnographer with the more mature Mervyn, now nineteen, who has, according to his own estimation, grown more in the previous plague year than in all the others combined (292). On his southern journey, Mervyn demonstrates that he has graduated to a different *species* of racial discourse.[15]

Although the regulatory mechanisms of classification remain similar, Mervyn's travel narrative reveals how his classificatory discourse evolves to adapt to his radically altered subjectivity and the circumstances of his immediate surroundings. Anxious to discipline the specter of the "marauding West Indian slave," and of West Indian culture's unsettling effect on U.S. national character, he once again seeks to assign positions, regulate groups, and enforce boundaries, but this time his disciplining gaze focuses on the West Indies and not the "vulgar" rustics of his hometown. Mervyn exploits figures affiliated with the West Indian plantation economies in relation to the U.S. environment as a way of deflecting, or at a minimum repressing, Northern investments in the evils of Southern slavery. More overtly, he suggests the need to police the cultural contaminants and economic excesses devolving from U.S. participation in the West Indian trades. Early in his account Mervyn lays bare the classificatory apparatus that he relies on in territorializing the spaces of his narrative. Later, as he proceeds through Baltimore's urban spaces, he covers over the skeleton of ethnographic racialism with storytelling flesh, most conspicuously the language of sentiment. Mervyn alternates between the two modes so as to best express the extent of West Indian blight on the national character.

The occasion for Mervyn's trip arises when he volunteers to transport profits resulting from the West Indian trades to two families living in Baltimore. Like the moneys banditti discover in an ancient Italian tomb in the novel Mervyn translates, a book in whose pages are stitched twenty thousand dollars in West Indian specie that Mervyn later burns out of fear for their cultural contagion, these profits have been entombed in the grave of one of Welbeck's many victims. Hoping to rehabilitate his fragile reputation by successfully delivering the contaminated currencies, Mervyn sets out for Baltimore in a highly constructed "stage":

I mounted the stage-coach at day-break the next day, in company with a sallow Frenchman from Saint Domingo, his fiddle-case, an ape, and two female blacks. The Frenchman, after passing the suburbs, took out his violin and amused himself with humming to his own *tweedle-tweedle*. The monkey now and then mounched an apple, which was given to him from a basket by the blacks, who gazed with stupid wonder, and an exclamatory *La! La!* upon the passing scenery;

or chattered to each other in a sort of open-mouthed, half-articulate, monotonous, and sing-song jargon. (370)

The "stage" show that Mervyn describes is not a performance that his traveling companions wittingly offer up for scrutiny. What the scene is obviously meant to denote are the grotesque effects of cultural and racial mutations between ostensibly discrete species. Notably, Brown had been to see Lailson's Pantomimes, the circuslike theater act in which West Indians, particularly Saint-Dominguan refugees, performed (Warfel 78–79). Such performances included acts with live animals, notably monkeys and orangutans, rope dancers, and whites and blacks alike performing "creole" dances. As Chapter 4's analysis of Robinson's *Yorker's Stratagem* suggests, to protectors of the U.S. literary and cultural establishment, such performances raised the specter of excessive democratic and liberalizing tendencies within the national culture. The combined needs of policing the effects of West Indian racial and cultural contamination are reified through Mervyn's use of racist ethnological discourse to frame this scene. His characterizations of his four traveling companions evince the ways in which he has related the "visible" to the invisible and then sought additional signs on the surfaces of their bodies and faces to confirm his logically circular discoveries. While Mervyn does not possess the verbal mastery necessary to decipher the "singsong jargon" of the two black West Indian women, the implications of what the Frenchman says to his monkey are startlingly clear: "The man looked seldom either on this side or that; and spoke only to rebuke the frolics of the monkey, with a Tenez! Dominique! Prenez garde! Diable noir!" (370). The exchange between the French creole and his primate suggests their shared buffoonery, but translated—"Stop! Dominique! Mind you! Black devil!"—the line also functions as an admonition about Saint-Dominguan creoles' too-permissive and promiscuous behavior, conduct that many U.S. observers felt foreordained the Haitian Revolution. The passage implies that, unlike this French creole but like the racial scientist, Americans will need to look on both sides, and frontward and backward, in order to prevent such a rebellion from occurring in the United States.

Given his traumatic experience during the yellow fever epidemic, Mervyn has trained himself to look in multiple directions:

As to me my thought was busy in a thousand ways. I sometimes gazed at the faces of my *four* companions, and endeavoured to discern the differences and samenesses between them. I took an exact account of the features, proportions, looks, and gestures of the monkey, the Congolese, and the Creole-Gaul. I compared them together, and examined them apart. I looked at them in a thousand different points of view, and pursued, untired and unsatiated, those trains of reflections which began at each change of tone, feature, and attitude. (370)

Rather than acknowledge the achievements of freed Northern blacks, as Jones and Allen urged, and recognize what was transpiring in Saint-Domingue as a further sign of blacks' common humanity with whites, many white Americans sought to reinforce their racist institutions and governing discourses by amassing racial inventories. The synecdochic bodies of Saint-Dominguan émigrés, powerfully situated in the context of the highly figurative yellow fever epidemic and rebellion, signify renewed investments in the racialized body. Such an inventory, crucially voiced by Dr. Stevens's model American citizen, reveals the ways in which national character came to be defined according to the bogus terms of racial classification and suggests the necessity of Mervyn's evolution from precocious natural historian to Jeffersonian racial scientist—an unsettling transformation that occurs, in the temporalities of the novel, within twelve months' time. The influx of Saint-Dominguan refugees, the presence of ghostly West Indian mulattos, the phantom yellow fever, and a turbulent commercial climate made such drastic transformations necessary not only in Mervyn's mind but also in the thinking of an increasingly racist nation. Mervyn's racialist juxtapositions, his careful measurements of the facial features and gestures of the subjects in his traveling ethno-laboratory—a carnival reenactment, one might suggest, of Charles White's brand of racial science—reveal the shifting attitudes in the North in the wake of the Haitian Revolution. As this passage demonstrates, one did not have to be *born* in the South, or live in and around the Southern plantation economy, to become racial in one's thinking by the turn of the nineteenth century.[16]

Even as Mervyn catalogues the similarities and differences of his *"four companions,"* he also "marked the country as it successively arose before me." He "examin[es] the shape and substance of the fence, the barn and the cottage, the aspect of earth and of heaven. How great are the pleasures of health and of mental activity!" (370–71). On one level, Mervyn retreats here, as he had on being assaulted by the West Indian mulatto, to the surety of a depopulated country scene for purposes of relation. Clearly, the distinctions between the mixed-up, mottled "equipage" in which he rides and the picturesque landscape outside are being foregrounded. Less transparently, the awkward shift marks a carefully orchestrated effort to repress and deflect onto the West Indies the nation's responsibility for its own inhumanity toward its ethnic and racial others as a result of an ongoing exploitative paracolonial commercial relationship with the West Indies and, in the case of the North, a parasitic one with the South. As Mervyn proceeds farther southward on his mission, such contradictory desires become clear as he marshals a range of discourses in order to posit the inferiority of the West Indian creole to European and American standards of morality and character.

More precisely, his tale about how he virtuously restores "lost" properties to two families, a transplanted Charleston *mercantile* family and a *plantation-owning* Jamaican one, is filtered through the racially scientific gaze he trains on them. His evolving racial discourse "naturalizes" classificatory patterns of thought by overlaying them with the discourses of travel writing and sentimentalism. By so doing, he (not very successfully) attempts to mystify the sorts of scientifically unsound judgments he arrives at while positioning himself in relation to the French West Indians on the stagecoach so as to assert his superiority in the hemispheric "creole" chain of being.

The context behind how Mervyn has come to possess the moneys that he is destined to restore to these two families suggests the complex associations between West Indian specie and the U.S. political economy.[17] When Welbeck murders Amos Watson secretly, Welbeck and Mervyn bury him without realizing that strapped around Watson's waist is a girdle containing bills of exchange worth tens of thousands of dollars. Although Watson's trading venture to Saint-Domingue and Jamaica resulted in the British seizing his vessel for what they claimed to be illegal trading practices with the French colonies, the bills of exchange he carried represent his success in another kind of commercial transaction with the West Indies. The smaller portion of these moneys belong to Watson while the much larger portion, the result of a plantation sale Watson was commissioned to oversee, belongs to the Maurices. During his expedition, Mervyn carefully scrutinizes both the Watsons and the Maurices, who immigrate to Baltimore in order to escape an increasingly volatile and rebellious Jamaica.

The Maurices, Mervyn's account quickly makes apparent, have made an otherwise familiar landscape corrupt and unfamiliar. Mervyn relates that although they appear to live in "a neat dwelling," on closer inspection the seemingly picturesque estate is "naked and dreary" (377). Thus the anticipations of picturesque scenery that set him off on flights of fancy in the stagecoach are replaced by a foreboding setting of West Indian gloom and doom. The corrupted landscape reflects the occupants of the plantation. If the French West Indians are contemptible for their lack of probity and their infantile and hedonistic pursuit of pleasure, the British West Indian Maurices lack any sense of charm and, according to Mervyn's account, are ruthless, avaricious, and utterly miserable. Having outgrown his earlier fancy for West Indian frocks, Mervyn scrutinizes the Maurices' clothing. Like the estate in which they live, their clothes become indices of their degeneracy, which in turn registers itself in a host of other cultural signs that justify Mervyn's essentialist classification. Creole exaggerations of European styles tend to obscure or, more accurately, adulterate the physical features of the wearer rather than accentuate them. These outward cultural signs correspond to the characters of the women, who are rude, peevish, and unhelpful.

While Mervyn has no problem reading from the outside inward, he mocks the Maurices for doing the same with him, even as he confesses to his unprepossessing appearance. The conveyor of not only "competence but riches," he confesses that his "age and guise would be the least suspected of being able to restore [them]" (377). Despite this admission about his appearance, he professes to be surprised and insulted when he is not welcomed into the Maurice household. The door is answered by a black of "a very unpropitious aspect" who looks at Mervyn initially "in silence" before proceeding to respond "in a jargon which I could not understand" (378). As on the stagecoach, Mervyn attributes the indecipherability of West Indian blackness and creole dialect to ignorance and corruption. And once again, he proceeds to decipher the indecipherable. When Bob and Cato, "two sturdy blacks" (379), are summoned to throw him out of the house, Mervyn seems to have no difficulty identifying their motivations: "The blacks looked upon each other, as if waiting for an example. Their habitual deference for everything *white*, no doubt, held their hands from what they regarded as a profanation" (379). Yet we do have "doubt" about what it is Bob and Cato think about *whiteness*, because Mervyn persists in interpreting *blackness* according to his own "profanation[s]," as if each succeeding West Indian black he meets with is but another version of the last. The blacks' "sturdiness," their indecipherable creole, their pent-up rebellion that awaits only an "example" like the slave who murders the senior Lodi in Guadeloupe, the specter that assaults Mervyn during the epidemic, and the revolutionaries in Haiti: all these things have conditioned Mervyn to mark his encounters with West Indian blacks and West Indian culture in unfavorable ways.

When Mrs. Maurice suggests that "this is a suspicious case. Watson, to be sure, embezzled the money; to be sure, you are his accomplice" (382), Mervyn's innocence is not nearly as "pure" as he implies in his mocking reply. Mervyn has not informed Mrs. Watson about the circumstances that led to Watson's disappearance, nor has he come to terms with the fact that indeed he is implicated in that disappearance. He is not a neutral party to the affair, and perhaps most significantly, he might *not* have—as he jests—kept the missing funds without "suspicion" (382). Their restoration to the Maurices and Watsons is a test of his criminality or virtuousness by Stevens and others. By accusing him of theft and refusing to be "properly" grateful for the return of their money, the Maurices invert the power of the gaze, place Mervyn on the defensive, and unsettle his pursuits of commercial confidence.

At the Watsons, Mervyn once again is both seer and seen, but in such a way that identities—both black and white—remain comforting and fixed. Slipping through the gate to the family property at nighttime, Mervyn peers through the window of the home. The scene he witnesses is a textbook case of domestic tranquility, with two exceptions:

I . . . beheld a plain but neat apartment, in which parlour, kitchen, and nursery seemed to be united. A fire burnt cheerfully in the chimney, over which was a tea-kettle. On the hearth sat a smiling and playful cherub of a boy, tossing something to a black girl who sat opposite, and whose innocent and regular features wanted only a different hue to make them beautiful. Near it, in a rocking-chair, with a sleeping babe in her lap, sat a female figure in plain but neat and becoming attire. Her posture permitted half her face to be seen, and saved me from any danger of being observed.

This countenance was full of sweetness and benignity, but the sadness that veiled its lustre was profound. Her eyes were now fixed upon the fire and were moist with the tears of remembrance, while she sung, in low and scarcely audible strains, an artless lullaby. (372)

The two images that threaten to upset this idyllic view are race—the black girl who "wanted a different hue"—and mourning. Yet both are cast in ways that are meant to augment, rather than mitigate, the sentimental transaction between the images described and the reader. We too are meant to pity the benighted black and shed a tear for the widow of a virtuous American man of commerce gunned down by a rogue in West Indian clothes, Welbeck. Our gaze is like Mervyn's, that of the master (the slave girl) and patriarch (bearers of West Indian goods).

Mervyn claims that the "spectacle" of domesticity exercises an unfamiliar "power" over his "feelings," yet what the evidence suggests is that he delights in exercising a measured terror over the feelings and emotions of the subjects he observes. For example, Mervyn states that the black girl, having momentarily altered her position, "unluckily caught a glance of my figure through the glass," and cried out in a tone mixed with terror and surprise, "Oh! see dare! a man!" (373). In the previously described scene, Mervyn fantasizes that his "whiteness" kept the Maurices' male black creole servants from lunging at his throat despite their "profanation" for everything white. Here, Mervyn exults in a setting of romanticized U.S. racial slavery in seeing a black girl recoil from his spectral whiteness set off against the blackness of the night. Seen through the glitter of the windowpane, this time Mervyn is the apparitional attacker rather than a surprised victim. If Mervyn claims not to have enjoyed alarming the black girl—he "felt a sort of necessity for apologizing for my intrusion" (373)—the "sort of" in his equation belies his sincerity. Perhaps not so ironically, Mervyn momentarily occupies the disembodied, horrifying heart of racial darkness that the West Indies have come to represent in his mind, as well as in the hearts and minds of white Southerners and Northerners during the 1790s. These contrasting apparitions—the ghostly, marauding West Indian mulatto; the terrorizing face of whiteness—manifest themselves by 1800 in the nation's fatal movement toward proslavery and/or plans for black colonization according to the terms of scientific racisms denoting the innate inferiority of blacks.

When Mervyn leaves Baltimore a fortnight later, his "heart [is] buoyed up by a kind of intoxication" (391). He emerges from his trip, he believes, a heroic exemplar of a renovated and virtuous U.S. hemispheric empire for commerce after having restored the "lost" West Indian riches to their rightful owners, however ungrateful or grateful they might be. Mervyn has no qualms about accepting the thousand-dollar reward for the restoration of Mrs. Maurice's lost goods, despite his conflicted relationship to their disappearance and his self-interested motivations for returning the missing funds according to his need to restore the confidence of his tale's auditors in his questionable virtue. The "reward" signifies the complicity of the United States in West Indian slavery, a participation marked by the wielding of debasing figurations of the West Indies in support of an assumed racial and ethnic superiority and the championing of a more enlightened republicanism. It also represents U.S. involvement in a parallel U.S. plantation economy, which Mervyn's narrative romanticizes by depicting the domestic sphere of a Southern white mercantile family transplanted from Charleston to Baltimore, rather than the domestic scene of a Southern plantation in South Carolina. As Mervyn leaves Baltimore for Philadelphia, he departs with a new confidence founded on the logical structures of racial science. Given such ideological investments, he willfully refuses to see how U.S. commerce, however modest its ambitions, will not ever be "virtuous" without the emancipation of black slaves and the acknowledgment of U.S. paracolonial complicity in the West Indian slave economies.

Returning to Philadelphia uplifted from his descent into the overlapping worlds of West Indian and U.S. commerce and slavery, Mervyn also returns to the comforting fictions of classifiable and controllable life. Yet his pending marriage to the considerably older heiress Ascha Fielding at novel's end has disturbed generations of readers for what they suggest is its unfathomability given all that has come before. I would suggest that both Mervyn's representative impulse to "fix" and classify racial others, and his penchant for rescuing the female "victims" of empire's excesses, dictate the logic of the marriage. Having recently emigrated to the United States from Europe, where she has grown tired of the revolutionary climate, Ascha brings her considerable fortune to American shores, where she announces unequivocally that she is willing to "stay for . . .

the rest of her days" (426).[18] Moreover, Ascha voices appropriately republican virtues. As Mervyn states, "I have heard her reason with admirable eloquence, against the vain distinctions of property and nation and rank . . . she, herself, has felt so often the contumelies of the rich, the high-born, and the bigoted" (433). Even more importantly, Ascha's inferior physical traits—"in stature she is too low; in complexion dark and almost sallow" (414)—constitute a distinction that Mervyn can both classify and accept in relation to himself. As we have seen, Mervyn exults in making "vain distinctions" (433), and he is particularly pleased with himself when he deduces from Ascha's eyes that she is a Portuguese Jew. Her ethnic identity a test to the classifying abilities that Mervyn has been cultivating and her wealth an avenue to a lifestyle that will enable him to continue his intellectual pursuits, Ascha grants Mervyn that which he would extract from the West Indies—the distinction of species and a specie of distinction—without the accompanying guilt or the threat of West Indian rebellion.

Yet Mervyn's and many of the nation's foremost leaders' shared vision of U.S. commercial and cultural ascendance in the hemisphere are issues of mastery and control the Constitution ostensibly resists. *Arthur Mervyn*'s narrative creole complex reveals that mastery and control of the United States nation-space, let alone the hemispheric waterways, has been replaced at the turn of the century by chaos and instability. Brown's sensitivities to increasingly democratic, creolized, and fractious societies in the West Indies *and* the United States are elaborate and unsettling. Within and without the borders of Brown's text, West Indian and Anglo-American cultures and commodities clash and cohere in ways that resist hegemonic attempts to domesticate West Indian figures within their discursive constructions of a resolutely *white* empire.

Given what generations of Brown scholars have noted are the work's manifold ambiguities, tantalizing questions persist about the ideological implications of *Arthur Mervyn*. The novel's abolitionist politics, for one, would seem to be far less transparent than present-day readers might prefer. Brown crucially neglects to present positive, sustained portrayals of the characters and cultures of black U.S. and West Indian communities, both in the novel and elsewhere; the wish that he would have done so is perhaps more a product of our own desires and moment than of Brown's. Nor would I argue that the novel advocates a pluralist, multicultural society wherein "racial and ethnic purity are no more to be valued . . . than sexual purity is" (Tompkins 81). Brown stops well short of promoting, like Allen and Jones in *A Narrative*, the abolition, emancipation, and full integration of black slaves in the New Republic, although such a politics may be an effect of the novel for some readers.[19]

More legible, this chapter has demonstrated, are Brown's unconventional figurations of the West Indies and the text's insistence that its audience scrutinize ever more carefully the national drive toward racially motivated economic, social, and political policies. Because Brown illuminates the emergence of a racially supremacist consciousness in the exceptional ways that he does—both by staging such a formation through and against the novel's swirling testimonies and countertestimonies, and by deploying competing scenes of white and black, and U.S. and West Indian–authored, rebellion in order to effect the compelling transmutation of U.S. and West Indian faces—the reader *does*, to re-mark on Mervyn's words, begin to discern *the profanation of everything white*. In this way, Brown's novel anticipates appeals by African Americanists and "whiteness" scholars, most famously Toni Morrison, that we "examine the impact of notions of racial hierarchy, racial exclusion, and racial vulnerability," not just on the victims of racism (and slavery) but on "nonblacks who held, resisted, explored, or altered those notions" (*Playing* 11). Indeed, Brown's accomplishment in *Arthur Mervyn* is significant: by limning the contours of U.S.-West Indian relations, Brown dares us to come face-to-face with disturbing affiliations between U.S. and West Indian creole characters, cultures, and economies at the turn of the nineteenth century.

The Afterlife of Cora Munro

Peace, commerce, and honest friendship with all nations, entangling alliances with none.

—*Jefferson's First Inaugural Address, March 4, 1801*

Contamination is the wrong word to use here, but some notion of literature and indeed all culture as . . . encumbered, or entangled and overlapping with what used to be regarded as extraneous elements—this strikes me as the essential idea for the revolutionary realities today.

—*Edward Said,* Culture and Imperialism

To declare one's own identity is to write the world into existence. If, therefore, when we deal with our own history, we adopt (we Caribbean people) the various European languages and adapt them, no one will teach us how to do this. We will perhaps be the ones to teach others a new poetics and, leaving behind the poetics of not-knowing (counterpoetics), will initiate others into a new chapter in the history of mankind.

—*Édouard Glissant,* Caribbean Discourse

To exhume is to bring to light, to restore or revive after a long period of forgetting or neglect. To treat the paracolonial relationship of the United States with the West Indies according to its creole complex is to strive after an ethically responsible way of exhuming the "West Indian" body in the writings of the early national period. It is to reckon with the "entangled . . . revolutionary realities" of U.S. and West Indian hemispheric relations then *and* now. As paradigm, the creole complex lays bare the utter impossibility of a Jeffersonian notion, however seductive, of commerce without "foreign" entanglements; it belies what Glissant terms a "poetics of not-knowing" or what I have identified in the context of this study as a rhetoric of paracolonial negation.

It is difficult to recall a more undead figure in early U.S. literature than Cora Munro, the Jamaican creole with suspiciously dark eyes whose erotically charged complexion gushes with blood threatening to exceed its bounds. Such figurations of the ways in which "blood will tell" signal for readers of Cooper's novel Cora's creole confusion(s), the author's legerdemain making visible the invisible such that Cora's mixed "blood" betrays her not-quite-white white skin and provides "scientific" explanation, in the mode of Arthur Mervyn's classifying gaze, for her fiery, instinctual character. As Betsy Erkkila remarks, "Against the social degeneration and danger signified by Cora's mixed blood, pure blood functions in Cooper's narrative as a sign of good character between the sexes as well as among races, classes, tribes and nationalities" (15). Thus Cora's murder at novel's end, an act of hyperanxious removal, clears necessary space in Cooper's expansionist text for its various mytho(patho)logies to unfold. In order to accomplish this "monstrous" act, Cooper not coincidentally enlists the services of the novel's other most dangerously "creole" character, the archvillain Magua.

Cora's ghost has haunted generations of readers, in part because it is difficult to decipher how precisely Cooper's fetishistic summoning and banishment of Cora relates to his poetics of "not knowing." In order for critics to appease Cora's ghost and provide suitable libation for her restless spirit, we need to recognize how the violent act of dispossessing the North American continent of the "West Indian" body in the novel functions as a spectacular act of hemispheric *disentanglement*—especially if we recall that the text is set in the last years of the French and Indian War. Like Franklin's appeal in *The Canada Pamphlet* urging the return of Guadeloupe rather than Canada to the French as part of the Treaty of Paris, *The Last of the Mohicans* (1826) champions Western—not West Indian—expansionism, the Creole Republic emerging magically "uncrossed" in the novel by its would-be degenerative entanglements with creolizing West Indian bodies, commodities, and cultures. (Only in Michael Mann's recent Hollywood blockbuster can Cora be transmogrified into a "pure" white, non–West Indian woman suitable for romantic encounter with Natty Bumppo, the "American" man without a creole "cross" played by Irish actor Daniel Day Lewis.) Cooper—and Mann—thereby negate as Franklin and others before them what John Adams on the eve of the peace at Versailles anxiously terms "intimate combinations between the islands and the continent." Cooper disavows, too, not only his New York father's staunchly Federalist politics but also those of his father's most admired politician and close friend, the architect for the United States as an empire for commerce: Alexander Hamilton.

In Haitian vodoun's secret societies, when one wants to expel an undesirable member from the community a *bokor* is consulted, a sorcerer who might make of the living the living dead, much as the master in plantation times used the lash to make of the slave a socially dead and thus productive laborer. Yet a lasting fear is that a zombie or the spirit of an unceremoniously buried slave will return to haunt the living, the two practices being perhaps more intimately related than we have heretofore understood. As Joan Dayan remarks regarding the unstable boundaries between the Haitian living and dead and the past and present in her eloquent conclusion to *Haiti, History, and the Gods* (1995): "The landscape of Haiti is filled not only with spirits of the dead seeking rest and recognition but with other corporeal spirits who recall the terrors of slavery and the monstrous, institutionalized magic of turning humans into pieces of prized and sexualized matter" (264). Dayan directs our attention to how vodoun ritually reenacts the past, refiguring powerful myths of white domination into potent narratives of violence and seduction. In such a way, critics as vodouisants might endeavor to disinter the "magical" ways in which Cooper's trafficking in libidinally charged West Indian bodies mystifies the circuits of "damage" attending to the New Republic's paracolonial investments in the West Indies. Put differently, how might we rememorialize and by so doing rematerialize the West Indian undead in Cooper's novel in order to exhume not only Cora Munro but a creolizing, anticolonizing hermeneutics of knowledge?

I would like to conclude *Creole America* by focusing on representations of West Indian creole women in Anglo-American colonial and early U.S. American literary texts, representations that Cooper's work neither inaugurates nor forecloses. I undertake such an inventory in order to demonstrate, as I have attempted to do throughout this project, the possibilities of a critical reading practice that privileges a poetics of creolization over and against a "poetics of not-knowing" or creoleness. My critical strategy functions as an "effective history" or a "genealogy" does for Foucault, a network of meaning that "introduces discontinuity into our very being . . . not to discover the roots of our identity but to commit itself to its dissipation" (*Language* 154, 162). To attempt a genealogy of representations of West Indian creole women like Cora Munro is to confound, according to a critical practice of creolization, the figuration of the United States as "Columbia." Columbia licenses a proliferating nation-state as, for example, in Robinson's important drama whereby the "Sons of Columbia" usher in a utopian era of U.S. commercial empire in the West Indies. Chapter 4's examination of that play showed how the specter of a potentially inassimilable white West Indian creole woman—Sophia Bellange—threatens to infect the would-be inviolate Columbia, even as her body and fortune are seized or rescued, depending on one's assessment of the play's messianic republicanism, as the most desirable of commodities by heroic agents of the rising U.S. empire for commerce. Such a tension in Robinson's drama provides a foothold from which critics might assess Cooper's similarly unstable commodification of Cora.

An incorruptible Columbia is frequently depicted presiding over the hemisphere's many others—particularly blacks and Native Americans who, in tableaux after tableaux, kneel in adoration at Columbia's feet and in such a way license their own oppression according to the irrepressible U.S. empire's civilizing march across the continent and, this study has stressed, the tradeways of the Atlantic and the Caribbean Sea. The figure of the West Indian creole woman should be understood therefore as Columbia's constitutive double, Columbia's figuration signifying a Republic that violently exploits for purposes of power and prestige "monstrous," creolizing hemispheric realities that the figure of the West Indian creole woman is made to embody according to her "blood" entanglements. So we encounter in Charles Brockden Brown's novel *Ormond* (1799) charged scenes of homoeroticism between the Philadelphia heroine Constantia Dudley, who only narrowly escapes being raped by the novel's eponymous archvillain, and the sister of her attacker, the radical Martinette Beauvais, corrupted by her participation in the revolutions and uprisings of the circum-Caribbean world.

Chapter 1 referred to Samuel Keimer, the ungentlemanly rival printer whom Franklin banishes from Philadelphia according to his text's recurring acts of paracolonial negation. Keimer's *Caribbeana* (1741), a miscellany comprising writings from his *Barbados Gazette*, includes accounts of current events, letters to the editor, original verse, and other pieces authored by creole West Indians and visiting English "gentlemen," as well as many contributions by Keimer under various sobriquets, most prominent and intriguing among them "Christopher Creole." Widely circulated in England and in the West Indian colonies, *Caribbeana* is marked by a vexing tension between Keimer's project of creole uplift on the one hand, and his determination to present Barbados "as it is" on the other. These twin motives as often conflict as prove mutually ennobling. That is, Keimer frequently incurs the wrath of the *Barbados Gazette*'s readers, Barbadians not a little displeased that the Philadelphia immigrant has taken on himself the mission of exposing to the metropolitan center "our Nakedness" (1:64). Amplifying on this point, one of Keimer's most ardent detractors berates him for the ways in which his insinuation of a printing press into the Barbadian community formalizes the putatively flexible, informal terms of sociocultural relations between Barbadians that privilege oral rather than print-centered transactions and negotiations of disputes (1:35). The unnamed critic seems less concerned with having an oral society transformed by Keimer's press into a two-dimensional "imagined community" of print than with the ways in which such a print version of Bridgetown decontextualizes three-dimensional aspects of Barbadian "local knowledge," providing justification for stereotypical assumptions about creole West Indians promulgated by a privileged metropolitan center.

To return to the ways in which figurations of West Indian creole women can help us refocus our critical attention and exhume what otherwise has been forgotten, I look at two particular pieces from *Caribbeana*, letters treating the comedy of courtship between West Indian creole men and women. These letters evince competing creolizing and colonizing tendencies. In the first letter, Barbadian "Batchelors and Widowers," pseudonymously identified as "Century Lackwives," critique single Barbadian women, "*Creolia's*" (1:59), for their too-intimate relations with black female slaves and with "foreign" men. Regarding the first charge, the Batchelors hold, "You are accused of several great *Foibles*, such as valuing yourselves too much on your Negroes, lisping their Language; as Slaves, using them too familiarly" (1:56). Single Barbadian men charge white creole women therefore with embodying a transatlantic stereotype of creole degeneracy as a result of their too-close proximity with their female slaves such that it affects their carriage, their spoken language, and their willingness to participate in intimate relations with white creole men. Such interracial relationships prevent white West Indian creole women, the Batchelors argue, from becoming proper "British gentlewomen," something they could only accomplish were they to be "as polite in [their] Language as in [their] Dress; and learn to write a Stile, as well as direct a Negro" (1:56).

To deflect charges of a double standard, the Batchelors admit that they themselves have sexual relations "with your Sex of an inferior Species," which they confess "truly is base for White Men so to do," though they claim such relations are "chiefly owning to your Scorn of us" (1:58). Lest we get too carried away with the notion that black and mulatto creole women disrupt and thereby achieve a measure of agency over the economy of manners between white creole men and women— which, indeed, they did—the "Married Men" of Barbados in their own follow-up letter lay bare the coercive environment in which such subversions unfold when they propose that in all ages "a small Probation of Batchelors has been held necessary," and that by their having intimate relations with slave women, the would-be white creole wife is the recipient of two benefits. Namely, intimate relations with slave women provide for the carrying on of "Business and Diversion at the same Time; and improves our Estates, whilst it recreates our Sons" (1:62). The pseudonymous "Century Havewives" here reproduce a superstition that the firstborn of a white man's "seed" in the tropics is often a miscarried or a tempestuous child; by not subjecting the wife and the "white" family to such a danger, they profess in their sexual indiscretions to be performing a noble service on behalf of their spouses (1:62). Creole white men and women negotiate, then, the terms of their relations with one another over the bodies of their black female slaves, who achieve a kind of negative power over both given white creoles' concerns about actualizing in their conduct and deportment signs of their "inherent" creole degeneracy. Indeed, as we have seen, such a crisis in "intimate relations" between creole whites and blacks became fodder for charges of creole degeneracy in natural history accounts of the West Indies across the eighteenth century. By reproducing such letters in his miscellany for an English audience, "Christopher Creole" would seem to reinforce, indeed allow for, the proliferation of stereotypes about West Indian creole degeneracy.

The binary relation between metropolitan center and colonial periphery seemingly reinforced above is belied, however, by a sustained critique of the second major downfall of white West Indian women: their susceptibility to the wiles of the "Out-landish" (1:58)—non–West Indians from Great Britain, North America, and elsewhere:

Let those Persons be as worthy as they will, yet it must be allowed that the Bulk of them, who come here to prey upon us, are either of the Learned Professions, or are Merchants. . . . The Merchants, we allow furnish us with Provision for ourselves and our Negroes; but don't they, in the End, commonly take ourselves and our Negroes for their Provisions? . . . The Inference to be drawn from all this is evident, namely, that she who marries a Man who subsists on the Misfortunes of her Country, becomes one Flesh with the Enemy of her Country. (1:61)

Thus Barbadian white women are urged, as a sign of their allegiance to their "Country"—defined in opposition to England, Ireland, and the North American colonies—to avoid rewarding those who seek to exploit the island's plantation economies for purposes of self-interest and greed. The Batchelors and Married Men alike warn that foreign men are masters of artifice, thereby predicting the schemes by which Robinson's Sons of Columbia win the fortunes and bodies of creole women in his play, and the stratagems adopted by U.S. mercantile men like Thomas Welbeck in *Arthur Mervyn* or Thomas Craig in *Ormond* who impersonate "West Indians" or act like "West Indian" nabobs in order to exploit and defraud others—particularly West Indian and North American women. As the Batchelors argue, "When you wed your Countrymen, you know what you do. You *don't buy a Pig in a Poke.* WE don't chouse you with sham patch'd up Constitutions. . . . But, when you take up with a Stranger, you venture your Fortune, your Honour, yea, all your Lives future Happiness, for a Face, or Shape, or Mien you like; for a well-hung deceitful Tongue" (1:57).

Peter Stallybrass and Allon White have remarked on "a production of identity through negation" in British literature and culture that suggests "[t]he civic body is *topographically* reformed by the unceremonious exportation and dumping of libido in the countryside and in the far colonies, where, at the end of the next century, it will be miraculously rediscovered and hailed as a new life-source" (89), hence Bill Clinton's "Our nation is a Caribbean nation." The "Batchelors" and "Husbands" letters that incriminate the "patch'd up" nature of not West Indian but British and North American mercantile "Constitutions" thus endeavor to destabilize the sorts of topographical displacements that Stallybrass and White suggest structure the hierarchical relations between the "civilized" metropolitan centers of Europe and their "barbarous" colonies.

My first chapter treated Equiano's ingenious negation of Franklin's West Indian negations according to which he gives voice to the "other" Philadelphia that Franklin seeks to displace onto the West Indies. Likewise, a poem by Phillis Wheatley, if it does not negate, at least illuminates the entangled poetics of knowing and not-knowing informing the above letters in Keimer's *Caribbeana*. Perhaps unsurprisingly, the figure of the (black) creole woman provides a vantage point from which to mount such a critique. In her late colonial poetry, Wheatley scrutinizes the nexus between North American and West Indian creole societies and cultures across the various port cities of the continent and the islands. She does so from a gendered perspective distinct from Equiano's, powerfully redirecting our attention—according to a stealthily heterodox poetics—to the figure of the black female slave silenced in the above "comedy" of manners.

In the opening stanza of "To a Lady on Her Coming to North America With Her Son, for the Recovery of Her Health" (1773), Wheatley demarcates the profound distinction between the ways in which she was transported to the New World—via the Middle Passage—and the ways that the white creole Jamaican lady who is the poem's subject is conveyed to Boston via Philadelphia from Kingston:

> See from Jamaica's fervid shore she moves,
> Like the fair mother of the blooming loves,
> When from above the Goddess with her hand
> Fans the soft breeze, and lights upon the land;
> Thus she on Neptune's wat'ry realm reclin'd
> Appear'd, and thus invites the ling'ring wind. (7–8)

The evocative tone of Caribbean pastoral that Freneau in "Santa Cruz" strikes and that Chapter 3 systematically critiqued is operative here as well, except that the poem proceeds in an inverse topographical direction. Wheatley's white creole Jamaican woman is conveyed like Venus from a "malignant" (10) Jamaican climate to an ostensibly milder northern North America. If Freneau in occasional poems like "Lines Written at Port-Royal" provides a set of vernacular translations of the "pent-up" complaints of Jamaican blacks against their white masters, Wheatley inverts the power dynamics attending to such translations. She deftly ventriloquizes the privileged voice in relation to herself as a black slave woman of a West Indian creole "lady": "The Northern milder climes I long to greet, / There hope that health will my arrival meet" (11–12). Wheatley exploits eighteenth-century climatological theories of race holding that blacks and whites alike might improve not just their health but also their characters by relocating from a tropical climate to a more temperate Northern one. Writing as both poet and slave from the putatively more salubrious "Northern" climate, Wheatley suggests that the administration of the peculiar institution—in more or less harsh ways—across climates is what accounts for ill physical and mental health of white creole men and the central figure of her poem, the Jamaican "lady," not climate per se. In that regard, whereas the white creole lady gains passage from Jamaica to North America on vessels plying the West Indian trade routes in the poem, such vessels exploit, in paracolonial fashion, the West Indian plantation economies for material benefit at the expense of women of the black diaspora like Wheatley who, as a slave, does not enjoy the same "freedom" of mobility that her imaginatively figured West Indian creole woman does.

If what mortifies Barbados "Batchelors and Husbands" is West Indian creole white women's tendency to become "infected" with the manners of their black female slaves, Wheatley brilliantly de-authorizes the unidirectional nature of such anxieties. From her location as a black female slave marked by such debasing discourses across the circumatlantic world, she summons the "Indulgent muse!" that, in turn, provides the space necessary for Wheatley to interrogate the terms of relation between black female slaves and their white Jamaican creole mistresses as depicted in dominant accounts. Significantly, Wheatley inverts the hierarchical representations of West Indian speech acts by critiquing the "gentlewoman" speech that the "Batchelors" and "Husbands" in the above letters profess to desire as a sign of civilized/savage distinction.

More to the point, Wheatley's negation of the negation of black creole women's voices in white-authored texts is characteristic of the ways in which, according to Srinivas Aravamudan, "tropicopolitan" writers refigure the hierarchical terms of relation informing colonialist discourses in order to achieve a measure of agency as self-authorizing subjects. Aravamudan "propose[s] the term tropicopolitan as a name for the colonized subject who exists both as fictive construct of colonial tropology *and* actual resident of tropical space, object of representation *and* agent of resistance. In many historical instances, tropicopolitans—the residents of the tropics, the bearers of its marks, and the shadow images of more visible metropolitans—challenge the developing privilege of Enlightenment cosmopolitans" (4). When Wheatley as poet of creolizing relation speaks her white creole subject's command—"Waft me, ye gales, from this malignant shore; / The Northern milder climes I long to greet, / There hope that health will my arrival meet" (11–12)—she simultaneously pronounces her ironic relation as slave in that "milder climate" to that command. Such an inversion is emphasized when Wheatley's own voice inserts itself in the poem, re-imposing the division between the poet and the poem's subject as attendant and attendee respectively: "Thence I attend you to Bostonia's arms, / Where gen'rous friendship ev'ry bosom warms: Thrice welcome here! May health revive again" (22–24).

As Kathryn Bassard in a brilliant reading of Wheatley's poem argues, "the multiplication of perspectives at work in Wheatley's appropriated 'I' of this poem shifts the terms of signification by rendering the signifiers of Western cultural spaces unstable. Wheatley relativizes the meanings mapped onto Jamaica/North-America by shifting the referents of health/dis-ease, recovery/loss. In the process all signifiers become suspect" (51). Bassard thus anticipates the improvisational attributes that Aravamudan affords the "tropicopolitan" subject. Wheatley's de- and re-territorialization of the circuits of meaning become especially palpable in the poem's final stanza wherein a highly sentimentalized return of the white creole woman to her family in Jamaica exists in binary relation to the fact that Wheatley and the unnamed West Indian slave women of the letters in Keimer's *Caribbeanna*, regardless of the "clime" in which they live, will never enjoy such a "family" reunion. That resistant reality signifies in ironic ways on the highly stylized, anthropomorphic Jamaican landscape that welcomes the Jamaican lady "home": "shouts of joy Jamaica's rocks resound, / With shouts of joy the country rings around" (33–34). If such a melodramatic reunion is possible in Jamaica's ostensibly "fervid" and "malignant" climate, then the reader wonders what has changed to allow for the transformation of Jamaica's "dark recesses" (16) into salubrious environments that "resound" with "joy"?

Jamaica's black slaves are nowhere present in the poem; indeed, their strategically figured absence draws our attention all the more to them and to Wheatley's subversive voice. Wheatley's is the only "face" of hemispheric blackness in a text whose creolizing poetics of relation undermines what Aravamudan terms "the developing privilege of Enlightenment cosmopolitans" from a northern North American point of view characterized by Wheatley's "paracolonial" improvisations and exposures. In establishing her contentious relation to Enlightenment knowledges—the hierarchies of race and place that attend to climatological theory, the civilized/savage binary that maps itself on the back of the West Indian slave woman—Wheatley demonstrates her mastery of Enlightenment knowledges as a *black* "Gentlewoman," knowledges that provide for her ongoing enslavement, not in Kingston but in Boston where the white Jamaican woman in her poem goes to cure her nervous condition.

Likewise, if European and creole whites across the circumatlantic world believe that black female slaves "corrupt" and degenerate the tastes and manners of would-be West Indian gentlewomen, Wheatley by "talking too much English," to evoke a charge made by a white British man against Equiano, de-authorizes such arguments by redirecting our attention to how they foreclose the liberatory potential of such creolizing vernaculars—whether it be a white West Indian woman speaking too much black creole, or a black woman speaking too much gentlewoman's English, or the considered silence of a white European or creole male character or author who recognizes the value of listening to, rather than negating from a position of imperiled self-interest, such revolutionary exchanges.

In an act of extraordinary irony given his own revolutionary leanings and reputation for promulgating anarchy, Aaron Burr is thrust into the location of considered silence in Mary Hassal/Leonora Sansay's novel *The Secret History; or, the Horrors of St. Domingo* (1808). The man who shot and killed Hamilton and who was charged with plotting an insurrection in the Western territories of North America against the United States government is the silent addressee of the bundle of letters that constitute this extraordinary work. If "History seen from above and history seen from below are irreducibly different and . . . impose radically different perspectives on the question of hierarchy" (Stallybrass and White 4), then the secret behind Sansay's *Secret History* is how, like Wheatley's poem, it self-reflexively mobilizes history "from above" and "from below," a poetics of creoleness and another of creolization. Glissant has held that "creolized" people "do not 'need' the idea of Genesis, because they do not need the myth of pure lineage" (*Carribean Discourse* 141). The frame narrator, Mary, for much of the novel remains hostage to a poetics of creoleness. Yet her sister Clara recreates her identity, not as Genesis but as the culturally impure figure of postcolonial creolité, acquiring the ability during a West Indian odyssey that propels her across the Francophone, Hispanic, and Anglophone West Indies to reassemble languages and cultures, histories and philosophies fragmented by the violence of colonialism and countercolonial revolution.

Joan Dayan has provided the most influential assessment of *Secret History*, arguing that the novel's "insights into the relations between castes and colors during the last days of Saint-Domingue reveal more about the kinds of mixture and erosion of boundaries that prevailed there than any other document about this period" (172). Dayan demonstrates how Sansay's text, like vodoun itself, transfigures the monstrous excess of slave violence and revolution in its multiple scenes of domination, intrigue, and seduction in order to fracture and subvert dominant representations of these things. Powerful as it is, Dayan's reading focuses on the parts of the novel set in and around the French colony of Saint-Domingue during its "last days" as the Haitian Revolution achieves fruition. Instead, as Michael Drexler does in a compelling essay that focuses on the novel's multiple "modes of women's collectivity" responsive to "the world-shattering implications of the revolutionary collective formed against slavery on Saint-Domingue" (186), I want to treat the novel's various settings across the circum-Caribbean region, especially as they proliferate on the two sisters fleeing the scene of revolution in Saint-Domingue by stowing away on a light vessel. Across the novel's multiple topographical sites, the intricacies of form and character that Dayan identifies are heightened and extended in important ways. Whereas Mary remains hostage to a grammar of creoleness in relation to French, Spanish (especially), and British West Indian creole societies and cultures, Clara evolves into a figure of creolité—a creolized and creolizing West Indian goddess in the making.

At the novel's outset, Mary relates how she and Clara relocate from their native Philadelphia to Saint-Domingue with Clara's new husband, St. Louis, a Saint-Domingue planter who seeks to reestablish his fortune after having fled the country at the outbreak of the Haitian Revolution. The novel foregrounds how, amid the chaos of revolution, U.S. American urban economies and merchants operate paracolonially to benefit themselves. Clara's motives for marrying St. Louis mirror the motives of U.S. commerce, both exploiting the Haitian Revolution for purposes of self-interest and financial gain. Yet U.S. paracolonialism and Clara are imperiled when Toussaint L'Ouverture is seized and sent to France by agents of Napoleon on Clara's and her sister's arrival in Cape Francois. As U.S. merchants and sailors fight alongside the French army, they suffer significant casualties and are unable to stem the tide of the black generals' offensive. Not only are U.S. merchants helpless against the violence of the revolution but the integrity of their motives is immediately suspect. When the Haitian revolutionaries seize a U.S. ship suspected of secreting white and mulatto creoles fleeing the island, the captain saves himself by claiming to have no knowledge of the affair whereas everyone else on board is executed (145). Although U.S. merchants are able to save some white creoles from attack by "conceal[ing] them in stores" (146) on their vessels, British blockades make such rescue efforts highly dangerous, particularly given the resumption of war between the French and British. Even as Mary suggests that perhaps she and Clara as "Americans" may be allowed to pass through the blockade on fleeing Cape Francois, such hopes prove false: not only are they forced to flee the island in a tiny French boat instead of finding "protectors in [the] American merchants" (146), but the boat is immediately seized by the British as an "enemy" vessel and the women are transshipped to the Spanish West Indies. Whereas in Robinson's drama of commercial utopia heroic Sons of Columbia rescue West Indian creoles from tyranny, in Sansay's novel U.S. merchant men cannot even protect their own female compatriots from British search and seizure.

Although such traumas prove unsettling for Mary, Clara seizes on the opportunity of an escalating conflict to escape not only the revolution itself but her jealous and violently abusive husband, the Haitian revolutionaries' acts of rebellion seeming to enable and ennoble Clara's own. Such consanguinity is not just "seeming," I suggest, but actualized, materialized, and spiritualized across the balance of the novel; Clara forges a creolizing sensibility marked by her intricate relations with oppressed peoples across the islands of the West Indies, a development inversely related to Mary's inability to let go of her conservative bourgeois value system.

Much of the narrative is told from Mary's point of view and exhibits the sort of racialized melancholy found in nineteenth-century European and American travel writing in the Caribbean. The West Indies become the abject to Mary's untenably pure idea of "home." At the first sign of serious difficulty in the novel, Mary is "all anxiety to return to the continent" (35). Mary's investment in a nostalgic notion of Philadelphia contrasts with her sister's unwillingness for much of the narrative to even consider a return there. For Mary, hardship tends to reinforce her stereotypical views about foreign creoles and to heighten her desire to return "home." Clara responds quite differently, preferring "exile" in Cuba, her exilic consciousness a sign of her proliferating affiliations with poor and refugee populations across the "foreign" West Indies.

Not all of Mary's reflections on the scene of "horror" in Saint-Domingue prove racialist or colonizing in their impulse. As Dayan demonstrates, Mary progressively critiques the ways in which the French army wages a campaign of terror and brutality that almost seems to exceed in its horrors the one perpetrated by the black revolutionaries. Although creoles are accused in the metropolitan center of indulging in "monstrous" excess, Mary describes how the commanding generals Le Clerc and especially Rochambeau prove unparalleled in their capacity for vice, luxurious spending, and scandalous conduct. In such ways, Mary's account de-essentializes hierarchies between a civilized center and a barbarous periphery, between enlightened metropolitans and degenerate creoles. Accordingly, she reports how the creoles regret the departure of Toussaint, claiming that under his leadership they were "less vexed by the negroes than by those who have come to protect them" (34). Mary also acknowledges the black revolutionaries' right to fight for their "freedom" and recognizes that whites are not alone entitled to the "blessing of liberty" (25).

Still, progressive insights such as these exist alongside many less generous reflections, as for example her totalizing assessment of the black revolutionaries as "Monsters" (147), or her account of the residents of St. Jago de Cuba as a "degenerate race" (141) prone to promiscuity, gambling, and intrigue. Moreover, even as Mary anoints herself the protector of her sister, ironically she is the one who comes across as utterly dependent on Clara, incapable of functioning apart from her sister's far more dynamic, inspiring, and adventurous character. Indeed, Sansay almost seems to unmask Mary as an impostor, a too-stylized representative of the "cult of true womanhood" when Mary writes to Burr, "It is not often in the tranquility of domestic life that the poet or the historian seek their subjects!" (73). As such, Mary functions in the novel to a significant extent as a foil, a caricature in creoleness against whom Clara is cast in creolizing relief.

To my knowledge, there is no evidence that Sansay attended vodoun rituals or was a student of its mythologies and iconography. Neither is there evidence in the text that her seeming "double," Clara, is exposed in direct ways to vodoun, though there is evidence not only of her coming into contact with Afro-Caribbean faith traditions in the Spanish West Indies but of her becoming prepossessed—if not possessed—by the lwa Ezili/Erzulie. Crucially, this moment occurs in Letter 28, when Clara takes over narration of the novel for the first time. Clara writes after being separated from Mary, their separation the occasion for the call and response of letters across the remainder of the narrative. As Drexler suggests (191), Clara's letters reveal her increasing cross-cultural sensitivity and awareness. In Letter 28, which Clara writes from a desolate village fallen prey to imperial copper mining industries that have now forsaken it, she notes that Bayam's "inhabitants, almost all mulattos, are in the last grade of poverty." However, despite their poverty, there exists in the town "a magnificent temple, dedicated to the blessed Virgin. Its ornaments and decorations are superb. The image of the Virgin, preserved in the temple, is said to be miraculous and performs wonderful things. The faith of these people in her power is implicit" (195). Clearly this "temple" is not merely a shrine to Catholic deities.

This extended letter registers, I believe, Clara's "conversion" experience as a devotee to Mary/Erzulie, which, as it unfolds, becomes localized and materialized in Clara's increasing sensitivity to the poor, her contentment living among mixed-raced creole communities, her ever-expanding linguistic facility and talents, and her expressed resentment of tyrannical colonial governments and cultural imperialism. As Clara approaches the temple for the first time, she remarks that

the mind almost involuntarily yields to the belief of supernatural agency. On entering the church the image of the Virgin, fancifully adorned and reposing on a bed of roses, appears like the presiding genius of the place. . . . the obscurity that reigns within . . . fill[s] the mind with awe; and we pardon the superstitious faith of the ignorant votaries of this holy lady, cherished as it is by every circumstance that can tend to make it indelible! (196)

Clara's final note of condescension might seem to undermine the otherwise "supernatural agency" that descends on her and which she "indelibl[y]" feels, but she asks her sister, who has shown nothing but disgust for local Spanish creole faith practices, to "pardon" with her these villagers' devotion, suggesting that she herself has not only already done so but is herself taken by the Virgin's spirit. It is in Bayam where Clara aggressively insinuates herself into the fabric of creole society, and her communal awareness is ever more sensitive following this "initiation" experience. For example, when her friend attributes the mulatto villagers' "abject poverty" to their racial inferiority, Clara argues that she does so "unjustly," insisting instead that their poverty is "entirely owing to their vicious [colonial] government" (200). Thus Clara begins to demonstrate, as devotee to Mary/Erzulie, her inter-American creole commitments toward social justice, toward "destroy[ing] the cunning imperial dichotomy of master and slave, or colonizer and colonized" (Dayan 72), and toward an ethics of creolization as lived-faith practice.

There is one other important connection between Clara and Erzulie/Mary. Recall in the passage above that on entering the temple, Clara remarks how the "image of the Virgin, fancifully adorned and reposing on a bed of roses, appears like the presiding genius of the palace." This regal description recalls the way in which Clara is described when she first dons the creole fashions of Saint-Domingue for a party hosted in "in a fairy palace" by General Rochambeau: "A robe of white crape shewed to advantage the contours of her elegant person. Her arms and bosom were bare; her black hair, fastened on top with a brilliant comb, *was ornamented by a rose which seemed to have been thrown there by accident*" (30; emphasis added). Sansay thus proleptically figures Clara's initiation in the temple devoted to Mary/Erzulie at Bayam; Ezili/Erzulie, like Aphrodite, is known for her otherworldly beauty, precisely the sort of bewitching beauty that Clara seems to possess.

To align Clara with Erzulie is to align her with not only a resistant, creolizing force as lived experience but also to associate her with ways in which creolization is marked textually. According to Leslie Desmangles, Erzulie represents

the embodiment of human longing for an ideal in which human fantasy transcends the limitations of mundane reality and the exigencies of privation. . . . [S]he symbolizes not merely the mother of fantasy but the mother of mythopoeia as well, for around her persona Vodouisants have developed an oral literature: a large complex of poems, songs, and stories extolling her virtues. (132)

Eventually, Mary acknowledges Clara's "mental magic" (221), the deft ways in which she "surprise[s others] with ingenious combinations of their own materials, and with results which they did not dream of" (222), and her ability to "fascinate, intoxicate, [and] transport" (223). When Mary writes to Burr at novel's end that she hopes to be able to "infuse into your bosom those sentiments for my sister which glow so warmly in my own" (225), the *author* Mary Hassal/Leonora Sansay collapses the boundaries between Clara and herself and announces her own creolizing mythopoetic intentions, products of her own experiences while living in exile in the West Indies. On arriving in the Cape at the novel's outset, Mary announces that a "[n]ew world [was] opening to my view" (2). On embarking once more for Philadelphia, Sansay/ Clara, denizens of West Indian border territories and masters of mythopoetic creolization, promise to "open" a new world, too, to Burr's already revolutionary, radicalized vision, a *Secret History* as "seen from below" in the West Indies.

I end this project by suggesting, as a devotee of Sansay's creolizing mythopoeia, how as early U.S. Americanists we might provide a subaltern, symptomatic reading of Cooper's text. For Clara is at once the fore- and afterlife of Cooper's Cora Munro. She embodies at novel's end, on her departure for Philadelphia, the same potent, mythopoetic, revolutionary forces of creolization that Cooper must work so very hard to repress, or, more precisely, entomb.

To read Cooper from below is to attend to the novel's creole complex and to confront his conscious grammar of creoleness with the novel's creolizing unconscious. In that regard, I am certainly not the first critic to suggest Cooper's preoccupation with racial science and phobia for racial mixing. Nor am I the first critic to identify the threat that Cora poses to the "domestic" home front. Yet by juxtaposing the novel's conscious grammar of creoleness with its creolizing unconscious, we might be more sensitive to the precise kind of creolizing threat that Cora poses and exactly in what ways she augurs to corrupt the "home front" of the expansionist Republic as "Columbia." Such a reading pivots on Cooper's womb/tomb imagery as it relates to the specular politics involving the reader and the charged relationship between the Munro family and Magua.

The "spectres" (11) that haunt the novel's opening are also the ones buried and entombed at its end. The specular politics of the first chapter is intricate and telling: in seriatim we are witness to a Jamaican "war-horse" like one "never before . . . beheld" (8); a creole-confused "savage" characterized by "an air of neglect" ("The colors of the war-paint had blended in dark confusion about his fierce countenance, and rendered his swarthy lineaments still more savage and repulsive" [8]); and finally, Cora, whose "complexion was not brown, but rather appeared charged with the color of rich blood" (10). Magua's "spectre" frightens all but Cora, who "coldly" asks, "Should we distrust the man because his manners are not our manners, and that his skin is dark?" (12). Although Cora demonstrates no fear of Magua, this assemblage of images with which Cooper opens *Last of the Mohicans* emblematizes a fear of creole maroonage that by 1826 had materialized repeatedly in the hemisphere. Positioning Magua and Cora in relation to each other in this scene not only illuminates the extraordinary otherness betokened by their creole (con)fusions but also foregrounds the dangerous possibility of their affinity.

The Seminole Wars began in 1818 and would continue through 1859 in the Southeastern part of the United States. Some of the fiercest fighters in that conflict were the Black Seminoles, maroon communities formed of mixed African and Native American "blood." Simultaneously Denmark Vesey plotted a Haitian-inspired slave rebellion in South Carolina in 1823, and significant maroon wars transpired in the West Indies, including one in Jamaica in 1822–24 and another in Dominica in 1809–14. Moreover, the greatest maroon war in Jamaican history unfolded precisely as the Treaty of Paris negotiations were under way at the conclusion of the French and Indian War, the setting for *The Last of the Mohicans*. Maroons across the Americas established "African communities outside of and often in opposition to the great Euro-Creole Plantations" (Brathwaite, *Roots* 229) for purposes of mutual protection, cultural conservation, and violent resistance to colonial institutions. Thus in sketching the specular alignments between Cora, Magua, and the Jamaican warhorse, Cooper not so subtly creates a tableau suggesting that these figures are the constituent parts of a potential maroon resistance. That is, underlying Cooper's desire to populate the frontier with men who know "no cross of blood" (282) like Hawkeye is the national uncanny figured as a "monstrous," maroon-infested West Indies.

When Munro impulsively explains Cora's background, he, like Alexander Hamilton, claims noble Scottish ancestry to offset any misgiving

Cora's would-be betrothed Heyward might have about her mixed-race creole blood. Munro reports, "it was my lot to form a connection with one who in time became my wife, and the mother of Cora. She was the daughter of a gentleman of those isles, by a lady whose misfortune it was, if you will . . . to be descended, remotely, from that unfortunate class who are so basely enslaved to administer to the wants of a luxurious people. Ay, sir, that is the curse entailed on Scotland by her unnatural union with a foreign and trading people" (164). Tellingly, the "South" appears here as well, in the person of Heyward. In response to the charge that he seemed hesitant to marry into a "race inferior to your own," Heyward renounces such prejudice although "at the same time [he was] conscious of such a feeling . . . deeply rooted as if it had been grafted in his nature" (164).

These "deeply rooted" sentiments triumph at the end of Cooper's novel when one of Magua's accomplices kills Cora even as the novel, operating along the lines of a Foucauldian "genealogy," "introduces discontinuity . . . that commit[s] itself to its own dissipation" (*Language* 154, 162). That is, the injuries that Magua causes to be inflicted on Cora in a highly stylized "maroon" cave that is their womb/tomb, like the whip marks that Cora's father orders to be inflicted on Magua that inspire his spectacular vengeance, are what Guyanese writer Wilson Harris terms "symptoms of historylessness, rootlessness—stigmata of the void" ("Interior" 12). As such, they are the markings of subalternity. Our challenge as readers of Cooper's novel, then, is the one Harris poses in *Womb of Space*: to reverse the magical practice of the bokor by "making the dead let go" (xvii). Cora's wounds provide for a symptomatic reading of the ambiguous fissures in Cooper's novel; "seen from below," they are material referents to the text's floating West Indian signifiers.

To read Cooper from "below" is to read, as I have tried to do in this study, according to postcolonial creolité—to reassemble and re-empower "West Indian" images and bodies, histories and philosophies fragmented by the power of the figure of the United States as "Columbia." Exhuming Cora Munro, bringing her "back to life" as it were, entails the critical ability to reveal the ways in which creolizing syntaxes form themselves as mythopoeia in vexed relation to grammars of creoleness or colonization. Such conjurations are only possible when critics of early U.S. American literature and culture apprehend the ways in which the New Republic's creole complex and manifold acts of paracolonial negation people the literary terrain with West Indian ghosts like Cora's.

Notes

Introduction

1. My understanding of the publication histories of "Thoughts" and the Rendón letter derives from the fine editors' notes on the latter text. See Morris 467–70, 476–79.

2. For discussions of European natural history writings—including extensive treatment of New World creole discourse—see Glacken; Gerbi; Commager and Giordanetti; and Chinard. For analyses that focus on the U.S. response to European environmental theories about the New World, see Commager; and Boorstin. For a deft analysis of how racial discourse helped consolidate a predominantly "white" and "masculine" U.S. national identity in the post-Revolutionary period, see Nelson.

3. Although encounters between European Americans, Native Americans, and African Americans are not always discussed in specifically "creole" terms, there is a voluminous body of literature on such encounters. See, for example, Jordan; Axtell; Todorov; Hulme; Greene; Hoxie; Kolodny; and Shuffelton. For a fine essay that shares my interest in comparative creole identities in the Americas, see Bauer, "Creole Identities in Colonial Space: The Narratives of Mary White Rowlandson and Francisco Núñez de Pineda y Bascuñán." Bauer juxtaposes the two captivity narratives—one authored by an Anglo-American Puritan, the other by a Catholic Spanish American—so as to demonstrate "both the distinctiveness of America's various New World transculturations vis-à-vis the Old World and inter-American national and regional differences" (666). The essay is reproduced in Bauer, *The Cultural Geography of Colonial American Literatures*, which provides a compelling array of such comparative assessments. See, too, St. George's elegant introduction to his essay collection *Possible Pasts*, wherein he states, "Becoming 'colonial' was an intricate process. It involved both vernacular theories of lived experience of race and racial mixture, commercial exchange, kinship alliance, aesthetics, creolization, language, civility, savagery, and ambiguity concerning one's social position and personal power" (5).

4. The Alien Act authorized the President to order out of the country all U.S. aliens considered to be subversive, while the Alien Enemies Act gave the President the power to arrest, imprison, or banish aliens who were subjects of an enemy nation. For an analysis of these three acts, see Miller, esp. 144–53 and 188–89, for discussions of the effects of these acts on the refugees from Saint-Domingue; see also James Morton Smith.

5. For a brilliant study of the permutations of "creole" races and cultures in Haiti at the time of the Haitian Revolution, see Dayan. For discussion of the formation of Afro-Creole culture in Jamaica from 1655 to 1838, see Burton, esp. 13–46; and Brathwaite, *Development*. For two accounts of the politics of racial and

cultural admixtures in Latin America throughout the colonial period and into the nineteenth century, see Gruzinski; and see Morner. See also Bauer, *Cultural Geography*, which, as I describe above (see note 3), is comparativist in its approach to early Anglo- and Spanish American colonial literatures and identities. For the multiple and shifting meanings of "creole" contemporary to the acquisition of the Louisiana territories by the United States, see Hall; Dominguez; and Treagle.

6. For example, French creoles in Louisiana transformed what had been a more neutral racial, cultural, and national designation under Spanish colonialism—"creole"—into a term of identity that signified their resistance to Anglo-American imperialism in 1804.

7. Archer also uses the term "paracolonial" in *Old Worlds: Egypt, Southwest Asia, India, and Russia in Early Modern English Writing*. Consistent with our arriving at the term independently, Archer defines "paracolonial" according to literary and cultural traditions (Renaissance), periods (pre-1700), regions (Europe in relation to the "Old World"), and material conditions (European trading with those regions) in ways that are distinct from those that I treat in my study. Archer, nonetheless, arrives at the term "paracolonial" as I did: so as to understand aesthetic features of a literary and cultural tradition that forms itself in relation to a political economy not accounted for by extant terminology in postcolonial studies, which too frequently proceeds according to a colonized/colonizer binary. Writes Archer, "It is vital to avoid the notion of 'pre-colonial' studies . . . for the sixteenth and seventeenth centuries did not contain the germs of the inevitable colonization of the rest of the Old World by Europe; Russia and the Ottomans were never colonized in the conventional sense at all. A proper consideration of Europe amidst the Old World during the early modern period requires a concept like *para-colonial* studies" (16–17). If particular in definition, form and application, Archer's and *Creole America*'s respective accounts of paracolonialism suggest that a field of study that exists in relation to, but is not the same as, the larger field of postcolonial studies is perhaps emerging across periods, continents, traditions, and areas of study, the field of *paracolonial studies.*

8. The more widely recognized phenomenon of U.S. internal colonialism on the continent, which entails the expansion of the so-called U.S. empire for liberty westward according to federally sanctioned projects like chattel slavery and the removal and genocide of Native Americans amid ongoing and overlapping conflicts between the U.S. and European empires in the North American interior, between the nation's urban citizens and leaders and white settler colonists in the West, and between those settlers and blacks and Native Americans, might be understood as unfolding not apart from but in coterminous, if frequently tense, relation with the paracolonial push for an extranational U.S. empire for commerce in the late eighteenth and early nineteenth centuries in the West Indies (as well as the East Indies and Asia). For a treatment of the issue of internal colonialism according to "second world" postcolonial models, see Edward Watts, *An American Colony*. Watts's study "engages the entanglement of regional and national cultures and finds in it the markers of colonial asymmetries . . . a plurality too often hidden by a view of American culture as surveyed from the Old North Church" (xxv). See also Schueller and Watts's "Introduction" to their *Messy Beginnings* for a useful account of how early U.S. Americanists in their scholarship have been "building upon the work of theorists of settler colonialisms" (5), including many of the contributors to their collection. For a fine

adaptation of Gayatri Spivak's famed postcolonial concept of the "subaltern" to treat the phenomenon of rural rebellion in the United States as "subaltern" rebellion of a particular kind—the Paxton Riots, Pontiac's Conspiracy, Shays' Rebellion, the Whiskey Rebellion—see White. In this study, the "region" unsettling seamless notions of national character and identity is the West Indies, and its key "subaltern" figure is the West Indian creole (across races).

9. I adapt the phrase "creole complex" as well from Lawrence S. Kaplan's substantially more narrow usage of it in *Entangling Alliances with None*. Kaplan uses the concept to account for the commercial crisis that led to the U.S. War of 1812 with the British, a topic he treats with great range and insight.

10. In addition to Brathwaite and Glissant and the critics listed in n. 5 above, this study's account of creolization has profited from scholarship on the topic produced on a variety of subjects across a range of disciplines. The proliferation of such studies make it impractical to note them all here, nor is anything approaching a comprehensive account of them produced in the study's body. For influential studies of creolization in relation to Caribbean literature, see Dash, *The Other America*, and Antonio Benítez-Rojo, *The Repeating Island*; both texts employ theories of creolization as a way of reconciling modern/postmodern tensions in twentieth-century Caribbean writing, if in distinct ways. Similarly, in *Islands and Exiles*, Bongie treats a range of colonial and postcolonial texts, not all of them set in the Caribbean, to argue for their overlapping modern and postmodern tendencies, "a double space [of identity], neither here nor there, but always in between and in transit" (24). Raiskin, *Snow on the Cane Fields*, considers the transnational meanings of "creole" in comparative South African and Caribbean literary contexts. Finally, a recent issue of the *Journal of American Folklore* is devoted to "Creolization." See *JAF* 116 (Winter 2003).

11. In its exclusive focus on the early national period, *Creole America* complements recent efforts by American studies scholars to interrogate from a *hemispheric* vantage point dominant critical tendencies to understand nineteenth-century U.S. literary and cultural formation from a bounded "national" and thus "exceptional" perspective. See, for example, Amy Kaplan, *The Anarchy of Empire in the Making of U.S. Culture*, a work that shares *Creole America*'s impulse to understand conceptions of "nation" as interwoven with emergent ideas of the U.S. as empire, for Kaplan "movements that both erect and unsettle the ever-shifting boundaries between the domestic and the foreign, between 'at home' and 'abroad'" (1); Gruesz, *Ambassadors of Culture*, which argues for the mutually formative relation between U.S. and Latino writing in the nineteenth century and usefully directs our attention to the importance of lyric poetry as a mobile, "vernacular" genre providing for literary and cultural translations across borders, an insight to which this study's treatment of Philip Freneau's hemispheric lyrics in Chapter 3 is indebted; Kazanjian, *The Colonizing Trick*, which devotes substantial attention to the early national period and argues that universal and egalitarian ideas of U.S. "citizenship" are coextensive with contradictory hierarchical notions of race and nation that extend throughout the hemisphere, where U.S. "[c]olonizationists explicitly seek both to colonize Africa with Western economic, political, and religious systems, and to create a white nation-state by purging North America of African Americans" (5); Brickhouse, *Transamerican Literary Relations and the Nineteenth-Century Public Sphere*, which across an impressive range of authors and texts demonstrates the manifold ways in which, when considered in the context of U.S.–Latin American and Caribbean relations, the American Renaissance "might more accurately be reconfigured as a

*trans*american renaissance, a period of literary border crossing . . . [and] intercontinental exchange" (8); and Murphy, *Hemispheric Imaginings*, which focuses on the ways in which barely veiled U.S. imperialist ambitions in the nineteenth century, as embodied in the Monroe Doctrine, shape and form a literary culture that advocated transatlantic separation in favor of hemispheric unity. As such, Murphy cautions against uncritically embracing transamerican "hemispheric imaginings" of U.S. literary and cultural production lest critics replicate the imperialist tendencies of the Monroe Doctrine itself.

Chapter 1. Locating the Prenational Origins of Paracolonialism and the Creole Complex

1. This chapter's arguments concur with Warner's assessment that by the middle of the eighteenth century, "American" had come to function as a term of creole nationalism for many, though certainly not all, writers in North America (65). Warner is right to interrogate the critical impulse to label *all* Anglo-American colonial writing authored by those living in what would become the United States as "American" in the protonationalist sense (a point he adopts, in part, from Spengemann; see the arguments in *A Mirror for Americanists* and *A New World of Words*). Only "[l]ater in life," Warner argues, can Franklin be said to have "changed his image and played the American, a role he invented for the occasion [of the *Autobiography*]" (65). Of course, Warner might have noted that Franklin's "Englishness" is itself quite often a performance, an act of resistance to impure or imperfect "British" performances unfolding in the corrupted mercantilist epicenter of empire.

2. Mulford provides a nuanced understanding of the ways in which Franklin's creole nationalism results from his appropriation of European philosophical and scientific ideas for "local" purposes coupled with North Americans' complex relations to blacks and Native Americans: "In my view, the influence of the new science—along with what for the most part seemed to colonial Americans an exclusion of American intellectuals from the centers of European intellectual influence and along with colonial Americans' affiliative sense of their destiny's alignment with Native American and African peoples—worked to assist elite-group English colonials in their wringing a collective self-determination out of the wilderness they were said by Europeans to inhabit" ("New Science" 100).

3. Marc L. Harris treats the related issue of Franklin's "decision to write ethnicity out of Philadelphia" (288). Harris argues that by 1730 Franklin had adopted elite British standards of "politeness" that were "meant to extend virtue through regulating the behavior of men in groups" (288). Relevant is Harris's trenchant suggestion that politeness as a flexible construct was especially suitable for responding to the social and cultural realities of an increasingly commercial and ethnically, racially, and culturally diverse urban North America. The West Indies become the holding place of Philadelphia's "impolite" persons in this chapter's arguments. Franklin's politeness works to repress the diversity attending to Philadelphia's burgeoning commerce not only by suppressing diversity in Philadelphia itself but by actively relocating impoliteness, in marked contrast to a rhetorical tendency to omit or suppress, to the West Indies. The "monstrous" West Indies—its peoples, societies, and cultures—become necessary containers, as it were, for Franklin's anxieties about his and his North American homeland's "degenerate" creole identities as ascribed to them by European natural history discourses and as borne out, in part, according to eth-

nic and racial violence perpetrated by "polite" Anglo-American society in Philadelphia. On Franklin and gentility, see also Shields, *Civil Tongues* 37–39.

4. On Keimer, see Bloore 265–67, 283; and Carlson 385–86. Franklin's debasement and negation of Keimer may devolve, in part, from Keimer's having been the first to undertake a series of projects to which Franklin might otherwise have claimed a "foundational" relationship: to print and publish newspapers both in Philadelphia and the West Indies, to found a school for slaves, and so on.

5. In *Blues, Ideology, and Afro-American Literature*, Baker calls for a reexamination of "traditional" approaches to U.S. canon formation and literary study by reading the interdynamics of commerce and race in Equiano's slave narrative. This chapter extends his critique by urging scholars to read the narrative's "Philadelphia story" in order to comprehend the paracolonial origins of early U.S. American literature and culture. Even so, it is mindful that Equiano's narrative itself cannot be considered U.S. American precisely because of the ways in which he is refused citizen status according to his racial identity. As Kazanjian explains, such exclusions based on hierarchies of race and nation cause Equiano's dream of freedom and equality to be endlessly deferred across the mercantile world (152). In using Equiano to negate Franklin's paracolonial negation, this chapter does not mystify but strategically foregrounds that reality. Recently scholars have raised doubts about Equiano's African origins (see esp. Carretta). Such scrutiny does little to alter the shrewd ways in which an actual and/or fictionalized *Interesting Narrative* operates to negate Franklin's paracolonial negation.

6. See Gates, and see Smith, *Self-Discovery and Authority in Afro-American Narrative.*

7. Equiano first published his narrative two years *after* the passage of the Constitution. Accordingly, his double-voiced Philadelphia account might be said to critique the withholding from blacks of full and equal rights to citizenship. That Equiano ultimately purchased his freedom from King, his Philadelphia master, not in Philadelphia but *in the West Indies* is a development fraught with irony.

8. Franklin expresses in a letter to one of Mecom's Philadelphia creditors disappointment that his nephew has fallen into debt in the West Indies: "The People of those Islands expect a great deal of Credit, and when the Books are out of his hands, if he should die, half would not be collected; This I have learnt by Experience in the Case of poor Smith, whom I settled there" (*PBF* 6:277). Franklin here speaks as an absentee landlord who displaces responsibility for Mecom's inability to run an effective business onto West Indian "People" who traffic in bad credit.

9. This chapter has benefited considerably from several keen studies of Franklin's views on mercantilism and empire building. Works that have been especially helpful include Stourzh; Schlereth; and McCoy (see esp. chaps. 2 and 3).

10. See Douglas Anderson for an optimistic reading of "Observations" as urging assimilation rather than exclusion of what Anderson—drawing on Satan's address to Eve in *Paradise Lost* regarding the Garden "'of fairest colors mixt'"— terms North America's "human fruits" (166–67).

11. In December of 1763, Franklin wrote a letter to John Waring, who was an administrator for a charitable organization promoting black education in the colonies, in which he outlined his shifting attitudes toward blacks' intellectual abilities as a result of visiting a "Negro School" in Philadelphia: "I was on the whole much pleas'd, and from what I then saw, have conceiv'd a higher Opinion of the natural Capacities of the black Race, than I had ever before entertained"

(*PBF* 10:396). The paternalism undergirding Franklin's otherwise more forward-looking views on the "natural" intelligence of blacks reveals itself as Franklin remarks upon the black students' deportment as "orderly, show[ing] a proper Respect and ready Obedience to the Mistress" and as "very attentive to, and a good deal affected by, a serious Exhortation" (*PBF* 10: 395–96) delivered by a clergyman at the conclusion of Franklin's visit.

12. Mulford argues that twentieth-century critical views that characterize Franklin's "sympathy" for Native Americans as progressive in its racial and cross-cultural orientation misunderstand how Franklin commodifies Native Americans in his writings from the "pose of the 'good' Christian" ("Caritas" 347) in ways that ultimately reinforce Franklin's and the Pennsylvania Commonwealth's hegemonic relation to Native peoples. Such commodification functions in ways not unlike the rhetorical operations marking Franklin's Anglo-American Christian sympathy toward black schoolchildren in the passage in the previous note—sympathy as creoleness rather than creolization.

13. See *The Political Unconscious,* esp. 53 and 70.

14. Likewise, many critics have remarked on the self-interest underlying Franklin's Western expansionist ideology, including his investments in several settler colony schemes in the Ohio Valley area and elsewhere. Stourzh provides a candid assessment of Franklin's Western land dealings: "Franklin's interest in westward expansionism during the 1760's and early 1770's is to a large extent connected with his participation in the land speculations of the Illinois Company (founded 1766) and the Indiana Company (1767), which developed into the Grand Ohio Company" (306). See also Alvord 96.

15. It was customary for authors to keep their identities private when weighing in on controversial and momentous debates. For discussions of the pamphlet wars on the Canada-Guadeloupe question in which Franklin's text participates, see Namier; Alvord; and Stourzh.

16. While Franklin began a response to this particular critique of *The Canada Pamphlet,* he never actually completed it. See *PBF* 9:110.

17. For the editors' helpful summary of these four main objections to Franklin's *The Canada Pamphlet,* see *PBF* 9:108.

18. Sussman argues that in the post–Seven Years' War period the British novel registers anxiety about the proliferation of "colonial wealth and commodities" by imagining "British bodies to be under attack by the forces of mercantile accumulation, forces materialized in the catachrestic 'tide of luxury.' The novel reacts to this anxiety by producing fantasies of English economic and physical self-sufficiency—images of consumers able to abstain from purchasing commodities that disturb the social order" (19). Franklin's "*Concerning* SWEETS" thus reproduces the figures and themes of the eighteenth-century British novel as Sussman defines them, in particular the figure of "slave-grown sugar as a moral threat to British values, and, implicitly, as a physical threat to British consuming bodies" (19). He does so, however, from an emergent creole nationalist position that seeks to isolate itself from the British mercantilist project altogether, a project that Franklin and other North Americans believe privileges the interests of the West Indian sugar colonies over North American colonial concerns. Franklin's appeal to consume "native" sugar thus functions as nostalgia for a "pure" and uncorrupted North American creoleness retrieved from a mythic premercantile past masquerading as reformist project for the future whose anxious aim is, in actuality, to "extract" North American commodities, bodies, and institutions from their creolizing entanglements with the West Indies.

19. It is possible to read Franklin's proposed treaty articles as evidence of what Egan suggests is Franklin's cosmopolitan attempt to fashion notions of community and identity that transcend the structures of nationalism (206). Yet, in treating Franklin's elitist attitudes regarding whiteness, Schlereth instructively evokes M. H. Boehm's argument that "cosmopolitanism as a mental attitude always manifests itself in the form of compromise with nationalism, race consciousness, professional interests, caste feeling, family pride, and even with egotism" (126). In the neutrality article, Franklin does allude to a "celebrated philosophical writer" who has argued for the abolition of slavery by noting the extreme death toll suffered by Africans in order to "raise sugars in America," such that sugar for the philosopher is "spotted with human blood." Franklin, however, proceeds to critique the abolitionist's views along racial lines, suggesting that had he considered the great many white deaths as a result of ongoing European wars for control of the West Indies, "he would have imagined his sugar not as spotted only, but as thoroughly dyed red" (*WBF* 10:71). Thus the cosmopolitan Franklin who authors the proposed neutrality article bizarrely suggests that the deaths of whites in wars for the sugar trade, in terms of their sentimental value, ought to far outweigh the millions of deaths suffered by blacks in the slave trade and under slavery. As such, Franklin's neutrality article raises the specter of violence against slaves in relation to the West Indian plantation economy in negative terms for purposes of argumentative advantage rather than in order to advocate for abolition and emancipation as a constituent part of the article.

20. Greeson argues that the encounter "exposes the difficulty of maintaining an imaginatively colonialist space *within* the borders of the new nation" in that the scene "inscribes the repressed violence of U.S. economic production *onto* Farmer James himself" (114). For Greeson, in much literature of the nascent U.S. Republic the "South" is made strategically to occupy that "imaginatively colonialist space." Certainly that is true in Crèvecoeur's text and many others authored during the early national period. Yet *Creole America* argues that at least equally as many authors strive to project the reality of a "residual coloniality within the nation itself" onto the West Indies, with which the U.S. South, in the anxious minds of repressive non-Southern writers in the New Republic, is contiguous on actual and figural levels.

21. In *Runaway America* Waldstreicher goes a long way toward unsettling mythic ideas about Franklin's views on race, slavery, and national identity. Given the potentially controversial nature of the ideas in this chapter, it might be advisable to repeat here Waldstreicher's eloquent statement in his preface: "The problem of slavery"—and, this chapter demonstrates, the related "problem" of the West Indies in relation to North American/U.S. slavery—"touched Franklin to such an extent that its investigation actually permits, rather than prevents, a deeper appreciation of the man and the Revolution he helped lead" (xv).

22. Wallerstein suggests that in the aftermath of the Revolution, "the English and the Americans found themselves once again in tête-à-tête" whereby smooth-running trade relations resumed between the two: "Why did this happen? In large part, for all the reasons which explain the parallel resumptions of commercial links between the excolonizer and excolonized after the so-called decolonizations of the twentieth century: it is far simpler—in terms of existing commercial, social, and cultural networks—for the excolonized to resume their old ties (in somewhat altered form) than to transfer this relationship to other core powers" (83). Wallerstein perceptively spies out similarities between the

"so-called decolonizations" of the British West Indies in the last half of the twentieth century and the post-Revolutionary political economy of the United States. Yet such a linkage obscures the profound differences between a postcolonial Caribbean nation-state in the late twentieth century and a Republic with empire on its mind.

Chapter 2. Alexander Hamilton and a U.S. Empire for Commerce

1. See Fleming and Rogow for two other recently published works that reexamine the Burr-Hamilton duel. For a sympathetic reassessment of Hamilton's military politics, see Walling. Recently published biographies include Chernow; Randall; and Brookhiser. Several children's books on Hamilton have appeared in the past few years, and Jesse Pennington played Hamilton in a 2002 play, *The General from America* (Weber).

2. More accurately, these discourses tended to be mutually reinforcing, though literary representations sometimes unsettle received assumptions about creole character. For two fine treatments of eighteenth-century British literature depicting West Indians, see Sypher.

3. Long suggests this practice is an extension of the mulatto woman's illicit "commerce with more than one man," and he worries that her "venereal disease[s]" have caused white babies to be "murdered; and many more have sucked in diseases, which rendered their life miserable, or suddenly cut short the thread of it" (2:277). Thus he connects "creole" commerce to illicit racial, sexual, and domestic relations, a central focus of Dominican Jean Rhys's celebrated novel from the late colonial period in the Caribbean, *Wide Sargasso Sea* (1966).

4. See Seilhamer for late eighteenth-century play lists from theaters throughout the United States.

5. Indeed, Washington's role as a political and military mentor provided the "exotic" West Indian legitimacy and access to the highest reaches of government during the early national period. Upon hearing of Washington's death in 1799, a melancholic Hamilton remarked to U.S. diplomat Tobias Lear, "He was an *Aegis*, very essential to me" (qtd. Emery 207).

6. See Atherton's *Adventures of a Novelist*, in which she recalls the political intrigue of the 1790s surrounding Washington's alleged paternity to Hamilton and remarks, "Interesting if true." She provokes her reader's curiosity further by noting that her research (erroneously) revealed that Washington was on the island of Barbados in 1756, the same year that Hamilton's mother, Rachel, was on the island (352–53). In fact, Washington had been in Barbados with a convalescing brother in 1752—his experiences there left an indelible impression on him regarding what he perceived to be unnatural and destructive gaps in socioeconomic status between affluent whites and poor whites and black slaves in the West Indies. It was the only time Washington ever traveled outside the continental United States. The rumor reveals how the West Indies denoted contagion (Barbados; Rachel; Hamilton) to an ostensibly pure national character (Washington) and virtue (republicanism). John Hamilton inaugurated another legend about the legitimacy of his father's birth in his early nineteenth-century biography, a legend perpetuated by Hamilton's descendants (Schachner 1). John founded the myth, which subsequent examinations of deeds and records have disproved, that Hamilton's father and Rachel were legally married. The recent debate surrounding the paternity of Jefferson's black progeny can be compared

in interesting ways to the controversies over Hamilton's origins and suggests how crucial matters involving race and sexuality are to the "legitimacy" of national figures and icons. In that regard, consider Toni Morrison's comment in *The New Yorker* in which she identifies Bill Clinton as the nation's first "black" president. She argues that Clinton's origins—his poor, rural Southern upbringing, his close relationship with the black community—account for what she perceives to be an unwavering assault by the right on President Clinton's personal life and character. States Morrison, "the President's body, his privacy, his unpoliced sexuality became the focus of the persecution, [and] when he was metaphorically seized and body-searched, who could gainsay . . . black men who knew whereof they spoke? The message was clear: 'No matter how smart you are, how hard you work . . . we will put you in your place or put you out of the place you have somehow' " ("The Talk of the Town" 32). Like Morrison, this chapter's arguments are interested in the ways in which attacks directed at a politician's "body" (Hamilton's) disclose fears about that politician's contamination of the "body politic" (the early Republic).

7. Writes late nineteenth-century biographer John Morse, "It would be an interesting speculation . . . to inquire how far the peculiarities of the mind and character of Hamilton were due to the intermingling of the blood of two widely different races, and to the *superadded effect of his tropical birthplace*" (2; emphasis added). More recently, Ron Chernow, in what he terms a "will-o'-the-wisp" of his research that ultimately proved inconclusive, sought to determine once and for all if Hamilton had "fathered an illegitimate mulatto child," and he boasts that he "consulted two of the world's top geneticists" to see if they could "*yield up secrets* about [Hamilton's] racial ancestry" from a lock of Hamilton's hair (734–35; emphasis added).

8. While important, scholarly efforts to determine how the term "creole" was used in the West Indies prior to the twentieth century—did it denote "black," "white," either/or, both/and?—ironically reflect how the utterly inscrutable, racially neutral term "creole" might be deployed for malignant effect. Certainly a number of "white" creole characters, having acquired the prerequisite sense and sensibility, are ultimately accepted into white society in period literature, unlike black or mulatto creoles. Belcour in Richard Cumberland's drama *The West Indian* (1771), which like Shakespeare's *The Tempest* was singularly popular in American theaters in the late eighteenth century, is such a character. While purged of their "creole" contagions, even these characters remain "other" to their European or American counterparts.

9. Thus Hamilton's model for empire merits the sort of critical scrutiny that Jefferson's "empire for liberty" has received during the past two decades, particularly by scholars interested in the material effects of U.S. empire building (see, for example, Boorstin; Dimock; Jehlen; Onuf; and Shuffelton). Indeed, Hamilton's competing model was arguably more influential, and had greater currency, than "the empire for liberty" prior to 1800. We need to understand, too, that although the two visions of empire clashed, they were mutually dependent and formative. Thus this chapter gestures to the potential benefits awaiting scholars who treat Hamilton's "empire for commerce" alongside Jefferson's "empire for liberty." Succeeding chapters demonstrate the relevance of Hamilton's "empire for commerce" to the nascent republic's literary and cultural formations. For a balanced discussion of the differences between Jefferson's and Hamilton's notions of republicanism (though he doesn't treat issues of empire), see McCoy.

10. All quotes from Hamilton's letter about his West Indian birth can be found at this citation.

11. Hamilton's boss, Nicholas Cruger, was the son of Henry Cruger, a New York shipping magnate, prominent New York assemblyman, and a member of His Majesty's Royal Council for the New York province before independence. Nicholas Cruger's uncle, John Cruger, was mayor of New York City, and the first president of the New York Chamber of Commerce. John Harris Cruger, Nicholas Cruger's brother, ran the family's merchant house in Bristol, England, traded with his brother's merchant house in St. Croix and his father's in New York City, and became a close friend of Edmund Burke and a staunch defender of the American colonies during the Revolution. Teleman Cruger guided the commercial affairs of the Crugers on the Dutch island of Curacao, while John Harris Cruger ran the family operation on Jamaica. (See *PAH* 1:8.) For information on the late eighteenth-century New York merchant community, see Barrett and Harrington.

12. My discussion about Hamilton's merchant clerk experiences draws on letters he wrote while employed by Cruger. (See *PAH* 1:1–39.) My understanding of North American trade with the West Indies derives from reading in a range of primary and secondary materials. Secondary sources that have been especially helpful include Coatsworth; Curtin; Dunn; Liss; Liss and Knight; Doerflinger; Greene; and Matson. For a sustained treatment of North American–West Indian trade relations during the pre-Revolutionary period, see Pares; on the early nineteenth-century battle over West Indian commerce between the United States and Britain, see Benns.

13. Land-centered theories of colonialism and conquest do not sufficiently account for the commercial expansionism that Hamilton has in mind according to his model of empire. Rowe makes a related point when he suggests that "the United States developed *non-territorial* forms of colonial domination, ultimately systematized in an 'imperial' system that in the nineteenth century complemented American nationalism and in the twentieth century grew to encompass 'spheres of influence' ranging from the Western Hemisphere to the farthest corners of the earth" (11). Sustained attention to the New Republic era suggests that such "non-territorial forms of domination" are already operative according to Hamilton's empire for commerce ideology and U.S. commercial practice. As such, Hamilton envisions the waterways of the hemisphere as places/spaces to be mapped, exploited, and occupied by agents of U.S. commerce.

14. "Hemispheric man" is a term I have devised to account for the layered properties of Hamilton's U.S. "man of commerce," which elsewhere he refers to as a "species for empire."

15. Ironically, Jefferson is perhaps the politician most responsible for the onset of the industrial revolution in the United States during the first decades of the nineteenth century. His embargo on U.S. trade with Britain not only led to the War of 1812 but also to the emergence of a modern industrial complex. This is one of many ironic developments wherein Jefferson's political praxis more resembled Hamilton's ideological views than Jefferson's own. Indeed, his very use of commerce as a foreign policy weapon is borrowed from Hamilton. In Federalist 11, Hamilton suggests building up a powerful navy and then "excluding Great Britain from all our ports" in order to extract more reasonable "commercial privileges" from "that kingdom" (85–86). Other examples include Jefferson's metal works factory run by his slaves in the midst of Jefferson's "edenic" Monticello, and his use of the "doctrine of implied powers" to justify the Louisiana Purchase. Jefferson had fought this strengthening of the executive as a sign of Hamilton's monarchical leanings during the Washington

administration. Finally, largely U.S. commerce men infiltrating the Louisiana area—not "farmers"—secured the Louisiana Purchase.

16. For discussions of these smuggling terms, see Matson 211–14, and Harrington 250–76.

17. One wonders to what extent Hamilton, in advocating the use of guerrilla warfare by the colonies, was drawing on his knowledge of rebel tactics employed by the maroons, or escaped slave communities, throughout the French and British West Indies (particularly Jamaica). Hamilton is notable among the founding fathers for his unequivocal recognition of the bravery displayed by the Haitian revolutionaries and for his acknowledgment that the Louisiana Purchase was made possible by the maroons' brilliant battle tactics. On this, see *PAH* 21:131. Moreover, Hamilton urged the colonists to enlist blacks in the Continental Army, a proposition that was not warmly received. He wrote of the racialist overtones of those who objected to their plan to enlist black slaves, "[it is] so far from appearing to me a valid objection that I think [black slaves] want of cultivation (for their natural faculties are probably as good as ours) joined to that habit of subordination which they acquire from a life of servitude, will make them sooner become soldiers than our white inhabitants" (*PAH* 2:17–18).

18. In Federalist 24, Hamilton hints at the dangers that lurk on the borders of the "empire for commerce": "Though a wide ocean separates the United States from Europe, yet there are various considerations that warn us against an excess of confidence or security. On one side of us, and stretching far into our rear, are growing settlements subject to the dominion of Britain. On the other side, and extending to meet the British settlements, are colonies and establishments subject to the dominion of Spain. This situation *and the vicinity of the West India islands*, belonging to those two powers, create between them, in respect to their American possessions and in relation to us, a common interest. . . . And politicians have ever with great reason considered the ties of blood as feeble and precarious links of political connections. These circumstances combined admonish us not to be too sanguine in considering ourselves as entirely out of the reach of danger" (161; emphasis added). Collapsing and overlapping European empires, unholy alliances, and conspiratorial commingling of "commercial" bloods: all these things converge in the most bedeviling of empire's spaces, "the West India islands."

19. These crises include Hamilton's private and public deliberations with British Major George Beckwith in 1789, in which Hamilton sought an arrangement allowing U.S. vessels to legally trade with the British West Indies, in contradistinction to the United States' ongoing illegal trade relations with those colonies so as to, in Hamilton's words, avoid "a system of warfare in Commercial matters" (Elkins and McKitrick 125); the Washington administration's follow-up efforts in 1790 to secure such commercial arrangements with Britain, including diplomatic missions by Gouverneur Morris; charged negotiations surrounding the Jay Treaty, in which the United States sought, once more, to grant concessions to the British in exchange for formal admission to the British West Indies; the XYZ debacle with France in 1797, which resulted in a "Quasi-War" and an escalation of the spoliation of U.S. merchant vessels in the West Indies by both France and Great Britain amid ongoing trauma in the region owing to the Haitian Revolution; and Hamilton's fantastic plan to establish U.S. naval and commercial superiority in the West Indies as part of his failed military collaboration with Francisco de Miranda, a Venezuelan freedom fighter, and General James Wilkinson, a shady, power-seeking former officer in the Continental Army, in

1799–1800; their inter-creole arrangement aimed to rid the West Indies and Latin America of French and Spanish influence.

20. For an expert account of this rhetorical maneuver, see Onuf 80–108.

21. For an important political pamphlet that specifically identifies Hamilton as the chief target of Republican wrath for allegedly allowing U.S. Americans to be recolonized by the British, see Pendleton.

22. These anxieties and the subsequent acquisition of Louisiana and the Western territories spawned a set of Northern Confederacy schemes in 1803 and 1804 by ultraconservative factions within the Federalist party. For a discussion of the Northern secessionist controversies, and Hamilton's role in suppressing them, see McDonald 355–63, and Emery 222–28.

Chapter 3. Paracolonial Ambivalence in the Poetics of Philip Freneau

1. Freneau's spectral Franklin thus expresses contempt for the impracticality of verse, a sentiment to which Freneau would respond repeatedly in his condemnation of a U.S. audience too disinterested in arts and literature and, conversely, too preoccupied with earning, luxury, and vice. Freneau's Princeton classmate Hugh Henry Brackenridge was the editor of the *United States Magazine*, a periodical in which Freneau's first poems appeared. Upon the demise of the magazine in 1779 after only twelve issues, Brackenridge wrote that too many Americans "cannot bear to have the tranquility of their repose disturbed by the villainous shock of a book" (qtd. in *PPF* 1:xxix). In "Literary Importation" (1786), Freneau in his own act of poetic creole nationalism and critique indicts U.S. Americans for their privileging of British intellectual and cultural traditions rather than seeking to "plant . . . our own": "It seems we had spirit to humble a throne, / Have genius for science inferior to none," and yet "Can we never be thought to have learning or grace / Unless it be brought from that horrible place / Where tyranny reigns with her impudent face" (*PPF* 2:303–04). Freneau's misgivings about the ongoing cultural colonization of the post-Revolutionary United States correspond to his concerns about social and cultural ills stemming from U.S. involvement in the West Indian trades. Thus Freneau's related anxieties about the British origins of the nation's social culture as well as its political economy converge in his poetics of paracolonial ambivalence.

2. In a recent essay that treats elegies published in remembrance of George Washington, Cavitch urges "Americanists . . . to read more poetry," suggesting that by doing so we might gain an appreciation for its "role in the formation and deformation of national subjects" (249). Cavitch is particularly interested in how the nation imagines itself into being through its poetic commemorations of deceased heroes—mourning as "civic action" and "sympathetic union" on behalf of the formation of a "national sensibility" (268–69). Freneau's commercial lyrics are memorials of a sort in that they commemorate the vexing location of the United States in hemispheric commerce during the New Republic period. Moreover, they evince the challenges posed by individualism, acquisitiveness, and pro-commerce Federalist policies to the nation's foundational values and institutions. If Hamilton and the Federalists believed these things to be compatible, trader-poet Freneau anatomizes what he perceives to be the pitfalls of such a posture according to an ethos of empire building that emphasizes continental expansionism and agrarianism. As such, Freneau's commercial lyrics belie any notion that there was anything approaching "sympathetic union" or consensus

regarding the most appropriate political economy for forming a "national sensibility."

3. In many poems Freneau voices his support for Western expansionism. He articulates such a position perhaps most succinctly in "On the Emigration to America, and Peopling of the Western Country" (1785). In the "western woods," Freneau remarks, "mighty States successive [may] grow" by displacing the "unsocial Indian" who must instead "retreat, / To make some other clime his own" (*PPF* 2:280). According to Freneau's plan for the internal colonization and annexation of the Western territories, the combined removal of Native Americans and emancipation of black slaves will "happier systems bring to view / Than all the eastern sages knew" (*PPF* 2:281).

4. Many critics have remarked on Freneau's privileging of an agricultural over a commercial ethos. As Shields writes in the conclusion to his influential *Oracles of Empire*, "While trade had its celebrants, poems such as Freneau's 'The Village Merchant' attacked the commercial ethos of the early republic" (226). Shields marks a topical shift in Anglo-American poetry after the 1750s and 1760s according to which there was a "tipping of the balance from trade to land," a phenomenon characterized in print culture by a "vogue for letters and tracts by Americans who characterized themselves as farmers" (225). Although such a shift is detectable in the late colonial period, Shields acknowledges in his conclusion that during the New Republic era the "glorification of trade became an ideological component of federalism" (226). Accordingly, even if we grant Freneau's prevailing antimercantilist, pro-agriculture tendencies, his occasional poetry is characterized by considerable ambivalence in arriving at, and occupying, such a posture. The persistent power of the ethos of commerce, as Shields puts it, and its ideological effects on late colonial and early national writings is best understood by evaluating the mutually imbricated ways in which the competing visions for the United States as empire for commerce and empire for liberty respectively form literary culture in the early national period.

5. Freneau's disparagement of Hamilton and his virulent anti-Federalist writings in the partisan *National Gazette* and other media are well-worn topics in Freneau scholarship. On these matters, see Leary, 202–19; Axelrad, 200ff.; Bowden, 91–96; and Marsh, as well as the Hamilton biographies referenced in Chapter 2.

6. The use of lyric as a preferred genre of social and cross-cultural critique by Freneau jibes with Gruesz's understanding of lyric as "highly portable, readily translated and memorized . . . the genre through which an aspiring writer can most easily enter the literary field" (26). According to Gruesz, lyricists concern themselves less with originality and more with "imitativeness" or making "a new impression from a known template" (*Ambassadors* 26). Freneau's portable, democratic, impressionistic West Indian lyrics, published in the leading U.S. newspapers and periodicals, are not translations of preexisting foreign-language texts like many of the "border" texts responsive to U.S.–Latin American relations in the nineteenth century that Gruesz treats. Even so, Gruesz's account of transamerican lyricists as "vernacular"—or in the terms of this study, "creolizing"—recorders of the cultural borderlands is wonderfully applicable to Freneau as "West Indian" linguistic and cultural translator, with all the attendant possibilities and limitations that the term "translation" suggests. Across his West Indies lyrics, Freneau critiques the circumatlantic relations—social, cultural, and economic—between Europe, the United States, and the West Indies in the late eighteenth century, and as poet-speaker he propagates a particular ideology, this chapter argues, about what the terms of those relations ought to be. On the

importance of "translation" to a postcolonial studies lexicon in the Americas, see Gruesz, "Translation."

7. This chapter gestures to the importance of evaluating Freneau's practice of constantly revising and republishing his poetry. Although critics have sometimes dismissed the practice on purely aesthetic grounds as evidence of Freneau's manic obsession with his craft, the readings of "Santa Cruz" and several other poems below show how Freneau revised his poems so as to respond to shifting material conditions in ways that lyric as democratic, fluid genre allows for (unlike the novel, for example).

8. Relevant here is an essay entitled "General Character of the Insular West Indian Creoles" (1790), authored by Freneau in the pages of New York's *The Daily Advertiser*. In the essay Freneau draws on his firsthand experience in the West Indies, suggesting, "The two [*sic*] leading traits in this kind of character are revenge, sulkiness and pride. I cannot persuade myself, however, that the influence of the tropical climates has had any thing to do in the formation of these characteristic peculiarities ; they rather arise from the mode of education in use throughout that extensive cluster of islands known by the name of the Caribbees, or greater and less Antilles" (2). He proceeds to excoriate the ways in which male and female white creoles from their infancy in plantation society "are accustomed to be waited upon by a number of black and white slaves, whose business it is to watch the wants and wishes of the bratling, and even anticipate its most whimsical desires; the least neglect of which is sure to be punished with severe whipping" (2). While Freneau's account of the West Indian creole type bears resemblance to scathing accounts published in natural histories authored by the likes of Edward Long, Freneau crucially does not attribute such behavior in any way to climate but to the corruptive institutions affiliated with the islands' slave economies. Moreover, at the end of the essay he avails himself of the opportunity to condemn once more the British metropolitan center of empire for its implication in the deplorable state of slave society in the West Indies. He notes how some creole planters and overseers send their children to England for schooling in order to avoid their "miseducation" in the islands, "or as the common saying is, 'To have the devil whipp'd out of them betimes.'" Yet Freneau professes doubts about the possibility for a creole character makeover in London, which he views as being itself corrupt: "Happy would it be, could it be truly said that they always return with the devil completely eradicated!" (3).

9. A cursory examination of the pages of *The Daily Advertiser* reveals a staggering number of "advertisers" in each issue—mercantile outfits, independently operated trading vessels, and others—selling and buying stores of West Indian sugar-related products, most conspicuous among them Jamaica rum.

10. Upon the scuttling of the *Dromilly*, Freneau was stranded on the island of Jamaica from July 30 until September 23, 1784, when he secured passage home aboard the U.S. vessel *Mars* (Axelrad 145–49). Thus he had almost two months to observe and record colonial life in Jamaica at the very moment when U.S. ships were being banned from actively trading there as a result of the peace negotiations at Versailles and subsequent Orders of Parliament. Moreover, as his initial published versions of the Jamaica poems appeared variously from 1784 to 1792, Freneau was able to revisit his memory of his Jamaican "captivity" in 1784 in light of subsequent trading experiences in the West Indies as well as ongoing diplomatic, economic, and military negotiations between the United States and Britain over the vexing West Indian trade issue.

11. Freneau inserts a hyphen in the name "Port Royal" in the title and text

of the initial 1788 edition, although in subsequent versions of the poem he drops the hyphen, and no hyphen is used in other contemporary spellings of the town's name. Thus I use "Port-Royal" when I cite from Freneau's 1788 edition of the poem, whereas in my prose I refer to the town by its more common spelling, "Port Royal."

12. I reproduce here the more charged account of the black Jamaican creole population found in the revised 1809 edition of "Lines Written at Port-Royal, in the Island of Jamaica," which suggests that Freneau's stylization of West Indian creole freedmen and slaves became more animated across time. In the 1788 version of "Lines," Freneau's account of black slave life is more abbreviated and restrained; it includes only the first two lines cited here. How might we account for such a representational shift? I believe the more menacing caricature in the poem's revised version is perhaps attributable to its being published in the wake of the Haitian Revolution (1789–1804). Moreover, there were a series of slave revolts in Jamaica in the 1790s after a period of relative inactivity. Thus Freneau's two versions of "Lines" would seem to adapt and respond to the reality of an increasingly revolutionary, democratic, and volatile West Indies in the 1790s and early 1800s, both in Haiti and elsewhere, owing to the liberalizing influence of the U.S. and Haitian revolutions on West Indian nonwhite creole populations. Such an argument is supported by Freneau's ambivalent gesture to the Haitian Revolution in "Seventeen Hundred Ninety One" (1795): "Great things have pass'd the last revolving year; / . . . Rebellion has broke loose in St. Domingo— / Sorry we are that Pompeys, Caesars, Catos / Are mostly found with Negroes and Mulattoes" (*PPF* 3:65). I say ambivalent, because Freneau wonders why whites—particularly U.S. Americans—are not similarly fighting for freedom in the hemisphere. This poem is also notable for the ways in which Freneau's anti-Semitic, anti-Catholic, and anti-British sentiments are so prominently on display.

13. In considering the possibilities and limitations of Freneau's shifting translations of Jamaican black creole language, culture, and identity, we might recall Cheyfitz's account of translation in his landmark study *The Poetics of Imperialism* (1991): "We must be in translation between cultures and between groups within our own culture if we are to understand the dynamics of our imperialism. For our imperialism historically has functioned (and continues to function) by substituting for the difficult politics of translation another politics of translation that represses these difficulties" (xvi). In the case of Freneau's treatment of West Indian blacks in his poetry, for the difficult politics of translating white U.S. Americans' exploitative relations to blacks and slavery on the continent *and* in the West Indies, Freneau substitutes a politics of translating British imperialism and colonial violence in relation to West Indian blacks that represses the former difficulty.

14. For a candid scholarly assessment of the devastating impact of Parliament's embargoes on U.S. commerce to the West Indies in the 1780s, see Williams, *Capitalism and Slavery*. Williams writes, "Fifteen thousand slaves died of famine in Jamaica alone between 1780 and 1787, and American independence was the first stage in the decline of the sugar colonies" (121). Accordingly, Freneau's account of a brewing crisis between slaves and whites, and white creoles and British colonial forces, is not contrived but responds to shifting material conditions during the post-U.S. Revolutionary period in Jamaica.

15. As I suggest above, Freneau blames ongoing British depredations on U.S. commerce and impressment of the nation's merchant men on an Anglophilic

Federalist party. See, for example, "On the Prospect of War, and American Wrongs," wherein Freneau, like other leading Republicans, accuses the Federalists of allowing a monarchical Britain to recolonize the United States:

Since the day we declared, they were masters no
   More.
The day we arose from the *colony station*,
Has England attack'd us, by sea and by shore,
In war by the sword, as in peace by vexation ;
Impressment they claim'd, till our seamen, ashamed
Grew sick of our flag, that against the old hag
Of Britain, no longer their freedom protected
But left them, like slaves, to be lash'd and corrected. (*PAA* 11–12)

These are the very anxieties informing the creole complex that *Creole America* argues haunts Republicans and Federalists alike in the New Republic period.

16. We might draw a distinction, as Freneau does in the poem, between British metropolitan representatives—including the despised governor—on the island who are there to enforce Parliament's navigation acts against the United States and white Jamaican creoles, many of whom opposed such policies. The latter group was outspoken, even violent, in their protest of Parliament's restrictions on trade between the British West Indies and the United States. As O'Shaugnessy writes, "In contrast to their passive behavior between 1766 and 1774, the colonists exhausted every official channel to obtain the removal of the trade restrictions after 1783" (240). West Indians rioted against such restrictions, wrote copious pamphlets protesting them, and tarred and feathered colonial governors. Thus, *after* the U.S. Revolution many white Jamaican planters and merchants ironically began to resemble the U.S. Revolutionaries in many respects. Continues O'Shaugnessy, "In attempting to win exemption from the Navigation Acts to trade with the United States, West Indians challenged the traditional mercantilist principles of colonial policy that had attempted to enforce a balance of trade favorable to Britain and to encourage the expansion of British shipping. The post-war conflict of interests weakened their political influence in Britain" (241). Freneau's poem, then, must be considered as inter-creole in its ideology, speaking on behalf of U.S. Americans and many white Jamaican creoles alike in its argument for free and unrestricted trade between the islands and the continent and its protest of strict British mercantilist policies against such trade arrangements. White Jamaican creoles' engagement in commercial intrigue with U.S. merchants and traders against the will of the mercantile and metropolitan center of the British empire created potentially dangerous inter-American energies that a free trade policy might well have avoided (or perhaps further exacerbated). Even so, we should be wary of labeling such acts as "revolutionary." Given the sizable slave populations in each of the British West Indian colonies, white creoles maintained an allegiance to the crown because of their need for military protection against "invasions" from black slaves within and from competing European empires without.

17. A substantial poem set in Jamaica that the chapter does not treat, "The Jamaica Funeral," was written in 1776 and published in 1786. This poem is associated with Freneau's initial stay in the West Indies during the Revolution and thus, unlike Freneau's other Jamaica poems is not directly responsive to his ill-fated voyage to the island in 1784 aboard the *Dromilly*. In "The Jamaica Funeral," Freneau provides a portrait of a debased white creole community who

tend less to their responsibilities as mourners concerned about the deceased and the afterlife and more to the pleasures of this world, including imbibing the "bowls" of liquor that Freneau critiques in "Santa Cruz" as the downfall of European immigrants and white creoles in St. Croix (see *PPF* 1:239–48). See also "Carribbiana," which is an indictment of the entire history of slavery in the West Indies and a summons to Freneau's readers to usher in the day when "freedom to these coasts repair, / Assum'd the slave's neglected claim, / . . . And a new race, not bought or sold, / Springs from the ashes of the old" (*PWB* 319–20). Fascinatingly, "Carribbiana" calls and responds to "The Jamaica Funeral" in its redeployment of that poem's title figure. More precisely, in "Carribbiana" "The *funeral* is the joyous day" (*PWB* 319) of the African slave not because he debauches himself like the white creole mourners in "The Jamaica Funeral," but because in death he might at last shed the "galling chain" and return once more to "his native [African] climes" (*PWB* 319).

18. In a humorously self-reflexive poem entitled "The Newsmonger," Freneau as poet-trader-journalist remarks of himself, "He prophesies the time must come / When few will drink West-India rum— / Our *spirits* will be *proof* at home" (*PWB* 311). Yet the failure of the United States to fulfill Freneau's prophesy paradoxically undermines the notion that the U.S. republican "spirit" is "proof" that the New Republic is immune to the commercial, cultural, and political corruptions that mark European colonialism in the West Indies.

19. As Wertheimer argues in a fine reading of Freneau's "Rising Glory" poems, according to their anxious redeemer complex "The Spanish Conquest . . . performs a dual function that is related to [the poems'] quest for innocence; it is both a cautionary tale of empire and an emboldening story for Anglo-Americans. In Anglo-American mythology, Columbus, the Aztecs, and the Incas all stand as crucial secular types, the preeminent New World martyrs of corrupt empire" (50).

20. Of course, this is a critical adaptation of the ultimate move that Raymond Williams makes in his landmark study *The Country and the City*. In extending his thesis about the capitalist overdetermination of the relationship between the city and the country to that between the metropolitan center and the colonial periphery, Williams writes, "The terrible irony has been that the real processes of absolute urban and industrial priority, and of the related priority of the advanced and civilised nations, worked through not only to damage the 'rural idiots' and the colonial 'barbarians and semi-barbarians', but to damage, at the heart, the urban proletarians themselves, and the advanced and civilised societies over which, in their turn, the priorities exercised their domination, in a strange dialectical twist" (303). A consideration of U.S. port cities like Baltimore in the late eighteenth century causes us to think through what Williams provocatively terms the "damage" of capitalist expansionism in circumatlantic rather than merely transatlantic ways. Such circumatlantic circuits of "damage"— perhaps best grasped by following the roots and routes of the West Indian trades—Freneau strives to reconcile as he interrogates the unseemly connections between British colonialism and the post-Revolutionary U.S. political economy, which depended so heavily on slave labor at "home" and in the West Indies for its prosperity.

21. Although he does not include them in the "Rising Empire" series of state poems, Freneau did pen a number of works on South Carolina. Freneau frequently visited and traded in South Carolina, especially Charleston, where his brother operated a mercantile firm. Significantly, Freneau's South Carolina

poems are acts of pure nostalgia. Rather than indict South Carolina for its reliance on international commerce and plantation slavery for its financial well-being—as he does in his Maryland and Virginia poems, for example—Freneau foregrounds in "On Arriving in South Carolina, 1798" a romanticized South Carolina, "Placed in a climate ever gay, / From wars and commerce far away, Sweet nature's wilderness" (*PAA* 25). The pastoral pleasures of South Carolina are thanks to "her" Revolutionary "heroes, who redeem'd the land . . . And from their old dominions drove / The tyrants of the age" (*PAA* 23). Roman goddesses, not slaves, do the cotton picking and planting according to Freneau's pastoral substitutions: "And, Ceres, all that you can yield / To deck the festive board; / The snow white fleece, from pods that grows. / And every seed that Flora sows—/ The orange and the fig-tree shows / A paradise restored" (*PAA* 24). Freneau's exoticized landscapes ironically repeat the very colonialist topos that provide for the sorts of colonial "wars" that are said to be "far away." When Freneau does refer in specific terms to South Carolina's plantations, he does so in order to indict the British army, as in "The Royal Cockneys in America" (1797), for having "conquer[ed] and pillage[d] the *royal-plantations*" (*PAA* 37) during the Revolution rather than indicting Charlestonians post-Revolution for persisting in the plantation economies that mark Britain's hostility to that "*nuisance* democracy" (*PAA* 37). Freneau's fondness for his times spent in South Carolina with his brother coupled with his anti-British sentiment ultimately trump any sympathy he might have had for the state's enslaved population. In that regard, Freneau's nostalgia for a prelapsarian South Carolina seems to derive from ongoing trauma he sympathetically feels on white South Carolinians' behalf owing to British invasion of its plantations during the war. Thus the two states in which he spent much of his adult life—Pennsylvania and South Carolina—are examined far less systematically and critically than all others in his collective body of state poems.

Chapter 4. The West Indies, Commerce, and a Play for U.S. Empire

1. Nicholas Cruger was an important organizer of the ratification parade (Rogow 126). One wonders what emotions he felt on witnessing the spectacle surrounding his former West Indian creole clerk. A reproduction of a fascinating contemporary etching of the "Hamilton" float is provided by Vandenberg.

2. Noteworthy twentieth-century references to *The Yorker's Stratagem* include Odell, *Annals of the New York Stage*, which urges the play "should be considered in any history of the Stage Yankee or of the Stage Negro" (1:306–07); Meserve, *An Emerging Entertainment*, 134–35; and Cooley, "Literary Dialect in *The Yorker's Stratagem*," which treats the play in a consideration of "the validity of using literary dialect as primary evidence in historical research" (173); on Cooley, see also notes 25 and 30 below.

3. Robinson was a contract player with the Old American Company of Comedians in the early 1790s, and *The Yorker's Stratagem* was performed on several occasions in Philadelphia and at the company's then home theater on John Street in New York City. Founded by Lewis and William Hallam in London and relocated to the American colonies in the 1750s, the Old American Company removed to Jamaica on the eve of the U.S. Revolution. Even before that time the company was based in Jamaica, where it returned each year in the off-season after touring throughout the urban centers of British North America. The company remained in Jamaica during the Revolution until Lewis Hallam Jr. returned

to the United States in 1783 to reestablish the Old American Company in Philadelphia and later in New York. According to William Dunlap, whatever Hallam's
professions of support for the U.S. cause on his return, his political and cultural
allegiances, given the Old American Company's "runaway" status on the eve of
the war to a loyalist British West Indian colony, were considered suspect and
repeatedly challenged by detractors of the theater: "With peace returned the
players by profession, but not the whole company. Hallam arrived first [from
Jamaica], with a weak attachment, as if to gain a footing in the New Republic.
Philadelphia was the place chosen at which to effect a landing, but the people
received the runaways with frowns" (104; see also 120–21). Ambiguities in a play
dependent for its meaning on devices like imposture and stratagem are thus
further complicated by the circumatlantic circulation of actors, acting, and identities in the late eighteenth century, a phenomenon embodied by the Jamaican
affiliations of the manager and many of the players of the Old American Company.

   Like the more widely known novelist and playwright Susanna Rowson, who
emigrated from England to the United States, Robinson was almost certainly an
immigrant, given how native-born playwrights like Royall Tyler (Massachusetts)
had their "American" origins lionized by contemporary theater reviewers and
drama historians. In a 2005 article published in *Early American Literature* (an earlier version of this chapter), I suggest that Robinson was a "Jamaican immigrant." However, additional research conducted while completing final
revisions on *Creole America* has led me to conclude that the extent of Robinson's
Jamaican affiliations cannot be determined (as yet) with any degree of certainty.
Little is known about where Robinson was prior to joining the Old American
Company—there are to my knowledge no plays by "J. Robinson" published in
Britain in the late eighteenth or early nineteenth centuries, and he is not
referred to by critics who have studied the Old American Company in Jamaica
during the 1770s and 1780s (see Hill 127–28). Nor is much known about Robinson's whereabouts on departing the Old American Company in the mid-1790s,
though there is some indication that he might have spent time acting and living
in Boston. In addition, I note that a publisher named "J. Robinson" began operations in Baltimore in the early 1800s and published many literary and dramatic
texts. Might this be the same J. Robinson? My best speculation—which is what,
regrettably, determining Robinson's identity amounts to at the moment—is that
Robinson was born in either Great Britain or the West Indies and spent significant time living and working in Jamaica and/or elsewhere in the West Indies,
perhaps in a capacity other than acting; he was not a known actor (unlike many
of Hallam's Jamaican-affiliated performers) at the time of his appearance on the
U.S. stage, nor did he become one thereafter. Robinson could have immigrated
to the United States from either Europe or the West Indies, and he remained in
the United States for an unknown period of time.

   4. The notice in the *Federal Gazette* was printed shortly before Robinson wrote
the first of his two plays, *Constitutional Follies; or, Life in Demerara*, in 1791, which
was "performed before a full house with great applause" according to a review
in the *Federal Gazette* (qtd. Seilhamer 2:324). Another sentimental comedy, *Constitutional Follies* appears to have been a full-length, five-act production. Set in
the West Indian slave colony of Demerara, the action centers on various acts of
seduction and intrigue, and included in the cast are Irish servants and black
slaves. The title of Robinson's inaugural play suggests the work might have com-
mented in textual and/or metatextual ways on the Constitutional debates that

had taken place a few years earlier. This suggestion is consistent with Robinson's having written the play in response to a call for national drama. These questions will likely remain unanswerable. To my knowledge, no manuscript of the play exists and there is no indication that the play was ever published.

5. Although urban theater audiences were quite familiar with white characters performing "comic Negro" roles in blackface in European-authored plays performed on the U.S. stage in the late eighteenth century, *Yorker's Stratagem* is one of the first U.S.-authored plays to include such roles. Royall Tyler's little-known comic opera *May Day in Town, or New York in an Uproar* (1787) also includes a stylized Banana-esque figure, Pompey, who has a significant singing part and likely would have had an important speaking role as well, though only the play's songs survive. For an account of the recovery of the partial text of Tyler's *May Day*, see Jarvis. Errors abound in the plot synopses offered by the few critics who refer to *The Yorker's Stratagem*. Such critical inaccuracies are perhaps attributable to the play's aesthetic novelties, including its creole dialects and elaborate relationship to the West Indian material culture of which it is a part.

6. Wadlington identifies two predominant types of the "Yankee" in U.S. literature from the Revolutionary period onward: "*Yankee* became a synonym for both *American*, a man of confidence, and *New Englander*, a confidence man" (10). The *American* type, inaugurated in the U.S. literary tradition by Tyler, was "often scornfully attributed to Americans by foreigners . . . [but] was picked up by the national culture as a nose-thumbing badge of identification" (10). Most commonly figured as a bumpkin or peddler, the *American* type is a benign figure who advocates thrift, upholds U.S. virtues and the principles of democracy, and became an inspiration for the "rustic" figure of American Romanticism. The *New Englander* type, to which Jonathan Norrard bears some resemblance, was originally perceived as a character "whose slyness in trading was the harmlessly comic consequence of the national game of merchant self-reliance versus customer self-reliance" (11). By the mid-nineteenth century, this figure came to be depicted in far less benign ways as a swindler, a deceiver, and a con man—a duplicitous abuser of trust *and* virtue—in works like Melville's *The Confidence Man* (1856). Last, the "picaro" or wanderer type (Jonathan Norrard exhibits features of this type as well) is figured in Hugh Henry Brackenridge's *Modern Chivalry* (1792–1815), which chronicles the travels and travails of the bumbling, overreaching Irish manservant Teague O'Regan. Distinctions between these three types of Yankee figures are somewhat arbitrary, especially as the three become tricksters in the mid-nineteenth century. On this, see Wadlington; Kuhlmann; and Rourke.

For two accounts of the ways in which issues relating to sectional rivalry and tension, race and manifest destiny, and U.S. expansionism and imperialism caused the "Yankee" figure to evolve in relation to national character in the antebellum period, see Hodge, *Yankee Theatre* and Winifred Morgan, *An American Icon*. If, as Hodge points out, Jonathan became installed by the 1830s as a figure for an emergent, vernacular theater culture that sought to wean "audiences away from a strict diet of English plays and English actors by encouraging the view that native products had inherent merit" (262), Morgan suggests that in aiming for a kind of romantic realism in the antebellum period, what such stage—and popular culture—representations reveal is Jonathan as an "average American" type who holds "parochial, petty, anti-Semitic, racist, sexist, [and] anti-Catholic" (159) tendencies. Robinson's inventive use of the Yankee figure as *mask* not only predicts the postcolonial cultural nationalism that Hodge suggests informs the rise of the "Yankee theater" in the 1830s but also works in tandem with racial and expansionist ideologies like those operative in the antebellum heyday of "Jonathan" as national icon, according to Morgan (and Hodge; see also Richards, "Race and the Yankee").

7. "He stands like one, and he has salt fish in one hand, and a hen in the other."

8. Amant also "trades" on his identity by feigning ignorance about the distinctions between West Indian and New England commodities circulating in the West Indian trades. He especially puns on produce in order to convey Jonathan's ignorance. When Amant asks Acid for a "little apple toddy," Acid, baffled that the Yankee imbecile doesn't realize that apples don't grow in the "torrid zone," offers instead a "bowl of punch, and a slice of pine-apple in it." Amant responds in disgust, "apples don't grow on pine-trees" (6). He confuses a cashew for a "cow shoe" as well, and so the Yankee riddle goes.

9. What differentiates Jonathan Norrard, then, from Tyler's Jonathan and Jonathan Corncob is that he is a hybrid version of the two, and what distinguishes Amant from the three Jonathans is that "Jonathan" is only a disguise Amant manipulates in order to deceive others. This use of the Yankee figure as a mask is original to Robinson and raises interesting sets of questions within and without the text about agents of U.S. empire masking themselves according to ostensibly honorable motives. Amant is a forerunner of the many artful confidence men in nineteenth-century U.S. literature. The distinction between those characters and Amant according to the governing ideology of Robinson's play is that while the swindlers and cheats of the nineteenth century pursue games of confidence in order to affront virtue with vice, Amant does so in order to defend virtue against vice.

10. The notion that antimiscegenation statutes betray the ways in which U.S. republican and democratic principles are written in "blood" is not, of course, original to me. See, for example, the arguments in Sollors's *Neither Black nor White Yet Both*. Rather, this chapter's argument extends this discussion about the junctures between blood and the law in the formation of nation by introducing a fourth term, the West Indies.

11. Thus Robinson's play might profitably be treated in relation to "American Barbary captivity" texts, including captivity narratives (see Baepler), fiction such as Royall Tyler's novel *The Algerine Captive* (1797), and drama, especially Susanna Rowson's now familiar play *Slaves in Algiers; or, a Struggle for Freedom: A Play, interspersed with songs, in three acts* (1794). With Robinson's text, *Slaves in Algiers* is one of the only original U.S. American plays to be written and performed in the early 1790s. Rowson's drama—written two years after Robinson's text was published—shares a variety of dramatic figures, themes, and conventions with *Yorker's*. Briefly, *Slaves in Algiers* treats matters relating to the "captivity" of U.S. commerce representatives by the despotic Muslim governor Muley Moloc, Dey of Algiers, and involves the ultimate liberation of these "Sons"—and Daughters—"of Liberty" owing to their superior "stratagems," including a masked "slave uprising" not unlike the one that Ledger and Amant perform to thwart Fingercash in *Yorker's*. Also, the play's North Africa setting, like the West Indies in Robinson's play, functions, in part, as a screen onto which a host of crises occurring at "home" are projected "abroad." As such, the two texts might be compared in terms of their respective treatments of issues like race and ethnicity, and gender and sexuality in relation to the formation of a "national character" and the United States as an emerging empire for commerce. For a fine treatment of these concerns in Rowson's text, see Dillon.

12. Thus Ledger joins a long line of merchant clerks, both real and imagined, affiliated with the West Indian trades—Franklin, Equiano, Robert King, Hamilton, Amant, Fingercash, and a mystery merchant clerk or two to be named later—and on whom plots and themes that address the formation of nation and empire depend.

13. Several works by theater historians and critics during the past decade or so have done much to refocus scholarly attention on the importance of the theater and drama to the formation of a national literature and culture, including: Richards, *Theater Enough*; Brown, *Theatre in America during the Revolution*; Witham, ed., *Theatre in the Colonies and United States, 1750–1915*; Wilmeth and Bigsby, *Cambridge History of American Theatre, vol. 1;* Nathans, *Early American Theatre from the Revolution to Thomas Jefferson*. Historians and critics doing work in early U.S. American drama owe a substantial debt to these scholars and their works. The fact that none of these studies mentions Robinson's play signals its relative obscurity. However, see Richards, *Drama, Theater, and Identity in the American New Republic* (forthcoming), which I understand from the author will include a sustained account of *The Yorker's Stratagem.*

14. *In the Midst of Perpetual Fetes* by Waldstreicher and Nathans's *Early American Theatre* begin the work of examining the elaborate ways in which U.S. performance culture (Waldstreicher) and theater (Nathans) emerged through a process of what we might term *postcolonial invention;* that is, by adapting and appropriating European sources and influences for nationalist purposes.

15. In his important study *Love and Theft*, Lott demonstrates the ways in which "the insurrectionary resonances of black culture" (84) were manipulated by white laborers in blackface during the nineteenth century to register resentments about their social status. Also, Hartman argues in *Scenes of Subjection* that "both minstrelsy and melodrama (re)produced blackness as an essentially pained expression of the body's possibilities" (32) during slavery and Reconstruction. This chapter examines blackface in an earlier material context than the nineteenth-century ones that Lott and Hartman explore. The "insurrectionary resonances" that Lott identifies, and the repressed violence that Hartman notes, manifest themselves in the prohibitions against—rather than in the actualized performances of—blackface in Charleston during the late eighteenth century. In Robinson's play generally, I am interested in how blackface is employed not just in the service of racial and national formations but also in the formation of "empire."

16. For example, on February 23, 1795, *Oroonoko* was postponed and then removed from a play schedule "on account of some improper sentiments contained in it" (Curtis 272).

17. Martin Delany's novel *Blake* (1859) manipulates the figure of a West Indian festival as part an impending slave revolt destined for U.S. shores.

18. Versions of this debate were played out in newspapers across the nation during the first decades of the nation's existence. The following excerpt from an attack on the theater made in the Charleston *City Gazette & Daily Advertiser* on January 4, 1794, evinces the anxieties of theater critics about drama's alleged crime-inducing tendencies: "If the admirers and disciples of the stage wish to strengthen their love of virtue, and their dislike of vice, why need they visit the theatre for this good purpose! When every street, and lane, and wharf of Charleston, and every other populous city, may afford them scenes of mimickry, buffoonery, intrigue, chicanery, and every other vice that dishonors human nature, makes [*sic*] a man of feeling blush for the depravity of his species, and

wish to find some retreat where he could forget the follies and miseries of mankind. The stage a school of virtue! It is a ridicule of virtue."

19. Robinson's characterization of Banana is indebted to a number of burlesqued black characters in British drama, perhaps especially Mungo in Isaac Bickerstaff's *The Padlock* (1768). In complimenting the play for its "coding" of dialogue and dialect to suit particular characters, Dunlap remarks in specific terms on Robinson's debt to Bickerstaff in his acting role as Banana: "The author played in it as a mongrel creole, a kind of tawny Mungo" (222). For a discussion of the history of blacks on the U.S. stage, see Mitchell; E. G. Smith; and Hill and Hatch.

20. As such, Banana might be said to play the West Indian "double" to Amant's composite "Yankee" impersonation, the two characters emblematic of extreme versions of hemispheric creole degeneracy. Also, Fingercash's willingness to sell off Sophia to Jonathan Norrard for the right price represents a parallel breakdown of established creole hierarchies, the degenerate Norrard's proposed marriage to Sophia being obviously considerably less offensive to the play's contemporary audience than that between Louisa and Banana. Tellingly, Banana and Norrard are referred to in related pejorative terms by other characters, a relation that anticipates the overlap between "white trash" and Southern black stereotypes in U.S. modern and contemporary lexicons.

21. "You don't have any shame about using somebody? When you marry the lady [Louisa], her family will beat little Quaka [Priscilla and Banana's child], work him like a horse, such that the hunger will kill him. If he speaks, the overseer will beat him."

22.

MRS. BANANA:	. . . YOU, PRISCILLA, YOU MUST HAVE THE IMPUDENCE OF THE DEVIL TO MAKE SUCH A NOISE IN MY HOUSE.
PRISICILLA:	I don't have the right to come see my husband?
MRS. BANANA:	Who is your husband?
PRISCILLA:	Banana is my husband.
MRS. BANANA:	Who told you so?
PRISCILLA:	I told myself so.
MRS. BANANA:	Who, you, you?
PRISCILLA:	Me, me, me, me, Priscilla.
MRS. BANANA:	You, mulatto Seasar, go tell the overseer to come turn this impudent hussy out of doors.
PRISCILLA:	Lord almighty in a tap, I'm a poor one in a white country; have you ever heard the likes of that—me the impertinent hussy—yes—and who are you then?
MRS. BANANA:	I'm the lady.
PRISCILLA:	You are the devil who looks like a lady; watch it don't touch me with your dirty skin.
MRS. BANANA:	I have a plantation.
PRISCILLA:	You, you look like a cow, your mouth like a bull-frog.
MRS. BANANA:	I have black blood [or slaves?] like you.
PRISCILLA:	You lie . . . you cow nose, your daddy chews tobacco, sires a gun beem; I don't care much about that. [Snaps her teeth with her fingers.]
MRS. BANANA:	Cato, Quamina, somebody come and carry this here devil to justice, so they can tie her mouth. [Enter Negroes, who take hold of Prissey and carry her off.]

23. For all their stereotypical conduct, these characters *do* have substantial status in the political economy of the island, albeit a problematic one wherein

they are enslaving other blacks for material benefit. It would be difficult to gauge precisely the reaction of white Northern audiences to this fact. As the above discussion of the Charleston theater indicates, however, the use of miscegenation as a central trope, a black character as a plantation owner, and a black woman seeking to infiltrate white society would be grounds for proscribing the play's production in its theaters.

24. This exchange is, to my knowledge, the first example of what Gates has identified as the African diaspora phenomenon of "signifying" in a text by a U.S. author. Note here that Priscilla is the "winner" of the verbal joust, as Mrs. Banana resorts to force rather than verbal cunning in order to get the upper hand. Robinson's recording of Jamaican creole dialect is rare, not only in U.S. texts but also in texts authored by West Indians or Europeans prior to the nineteenth century. As Lalla and D' Costa remark, "Eighteenth-century writers in Jamaica seldom recorded any verbatim nonstandard speech. The speech of Africans and creoles is represented by sparse word lists, and few writers even attempted to comment on the language usage of the island" (129). Thus, along with their U.S. counterparts, scholars of eighteenth-century West Indian and British literature and culture will appreciate the recovery of Robinson's play. Royall Tyler's dialect in *May Day* (1787) is far more contrived—in style and form, delivered as it is in rhyming couplets—than the creole dialect in Robinson's play. Even so, the actor Lewis Hallam Jr., who lived a significant period of his life in Jamaica, purportedly improvised on Tyler's decidedly non–West Indian dialect so as to inflect Pompey's songs and speeches with the rhythms and cadences of West Indian creole (Jarvis 190). Eighteenth-century British plays that contain a version of creole dialect, though none with the sociolinguistic sophistication of Robinson's, include Samuel Foote, *The Patron* (1764); Isaac Bickerstaff, *Love in the City* (1767) and *The Padlock* (1768); and William Macready, *The Irishman in London; or, the Happy African* (1792).

25. Consistent with the argument that creole language functions as a sign of contagion and degeneration in the play, readers of Robinson's text will note that none of the white West Indian characters speaks in a creole dialect. White West Indians do, however, speak with an accent different from that of the white American characters, and with different expressions and word choices. For example, Jonathan Norrard (Amant), when asked by Sophia, "Pray, friend, how does all at home do?" (11), responds in a surprised tone, "Ay, now Miss, you speak as if you had been born in a christian country" (12). Jonathan is referring to the ways in which Sophia's language usage, tone, and inverted syntax marks her "christian"-inspired voice as American rather than West Indian owing to her time spent at university in the states. Along with her race, wealth, and beauty, this feature makes her an especially strong candidate for assimilating successfully into the American cult of domesticity. Cooley confirms my own sense (based on personal familiarity with present-day Caribbean creole dialects) that Robinson's literary representation of Jamaican creole is, for the time, progressive. Cooley writes that Robinson's play included "highly unusual words" and "grammatical features . . . [that] had not previously appeared or had little frequency in other plays. . . . What he did was to introduce new forms on the American stage, thereby extending the AAE [African American English] characteristics in represented literary dialect, some of which were incorporated into later plays" (180).

26. Thus virtue and industry, freedom and union, justice and wisdom underwrite not only the Federalist agenda of a strong union and a bolstered commerce at home, one driven by a glory-seeking Hamilton with the blessing of the

U.S. "Majesty Divine," George Washington. These principles also authorized the outward-looking plan by Hamilton to control the commercial trade routes of the hemisphere, an ambition that pivots on U.S. military and mercantile influence in the West Indies.

27. Unlike seventeenth- or eighteenth-century British literature and drama that includes West Indian characters, West Indians are redeemed (or not) in Robinson's play by U.S. political, economic, and cultural values, not the European ones that have left them, like the United States before independence, in a deplorable state of decline. Set in England, Richard Cumberland's *The West Indian* (1771) is perhaps the best-known drama in which a West Indian creole figure is purged of his creole contagions and embraced by polite British society, though he remains other to his English counterparts in many ways. An otherwise congenial character, Belcour displays stereotypical proclivities toward reckless economic and social conduct: "I am an idle, dissipated, unthinking fellow, not worth your notice: in short, I am a West-Indian; and you must try me according to the charter of my colony, not by a jury of English spinsters" (3.7). Cumberland's play strikes an unusually compassionate tone in regard to the West Indies when he reminds his English audience of their economic benefit from the lucrative sugar colonies in the "Prologue": "For sure that country has no feeble claim, / Which swells your commerce, and supports your fame" (qtd. in Sypher, *Guinea's* 239). Richards provides a reception history of *The West Indian,* one of the most popular of all plays performed on U.S. stages in the late eighteenth and early nineteenth centuries, in "How to Write an American Play: Murray's *Traveller Returned* and Its Source." Richards incisively demonstrates how, just as Belcour tries to establish himself as New World creole subject on his arrival in the British metropolitan center, so Judith Sargent Murray in her play *The Traveller Returned* (1796) appropriates elements of plot, character, and theme from Cumberland's well-loved play for U.S. postcolonial purposes. Writes Richards, "Murray . . . turned to a popular play that attempted to deal with transatlantic distinctions at a time when Americans were self-consciously trying to negotiate their way to understanding what their own culture would be," drama thereby "emerg[ing]" as a discourse of national formation" (279, 287). Robinson's play, too, remarks on eighteenth-century British drama that features West Indian creole characters for U.S. nationalist purposes. The most thoroughgoing account of the treatment of the West Indies and the West Indian creole "type" in eighteenth-century British literature and culture remains Sypher's *Guinea's Captive Kings*; see also "The West Indian as a 'Character' in the Eighteenth Century."

28. "I will tell you a story; I love you, I love you, like pepper pot my heart does burn, it burns like a fire coal."

29. "That something you have there looks angry. . . . shut up its mouth and don't let it talk, and I will tell you a story."

30. Although not foremost a reading of the play, Cooley's essay speculates that Banana might well be a "white creole or an octoroon" rather than a darker-skinned West Indian based on "onomastics, the play's story and plot, and historical cultural context" (188). As this chapter's analysis of how the play's meanings pivot on its intricate use of blackface as a device suggests, Banana is definitely not intended by Robinson to be a white creole (see especially the dialogue when Ledger and Amant's "Black Plot" is revealed to Fingercash [30–32]). However, Cooley does provide important textual cross-references to suggest that the name "Banana" could indicate the character's mixed-race status. Although Cooley doesn't cite him, William Dunlap's first-person account that Robinson played

Banana as "a mongrel creole, a kind of tawny Mungo" (222) would seem to confirm her theory that the playwright intended for Banana to be played as a mulatto or light-skinned black creole. Accordingly, Banana's not-quite-white creole status, given his proposed marriage to the white creole Louisa, poses the threat of category crises to ostensibly "pure" boundaries of race and ethnicity for U.S. audiences in ways that anticipate the function of the "tragic mulatto" figure in nineteenth-century U.S. literature and culture.

31. It is easier for Northern audiences to laugh at these perversions centered on race, rebellion, and imposture because they are represented in a West Indian setting, as opposed to a Southern United States one. Accordingly, Robinson's play would have been less overtly suggestive about challenges to national myths about purity and virtue. What does it say that a play about Southern U.S. slave culture had not to this point been written or produced on the Northern stage? What happens when the overlaps between United States and West Indian slave cultures is made explicit? What are the consequences on the (de)formation of the United States' political economy and culture, or its grand designs for hemispheric empire, when the distinguishing signs of West Indian and Southern U.S. slave societies begin to "bleed" together and blur?

32. In various Afro-Caribbean religions, black animals are offered up to the spirits of the dead. See Metraux 68–70.

33. Importantly, the mimetic miscegenetic marriage between the blackfaced Ledger and his white West Indian bride must occur off stage so as not to risk affronting the audience's sensibility with such a spectacle.

34. We might wonder then what Robinson's contemporary U.S. audience felt about an acting company with Jamaican ties and suspect political allegiances mimicking and mocking the islands from whence they came. Did they perceive them as especially apt advocates of empire owing to their experience in another of Britain's bastard colonies? This is what the play's conclusion, which advocates the renovation of the West Indies, seems to suggest. Or perhaps Robinson was engaging in a bit of mimicry himself by offering up to U.S. audiences the figurations of the West Indies they had come to expect from European literature, stylizations that he perceived they wished to co-opt according to their own meta-Caribbean designs.

35. Nathans argues that Federalist "elites" exerted substantial sway over the design and development of playhouses in the New Republic's urban centers; accordingly, urban theaters became sites for partisan bickering and demonstration. Writes Nathans, "The theater's supporters and detractors alike recognized it as a powerful tool for influencing thought and for disseminating visions of American national identity. But could it do so objectively? Democratically? Could a theater, run by an elite group of wealthy urban men (as most of the theaters were), fairly and accurately represent its audience?" (11–12). Perhaps no U.S.-authored dramatic work more ingeniously relates to Federalist domination of urban theater spaces for purposes of ideological control, this chapter suggests, than Robinson's play triumphing an embryonic U.S. commercial empire in the West Indies. In that regard, Robert Morris, who was appointed by Congress to be the nation's Financier in the early 1780s and who became a staunch Federalist, was largely responsible for Lewis Hallam Jr. being allowed to found a theater in New York in the postwar years, a theater in which Robinson's play would be performed (see Dunlap 106–9).

Chapter 5. Charles Brockden Brown's West Indian Specie(s)

1. Bordered on three sides by water, the city's streets teeming with refugees and their slaves from Saint-Domingue, Philadelphia becomes something of an actual West Indian island under siege in the novel and during the 1793 epidemic itself.

2. According to this interpretation, Thetford has exploited the Saint-Dominguan refugees, purloined Welbeck's substantial investment, and manipulated British laws governing forfeiture of "neutral" vessels carrying armaments or military personnel of the enemy, in this case France. Such trading practices are hardly the actions of a virtuous hemispheric man of commerce.

3. In several nonfiction works critical of Jefferson's abdication of a previously confirmed trade agreement governing commercial relations between the United States and Britain—the Monroe-Pinkney Treaty (1805–6)—as well as the Republican-dominated Congress's subsequent decision to impose the Embargo Act (1807–9), Brown demonstrates an acute appreciation for the contrasting effects that the West Indian carrying trade has on ideas about national character. He identifies the paradox of amassing national wealth through highly speculative and dangerous trading practices that he believes degenerate the nation's honor. This is so, according to Brown, not only because such paracolonial commercial strategies depend on carrying products produced by and for other empires, but also because "neutral" carriers are constant targets of empires (whether the British or French) resentful of the United States' parasitic role in supplying the enemy. Thus the carrying trade generally, and specifically the perversion of the nation's "neutral" status by traders employing duplicitous tactics, encourage rampant speculation according to Brown and obstruct the path toward a more virtuous empire. See, e. g., Brown's paracolonially ambivalent arguments on these matters in the *American Register,* vol. 1 (1807–8); *The British Treaty* (1807); and *An Address to the Congress* (1809).

4. Ultra-Federalist Timothy Pickering, for example, labeled Jefferson a "Parisian revolutionary monster" and asked Northerners, "Without a separation, can these states ever rid themselves of negro presidents and negro congresses and regain their just weight in the political balance?" (qtd. Emery 222). Pickering argued that a "servile war" like the one nearing its conclusion in Saint-Domingue would transpire if the nation acquired Louisiana.

5. By charting this mutually dependent relationship between racist environmentalisms, West Indian rebellion and unrest, and the shift away from abolition and emancipation toward colonization at the end of the eighteenth century, I do not mean to suggest that such an archeology is in any way absolute or comprehensive. It is, however, a dominant discursive trajectory in the United States by 1800. In arriving at this condensation of discourses, I am indebted to works by Jordan (*White Over Black*) and Nash (*Forging Freedom;* and *Race and Revolution*). Jordan provides significant insight into how the West Indies effected epistemological changes in the U.S. racial science community. Nash's works provide useful primary and secondary materials on these same issues, especially as they relate to shifting intellectual attitudes about race in the North.

6. Consider, for example, the May 8, 1797 diary entry of William Dunlap, which reveals the shift in mood in the North toward colonization in the 1790s and demonstrates the shaping influence of the West Indies on such a transformation: "'Perish our West India Islands rather than we should depart from the

principles of justice!' . . . *Fiat Justitia* is in the mouths of many who do not consider that to liberate the slave does not restore him to his original condition . . . but this is better understood now, and Colonization Societies are superseding the Abolitionists, who are to be blessed for beginning the good work" (327–28).

7. Christophersen argues that together with the nameless black servants who surface during the epidemic, Brown uses the gothic apparition of a marauding black slave in abolitionist ways (111). Even as Christophersen makes the unsteady assertion about the novel's abolitionist tendencies, he subordinates his discussion of race and rebellion to his main argument about tainted "virtue" in the novel. In a recent essay that shares my critical interest in locating Brown's novel in a hemispheric context, Smith-Rosenberg complicates Christophersen's account of race's function in the text by suggesting that blacks and women fracture attempts to cathect a hegemonic, bourgeois white male identity (see "Black Gothic").

8. Otter's important examination of race and ideology in Melville's fiction, particularly of the ways in which Melville systematically probes the rhetorical operations of various nineteenth-century pseudoscientific discourses including craniology, phrenology, and ethnology, provided a useful model for arranging my critical framework in this chapter. See especially chaps. 1–3 of *Melville's Anatomies*.

9. Although critics have noted Brown's satire of Jeffersonian agrarianism in the novel, they haven't remarked on the ways in which Mervyn comes to resemble Jefferson himself, a resemblance that is not transparently ironized by the novel. Mervyn *is* Jeffersonian in his training in natural history and, like Jefferson, comes to employ such knowledge in the service of a vicious racial ethnology that justifies a vigorous federal commercialism and an expanding empire.

10. My analysis of classification as a rhetorical figure in *Arthur Mervyn* is informed by a range of theoretical and critical sources. Foucault's foundational *The Order of Things* demonstrates how the eighteenth century is marked by "relations of similarity or equivalence between things, relations that . . . provide a foundation and a justification for their words, their classifications, [and] their systems of exchange" (xxiv). In *Imperial Eyes*, Pratt discusses the ways in which travel writers, natural historians, and other agents of European colonialism relied on classificatory structures to constitute empire's others. Relying on Foucault, Pratt, and other foundational figures in colonial/postcolonial studies, Spurr provides a highly readable and insightful account of the rhetorical operations of key figures in colonialist discourse in *The Rhetoric of Empire*, including a chapter on "classification." In *Describing Early America*, Regis shows how natural history discourse informs the ideological and structural features of writings by Bartram, Jefferson, and Crevecoeur.

11. Scholars have argued that the novel is about Mervyn's quest for stability or family. For example, Samuels maintains that Mervyn's homelessness reflects the prevailing view of the 1790s that the "threat to the mutually dependent institutions of family and state was . . . a contagious 'disease' imported from France" (243). Such an analysis is only partly true, I am suggesting. The "stability" that Mervyn seeks relates to his capacity to name and fix others according to his own ideological orientation. Conversely, he opposes others' efforts to name and fix identity unless such a naming reflects back to him a mirror image of his self-view, rather than a "phantom" of himself according to the subversion or inversion of his line of sight. "Family" then—a distinctly classifactory term—only works when Mervyn can choose and reject who may be placed in relation to himself. In this

way, he seeks "stability" in his character in precisely the same ways that the nation attempts to stabilize its "character" in the 1790s.

12. The novel hints that the epidemic originated in the West Indies. A predominant theory in Philadelphia in the 1790s, it had wide-sweeping implications, as I demonstrate in this chapter. For a discussion of the debate over the fever's origins, see Powell, 30–46.

13. Jefferson was a lifelong colonizationist, although his advocacy of such a position intensified after 1793 in reaction to events in the West Indies. In a 1793 letter to James Monroe, Jefferson wrote: "I become daily more and more convinced that all the West India Islands will remain in the hands of the people of colour, & total expulsion of the whites will sooner or later take place" (qtd. O'Brien 287). In 1797, he suggested that Saint-Domingue was only "the first chapter," arguing that "if something is not done and done soon, we shall be the murderers of our own children" (qtd. Jordan 434).

14. Stern maintains that the eponymous figure's blackface masquerade in Brown's *Ormond* repeats, "in theatrical form . . . the very dynamic of exploitation and commodification that marks slavery itself" (213). Stern's critical investment in the performative properties of race and ethnicity in *Ormond* nicely complements this chapter's interest in the "face" of those things in *Arthur Mervyn*.

15. Although he relates debasing accounts of black characters by other white characters, Mervyn himself does not author any such characterizations prior to his encounter with the spectral mulatto. Thus his evolution as a purveyor of scientific racisms is consistent with the patterns of racial representation that he presents in the narrative.

16. In arguing against biological theories of racial identity in favor of environmental ones in an essay entitled "On the Consequences of Abolishing the Slave Trade to the West Indian Colonies" (1805), Brown evinces a critical distance from Mervyn's brand of racial science: "[T]hose who argue about races, and despise the effect of circumstances, would have had the same right to decide upon the fate of all Russians [as inherently degenerate in the seventeenth century and thus not capable of improvement], from an inspection of the Calmuc skull, as they now have to condemn all Africa to everlasting barbarism, from the craniums, colour, and wool of its inhabitants" (377–78). Later in the essay, Brown cites the impressive achievements of the black revolutionaries in Haiti as evidence against claims of black West Indians' inherent inferiority to whites: "The war of St. Domingo reads us a memorable lesson. . . . We may be told, that brute force and adaptation to the climate, are the only faculties which the negroes of the West Indies possess. But something more than this must concur to form and maintain armies [in Haiti], and to distribute civil powers in a state. . . . There is nothing in the physical or moral constitution of the negro, which renders him an exception to the general character of the species, and prevents him from improving in all estimable qualities, when placed in favourable circumstances" (379–80).

17. Compelling examinations of the novel's commercial aesthetics and from which the discussion in this chapter has benefited include Decker; Goddu; Hinds; Justus; and S. Watts.

18. Ascha is quite unlike Martinette de Beauvais in Brown's *Ormond*, whose dark and exotic skin, coupled with her masculinity and her impulse toward revolution, ultimately horrifies the novel's heroine, Constantia Dudley, who at first desires a relationship with Martinette. Indeed, like Mervyn with the young Lodi, she considers Martinette a mirror image of herself. Ascha, for all her "exoti-

cisms," conforms to Mervyn's classifying gaze. She has fled from revolution and instability, rather than participated in it.

19. Locating Brown in relationship to the abolitionist debates and racial politics of his day has emerged as such a major critical obsession for contemporary scholars that Brown's status in the U.S. literary canon almost seems to hinge on determining these things. For instance, Robert Levine takes issue with Brown scholars, particularly Gardner, who distill from Brown's treatment of Native Americans, blacks, and "alien" others an author invested in the notion of the United States as a "white nation." In *Master Plots*, Gardner argues that in the novel *Edgar Huntly* and his 1803 Louisiana tracts, "Brown has arrived at nineteenth-century imperialism . . . an early formulation of Manifest Destiny . . . [;] in collapsing Indian and alien together and clearing both from the land, a unique national identity is born" (80). In contradistinction to what we might term "complicity critics" such as Gardner, Levine argues provocatively on behalf of what we might call "transcendence critics," or Brown apologists, who see in Brown an author at an ironic or privileged distance from the conspiratorial, proslavery, genocidal, white nationalist, and/or monomaniacally expansionist tendencies exhibited by some of his texts' main characters (Mervyn, Edgar, Ormond, and so on). Treating Brown's 1803 Louisiana writings alongside anonymously and pseudonymously authored pieces from literary magazines edited by Brown (and to whom Levine confidently attributes these pieces' authorship), Levine argues for a Brown "dependent upon antislavery . . . and a pragmatic expansionism that creates 'a complete barrier' not between white and red, or white and black, but between a still vulnerable nation and those European nations . . . that are willing to exploit racial and ethnic conflicts for their own colonizing ends" ("Race" 409). However, being the careful reader of Brown's works that he is, Levine acknowledges, "There are, I concede, suggestions in his major novels and in some of his nonfictional writings that [Brown] imagines the U.S. nation as a white nation" ("Race" 408), thereby granting a measure of credence to positions set forth by the complicity critics against whom Levine ostensibly argues in his essay.

At the risk of incurring the wrath of "complicity" and "transcendence" critics alike, I would submit that scholarly efforts that aim definitively to condemn or apologize for Brown's racial or expansionist politics, or to insist on his abolitionist or proslavery tendencies (the crux being, it seems to me, whether Brown was integrationist, colonizationist, or something else: to be pro-abolitionist during the period, on its own, tells us very little about a person's notions about race and nation formation), whether in a particular work or across Brown's writings, are ultimately misplaced. I would argue instead for a Brown (1) singularly capable of probing the contours and central concerns of discourses about race, nation, and empire, including a full range of abolitionist and proslavery arguments that were prominent in the United States during the late eighteenth century, and (2) whose works consistently register the manifold ambiguities and ambivalences attending those discourses, especially the nation's tangled investments in them, without himself being wholly complicit with, ironically detached from, or unaffected by their appeal and suasion. Indeed, Levine himself advocates a related critical orientation in influential earlier scholarship, wherein he argues "Brown's literary career writ large constitutes a dialogue without an authoritative center" (*Conspiracy* 26).

Like a double-helix, Brown's works, his fiction, and some of his nonfiction (especially the Louisiana writings that Levine and Gardner treat), interrogate these discourses from multiple vantage points at once, their narrative and plot structures frequently spiraling in several directions before doubling back on themselves, thereby rendering treacherous any effort to assert with any degree of certainty Brown's authorial—as opposed to the text's or his characters'—ideology on matters involving the intersections between race, nation, and empire building. If Mervyn resurfaces from his Southern mission supremely confident about having mastered the scene of West Indian and U.S. Southern slavery that he finds there, the arguments in this chapter suggest that Brown intends we not rest easily with any decision to adopt Mervyn's resolutions as our own. In that vein, the novel lays bare Brown's anxieties and ambivalences about the contradictory—to would-be purveyors of U.S. exceptionalist beliefs—commercial, cultural, and social cross-currents between the newly emergent Republic and the West Indian slave colonies.

Bibliography

Adams, John. *Diary and Autobiography of John Adams*. Ed. L. H. Butterfield. Cambridge, Mass.: Harvard University Press, 1962.

———. *Life and Works of John Adams (LWJA)*. Ed. Charles Francis Adams. Vol. 8. Boston: Little, Brown, 1853.

Adams, John, and Benjamin Rush. *The Spur of Fame: Dialogues of John Adams and Benjamin Rush, 1805–1813*. Ed. Douglass Adair and John A. Schutz. San Marino, Calif.: Huntington Library, 1966.

Adventures of Jonathan Corncob, Loyal American Refugee. London: n.p., 1787.

Alvord, Clarence Walworth. *The Mississippi Valley in British Politics: A Study of the Trade, Land Speculation, and Experiments in Imperialism Culminating in the American Revolution*. New York: Russell and Russell, 1959.

Ames, Fisher. *The Works of Fisher Ames*. Ed. W. B. Allen. Vol. 1. Indianapolis: Liberty Fund, 1983.

Anderson, Benedict. *Imagined Communities: Reflections on the Origin and Spread of Nationalism*. Rev. ed. London: Verso, 1991.

Anderson, Douglas. *The Radical Enlightenments of Benjamin Franklin*. Baltimore: Johns Hopkins University Press, 1997.

Aravamudan, Srinivas. *Tropicopolitans: Colonialism and Agency, 1688–1804*. Durham, N.C.: Duke University Press, 1999.

Archer, John Michael. *Old Worlds: Egypt, Southwest Asia, India, and Russia in Early Modern English Writing*. Stanford, Calif.: Stanford University Press, 2001.

Atherton, Gertrude. *Adventures of a Novelist*. New York: Blue Ribbon, 1932.

———. *The Conqueror, Being the True and Romantic Story of Alexander Hamilton*. New York: Macmillan, 1901.

Axelrad, Jacob. *Philip Freneau: Champion of Democracy*. Austin: University of Texas Press, 1967.

Axtell, James. *The European and the Indian: Essays in the Ethnohistory of Colonial North America*. New York: Oxford University Press, 1981.

Baepler, Paul, ed. *White Slaves, African Masters: An Anthology of American Barbary Captivity Narratives*. Chicago: University of Chicago Press, 1999.

Baker, Houston A., Jr. *Blues, Ideology, and Afro-American Literature—A Vernacular Theory*. Chicago: University of Chicago Press, 1984.

Barnard, Philip, Mark Kamrath, and Stephen Shapiro, eds. *Revising Charles Brockden Brown: Culture, Politics, and Sexuality in the Early Republic*. Knoxville: University of Tennessee Press, 2004.

Barrett, Walter. *The Old Merchants of New York*. 5 vols. 1870. New York: Greenwood, 1968.

Bassard, Katherine Clay. *Spiritual Interrogations: Culture, Gender, and Community in Early African American Women's Writing*. Princeton, N.J.: Princeton University Press, 1999.

Bauer, Ralph. "Creole Identities in Colonial Space: The Narratives of Mary

White Rowlandson and Francisco Núñez de Pineda y Bascuñán." *American Literature* 69.4 (1997): 665–95.

———. *The Cultural Geography of Colonial American Literatures: Empire, Travel, Modernity.* Cambridge: Cambridge University Press, 2003.

Benítez-Rojo, Antonio. *The Repeating Island: The Caribbean and the Postmodern Perspective.* Trans. James Maraniss. Durham, N.C.: Duke University Press, 1992.

Benns, F. Lee. *The American Struggle for the British West Indian Carrying Trade, 1815–1830.* Bloomington: Indiana University Press, 1923.

Bingham, Deborah M. "The Identity of Charles Brockden Brown." Ph.D. diss., Bowling Green State University, 1977.

Bloore, Stephen. "Samuel Keimer: A Footnote to the Life of Franklin." *Pennsylvania Magazine of History and Biography* 54 (1930): 255–87.

Boehm, Max Hilbert. "Cosmopolitanism." In *Encyclopedia of the Social Sciences*, 457–61. New York: Macmillan, 1937.

Bongie, Chris. *Islands and Exiles: The Creole Identities of Post/Colonial Literature.* Stanford, Calif.: Stanford University Press, 1998.

Boorstin, Daniel J. *The Lost World of Thomas Jefferson.* 1948. Chicago: University of Chicago Press, 1993.

Bowden, Mary W. *Philip Freneau.* Boston: Twayne, 1976.

Brathwaite, Edward Kamau. *The Development of Creole Society in Jamaica, 1770–1820.* Oxford: Oxford University Press, 1971.

———. *Roots.* Ann Arbor: University of Michigan Press, 1993.

Brickhouse, Anna. *Transamerican Literary Relations and the Nineteenth-Century Public Sphere.* Cambridge: Cambridge University Press, 2004.

Broadus, Mitchell. *Alexander Hamilton: The National Adventure, 1788–1804.* 2 vols. New York: Macmillan, 1962.

Brookhiser, Richard. *Alexander Hamilton, American.* New York: Free Press, 1999.

Brown, Jared. *Theatre in America during the Revolution.* Cambridge: Cambridge University Press, 1995.

Brown, Charles Brockden. *An Address to the Congress of the United States, on the Utility and Justice of Restrictions upon Foreign Commerce. With Reflections on Foreign Trade in General, and the Future Prospects of America.* Philadelphia: C. and A. Conrad, 1809.

———. *An Address to the Government of the United States, on the Cession of Louisiana to the French; and on the Late Breach of Treaty by the Spaniards: Including the Translation of a Memorial, on the War of St. Domingo, and Cession of the Missisippi to France, Drawn Up by a French Counsellor of State.* Philadelphia: John Conrad; Baltimore: M. and J. Conrad; Washington City: Rapin, Conrad, 1803.

———. *The American Register, or General Repository of History, Politics, and Science.* 8 vols. Philadelphia: n.p., 1806–10.

———. *Arthur Mervyn: or, Memoirs of the Year 1793.* 1799–1800. Ed. Sydney J. Krause et al. Kent, Ohio: Kent State University Press, 1980.

———. *The British Treaty.* [Philadelphia, 1807].

———. "On the Consequences of Abolishing the Slave Trade to the West Indian Colonies." *Literary Magazine* 4 (November 1805): 375–81.

———. *Ormond; or, The Secret Witness.* 1799. Ed. Sydney J. Krause et al. Kent, Ohio: Kent State University Press, 1982.

Burton, Richard D. E. *Afro-Creole: Power, Opposition, and Play in the Caribbean.* Ithaca, N.Y.: Cornell University Press, 1997.

Carlson, C. Lennart. "Samuel Keimer: A Study in the Transit of English Culture to Colonial Pennsylvania." *Pennsylvania Magazine of History and Biography* 56 (1937): 357–86.

Carretta, Vincent. "Olaudah Equiano or Gustavus Vassa? New Light on an Eighteenth-Century Question of Identity." *Slavery and Abolition* 20.3 (1999): 96–105.

Cavitch, Max. "The Man That Was Used Up: Poetry, Particularity, and the Politics of Remembering George Washington." *American Literature* 75.2 (2003): 247–74.

Chernow, Ron. *Alexander Hamilton.* New York: Penguin, 2004.

Cheyfitz, Eric. *The Poetics of Imperialism: Translation and Colonization from* The Tempest *to* Tarzan. New York: Oxford University Press, 1991.

Chinard, Gilbert. "Eighteenth Century Theories on America as a Human Habitat." *Proceedings of the American Philosophical Society* 91.1 (1947): 25–57.

Christopherson, Bill. *The Apparition in the Glass: Charles Brockden Brown's American Gothic.* Athens: University of Georgia Press, 1993.

Clinton, William Jefferson. "U.S. Interests in the Caribbean: Building a Hemispheric Community of Democracies." *U.S. Department of State Dispatch* 4.36 (1993): 1.

Coatsworth, John H. "American Trade with European Colonies in the Caribbean and South America, 1790–1812." *William and Mary Quarterly* 24 (1967): 243–65.

Commager, Henry Steele. *The Empire of Reason: How Europe Imagined and America Realized the Enlightenment.* 1977. Garden City, N.Y.: Anchor, 1978.

Commager, Henry Steele, and Elmo Giordanetti, eds. *Was America a Mistake? An Eighteenth-Century Controversy.* Columbia: University of South Carolina Press, 1967.

Cooley, Marianne. "Literary Dialect in *The Yorker's Stratagem.*" *Journal of English Linguistics* 28 (2000): 173–92.

Cooper, James Fenimore. *The Last of the Mohicans.* 1826. New York: Bantam, 1981.

"Creolization" [special topic]. *Journal of American Folklore* 116 (Winter 2003): 1–115.

Crèvecoeur, J. Hector St. John de. *Letters from an American Farmer.* 1782. New York: Dutton, 1912.

Cumberland, Richard. *The West Indian.* In *Eighteenth Century Plays,* ed. John Hampton. London: J. D. Dent, 1929.

Curtin, Philip D. *The Rise and Fall of the Plantation Complex.* 2nd ed. London: Cambridge University Press, 1998.

Curtis, Mary. *The Early Charleston Stage: 1703–1798.* Bloomington: University of Indiana Press, 1968.

Dash, J. Michael. *The Other Caribbean: Caribbean Literature in a New World Context.* Charlottesville: University of Virginia Press, 1998.

Dayan, Joan. *Haiti, History, and the Gods.* Berkeley: University of California Press, 1995.

Decker, Mark. "A Bumpkin Before the Bar: Charles Brockden Brown's *Arthur Mervyn* and Class Anxiety in Postrevolutionary Philadelphia." *Pennsylvania Magazine of History and Biography* 124.4 (2000): 469–87.

DeConde, Alexander. *This Affair of Louisiana.* New York: Scribner's, 1976.

Desmangles, Leslie G. *The Faces of the Gods: Vodou and Roman Catholicism in Haiti.* Chapel Hill: University of North Carolina Press, 1992.

Dillon, Elizabeth Maddock. "*Slaves in Algiers*: Race, Republican Genealogies, and the Global Stage." *American Literary History* 16 (2004): 407–36.

Dimock, Wai-chee. *Empire for Liberty: Melville and the Poetics of Individualism.* Princeton, N.J.: Princeton University Press, 1986.

Doerflinger, Thomas. *A Vigorous Spirit of Enterprise: Merchants and Economic Development in Revolutionary Philadelphia*. Chapel Hill: University of North Carolina Press, 1986.

Dominguez, Virginia. *White by Definition: Social Classification in Creole Louisiana*. New Brunswick, N.J.: Rutgers University Press, 1994.

Dowling, William. *Literary Federalism in the Age of Jefferson*. Columbia: University of South Carolina Press, 1999.

Drexler, Michael. "Brigands and Nuns: The Vernacular Sociology of Collectivity after the Haitian Revolution." In *Messy Beginnings: Postcolonialists and Early American Studies*, ed. Malini Johar Schueller and Edward Watts, 175–202. New Brunswick, N.J.: Rutgers University Press, 2003.

Dunlap, William. *History of the American Theatre*. 1797. New York: Burt Franklin, 1963.

Dunn, Richard. *Sugar and Slaves: The Rise of the Planter Class in the English West Indies, 1624–1713*. London: Cape, 1973.

Eames, Wilberforce. "The Antiguan Press and Benjamin Mecom, 1748–1765." *Proceedings of the American Antiquarian Society* 38.2 (1928): 303–48.

Edwards, Bryan. *The History, Civil and Commercial, of the British West Indies*. 5 vols. 1798. New York: AMS, 1966.

———. *Thoughts on the Late Proceedings of Government Respecting the Trade of the West India Islands with the United States of North America*. London: Weeden, 1784.

Egan, Jim. "Turning Identity Upside Down: Benjamin Franklin's Antipodean Cosmopolitanism." In *Messy Beginnings: Postcolonialists and Early American Studies*, ed. Malini Johar Schueller and Edward Watts, 203–22. New Brunswick, N.J.: Rutgers University Press, 2003.

Elkins, Stanley, and Eric McKitrick. *The Age of Federalism*. London: Oxford University Press, 1993.

Emery, Noemie. *Alexander Hamilton: An Intimate Portrait*. New York: Putnam's, 1982.

Equiano, Olaudah. *The Interesting Narrative of the Life of Olaudah Equiano, or Gustavus Vassa, the African, Written by Himself*. 1789. In *The Classic Slave Narratives*, ed. Henry Louis Gates, Jr., 1–182. New York: Mentor, 1987.

Erkkila, Betsy. *Mixed Bloods and Other Crosses: Rethinking American Literature from the Revolution to the Culture Wars*. Philadelphia: University of Pennsylvania Press, 2005.

Ferling, John. *John Adams: A Life*. Knoxville: University of Tennessee Press, 1992.

Fleming, Thomas. *Duel: Alexander Hamilton, Aaron Burr, and the Future of America*. New York: Basic Books, 1999.

Flexner, James Thomas. *The Young Hamilton: A Biography*. Boston: Little, Brown, 1978.

Foucault, Michel. *Language, Countermemory, Practice*. Ed. Donald Bouchard. Oxford: Oxford University Press, 1977.

———. *The Order of Things: An Archaeology of the Human Sciences*. 1966. New York: Vintage, 1973.

Franklin, Benjamin. *Autobiography*. Ed. J. A. Leo Lemay and P. M. Zall. 1818. New York: Norton, 1986.

———. "Information to Those Who Would Remove to America." In *Writings*, ed. J. A. Leo Lemay, 975–83. New York: Library of America, 1987.

———. *The Papers of Benjamin Franklin* (*PBF*). Ed. Leonard W. Labaree et al. 37 vols. New Haven, Conn.: Yale University Press, 1959–2003.

———. *The Works of Benjamin Franklin* (*WBF*). Ed. John Bigelow. 12 vols. New York: Knickerbocker Press, 1904.

Freeman, Joanne B. *Affairs of Honor: National Politics in the New Republic.* New Haven, Conn.: Yale University Press, 2001.

"French West-Indies." *The Daily Advertiser.* November 23, 1790: 2.

Freneau, Philip. *A Collection of Poems on American Affairs and a Variety of Other Subjects Chiefly Moral and Political (1815) (PAA).* Intro. Lewis Leary. Delmar, N.Y.: Scholars' Facsimiles and Reprints, 1976.

———. "General Character of the Insular West Indian Creoles." *The Daily Advertiser.* November 11, 1790: 2.

———. *The Poems of Philip Freneau, Poet of the American Revolution (PPF).* Ed. Fred Lewis Pattee. 3 vols. Princeton, N.J.: The University Library, 1902–7.

———. *Poems Written between the Years 1768 and 1794 (PWB).* Intro. Lewis Leary. Delmar, N.Y.: Scholars' Facsimiles and Reprints, 1976.

———. *Poems Written and Published during the American Revolutionary War (PWD).* Intro. Lewis Leary. Delmar, N.Y.: Scholars' Facsimiles and Reprints, 1976.

Frisch, Morton J. *Alexander Hamilton and the Political Order: An Interpretation of His Political Thought and Practice.* Boston: University Press of America, 1991.

Gardner, Jared. *Master Plots: Race and the Founding of an American Literature, 1787–1845.* Baltimore: Johns Hopkins University Press, 1998.

Gates, Henry Louis Jr. *The Signifying Monkey: A Theory of African-American Literary Criticism.* New York: Oxford University Press, 1988.

Gerbi, Antonello. *The Dispute of the New World: The History of a Polemic, 1750–1900.* Trans. Jeremy Moyle. 1955. Pittsburgh: University of Pittsburgh Press, 1973.

Gilman, Sander L. *Freud, Race, and Gender.* Princeton, N.J.: Princeton University Press, 1993.

Glacken, Clarence. *Traces on the Rhodean Shore: Nature and Culture in Western Thought from Ancient Times to the End of the Eighteenth Century.* Berkeley: University of California Press, 1967.

Glissant, Édouard. *Caribbean Discourse.* Trans. J. Michael Dash. Charlottesville: University of Virginia Press, 1992.

———. *Poetics of Relation.* Trans. Betsy Wing. Ann Arbor: University of Michigan Press, 1997.

Goddu, Teresa A. *Gothic America: Narrative, History, and Nation.* New York: Columbia University Press, 1997.

Goudie, Sean X. "On the Origin of American Specie(s): The West Indies, Classification, and the Emergence of Supremacist Consciousness in *Arthur Mervyn.*" In *Revising Charles Brockden Brown: Culture, Politics, and Sexuality in the New Republic,* ed. Philip Barnard et al., 60–87. Knoxville: University of Tennessee Press, 2004.

———. "The West Indies, Commerce and a Play for U.S. Empire: Recovering J. Robinson's *The Yorker's Stratagem* (1792)." *Early American Literature* 40.1 (2005): 1–35.

Gould, Philip. *Barbaric Traffic: Commerce and Antislavery in the Eighteenth-Century Atlantic World.* Cambridge, Mass.: Harvard University Press, 2003.

Greene, Jack P. *Pursuits of Happiness: The Social Development of Early Modern British Colonies and the Formation of American Culture.* Chapel Hill: University of North Carolina Press, 1988.

Greene, Jack P., and J. R. Pole, eds. *Colonial British America: Essays in the New History of the Early Modern Era.* Baltimore: Johns Hopkins University Press, 1984.

Greeson, Jennifer Rae. "Colonial Planter to American Farmer: South, Nation, and Decolonization in Crèvecoeur." In *Messy Beginnings: Postcoloniality and Early American Studies,* ed. Malini Johar Schueller and Edward Watts, 103–20. New Brunswick, N.J.: Rutgers University Press, 2003.

Grosz, Elizabeth. *Volatile Bodies: Toward a Corporeal Feminism.* Bloomington: Indiana University Press, 1994.

Gruesz, Kirsten Silva. *Ambassadors of Culture: The Transamerican Origins of Latino Writing.* Princeton, N.J.: Princeton University Press, 2002.

———. "Translation: A Key(word) into the Language of America(nists)." *American Literary History* 16.1 (2004): 85–102.

Gruzinski, Serge. *The Mestizo Mind: The Intellectual Dynamics of Colonization and Globalization.* Trans. Deke Dusinberre. 1999. London: Routledge, 2002.

Hall, Gwendolyn Midlo. *Africans in Colonial Louisiana: The Development of Afro-Creole Culture in the Eighteenth Century.* Baton Rouge: Louisiana State University Press, 1992.

Hamilton, Alexander. *Papers of Alexander Hamilton* (*PAH*). Ed. Harold C. Syrett. 26 vols. New York: Columbia University Press, 1961–79.

———. *Works of Alexander Hamilton.* Ed. Henry Cabot Lodge. 12 vols. New York: G. P. Putnam's Sons, 1904.

———. *Writings.* Ed. Joanne B. Freeman. New York: Library Company of America, 2001.

Hamilton, Alexander, John Jay, and James Madison. *The Federalist Papers* (*FP*). 1787. New York: Mentor, 1961.

Hamilton, Allan McLane. *The Intimate Life of Alexander Hamilton.* New York: Scribner's, 1911.

Hamilton, John C. *The Life of Alexander Hamilton.* 2 vols. New York: Appleton, 1834, 1840.

Haraszti, Zoltán. *John Adams and the Prophets of Progress.* Cambridge, Mass.: Harvard University Press, 1952.

Hardt, Michael, and Antonio Negri. *Empire.* Cambridge, Mass.: Harvard University Press, 2000.

Harrington, Virginia D. *The New York Merchant on the Eve of the Revolution.* New York: Columbia University Press, 1935.

Harris, Marc L. "What Politeness Demanded: Ethnic Omissions in Franklin's *Autobiography.*" *Pennsylvania History* 61 (1994): 288–317.

Harris, Wilson. "Interior of the Novel: Amerindian/European/African Relations." In *Explorations: A Selection of Talks and Articles, 1966–1981,* 10–19. Mandelstrup, Den.: Dangaroo, 1981.

———. *The Womb of Space.* Westport, Conn.: Greenwood, 1983.

Hartman, Saidiya. *Scenes of Subjection: Terror, Slavery, and Self-Making in Nineteenth-Century America.* New York: Oxford University Press, 1997.

Heilman, Robert Bechtold. *America in English Fiction, 1760–1800.* Baton Rouge: Louisiana State University Press, 1937.

Hill, Erroll. *The Jamaican Stage, 1655–1900: Profile of a Colonial Theatre.* Amherst: University of Massachusetts Press, 1992.

Hill, Erroll, and James Hatch. *History of African American Theatre.* Cambridge: Cambridge University Press, 2003.

Hinds, Elizabeth Jane Wall. *Private Property: Charles Brockden Brown's Gendered Economics of Virtue.* Newark: University of Delaware Press, 1997.

Hirsch, Arnold R., and Joseph Logsdon, eds. *Creole New Orleans: Race and Americanization.* Baton Rouge: Louisiana State University Press, 1992.

Hodge, Francis. *Yankee Theatre: The Image of America on the Stage, 1825–1850.* Austin: University of Texas Press, 1964.

Hoxie, Frederick E., ed. *Indians in American History: An Introduction.* Arlington Heights, Ill.: Harlan Davidson, 1988.

Hulme, Peter. *Colonial Encounters: Europe and the Native Caribbean, 1492–1797.* 1986. London: Routledge, 1992.

Jameson, Fredric. *The Political Unconscious: Narrative as a Socially Symbolic Act.* Ithaca, N.Y.: Cornell University Press, 1981.

Jarvis, Katherine Schall. "Royall Tyler's Lyrics for *May Day in Town.*" *Harvard Library Bulletin* 23.2 (1975): 186–98.

Jefferson, Thomas. *Notes on the State of Virginia.* Ed. William Peden. 1785. Chapel Hill: University of North Carolina Press, 1954.

Jehlen, Myra. *American Incarnation: The Individual, the Nation, and the Continent.* Cambridge, Mass.: Harvard University Press, 1986.

Jones, Absalom, and Richard Allen. *A Narrative of the Proceedings of the Black People During the Late Awful Calamity in Philadelphia in the Year 1793.* Philadelphia: William W. Woodward, 1794.

Jordan, Winthrop D. *White over Black: American Attitudes toward the Negro, 1550–1812.* 1968. Baltimore: Penguin, 1969.

Justus, James H. "*Arthur Mervyn,* American." *American Literature* 42 (1970): 304–24.

Kaplan, Amy. *The Anarchy of Empire in the Making of U. S. Culture.* Cambridge, Mass.: Harvard University Press, 2002.

Kaplan, Lawrence S. *Colonies into Nation: American Diplomacy, 1763–1801.* Toronto: Macmillan, 1972.

———. *Entangling Alliances with None: American Foreign Policy in the Age of Jefferson.* Kent, Ohio: Kent State University Press, 1987.

Kazanjian, David. *The Colonizing Trick: National Culture and Imperial Citizenship in Early America.* Minneapolis: University of Minnesota Press, 2003.

Keimer, Samuel. *Caribbeana.* 1741. Millwood, N.Y.: Kraus Reprint, 1978.

Kerber, Linda. *Federalists in Dissent: Imagery and Ideology in Jeffersonian America.* Ithaca, N.Y.: Cornell University Press, 1970.

Knight, Franklin W., and Peggy K. Liss, eds. *Atlantic Port Cities: Economy, Culture, and Society in the Atlantic World, 1650–1850.* Knoxville: University of Tennessee Press, 1991.

Knott, Stephen F. *Alexander Hamilton and the Persistence of Myth.* Lawrence: University Press of Kansas, 2002.

Kolodny, Annette. "Letting Go Our Grand Obsessions: Notes Toward a New Literary History of the American Frontiers." *American Literature* 64.1 (1992): 1–18.

Kuhlman, Susan. *Knave, Fool, and Genius: The Confidence Man as He Appears in Nineteenth-Century American Fiction.* Chapel Hill: University of North Carolina Press, 1973.

Lalla, Barbara, and Jean D'Costa. *Language in Exile: Three Hundred Years of Jamaican Creole.* Tuscaloosa: University of Alabama Press, 1990.

Lambert, John. *Travels through Lower Canada, and the United States of North America, in the Years 1806, 1807, and 1808.* London: Richard Phillips, 1810.

Leary, Lewis. *That Rascal Freneau: A Study in Literary Failure.* New Brunswick, N.J.: Rutgers University Press, 1941.

Levine, Robert. "Race and Nation in Brown's Louisiana Writings of 1803." In *Revising Charles Brockden Brown: Culture, Politics, and Sexuality in the Early Republic,* ed. Philip Barnard et al., 332–53. Knoxville: University of Tennessee Press, 2004.

———. *Conspiracy and Romance: Studies in Brockden Brown, Cooper, Hawthorne, and Melville.* New York: Cambridge University Press, 1989.

Liss, Peggy. *Atlantic Empires: The Network of Trade and Revolution, 1713–1826.* Baltimore: Johns Hopkins University Press, 1983.

Long, Edward. *The History of Jamaica.* 3 vols. 1774. New York: Arno, 1972.

Lott, Eric. *Love and Theft: Blackface Minstrelsy and the American Working Class.* New York: Oxford University Press, 1992.

Madison, James. "Foreign Influence." In *The Papers of James Madison,* ed. David B. Maltern et. al. 17:211–20. Charlottesville: University of Virginia Press, 1991.

Marsh, Philip M. *The Works of Philip Freneau: A Critical Study.* Metuchen, N.J.: Scarecrow, 1968.

Marx, Karl. *Grundrisse: Foundations of the Critique of Political Economy.* Trans. Martin Nicolaus. 1857–61. New York: Vintage, 1973.

Matson, Cathy D. *Merchants and Empire: Trading in Colonial New York.* Baltimore: Johns Hopkins University Press, 1998.

McCoy, Drew R. *The Elusive Republic: Political Economy in Jeffersonian America.* New York: Norton, 1980.

McDonald, Forrest. *Alexander Hamilton: A Biography.* New York: Norton, 1979.

Meserve, Walter. *An Emerging Entertainment: The Drama of the American People to 1828.* Bloomington: Indiana University Press, 1977.

Metraux, Alfred. *Voodoo in Haiti.* 1959. New York: Schocken, 1972.

Miller, John. *Crisis in Freedom: The Alien and Sedition Acts.* Boston: Little, Brown, 1951.

Mitchell, Loften. *Black Drama: The Story of the American Negro in the Theatre.* New York: Hawthorne, 1967.

Morgan, Edmund Sears. *Benjamin Franklin.* New Haven, Conn.: Yale University Press, 2002.

Morgan, Winifred. *An American Icon: Brother Jonathan and American Identity.* Newark: University of Delaware Press, 1988.

Morner, Magnus. *Race Mixture in the History of Latin America.* Boston: Little, Brown, 1967.

Morris, Robert. Letter to Francisco Rendón. August 30, 1783. *The Papers of Robert Morris: 1781–1784.* Ed. Elizabeth M. Nuxoll and Mary A. Gallagher. 8: 467–79. Pittsburgh: University of Pittsburgh Press, 1995.

Morrison, Toni. *Playing in the Dark: Whiteness and the Literary Imagination.* Cambridge, Mass.: Harvard University Press, 1990.

——. "The Talk of the Town." *New Yorker.* October 4–11, 1998: 31–32.

Morse, Jedidiah. *American Universal Geography.* Boston: Thomas and Andrews, 1789.

Morse, John T. *The Life of Alexander Hamilton.* Boston: Little, Brown, 1876.

Mulford, Carla. "*Caritas* and Capital: Franklin's *Narrative of the Late Massacres.*" In *Reappraising Benjamin Franklin: A Bicentennial Perspective,* ed. J. A. Leo Lemay, 347–58. Newark: University of Delaware Press, 1993.

——. "New Science and the Question of Identity in Eighteenth-Century British America." *Finding Colonial Americas: Essays Honoring J. A. Leo Lemay,* eds. Carla Mulford and David S. Shields, 79–103. Newark: University of Delaware Press, 2001.

Murphy, Gretchen. *Hemispheric Imaginings: The Monroe Doctrine and Narratives of U.S. Empire.* Durham, N.C.: Duke University Press, 2005.

Namier, Lewis Bernstein. *England in the Age of the American Revolution.* London: Macmillan, 1930.

Nash, Gary. *Forging Freedom: The Formation of Philadelphia's Black Community, 1720–1840.* Cambridge, Mass.: Harvard University Press, 1988.

————. *Race and Revolution*. Madison, Wisc.: Madison House, 1990.

————. *The Urban Crucible: The Northern Seaports and the Origins of the American Revolution*. London: Cambridge University Press, 1986.

Nathans, Heather. *Early American Theatre from the Revolution to Thomas Jefferson*. Cambridge: Cambridge University Press, 2003.

Nelson, Dana. *National Manhood: Capitalist Citizenship and the Imagined Fraternity of White Men*. Durham, N.C.: Duke University Press, 1998.

O'Brien, Conor Cruise. *The Long Affair: Thomas Jefferson and the French Revolution, 1785–1800*. Chicago: University of Chicago Press, 1996.

Odell, George C. D. *Annals of the New York Stage*. Vols. 1–2. New York: Columbia University Press, 1927.

Onuf, Peter. *Jefferson's Empire*. Charlottesville: University of Virginia Press, 2000.

O'Shaugnessy, Andrew Jackson. *An Empire Divided: The American Revolution and the British Caribbean*. Philadelphia: University of Pennsylvania Press, 2000.

Otter, Samuel. *Melville's Anatomies*. Berkeley: University of California Press, 1999.

Pares, Richard. *Yankees and Creoles: The Trade between North America and the West Indies before the Revolution*. 1956. London: Archon, 1968.

Patterson, Orlando. "Context and Choice in Ethnic Allegiance: A Theoretical Framework and Caribbean Case Study." In *Ethnicity: Theory and Experience*, ed. Nathan Glazer and Daniel Moynihan, 305–49. Cambridge, Mass.: Harvard University Press, 1975.

Pendleton, Edmund. *Address of the Honorable Edmund Pendleton, of Virginia, to the American Citizens, on the Present State of Our Country*. Boston: Benjamin Edes, 1799.

Powell, J. H. *Bring Out Your Dead*. 1949. New York: Time, 1965.

Pratt, Mary Louise. *Imperial Eyes: Travel Writing and Transculturation*. London: Routledge, 1992.

Raiskin, Judith. *Snow on the Cane Fields: Women's Writing and Creole Subjectivity*. Minneapolis: University of Minnesota Press, 1996.

Randall, William Sterne. *Alexander Hamilton: A Life*. New York: HarperCollins, 2003.

Regis, Pamela. *Describing Early America: Bartram, Jefferson, Crèvecouer, and the Rhetoric of Natural History*. DeKalb: Northern Illinois University Press, 1992.

Richards, Jeffrey H. *Drama, Theater and Identity in the American New Republic*. Cambridge: Cambridge University Press, forthcoming.

————. "How to Write an American Play: Murray's *Traveller Returned* and Its Source." *Early American Literature* 33 (1998): 277–90.

————. "Race and the Yankee: Woodworth's *The Forest Rose*." *Comparative Drama* 34.1 (2000): 33–51.

————. *Theater Enough: American Culture and the Metaphor of the World Stage, 1607–1789*. Durham, N.C.: Duke University Press, 1991.

Robinson, J. *The Yorker's Stratagem; or, Banana's Wedding*. New York: Sword's, 1792.

Rogow, Arnold. *A Fatal Friendship: Alexander Hamilton and Aaron Burr*. New York: Hill and Wang, 1998.

Rossiter, Clinton. Introduction. *The Federalist Papers*. New York: Mentor, 1961.

Rourke, Constance. *American Humor: A Study of the National Character*. 1931. Garden City, N.Y.: Doubleday, 1953.

Rowe, John Carlos. *Literary Culture and U. S. Imperialism: From the Revolution to World War II*. New York: Oxford University Press, 2000.

Said, Edward. *Culture and Imperialism*. New York: Vintage, 1993.

Samuels, Shirley. "Plague and Politics in *Arthur Mervyn.*" *Criticism* 23.3 (1993): 225–46.

Sansay, Leonora. *Secret History; or, the Horrors of St. Domingo, in a Series of Letters, Written by a Lady at Cape Francois, to Colonel Aaron Burr.* Philadelphia: Bradford and Inskeep, 1808.

Schachner, Nathan. *Alexander Hamilton.* New York: Thomas Yoseloff, 1946.

Schlereth, Thomas J. *The Cosmopolitan Ideal in Enlightenment Thought: Its Form and Function in the Ideas of Franklin, Hume, and Voltaire, 1694–1790.* Notre Dame, Ind.: University of Notre Dame Press, 1977.

Schueller, Malini Johar, and Edward Watts, eds. *Messy Beginnings: Postcoloniality and Early American Studies.* New Brunswick, N.J.: Rutgers University Press, 2003.

Seilhamer, George O. *History of the American Theatre.* 3 vols. 1888–91. New York: Benjamin Blom, 1968.

Shields, David S. *Civil Tongues and Polite Letters in British America.* Chapel Hill: University of North Carolina Press, 1997.

———. *Oracles of Empire: Poetry, Politics, and Commerce in British America, 1690–1750.* Chicago: University of Chicago Press, 1990.

Shuffelton, Frank. "Thomas Jefferson: Race, Culture, and the Failure of Anthropological Method." In *A Mixed Race: Ethnicity in Early America,* ed. Frank Shuffelton, 257–77. New York: Oxford University Press, 1993.

Smith, Edward G. "Black Theatre." In *Ethnic Theatre in the United States,* ed. Maxine Schwartz Seller, 37–66. Westport, Conn.: Greenwood, 1983.

Smith, James Morton. *Freedom's Fetters: The Alien and Sedition Laws and American Civil Liberties.* Ithaca, N.Y.: Cornell University Press, 1956.

Smith, Samuel Stanhope. *An Essay on the Causes of the Variety of Complexion and Figure in the Human Species.* Ed. Winthrop D. Jordan. 1787. Cambridge, Mass.: Harvard University Press, 1965.

Smith, Valerie. *Self-Discovery and Authority in Afro-American Narrative.* Cambridge, Mass.: Harvard University Press, 1987.

Smith-Rosenberg, Carroll. "Black Gothic: The Shadowy Origins of the American Bourgeoisie." In *Possible Pasts: Becoming Colonial in Early America,* ed. Robert Blair St. George, 243–69. Ithaca, N.Y.: Cornell University Press, 2000.

Sollors, Werner. *Neither Black nor White yet Both.* New York: Oxford University Press, 1997.

Spengemann, William C. *A Mirror for Americanists: Reflections on the Idea of American Literature.* Hanover, N.H.: University Press of New England, 1989.

———. *A New World of Words: Redefining Early American Literature.* New Haven, Conn.: Yale University Press, 1994.

Spurr, David. *The Rhetoric of Empire.* Durham, N.C.: Duke University Press, 1993.

St. George, Robert Blair, ed. *Possible Pasts: Becoming Colonial in Early America.* Ithaca, N.Y.: Cornell University Press, 2000.

Stallybrass, Peter, and Allon White. *The Politics and Poetics of Transgression.* Ithaca, N.Y.: Cornell University Press, 1986.

Stern, Julia. *The Plight of Feeling: Sympathy and Dissent in the Early American Novel.* Chicago: University of Chicago Press, 1997.

Stourzh, Gerald. *Benjamin Franklin and American Foreign Policy.* Chicago: University of Chicago Press, 1969.

Strachan, Ian Gregory. *Paradise and Plantation: Tourism and Culture in the Anglophone Caribbean.* Charlottesville: University of Virginia Press, 2002.

Sussman, Charlotte. *Consuming Anxieties: Consumer Protest, Gender, and British Slavery, 1713–1833.* Stanford, Calif.: Stanford University Press, 2000.

Sypher, Wylie. *Guinea's Captive Kings: British Anti-Slavery Literature of the Eighteenth Century*. 1942. New York: Octagon Books, 1969.

———. "The West Indian as a 'Character' in the Eighteenth Century." *Studies in Philology* 36 (1939): 503–20.

Taussig, Michael. *Mimesis and Alterity: A Particular History of the Senses*. London: Routledge, 1993.

Thomas, James. *The Young Hamilton: A Biography*. Boston: Little, Brown, 1978.

Thomas, Nicholas. *Colonialism's Culture: Anthropology, Travel, and Government*. Cambridge: Polity, 1994.

"Thoughts on the West India Trade" [untitled as such]. *Miscellaneous Papers of the Continental Congress, 1774–1789*. General Records of the United States Government. September 5, 1782. Microcopy 332, Roll 9: 282–84.

Todorov, Tzvetan. *The Conquest of America: The Question of the Other*. Trans. Richard Howard. New York: Harper and Row, 1982.

Tompkins, Jane. *Sensational Designs: The Cultural Work of American Fiction, 1790–1860*. New York: Oxford, University Press, 1985.

Treagle, Joseph G., Jr. "Creoles and Americans." In *Creole New Orleans: Race and Americanization*, ed. Arnold R. Hirsch and Joseph Logsdon, 131–88. Baton Rouge: Louisiana State University Press, 1992.

Vandenberg, Arthur Hendrick. *The Greatest American: Alexander Hamilton*. New York: Putnam's, 1922.

Vitzthum, Richard C. *Land and Sea: The Lyric Poetry of Philip Freneau*. Minneapolis: University of Minnesota Press, 1978.

Wadlington, Warwick. *The Confidence Game in American Literature*. Princeton, N.J.: Princeton University Press, 1975.

Waldstreicher, David. *In the Midst of Perpetual Fetes: The Making of American Nationalism, 1776–1820*. Chapel Hill: University of North Carolina Press, 1997.

———. *Runaway America: Benjamin Franklin, Slavery, and the American Revolution*. New York: Hill and Wang, 2004.

Wallerstein, Immanuel. *The Modern World-System III: The Second Era of Great Expansion of the Capitalist World-Economy, 1730–1840s*. San Diego: Academic Press, 1989.

Walling, Karl-Friedrich. *Republican Empire: Alexander Hamilton on War and Free Government*. Lawrence: University Press of Kansas, 1999.

Walvin, James. *Fruits of Empire: Exotic Produce and British Taste, 1660–1800*. Basingstoke: Macmillan, 1997.

Warfel, Harry F. *Charles Brockden Brown: American Gothic Novelist*. Gainesville: University of Florida Press, 1949.

Warner, Michael. "What's Colonial about Colonial America?" In *Possible Pasts: Becoming Colonial in Early America*, ed. Robert Blair St. George, 49–70. Ithaca, N.Y.: Cornell University Press, 2000.

Warshow, Robert Irving. *Alexander Hamilton: First American Business Man*. Garden City, N.Y.: Garden City Publishing Company, 1931.

Watts, Edward. *An American Colony: Regionalism and the Roots of Midwestern Culture*. Athens: Ohio University Press, 2002.

———. *Writing and Postcolonialism in the Early Republic*. Charlottesville: University of Virginia Press, 1998.

Watts, Steven. *The Romance of Real Life: Charles Brockden Brown and the Origins of American Culture*. Baltimore: Johns Hopkins University Press, 1994.

Weber, Bruce. "A Historic American Sure to Fall." Rev. of *The General from America*, by Richard Nelson. *New York Times*. November 23, 2002: B7.

Wertheimer, Eric. *Imagined Empires: Incas, Aztecs, and the New World of American Literature, 1771–1876.* Cambridge: Cambridge University Press, 1999.

Wheatley, Phillis. "To a Lady on Her Coming to North America With Her Son, for the Recovery of Her Health." In *Life and Works of Phillis Wheatley,* ed. G. Herbert Renfro. 1916. Miami: Mnemosyne, 1969.

White, Ed. "Carwin the Peasant Rebel." In *Revising Charles Brockden Brown: Culture, Politics, and Sexuality in the Early Republic,* ed. Philip Barnard et al., 41–59. Knoxville: University of Tennessee Press, 2004.

Williams, Eric. *Capitalism and Slavery.* 1944. Chapel Hill: University of North Carolina Press, 1994.

Williams, Raymond. *The Country and the City.* New York: Oxford University Press, 1973.

Wilmeth, Don B., and Christopher Bigsby, eds. *The Cambridge History of American Theatre, Volume I: Beginnings to 1870.* Cambridge: Cambridge University Press, 1998.

Witham, Barry, ed. *Theatre in the Colonies and United States, 1750–1915, A Documentary History.* Cambridge: Cambridge University Press, 1996.

Index

abolitionism: and Brown's *Arthur Mervyn*, 198, 246 n.19; and climatology/natural history discourse, 180–81; and Franklin, 40–41, 59–61, 223 nn.19, 21; and slave rebellions, 180–81

Adams, John: and creole colonialist discourse, 76–78, 81–82; and Hamilton, 7, 73–81, 96–97; Hamilton and the anonymous Adams letter, 78–81; and Hamilton's creole status, 76–78, 81–82; and the Peace of Versailles, 54, 61–63, 201; and Quasi-War with France, 96–97; and U.S.-West Indian trade relations, 4–5, 61–63; and West Indians' citizenship requirements, 8

Aeneid (Virgil), 140

Affairs of Honor (Freeman), 64

The Age of Federalism (Elkins and McKitrick), 96

agrarianism: and Brown's *Arthur Mervyn*, 182, 184, 244 n.9; and Freneau's "Rising Empire" series, 146–48; and Freneau's "The Rising Glory of America," 143; Jeffersonian, 16, 182, 184, 244 n.9

Alexander Hamilton and the Persistence of Myth (Knott), 65

The Algerine Captive (Tyler), 237 n.11

Alien Act, 8, 186, 217 n.4

Alien Enemies Act, 8, 217 n.4

Allen, Richard, 15, 181–82, 193, 198

ambivalence. *See* creole ambivalence; paracolonial ambivalence

"American Literature" (Ames), 104–7, 177–78

American Revolution (1776–84): and creole nationalism, 97; and Freneau's "Port Royal," 134; and Freneau's "Santa Cruz," 122–23, 127; and guerrilla warfare, 93–94, 227 n.17; and neutrality, 94

Ames, Fisher, 20–21; "American Literature," 104–7, 177–78; and representations of creole degeneracy, 71, 104–7, 178; "A Sketch of the Character of Alexander Hamilton," 106

Anderson, Benedict, 26

Anderson, Douglas, 221 n.10

Anglo-Americanness and Franklin's Empire Tracts, 45

anti-creolization, 102, 103. *See also* creolization

anti-mercantilism: Franklin's, 37–39, 43–45, 47–50, 54–57; Freneau's, 119–20, 124–25, 126–27. *See also* mercantilism, British

antimiscegenation statutes, 160, 237 n.10. *See also* miscegenation

antislavery. *See* abolitionism; slavery

Apparition in the Glass (Christophersen), 182

Aravamudan, Srinivas, 207–8

Archer, John Michael, 218 n.7

Arthur Mervyn (Brown) and West Indian specie(s), 11, 21, 174, 175–99, 205; and abolitionist politics, 198, 246 n.19; and agrarianism, 182, 184, 244 n.9; and classification, 183–86, 190–94, 244 nn.9–11; and colonization schemes, 189; and creole complex, 178, 198; and creole degeneracy, 178; faces in, 182–84, 192–93; and the Haitian Revolution, 192–93, 245 n.16; ideological implications of the novel, 198–99; Mervyn as farmer, 182, 184–85; Mervyn as natural historian, 184–86, 190, 244 n.9; Mervyn's racist ethnological discourse and racial inventories, 191–94, 197–98, 245 n.16; and the nabob, 175, 177, 186–87; and "phantom" identities/limbs, 185, 188–89, 244 n.11; and Philadelphia's yellow fever epidemic, 184, 186–87, 245 n.12; and racially supremacist consciousness/racial hierarchy, 199; and racial sci-

Acknowledgments

Although listed as author of *Creole America*, I think of myself as place-holder for the book's many collaborators—colleagues, family, students, friends, and acquaintances—whose inspiration and support made writing it possible.

In its early stages, *Creole America* benefited from the insights and expertise of several scholars whose collective interests are reflected in the book's focus: Sam Otter's brilliance as an "anatomist" of American literature and culture (Sam is a constant mentor and friend); Abdul JanMohamed's splendid writings on postcolonialism and minority discourse; and Michel Laguerre's prolific contributions to Caribbean and ethnic studies. I owe a substantial debt, too, to Deborah Baker Wyrick, who influenced my intellectual and professional development as a young scholar in countless ways and who first inspired me to believe that pursuing a career as an academic was a worthwhile endeavor.

I have been sustained in my scholarship and teaching at Vanderbilt as a result of consideration extended to me by colleagues and staff from all corners of the university. Vereen Bell, my first department chair, was responsible for hiring me—his quirky Southern charm is hard to resist. Along with Vereen, the following colleagues have supported me by providing feedback: Jay Clayton, my present chair, who has lent me much useful counsel during lunches together; Teresa Goddu, who is a valued colleague and friend to me and my family; Michael Kreyling, whose professional humility is exemplary; Vera Kutzinski, who as director of the Center for the Americas has provided opportunities for me to collaborate with other faculty members on meaningful interdisciplinary projects that strive to make our hemisphere a better place; Jonathan Lamb, with whom conversation is always a delight and who has emerged of late as a welcome comrade in creole studies; Mark Wollaeger, whose concern for, and defense of, good teaching has been inspiring; Cecelia Tichi, who has provided much helpful advice and welcome reassurance while we've sipped cocktails together at various university and social functions; and Thadious Davis, who recently left our department for the University of Pennsylvania but who has been a vocal backer of me and my work, for which I will always be grateful. Like Vera, Dana Nelson and Colin (Joan) Dayan became my colleagues as I was finishing *Creole America*. As Americanists around the country know, in addition to being a terrific scholar, Dana may be the single most motivated advocate in the profession for the concerns of junior scholars and minority and women faculty members. My debt to Colin's cutting-edge scholarship is apparent in the preceding pages.

I appreciate, too, the following colleagues, who have performed many acts of kindness and support on my behalf: Kate Daniels, Sam Girgus, Mark Jarman, Leah Marcus, and Mark Schoenfield. Faculty colleagues Lorraine Lopez and Tony Earley are exceptional fiction writers and friends. Finally, the superb staff in the English department, including Natalie Bagget, Sara Corbitt, Carolyn Levinson, Janis May, Dori Mikus, and Red Sox hater August Johnson, have provided a wonderful working environment in which to teach and write.

Many colleagues affiliated with the Circum-Atlantic Studies Working Group at the Robert Penn Warren Center for the Humanities have been uplifting in ways they are perhaps unaware of, including historians Richard Blackett, Jim Epstein, Ron Messier, and Dan Usner. Indeed, the history department has been like a second home department for me, and foremost among the historians who have taken an interest in my work and professional development is Jane Landers, co-organizer of the CASWG and devoted partner in all things early American and Caribbean.

I am appreciative of the generous funding for this project that I received at various stages of its development, including financial support from the University of California, Berkeley; a Mellon Foundation fellowship; a Vice Chancellor for Research Award from Vanderbilt; and a Barra Foundation Postdoctoral Fellowship from the McNeil Center for Early American Studies at the University of Pennsylvania. I am fond of times spent in conversation with McNeil Center fellows and friends; there are too many to list here, but worthy of special mention is noted historian Michael Zuckerman, who wrote me a trenchant eight-page, single-spaced comment in response to a seminar paper I presented on Alexander Hamilton.

I wish every first-time author could have the experience I have had in publishing with the University of Pennsylvania Press. Jeffrey Richards wrote the most generous, incisive, and eloquent reader's report that any author could hope for, and Amy Kaplan, the second press reader, provided a buoyant, discerning report in which she offered several keen suggestions for revision that contributed to a markedly improved final manuscript. Also, Jerry Singerman must be the most talented, witty, and patient editor on the planet—he has truly looked after my best interests. In short, it is hard to imagine a more supportive treatment of a book than the one mine has received at each stage of the publication process, the final stages of which were managed expertly by Erica Ginsburg.

Part of Chapter 4 was first published in the journal *Early American Literature* 40.1 (2005): 1–35. Part of Chapter 5 was first published in *Revising Charles Brockden Brown: Culture, Politics, and Sexuality in the Early Republic* (2004), edited by Philip Barnard, Mark Kamrath, and Stephen Shapiro. I am grateful to the University of North Carolina Press and the University of Tennessee Press for permission to republish this material here. I received feedback on this book's ideas at gatherings sponsored by the following organizations and institutes: the American Literature Seminar at the University of Pennsylvania, the American Studies Association, the Charles Brockden Brown Society, the Circum-Atlantic Studies Working Group at Vanderbilt, the David Library of the American Revolution, the Electronic Text Center at the University of Virginia, and the Modern Language Association. I appreciate the assistance of research librarians at the American Philosophical Society, the Library Company of Philadelphia, the South Carolina Historical Society, the South Caroliniana Library, the South Carolina Department of Archives, and the rare book and main libraries at Harvard University, the University of California, the University of Pennsylvania, and Vanderbilt University.

As the dedication suggests, I am much indebted to the town of Dangriga, Belize, where, as a physical education instructor and English teacher at Ecumenical High School, I first came to think about the United States from a Caribbean perspective. Owing largely to the inspiration of my colleagues, friends, and students in Dangriga, I became a student of the Caribbean. *Creole America* is dedicated as well to my great (in every sense of the word) family, including my mom, Kathleen Donovan Goudie, whose example as a single parent raising nine children and as a talented middle-school English teacher has been a constant inspiration, as have been my seven surviving brothers and sisters, the "pecking order" being: Robert (who has always shown a serious, if at times skeptical, interest in this project), Kathy, Colleen, Michael, Brian, Douglas, and Kara. Also on the Goudie side of things, thanks to my sisters-in-law Gina and Denise, brother-in-law Sarino, niece Michaela, and nephews Christopher and Connor. I am grateful, too, to my more recent parents, Dr. Jason and Sophie Chen, who provided crucial support while my wife and I were completing our books just as we were having our first child— Nora Sabella, whose eyes really do shine like diamonds—and to my brother-in-law John, his wife Kim, and their daughter Kylie. My best friend, Charles Potee, did not live to see this book in print, but his memory sustained me during the many early morning hours spent writing it.

The person who warrants my gratitude above all others is Tina Chen, without whose devotion the completion of this project would not have been possible. Her imprint is on my heart and each and every page of *Creole America.*